Beyond Timbuktu

BEYOND TIMBUKTU

An Intellectual History of Muslim West Africa

OUSMANE OUMAR KANE

HARVARD UNIVERSITY PRESS

Cambridge, Massachusetts
London, England
2016

Second printing

Library of Congress Cataloging-in-Publication Data
Names: Kane, Ousmane, author.
Title: Beyond Timbuktu : an intellectual history of
Muslim West Africa / Ousmane Oumar Kane.
Description: Cambridge, Massachusetts : Harvard University Press, 2016. |
Includes bibliographical references and index.
Identifiers: LCCN 2015050589 | ISBN 9780674050822
Subjects: LCSH: Islamic learning and scholarship—Africa, West—
History. | Islamic learning and scholarship—Mali—Tombouctou—History. |
Education—Africa, West—History. | Education—Political aspects—Africa,
West—History. | Africa, West—Intellectual life. | Africa, West—
Civilization—Islamic influences.
Classification: LCC DT474.5 .K36 2016 | DDC 966.0088/297—dc23
LC record available at http://lccn.loc.gov/2015050589

In loving memory of my grandfather,
Shaykh al-Islam Al-Hajj Ibrahim Niasse

Contents

Note on Transliteration

This book uses materials in several foreign languages, including Wolof, Pulaar, Hausa, and Arabic. I have opted for as simplified a transliteration of words and names as possible. I have omitted most diacritics as well as elongating Arabic vowels. The Arabic consonant *'ayn* has been transliterated as ' (as in Shari'a). Exceptions to the rule include when it appears in a name without 'ayn (as The College of Sharia and Islamic Studies Thika) and when mentioning West African Muslim names best known in their European form (for example, Uthman Dan Fodio, Umar Tall, Abdullahi Dan Fodio). I have transcribed these names with 'ayn only when they so appear in a citation. I have used the 'ayn, however, in transcribing Arab authors whose name are best known in Arabic form (for example, 'Umar Rida Kahhala, 'Ali Harazim, Ibn 'Ata Allah). The initial and final hamza have been omitted and the median hamza is transliterated as '. For the plural of certain Arabic words, especially when it comes to ideologies, such as Wahhabis or Salafis, or Sufis, I have opted to use the English plural *s,* in keeping with general English usage. For other Arabic plurals, such as *ulama,* I have opted to use the Arabic plural because that is how they are most commonly used in English writing.

Beyond Timbuktu

Prologue

> If the University of Sankore had not been destroyed; if Professor
> Ahmad Baba, author of forty historical works, had not had his
> works and his university destroyed; if the University of Sankore as
> it was in 1591 had survived the ravages of foreign invasions;
> the academic and cultural history of Africa might
> have been different from what it is today.
>
> —*Kwame Nkrumah*[1]

I N 1960, Senegal formally became independent from French colonial rule. As a young child, I have a vivid memory of people marching in the streets of Dakar chanting "Independence! Independence!"[2] with the strong conviction that independence would be the solution to all their problems. As opined by Ghana's first president—"Seek ye first the political Kingdom, and all things shall be added unto you"[3]—the end of foreign rule created high expectations among the people that they not only would recover their dignity as citizens of an independent country but also that such political autonomy would usher in a bright future, a future of prosperity.

Another slogan I heard time and again when I was growing up was "Development!" Although many African countries possessed rich natural reserves and / or arable lands, they lagged behind in most indicators of development. Life expectancy was low, child and maternal mortality high, illiteracy appalling. The little health and educational infrastructure that was available was concentrated in a few urban areas and particularly in capital cities. Rural areas, where more than 80 percent of the population lived, provided the bulk of the income of these countries, yet the development policies devised during and immediately after colonialism favored urban populations. The elites that inherited the apparatus of the state from colonialism were educated in Western languages—in the case of Senegal, in French. Léopold Sédar Senghor, the first president of independent Senegal, had received the degree of *aggrégation* in French grammar in France. His knowledge of the French language was so

outstanding that, after retiring from office in 1980, he was elected to the elite
Académie française.

During colonial rule, many African Muslims resisted Western education
because they feared—and rightly so—that it would acculturate their children
to Western values and alienate them from much-cherished Islamic and African
traditional values. Yet many others saw the tangible benefits of Western education and sent their children to the post-colonial modern schools. Although
quite a few French people were brought to the former colonies from France to
staff the administration of the newly independent state, independence also
allowed for the first time the appointment of Western-educated Africans to
senior levels of administration of the state and the economy. Like most African
countries, Senegal had adopted state-led industrialization as a development
policy and had created new industries, their management composed of
Western-educated Senegalese. Given the linguistic pluralism of most countries, imposing one African language as official could potentially frustrate other
linguistic groups and fuel ethnic irredentism, so French was adopted as the
language of the administration. The national radio broadcast essentially in
French. The only newspaper of the country, *Dakar Matin,* was published
entirely in French. Speaking French was a mark of distinction and education.
Although the overwhelming majority of the Senegalese spoke no French,
political leaders nonetheless typically addressed the country in French.

It therefore made sense for parents who wished to see their children achieve
social mobility to enroll them in the very few schools that offered education in
the French language. Named after the French statesman Georges Benjamin
Clemenceau (1841–1929), the École Clemenceau was one such school, and the
one to which I first went in October 1961. Like most kids, I woke up early in
the morning and put on my new clothes and new shoes, excited to go to school.
To enroll in school in those days, all a parent needed to do was show their
child's birth certificate. My mother and I queued to enroll. What a disappoint-
ment when we were told that because I was only six, I was a year too young to
enroll! Yet this was not enough to discourage us. We spent most of the day
begging the school principal to make an exception for me. At the time, a French
couple—Monsieur Poisson, the school principal, and his wife and assistant,
Madame Poisson—administered the school. By midday, virtually all nonad-
mitted kids had left. Tired of seeing me cry, Madam Poisson compassionately
took my hand from my mother and asked me to say, "Merci, Madam Poisson."
Although I spoke no French at all, I understood that she wanted me to thank

her, and acquiesced. Madame Poisson took me to the class where the master was a Senegalese, Mr. Diagana. I was enrolled in the first of six grades in the primary school system. This was the beginning of a childhood with very little leisure and free time.

Three years earlier, when I barely knew how to speak in Wolof, my mother tongue, I had been enrolled in a school to learn Arabic and the Qur'an. As it turned out, the school had no classroom. Schooling took place in the yard of our family house in Dakar, and the teacher was none other than my own mother. Part of a clerical Muslim family, my mother started her own school as soon as she got married to my father and settled in Dakar, the capital city of Senegal, in 1951. Between 1959 and 1961, I attended the Qur'anic school exclusively. It operated five days a week; Wednesday afternoons, all day Thursday, and Friday mornings were times of rest. Thus, after I enrolled in the Clemenceau School in 1961, I had to commit to two systems of education. The French school was important because it led to the award of a degree and recognition, and the Qur'anic school because it shaped its students' sense of belonging to a Muslim personality.

Like my siblings, I pursued Islamic and Western education simultaneously. I woke up around 6 A.M. to perform the first of the five daily Muslim prayers and then to study a set of verses of the Qur'an at home; at 7:45 A.M. it was time to walk to École Clemenceau. At noon, the beginning of the break at Clemenceau, I returned home to resume Qur'anic studies and have a brief lunch. At 2.45 P.M. it was time to walk back to Clemenceau. The school day at Clemenceau ended at 5 P.M. But at 5:15 P.M., when I arrived home from Clemenceau, I would right away resume Qur'anic studies until the Muslim prayer of the Maghreb, or sunset, around 7 P.M. Right after the prayer, I would do my public school homework with the help of my older siblings. I would have a short fifteen-minute break for dinner and would go to bed between 10 and 11 P.M. after completing my homework. On Saturdays and Sundays and during the other school holidays such as Christmas and Easter (two weeks each), and over summer break (three months), I studied the Qur'an full time.

When did I rest? Only at night! There was no other time to rest. My greatest childhood regret is never having learned to play soccer, a very popular sport in urban Senegal in the 1960s. There were the few well-designed stadiums for professional soccer, but kids of my and subsequent generations improvised soccer fields in most neighborhoods. When they returned from school around 5 P.M., most would join their team in playing soccer. Good players had fans.

Neither I nor any of my siblings ever had the time to learn how to play soccer, but we have all learned the Qur'an. Adults in my family taught us that learning soccer was the fastest way to perdition. They disparaged leisure and rest. One had to choose as a young person between the path of suffering and privation and therefore being successful in this world and the next and having leisure, knowing how to play soccer, and consequently failing in life.

I spent most summer vacations (July, August, and September) in Madina Kaolack, 192 kilometers from Dakar, where my mother's family resided. But once there, it was business as usual, meaning continued Qur'anic studies. In my mother's family, men and women were educated in Arabic and Islamic studies. According to his biographer, Ruediger Seeseman, my maternal grandfather, Shaykh Ibrahim Niasse (1900–1975), "can be counted among the most influential and versatile Sufi authors of the twentieth century."[4] His followers numbered in the millions and lived in areas from Senegal, as far west as one can get in Africa, to the Republic of Sudan in East Africa. Historian Mervyn Hiskett argued further that there is little doubt that Shaykh Niasse headed the single largest Muslim organization in West Africa by the end of European colonial rule.[5] More recent research on Niasse's community reveals that it has been expanding significantly in the past fifty years.[6]

Shaykh Ibrahim was taught in Senegal by his father, Abdoulaye Niasse (d. 1922), another central Muslim figure of late nineteenth and early twentieth-century Senegal. Unlike their father, who received his entire education in Senegal, many sons and disciples of Shaykh Ibrahim Niasse, after completing their traditional Islamic education in their home country, received higher education leading to the granting of formal degrees in North Africa and the Middle East. The majority of them graduated from Al-Azhar University in Cairo, but many studied in Morocco, Tunisia, Algeria, the Sudan, Qatar, and Saudi Arabia.

All my mother's sisters received Islamic education. Quite a few were married to disciples of my grandfather, men who were based in various countries of West Africa, though the majority were Arab-Berbers from Mauritania; Hausa, Fulani, or Yoruba from Nigeria; Zarma from Niger; or Bambara from Mali. Madina Kaolack, the city founded by my grandfather in the late 1920s, is the spiritual capital of Jama'at al-Fayda al-Tijaniyya (The Community of Grace), the revivalist movement within the Tijaniyya that he initiated. During his lifetime, thousands of people from all over West Africa visited to study Arabic and Islam or to receive spiritual initiation and to seek blessing. Among his disciples, intermarriage was very frequent, particularly between Arab-Berbers and other African groups. As a result, I have cousins, nephews, and nieces in most West African countries. Madina Kaolack is a microcosm of West African integration, which tells a different story of ethnic and racial politics than does the dominant academic discourse of an ethnically and racially fragmented West Africa. The glue holding these different communities together was of course the faith in Islam and in the Tijaniyya tariqa founded by Shaykh Ahmed al-Tijani (1735–1815). My grandfather claimed and was believed by all these people to be the spiritual heir of Al-Tijani.

It was not just in Kaolack that I experienced West African cosmopolitanism. Many members of my grandfather's large spiritual community that visited Senegal stayed at our huge family house that accommodated dozens of people, in Dakar where the only airport close to Madina Kaolack was located. Often, non-Senegalese guests and temporary residents in our house outnumbered family members. On the one hand, this meant that I grew up navigating easily between ethnic, racial, cultural, and epistemological boundaries. On the other hand, I heard time and again in school or read in books the narrative of Arabs enslaving and looking down upon blacks, of Africa being torn by ethnic warfare, and of the civilizing impact of Western colonialism, which introduced literacy to hitherto exclusively oral African societies. This colonial narrative contrasted with what I experienced in everyday life. Growing up, I often heard stories about my ancestors and the many clerical communities they created in central Senegal. In the many religious lectures and festivals that I attended—not just in Senegal but also in other West African countries—I heard testimonies of their erudition and also the devotional poetry that they wrote and that was chanted by the masses of disciples during the religious festivals organized throughout the year. Yet most of my Western-educated schoolmates believed more narrowly that literacy meant literacy in European languages.

In Freetown, Sierra Leone, the Church Missionary Society created the Fourah Bay College in 1827 as the first college to offer instruction in a European language in West Africa. At that time, several Islamic centers of higher learning already existed in West Africa. One of the oldest is Sankoré, which had been in Timbuktu since the fourteenth century. Sankoré compared favorably with the best centers of Islamic learning in the Muslim world in the sixteenth century and attracted students and scholars from West Africa, the Maghreb, and beyond.[7] The rise of spiritual and intellectual centers such as Sankoré rested largely on the economic prosperity of the Niger Bend region. Though Mali is today one of the poorest countries on earth, the predecessor empire whose name it adopted was a global supplier of gold. When Sankoré was established two centuries after the creation of Timbuktu, an estimated two-thirds of the world's gold came from West Africa, a large part of which passed through Timbuktu.[8] I hasten to add that historians are unsure of exactly how much gold was exported from sub-Saharan Africa to the north. According to the best estimates, it was slightly above one ton a year between the ninth and fifteenth centuries.[9] But, as Ralph Austen notes, although this may look insignificant compared with the amount of gold produced with the support of modern extracting technologies, medieval mining techniques limited the quantity of gold that could be obtained anywhere in the world, and limited geographical knowledge kept the gold of the New World outside global markets.[10]

The emergence of the Portuguese as a naval power and the discovery of gold in the Americas somewhat shifted the center of gravity of regional trade and led to a reduction in Timbuktu's prominence over the course of the sixteenth century, but Timbuktu remained an important regional commercial and intellectual hub until the Moroccan invasion, which precipitated the decline of Songhay. The Moroccan expeditionary force was composed of Spanish, Arab, and Berber soldiers called Arma, from the Arabic word *rumat*, or musketeers. Subsequently, the Arma settled in the region, declared their independence from the Saadian monarchy, and intermarried with the local elites. The 1591 expedition precipitated the collapse of the last and most prosperous and powerful medieval West African state, undermining its economic prosperity, which supported a vibrant intellectual life. This in turn led to the decline of intellectual centers that had flourished in West Africa prior to the invasion, including Timbuktu in the sixteenth century.[11] Moroccan vassal rule did not last long in the Songhay state. Though the Arma expeditionary force quickly declared its independence from the Saadian dynasty, relations between Muslims in North and West Africa survived Arma secession and indeed persist in the twenty-first century.

Throughout the second millennium, black Africans, Berbers, and Arabs maintained close contacts. As shown by the Moroccan invasion lamented by Nkrumah in his Flower of Learning address cited above, and the no-less-infamous Oriental slave trade, their relations at times have been violent. But as shown by my own family history, they have also been mutually beneficial through intermarriage, trade, diplomacy, and above all spiritual and intellectual exchange.[12] Yet those intellectual exchanges so far have been the least studied aspect of North African/sub-Saharan relations, due to the ways the Western academy has invented and studied Africa. Western universities nowadays typically divide academic study of Africa so that North Africa (Morocco, Libya, Tunisia, Algeria, and Egypt) falls within the realm of Middle Eastern studies, whereas the area south of the Sahara, considered Africa proper, is studied within the field of African studies. Such a division and its underlying assumptions overlook the fact that the Arabic language, as the language of Islamic learning and liturgy, was the glue holding together large populations of the Maghreb, the Sahara, and sub-Saharan Africa.

During the second millennium, the Arabic language played a transformative role in West African history. Some Islamized people in the Sahara gradually deserted their linguistic, cultural, and ethnic identities to claim exclusive Arab identities. Others have retained their African languages but have used the Arabic script to transcribe them, to compose scholarly treatises, to chronicle history, and to write poetry. Arabic as a linguistic vehicle of knowledge transmission was as important in the history of Muslim peoples as Latin was in Europe. Non-Arabs wrote much of what was written in Arabic in the formative period of Islamic civilization (eighth to fifteenth centuries).[13] As more people converted to Islam in subsequent centuries, Arabic became a language of learning for even more people, including in West Africa. Arabic (and to a lesser extent Ajami, African languages transcribed with the Arabic script) was a major medium of instruction for Muslims until the rise of Western hegemony. By the eighteenth century, several clerical communities flourished in West Africa. We know this not just from the Arabic sources, but also from testimonies of European travelers.

The governor of Senegal, Baron Roger, wrote that there were in Senegal "more negroes who could read and write in Arabic in 1828 than French peasants who could read and write French."[14] Francis Moore, an employee of the Royal African Company of England, a chartered company established in England and active in Senegambia, wrote in his travel narratives that in "every Kingdom and Country on each side of the River of Gambia," Pulaar-speaking communities spoke Arabic and that they were "generally more learned in the Arabick, than the people of Europe are in Latin, for they can most of them speak it, tho' they have a vulgar tongue besides, call'd Pholey."[15] Several other explorers before and after Moore, including Ibn Battuta in the fourteenth century, Leo Africanus in the fifteenth century, the European explorer Mungo Park in the eighteenth century, and others in the nineteenth century testified to Islamic

erudition in West Africa long before the colonial scramble of the late nineteenth century. The French explorer René Caillié, who visited Timbuktu in the
early nineteenth century, stated that "all the negroes of Timbuktu are able to
read the Qur'an and even know it by heart."[16]

Timbuktu was conquered by the French three centuries after the Moroccan
invasion of 1591. European colonial rule paved the way for the spread of modern
colleges in West Africa. In the late nineteenth century, Fourah Bay College was
one such island of Western higher education in an ocean of Arabic-speaking
colleges in West Africa. In the late twentieth century, the impact of European
colonialism had reversed this, and French, English, and Portuguese had become
the official languages of schooling and administration in the whole of West
Africa. Of the hundreds of modern colleges and universities created in West
Africa at the beginning of the second decade of the twenty-first century, less
than 5 percent offer instruction in Arabic,[17] and the oldest among them is the
Université islamique de Say (Islamic University of Say), inaugurated in Niger
in 1987. Between the building of the mosque/college of Sankoré in the fourteenth century and the inauguration of the Université islamique de Say in 1987,
higher Islamic studies waxed and waned in West Africa, but the Arabic language itself has remained central to the social and intellectual life of Muslim
communities. By 2009, Arabic had become the language in which 241 million
Muslims said their daily prayers in sub-Saharan Africa, and they represent
fifteen percent of the global Muslim population.[18] They share this language and
many aspects of Islamicate culture with North Africa. However, as a language
of administration and scholarly production, Arabic had been displaced by the
rise to prominence of intellectuals educated in European languages. Philosopher
Kwame Anthony Appiah called these the "Europhone" intellectuals.[19] Through
education in the colonial language, colonialism produced the intellectual ingredients through which colonial subjects educated in European languages understood their own universe.

In 1912, French scholar and colonial administrator Maurice Delafosse produced a magisterial socio-anthropological work on the French colony of Upper
Senegal and Niger that had been created in 1904. This book provided a detailed
historical ethnography of the people, cultures, and religions of what would
become a central part of Francophone Africa. Following the steps of Delafosse,
colonial scholars in charge of Muslim affairs wrote abundantly about Muslim
communities. The most prolific of them was Paul Marty, director of the Office
of Muslim Affairs, who authored six studies on Islam and Muslims totaling

thousands of pages.[20] Colonial writings produced analytical categories to make sense of the social organization of the people. Borrowing from French social theorist Michel Foucault, Congolese philosopher Valentin Mudimbe called this documentary field "the colonial library"[21]—that is, a body of writing by colonial scholars that creates a system of representation of African societies. This colonial library produced an intellectual framework to make sense of Africa, and that framework informed writings in European languages about Africa, including some by Africans. Linguistic dependence implied for African intellectuals writing in a Western language the adoption of Western analytical categories and thus an epistemological dependence on the colonial library. As more and more Africans and others wrote in European languages, the library expanded. According to Mudimbe, the "expanded library" operates in the same Western epistemological order as the colonial library that provided its conceptual categories.

Yet Mudimbe tells only one part of the complex story of higher learning in West Africa. Throughout the post-colonial period, debates on the production of knowledge in and about Africa in English and French were conducted with little mention of Sankoré and similar centers of learning. As I will show in this book, the breadth and depth of this intellectual tradition and its vitality and versatility are still something of which very few Europhone intellectuals, both African and Western, are aware. The history of African literacy did not begin with the colonial encounter. A discussion of the African library or intellectual history does little justice to the vibrant intellectual life between the formation of Sankoré and the creation of the Fourah Bay College if it begins with the colonial period. The dominant epistemological framework of this long period could not possibly have been Western for the simple reason that the West or modern civilization did not yet exist or was still in its infancy when the Islamic scholarly tradition was already flourishing in West Africa.

"The West" or "modern civilization," as Hall and others note, refers to a civilization built on the ruins of feudal Europe. Its formation involved several interrelated processes that affected the economy, politics, society, and culture over several centuries. But it was during the nineteenth century that it attained the maturity and the technological supremacy that enabled Europeans to dominate the whole world.[22] Europe is just one of the many regions of the world. Yet it has been central in the geographic representation of the world as shown by the Mercator projection, a cylindrical and thus distorted mapping of the world, and as omnipresent in the historical reconstructions in European languages of the other parts of the world. To fully appreciate the African library in the *longue durée,* I propose to turn the discussion of the African library on its head and start with Sankoré as a paradigm for knowledge production and transmission. Then I will address how only much later the rise of colonial hegemony displaced this paradigm and placed Europhone intellectuals at the center of West African public life.

The Precolonial Paradigm of Knowledge Transmission in West Africa

Islamic education in West Africa started at the beginning of Islamization during the first millennium. Among the eyewitness accounts of this scholarly tradition is, notably, the globetrotter Ibn Battuta, who wrote the following about the people of Mali a century after the creation of Sankoré:

> They are very zealous in their attempts to learn the holy Qur'an by heart. In the event that their children are negligent in this respect, fetters are placed on the children's feet and are left until the children can recite the Qur'an from memory. On a holiday, I went to see the judge, and seeing his children in chains, I asked him, "Aren't you going to let them go"? He answered, "I won't let them go until they know the Qur'an by heart." Another day I passed a young Negro with a handsome face who was wearing superb [clothes] . . . and carrying a heavy chain around his feet. I asked the person who was with me, "What did that boy do? Did he murder someone?" The young negro heard my question and began to laugh. My colleague told me, "he has been chained up only to force him to commit the Qur'an to memory."[23]

An important element of Sankoré epistemology that transpires from this testimony is the centrality of memorization of the Qur'an, if necessary through harsh punishment inflicted on the body. Memorization was valued in the classical period of Islamic scholarship and beyond.[24] Islamic studies in West Africa started at the Qur'anic school, where pupils as young as four were admitted and taught to memorize the Qur'an and write in the Arabic script. Students, including native speakers of Arabic, could not understand a text such as the Qur'an at the beginning of their education. Successful completion of Qur'anic studies paved the way to what we call higher Islamic studies, in which advanced students were taught a wide variety of subjects. Unlike beginners, who learned mostly by memorization, higher Islamic studies students developed the linguistic proficiency required to understand the Qur'an and other religious texts and to speak Arabic. They learned the science of the exegesis of the Qur'an to understand the text; Islamic jurisprudence to know what is allowed, forbidden, recommended or neutral; the scientific study of the Arabic language; and even some Greek philosophy. But at this stage of higher education too, memorization remained important in the pedagogy of Islamic studies. This was not due to the rarity of books and the relatively high cost of paper, but rather to the fact that committing a text to memory was a mark of scholarly distinction. Illustrative of this approach to learning are the following statements of Ibn Najjar (d. 643/1245):

Idha lam takun hafizan wa'iyan,	If retentive memory is not what you possess,
Fa-jam'uka li l-kutubi la yanfa'u,	Your collecting of books is quite useless,
A-tantuqu bi- l-jahli fi majlisin,	Would you dare, in company, nonsense say,
Wa-'ilmuka fil-bayti mustawda'u?	When your learning at home is stored away?[25]

Ibn Battuta's testimony validates the notion that harsh physical punishment was an element of Islamic schooling pedagogy. The goal of religious education was to create a virtuous Muslim subject. Achieving such a noble goal for Muslims justifies inflicting substantial physical pain on others or the self. When speakers of Wolof, a predominant language in Senegambia, describe a person as a walking Qur'an (*al-xuraan buy dokh*), they mean that he was transformed through education to become a virtuous Muslim, someone who throughout his life follows the teachings of the Qur'an and refrains from its prohibitions.[26] Michel Foucault, Talal Asad, and others note that the cultivation of technologies of the self were known in ancient societies, including in Ancient Greece and during early and medieval Christianity.[27] Foucault argued that those technologies "permit individuals to effect by their own means, or with help of others, a certain number of operations on their own bodies and souls, thoughts, conduct, and way of being, so as to transform themselves in order to attain a certain state of happiness, purity, wisdom, perfection, or immortality."[28]

In certain circles, this rigorous tradition of Qur'anic education was never abandoned. The majority of Muslim families continued to invest in the Islamic education of their children, even if they also attended schools offering education in Western languages, as I did. This is because schooling was not just about receiving instruction—it was about receiving a more holistic education under the supervision of a master. Such close master/disciple relations were an important element of Sankoré pedagogy and epistemology.

Master / Disciple Relations

Sankoré was a place of worship and learning in which highly knowledgeable scholars engaged in sophisticated intellectual conversation. But Sankoré (or for that matter other Islamic institutions of higher learning in North Africa or elsewhere) did not operate like the universities we tend to call to mind. Georges Makdisi's comparative study of medieval higher education in Islam and the West highlighted parallels in the methods of instruction and posts, but also differences. A notable difference was the possibility given to Western colleges to register as a corporation.[29] As such, Western colleges enjoyed the flexibility to reform and adjust to new conditions. In contrast, Islamic law recognizes only individuals (not corporations) as legal entities.[30] Based on endowment (*waqf*), premodern Islamic colleges, according to Islamic law, were supposed to be governed forever by the will of their endower. It was the rise of Western imperial hegemony that prompted the changes leading to the emergence in the Muslim world of universities in the modern sense of the term.

There was no single unified curriculum in the Sahel region in general and in the city of Timbuktu in particular. Unlike in modern universities, there was no central administration, no recruitment or graduation exam, and no school degree. University libraries as we know them now did not exist then. However, teachers typically were very learned scholars, some of whom had studied in Egypt or in the Bilad al-Sudan (name given by Arab authors to the regions south of the Sahara) with the highest intellectual authorities of their time. Many Timbuktu scholars possessed personal libraries of hundreds or thousands of books. Scholars offered instruction inside mosques such as Sankoré, Sidi Yahya, and Jingerer Ber, the largest mosque colleges in Timbuktu, but most scholars imparted knowledge to students in a special room in their own homes, which also housed their books. Masters delivered authorization to teach specific texts to their students. The prestige of the authorization depended on the pedigree of a scholar. The expectation still today is that a scholar authorized by a famous master who himself is a former student of another famous master to transmit knowledge will have more solid credentials than a scholar taught by a less famous master. Pursuing higher education consisted of studying with a shaykh either in his own house, in a mosque, in a *zawiya,* or in a public space (often called *majlis*).

In major centers such as Timbuktu, students found instructors who could teach most subjects. But most students did not live in such centers. For them, peripatetic scholarship was the rule. Qur'anic education and initiation into the basic texts might have been available in many rural and urban centers in the Sahel, but study of advanced texts required most students to travel tens if not hundreds or thousands of miles to the village of a shaykh with expertise on a specific subject or book. Unlike in modern times, when anybody can seek knowledge by ordering a book from Amazon.com or another bookseller and studying it, only a scholar who received certification or permission was allowed to teach a text. This is a fundamental difference between precolonial Islamic epistemology and that of Western schools.

In addition to lectures addressed to sizable student groups, a system of mentorship linked masters to a smaller number of promising students to whom they imparted knowledge on an individual basis. Members of inner circles of established scholars also served as assistants or secretaries. Through this system of intellectual patron / client relationship called *mulazama*,[31] students not only studied important books from a master, but they also had access to prestigious authorizations to transmit knowledge (*ijaza*). In addition, they learned from their masters other forms of knowledge not available in books, such as mystical secrets on how to acquire wealth, influence, or greater piety. The most zealous teaching assistants were likely to obtain the relevant credentials that ensured their gradual acceptance into the ranks of respected scholars.

The search for knowledge was linked to the struggle for self-improvement. Unlike in modern colleges, there was no fixed timeframe for studying a text or a particular subject. Students could study for many, many years, and often had to read and listen to a commentary of a major text several times. Students were also taught the virtue of humility. Typically, the master alone would sit in a chair, surrounded by students who sat on the floor and listened. This tradition is still maintained today in most theological schools of West Africa. Students showed their devotion to the master through physical work (*khidma*) but also by writing poems in praise of him. Indeed, in the surviving Arabic literature of West Africa, the most common genre is devotional literature in praise of the Prophet Muhammad, a shaykh, or a teacher. These works may consist of writing an original poem or expanding and commenting on an original poem by adding more verses of a similar meter.

In modern colleges of Africa, a teacher provides instruction and may continue to serve as a mentor even after the student graduates. He may write letters of reference in support of a student's application, but he is not believed to have supernatural powers to influence the course of things. In medieval Islamic centers of learning, in contrast, the teacher taught the Qur'an or rules of grammar, *fiqh* (jurisprudence), or other subjects. But he did more than that: the *murabit* among Arabic speakers of southern Sahara, the *malam* among the Hausa, the *ceerno* among Pulaar speakers, the *serin* among the Wolof of Senegambia, and the *mori* among the Manding played a central role in most life cycle events. Whether it is birth, death, illness, employment, harvest, travel, or elections, the teacher intervened before and after to pray that his following or disciples might succeed, survive, and be safe from reversal of fortunes. The cleric is able to do that because he was born as a wali, or friend of God. Sufi saints such as Ahmad al-Tijani (1735–1815) or 'Abd al-Qadir al-Jilani (d. 1166) were such wali. But it was also possible to reach high spiritual status through learning and piety. Performing spiritual exercises combining *khalwa* (retreat from the world), *dhikr* (repeated recitation of one of the beautiful names of God), fasting, and nightly vigils are efficient ways to be promoted to a higher spiritual rank.[32] Once this rank is reached, the cleric can bestow his baraka on his friends and disciples for good, but also to harm his enemies. A saint is supposed to have a "spiritual power" (*martaba* in Arabic) that can strike anybody who misbehaves toward him even if the saint thus offended does not seek revenge.

This level of spiritual dynamics found its most vivid expression within Sufi orders. Before the twentieth century, most of the shaykhs were initiated into Sufism and transmitted *wird* of Sufi orders. Some students received higher Islamic education but also were initiated into Sufi orders with the possibility of being promoted to the rank of *muqaddam* (deputy) and allowed to transmit wird (formal initiation). Sufi orders held a rich arsenal of talismanic secrets. A loyal disciple would accumulate all the secrets, but by then he would have served his shaykh (*khidma*) in addition to performing spiritual exercises. If the master was pleased with the disciple, the latter was guaranteed to succeed in this life and the next. A trusted disciple with whom the master is pleased becomes a spiritual child of the master. He will be given all the secrets, and sometimes the daughter of the shaykh in marriage. Marrying a daughter of a religious leader increased the prestige and legitimacy of students or disciples.[33] Most scholarly communities in West Africa significantly expand their membership and enhance their status through intermarriage.

Identity, Intertextuality, and Imagined Community

Reverence for authority, either personal or textual, was a fundamental tenet of precolonial Islamic intellectual and spiritual life. The teacher accredited the transmission of knowledge, whether an introductory text of grammar or a talismanic secret, by a permission (*ijaza*) given to the learner. In this way, Muslim scholars connected their writings to the "Islamic discursive tradition."[34] But did they mechanically replicate what masters taught, as the notion of *taqlid* (imitation) suggests? An insight of linguistic anthropology is that the relation between a text and a genre, or "generic intertextuality," is always a constructed one and that, in the process of linking a text to a genre, producers of discourse necessarily create an intertextual gap and use various ideologically motivated strategies to either minimize or maximize the gap.[35] Strategies of gap minimization or maximization in turn relate to a variety of factors (social, economic, cultural, and historical).[36] Although generic intertextuality is critical to identity and creating what Benedict Anderson called imagined communities, individuals in particular discursive contexts may choose either to maximize or minimize the gap, depending on the kind of authority they want to establish.

> Texts framed in some genres attempt to achieve generic transparency by minimizing the distance between texts and genres, thus rendering the discourse maximally interpretable through the use of generic precedents. This approach sustains highly conservative, traditionalizing modes of textual authority. On the other hand, maximizing and highlighting these intertextual gaps underlies strategies for building authority through claims of individual creativity and innovation.[37]

Sunni Islam based on Maliki jurisprudence, which imposed itself in the Islamic West following the eleventh-century Almoravid expansion, was central to the practice of Islam. But Maliki, and Islamic jurisprudence in general, is characterized by pluralism.[38] Maliki jurists often expressed conflicting views on the same question. The nineteenth century, more than any other period in the history of West Africa, witnessed the political triumph of the Islamic clerisy. From the Lake Chad region through the Niger Bend to Senegambia, Muslim clerics seized political power through jihad. These jihads in some instances involved clerics toppling illiterate rulers for being unsuited to rule. As shown by the attack of Umar Tall (1797–1864) against Masina or the followers of Uthman Dan Fodio (1754–1817) against Borno, some of these jihads involved attacking Islamic emirates. A huge nineteenth-century polemical literature features polemics within the Muslim clerisy in which conflicting parties invoked Maliki jurisprudence to back their claims.

So, for example, as I will discuss in greater detail in Chapter 5, in order to attack Hausaland in the late eighteenth century, Uthman Dan Fodio spun a sophisticated argument to prove that Hausaland is not part of the Abode of Islam (*Dar al-Islam*). In the process, he departed from an authoritative fatwa issued by the famous Maliki jurist, Ahmad Baba (1556–1627) of Timbuktu, who in the seventeenth century ruled that the Hausa were Muslims. Dan Fodio argued instead that the status of a land is that of its ruler, not the religion claimed by the majority of the people. Furthermore, he proclaimed the Hausa rulers (who professed Islam) to be non-Muslim and concluded that not only must true Muslims emigrate from Hausaland, but it was also licit to wage war against them. Analysis of the Islamic archive of West Africa reveals how scholars and activists successfully manipulated texts to establish their own authority. While their intellectual production is often rooted in a theological line of argument, Muslim scholars' writings, as we will see in Chapter 5, were often a response both to the historical circumstances they encountered and to the expectations of their followers.

The Colonial Library and the Disembodiment of Knowledge

During the formation of Western civilization, the Enlightenment played a central role. Above all, the political project of the Enlightenment was about freeing individuals from two main holders of power and authority in medieval Europe: the church and the monarchy. New conceptions of human welfare and freedom gradually imposed themselves in Europe and elsewhere, and various forms of human unfreedom (serfdom, chattel slavery) were attacked. In most Western societies, a separation between church and religion was successfully enforced. Freedom, reason, the individual, autonomy, and secularism were therefore central tenets in Western societies on the eve of their colonial conquest of West Africa. Western methods of learning imported to West Africa were influenced by those ideas. Ideas of absolute devotion to a master, the search for knowledge as an act of devotion, physical pain and suffering as central in character building—all those ideas differed markedly from conceptions of human welfare and freedom embodied in colonial pedagogy and epistemology. Memorization, which had been the key method of storing information in the classical epistemology, was now decried as the polar opposite of rational reasoning. Above all, it is the paradigm of the embodiment of knowledge that the new Western pedagogy challenged.

By the time West African countries became independent, Western conceptions of schooling had become very influential. Indeed, Muslims in West Africa realized that modern education leading to the receipt of a degree also facilitated securing a well-paid job. Many Muslims received education in colonial languages. Among those who opted for Arabic-language education, many embraced the organization of schooling into age groups, according to a specific time frame and using a unified curriculum, which is largely the European model. Traditional master/disciple relations have been criticized by a few, but such practices are still alive and well. Muslims do not so much have to choose between the old and the new, the Sankoré or the Western model, but can embrace both, as each fulfills a function that the other does not. The idea is that different visions of knowledge can coexist and enrich one another. But still, those who do not receive Western education are seen as backward.

Book Argument and Road Map

Black Africa has been represented in academia as well as in popular representations as a continent of warring tribes. One of the main challenges of nation building, so the story goes, was to create a sense of belonging among different tribes separated by colonial and post-colonial boundaries. This has been so well documented that it has become, if not the single story, at least the dominant narrative. I argue that large sections of West African peoples have, in the past and the present, proven their ability to transcend parochial identities and differences in a common cause and have indeed claimed their independence of thought and common destiny. More than anything else, this is embodied in a long literary tradition that has been obscured by European colonial hegemonic discourses of the past century. That dialogue tended to represent black Africa essentially as a continent of orality and obscured its literary tradition.

By 2013, people worldwide had heard about Timbuktu as a center of learning where thousands of Arabic manuscripts are preserved, some of which were destroyed by fanatics during the French counteroffensive to halt the expansion of Islamists in Mali. But few people know that Timbuktu was only one of many centers of Islamic learning in precolonial West Africa. This book seeks to fill that gap. It analyzes the rise and transformation of Arabo-Islamic erudition in West Africa from the sixteenth century through the colonial period to the twenty-first century. It highlights the contribution of Muslim scholars in the production and transmission of knowledge and in shaping state and society in West Africa. It refutes the notion of a dominant post-colonial Western epistemological order and argues that no study of the history of education or knowledge production in West Africa will be complete unless it pays attention to this intellectual tradition.

Titled "Timbuktu Studies: The Geopolitics of the Sources," Chapter 1 discusses the formation of the field that I call Timbuktu studies. It focuses on mapping the intellectual field—essentially the collection, archiving, cataloguing, digitizing, and translation into European languages of the Islamic archives of West Africa. Translated works were for the most part authored by prominent intellectual or religious/political leaders. Philosophers and intellectual historians writing in European languages have been largely unaware of those translations. This chapter stands on its own as a textual history. It might be of interest to specialists but can probably be skipped by the average educated reader who does not know Arabic.

In Chapter 2, entitled "The Growth and Political Economy of Islamic Scholarship in the Bilad al-Sudan," I trace the development of Islamic education back to the introduction of Islam in West Africa. By looking at accounts of medieval geographers and travelers, I discuss the routes by which Islamic influences found their way to the Bilad al-Sudan from North Africa through the Sahara, paying particular attention to the material culture and political economy of learning and writing in Arabic before colonialism.

Chapter 3, "The Rise of Clerical Lineages in the Sahara and the Bilad al-Sudan," identifies teachers of Arabic who were messengers of Islam in West Africa. The formation of an Islamic clerisy was also a story of racial, linguistic, and ethnic reconfiguration. Arab immigrants and their descendants, Saharan Berbers, and black Africans were the main actors in this process. New lineages resulted from this melting pot, some of which specialized in learning. They were responsible for the dissemination of learning in Arabic and/or Ajami before European colonialism.

In Chapter 4, "Curriculum and Knowledge Transmission," I discuss some of the most studied texts and subjects, with the understanding that there was regional variation in the curriculum. I analyze the main subjects that constituted Islamic knowledge as well as the main sources of intellectual influence. In major centers of learning, an identifiable set of core texts has been taught in the southern Sahara, North Africa, the Niger Bend, and the central Sudan. Some of them are still taught in traditional Islamic education settings today.

Chapter 5, entitled "Shaping an Islamic Space of Meaning: The Discursive Tradition," identifies the main genres to be found in available manuscripts. Focusing on works translated into European languages, it also analyzes major issues debated by Muslim scholars in the Bilad al-Sudan in the eighteenth and nineteenth centuries. As Muslim scholars and communities sought more converts and strove to expand the Islamic space of meaning, they were confronted with issues such as slavery, jihad, and state building, as well as relations with non-Muslims.

Chapter 6, "Islamic Education and the Colonial Encounter," looks at the impact of colonialism on education in West Africa. This is a landmark period in the history of education in West Africa. A great diversity of schools was created; some of the institutions taught in European languages exclusively, while others were bilingual in Arabic and French or English. Their increase notwithstanding, the old Islamic two-tier system of education still exists and attracts students and teachers from a variety of backgrounds, including graduates of Western-language schools.

The best illustration of the resilience of Arabic education in West Africa is the creation of modern degree-awarding Islamic universities and colleges. Their number is insignificant compared to that of Europhone universities, yet a couple dozen Islamic colleges created in sub-Saharan Africa since the mid-1980s have enabled Arabic-educated students to pursue modern higher education leading to a degree at home. This is in contrast with earlier cohorts, who attended North African universities. Titled "Modern Islamic Institutions of Higher Learning," Chapter 7 looks at the newer West African colleges.

Throughout the twentieth century, those I refer to as Arabophones[39] had to negotiate the post-colonial dispensation dominated by European languages. Some attempted to learn European languages, whereas others sought to promote Arabic with the help of Arabic petrodollars. Many saw in re-Islamization a way to assert the supremacy of the Arabic language and reestablish the influence of intellectuals educated in Arabic. They created mass social organizations of their own and preached against the separation of religion and state. They won disciples from different segments of West African societies, including Western-educated intellectuals. In Chapter 8, "Islam in the Post-colonial Public Sphere," and Chapter 9 "Arabophones Triumphant: Timbuktu under Islamic Rule," I analyze the growing success of advocates of Islamization and Arabization. Most West African states that adopted the policy of the separation of religion and state are now making substantial compromises to the Arabophone coalition. Reflecting on what Ali Mazrui calls "Africa's triple heritage,"[40] the conclusion to this volume addresses the multiple approaches to learning and knowledge that coexist in West Africa in the twenty-first century.

Chapter 1

Timbuktu Studies

The Geopolitics of the Sources

> At this point we leave Africa, not to mention it again. For it is no
> historical part of the World; it has no movement or development
> to exhibit. Historical movements in it—that is in its northern
> part—belong to the Asiatic or European World. Carthage
> displayed there an important transitionary phase of civilization;
> but, as a Phoenician colony, it belongs to Asia. Egypt will be
> considered in reference to the passage of the human mind from its
> Eastern to its Western phase, but it does not belong to the
> African Spirit. What we properly understand by Africa, is
> the Unhistorical, Undeveloped Spirit, still involved in the
> conditions of mere nature, and which had to be presented here
> only as on the threshold of the World's History.
> —*Georg Wilhelm Friederich Hegel*[1]

I N THE FIRST DECADE of the twenty-first century, a few treaties on Sufism
written by West African scholars were translated into European languages,
including Shaykh Ibrahim Niasse's magnum opus, *Kashif al-Ilbas* (Removal of
Confusion).[2] In this treatise centered on clarifying the doctrines of the Tijaniyya
tariqa and establishing his own authority as the spiritual heir of Ahmad
al-Tijani, Shaykh Ibrahim Niasse cites works on exegesis of the Qur'an (*tafsir*),
prophetic traditions (hadith), jurisprudence (*fiqh*), theology (*'aqida*), grammar
(*nahw*), religious principles (*usul*), the biography of the Prophet (*sira*), and of
course Sufism (*tasawwuf*). Authors cited by Shaykh Ibrahim Niasse, as well as
many other West African Sufis, come from a variety of regions, including Turkey,
India, North and West Africa, Persia, and Al-Andalus, which is evidence that
they participated in a global network of intellectual exchange.[3]

As I grew up, I often heard conversations about the *Kashif al-Ilbas* and Sufi
worldviews during the religious festivals and lectures that punctuated our lives.
In the past eight decades, *Kashif al-Ilbas* has been widely debated in West

Africa, not only by learned scholars who could read and grasp its meaning in Arabic, but also by individuals from a variety of linguistic and ethnic backgrounds, most of whom knew little to no Arabic and were taught the content of *Kashif al-Ilbas* orally in their mother language (Hausa, Hassaniyya, Pulaar, Yoruba, etc.) by literate shaykhs. Quite a few shaykhs or shaykhas of the Tijaniyya who were taught *Kashif al-Ilbas* orally have been teaching it to larger audiences in West Africa. It is only one of the many Sufi treatises taught in West Africa. By the time of the publication of the English and French translations, the field I call Timbuktu studies (meaning the inquiry into the intellectual history of Islam in Africa) had matured considerably.

Here I try to shed light on the invisibility of the Bilad al-Sudan in the academic study of Islamic ideas in the West until the recent developments in the early twenty-first century. I cannot overemphasize the extent to which colonialism was responsible for this neglect. As highlighted by late Columbia University professor Edward Said[4] in his study linking the intellectual labor of eighteenth- and nineteenth-century scholars of the Orient to the European project of imperial hegemony, the interaction between power and knowledge has been obvious in the creation of European representations of the Orient in general, and of Islam in particular. Especially in early colonial West Africa, the construction of imperial hegemony—that is, domination based more on consent than coercion—shaped the academic division of labor. Because they faced fierce opposition from Muslim leaders in North and West Africa during the colonial conquest, one of the greatest fears of European colonial powers throughout their rule was Pan-Islamism (i.e., a large transnational coalition of African Muslims against colonial rule). To exorcize that fear, the powers conceived of Africa as two main zones along the lines of Hegel's representation: the North and the South separated by the Saharan desert, a barrier that they strove to maintain both by restricting the movement of colonial subjects between North and West Africa and by colonial hegemonic discourses. Considered part of the center of the Islamic world, the Arabic-speaking North received greater attention from Orientalists trained in Semitic philology, who focused on the collection, edition, and translation of Arabic texts. Assumed to be superficially Islamized, peripheral to the Islamic world, intellectually inferior, and completely outside of history, West Africa was to a large extent left to African studies scholars who had little interest in Islam.

The Neglect of Orientalists and Arab Compilers

A look at two early Orientalist reference works on Islamic intellectual history will confirm this neglect of West African Muslim communities. The first is the *Encyclopaedia of Islam,* of which two complete editions have been published and a third is being compiled. The first edition was started at the beginning of the twentieth century and completed in 1938. Published by the world-renowned publisher in Islamic studies E. J. Brill, it covered essential aspects of the social, political, and intellectual history, as well as the geography, theology, and culture of the Islamic world. The first edition provides a thorough coverage of the Arabic, Turkish, and Persian world that hosted the largest historical Islamic empires, such as the Umayyad, the Abbasid, and the Fatimid, as well as the Ottoman and Sassanid Empires.

The first edition was published in the heyday of European imperial hegemony and consequently was influenced by its epistemologies and stereotypes. West African Islam was largely absent from this edition of the *Encyclopaedia of Islam.* To a great extent, the same prejudice affected the second edition, work on which started in the early 1960s. It was only from the 1990s on, when Islam in sub-Saharan Africa became a recognized field of research, that its experts were invited to contribute entries to that second edition. The ongoing third edition is likely to devote greater attention to Sudanic Africa, not least because its editorial team includes one Africanist, Dr. Roman Loimeier, who is in charge of selecting and assigning entries dealing with the Bilad al-Sudan.

Another notable effort at mapping Islamic intellectual history in a European language was the work of the German Orientalist Carl Brockelmann (1868–1956). Titled *Geschichte der Arabischen Litteratur* (History of Arabic Literature),[5] it was first published in 1909 in Leipzig, Germany, and later republished by the Dutch publisher E. J. Brill. Divided into chronologically organized sections subdivided by literary genres, this five-volume compilation of several thousand pages provides biographic and bibliographic information about Arabic writings and authors, with particular reference to the classical period. It devotes only four pages to West Africa, despite the fact that a couple of libraries including writings from the Bilad al-Sudan had been confiscated and taken to Europe by the colonizing armies in the late nineteenth century.[6] However, until the 1980s, none of them was analyzed, let alone catalogued.[7]

A look at encyclopedic dictionaries in Arabic shows the same neglect on the part of Arab compilers. Two examples of major compilations in Arabic are the *Al -A'lam* by Khayr al-Din Al-Zirikly (1979) and the *Mu'jam al-Mu'allalifin* by 'Umar Rida Kahhala (1957). Entitled *Biographical Dictionary of Arab Authors, Arabophones, and Orientalists*, Al-Zirikly's work, which was first published in 1927, has since appeared in three updated editions in 1957, 1969, and 1979.[8] It is composed of eight volumes and contains biographical information on many Arab and Orientalist authors and their works. The *Mu'jam al-Mu'allalifin* (Dictionary of Authors) of 'Umar Rida Kahhala (1957)[9] is another encyclopedic reference work on Arabic writings. In fourteen volumes, the *Mu'jam*, as its title indicates, aims to give maximum information about works written in Arabic, their authors, the genealogy of those authors, and their field of specialization. However, these two major reference works give the impression, left by the *Encyclopaedia of Islam* and the *Geschichte* of Brockelman, that sub-Saharan Africa has not contributed to Islamic intellectual history.

Early Mapping Efforts

The first notable effort to map Arabic sources in African history can be traced to the work coordinated by Prince Youssouf Kamal. Entitled the *Monumenta Carthographica Africae and Aegypti* and compiled by a team of researchers of different nationalities,[10] it remained until the late twentieth century the greatest cartographical work ever undertaken in terms of its broad range. The *Monumenta* include an inventory of written texts in Greek, Latin, Arabic, and other medieval European languages that concern Africa from Pharaonic Egypt to the arrival of the Portuguese in 1434. But until recently, they were very little cited, for two main reasons: first, because only one hundred copies of the first edition were produced by Brill between 1926 and 1951, of which seventy-five were offered to libraries; second, because the sixteen volumes that composed the work measured 75 × 60 centimeters and were very heavy.[11] This made the resource cumbersome to use, until 1987, when Fuat Sizgin prepared a second more accessible edition.[12] Thus, for a long time, the *Monumenta* were very seldom cited in African historiography.[13]

This endeavor was followed by the work of Father Joseph Cuoq entitled *Recueil des sources arabes concernant l'Afrique occidentale du VII au XVe siècle*, published in 1975.[14] It covered all Arabic sources concerning West Africa west of the Nile and south of the Sahara. This corpus, which includes twenty-five authors not mentioned in the *Monumenta*, dealt only with Arabic sources and provided crucial testimonies on the medieval states of Ghana, Mali, Songhay, and Kanem Borno, among others.

A third compilation of Arabic sources on African history[15]—this one much cited by historians—was sponsored by the University of Ghana in 1957 at a time when Pan Africanist agitation had reached its peak. It generated a great deal of interest in the African precolonial intellectual legacy. Historian John Fage established a provisional list of materials based mainly on the *Monumenta*.[16] Witold Rajkowski of the University of London translated a third of the material, but his premature death prevented its completion. The rest of the translation and the edition of the whole work was then carried out by John Hopkins and Nehemia Levtzion and published in 1981 under the title *Corpus of Early Arabic Sources for West African History*; it listed sixty-six Arab authors who wrote between the ninth and seventeenth centuries. These resources supply both first- and secondhand information concerning the political and social history of the Bilad al-Sudan.

Since the publication of the *Corpus*, many commendable efforts have been made to retrieve the Islamic library of West Africa. They consist of cataloguing and publishing collections of manuscripts in Arabic and Ajami as well as translations in English and French of the works of the most prominent intellectuals of the Bilad al-Sudan. Particularly worthy of note among them are these works: the seventeenth-century chronicler Al-Burtuli's *Fath al-Shakur fi ma'rifat a'yan 'ulama al-Takrur* (Key Given by God for Making Known the Noteworthy Scholars of Takrur);[17] nineteenth-century scholar of Hausaland, Uthman Dan Fodio's *Bayan wujub al-hijra*[18] (On the Obligation to Emigrate) and his *Ihya al-Sunna wa Ikhmad al-Bid'a* (Revivification on the Sunna and Destruction of Blamable Innovations);[19] four major works by Abdullahi Dan Fodio (1766– 1828) on political theory, which include *Diya Hukkam fi-ma lahum wa 'alayhim min ahkam* (Enlightening Rulers Concerning Their Rights and Duties), *Diya al-Sultan wa ghayrihi min al-ahkam* (Enlightening the Ruler and All the Brothers Concerning Their Rights and Duties), *Diya al-Siyasa wa fatawa wa nawazil* (Enlightening People on the Art of Governing and Verdicts on Events), and *Tazyin al-waraqat bi-ba'd min al-abyat* (Aspects of My Life Narrated in Verses);[20] Bello's *Infaq al-Maysur fi Tarikh Bilad al-Takrur* (Accomplishing the Feasible Concerning the History of the Land of Takrur);[21] Musa Camara's *Zuhur al-Basatin fi Tarikh al-Sawadin* (Flowers of the Gardens in the History of the Blacks);[22] Ibrahim Niasse's *Kashif al-Ilbas* (Removal of

Confusion);[23] two major works by Senegalese scholar Malik Sy, i.e., *Ifham al-Munkir al-Jani* (Silencing the Criminal Detractor) and *Kifayat al-Raghibin* (That Which Aspirants Need);[24] the long-overdue translation of Ali Harazim's *Jawahir al-Ma'ani* (Jewels of Meanings), the most important doctrinal source for the study of the Tijaniyya;[25] the edition and translation of Nana Asma'u's complete work by Beverly Mack and Jean Boyd;[26] the translation of Ahmadu Bamba's collection of poems;[27] and the translation into French of Umar Tall's *Bayan ma waqa'a* (Explaining What Happened).[28] In less than two decades, Islam in the Bilad al-Sudan (and particularly its intellectual history) has become a recognized field of study in Western universities, with several professorships filled by leading scholars of African Islam in France, Germany, and the United States and the emergence of leading international journals.

The most important task that scholars in the field undertook was to map the intellectual production, by localizing the writings, and producing printed lists as well as an online catalogue. The writings of West African countries such as Mauritania, Mali, Senegal, and Niger have been widely covered in the past fifty years, whereas Central African countries such as Chad and Cameroon have remained largely understudied.

Situated in the western Sahara between North and West Africa, Mauritania has historically bridged these two regions. It boasts a rather rich history of writings in Arabic, which have remained unknown for a long time, even in the Arab world.[29] Of limited circulation in the larger Islamic world had been the biographic dictionaries of Mauritanian scholars such as *Fath al-Shakur* by Al-Burtuli, produced in the eighteenth century,[30] and the *Al-Wasit fi tarajim udaba Shinqit*, a biographical dictionary of scholars of Mauritania by Muhammad al-Amin al-Shinqiti written in the early twentieth century.[31] Most Islamic manuscripts of Mauritania have remained in traditional centers of learning and have therefore been inaccessible to modern historians. The cataloguing of Mauritanian manuscripts started in the 1960s with the *Catalogue provisoire*, drawn up by Adam Heymouski, former curator of the Royal Swedish Library, and Moukhtar Ould Hamidoun, the doyen of modern Mauritanian historians.[32] Only a few examples of this catalogue were printed in Arabic with a Latin transliteration. The *Catalogue provisoire* included, in alphabetical order, a list of 425 authors, among the best known in Mauritania, as well as two thousand works by these authors, with a brief description of their manuscripts.

Twenty years later, German Islamicist Ulrich Von Rebstock[33] led a team composed of scholars from the University of Tübingen and the Mauritanian

Institute for Scientific Research to produce a catalogue of Mauritanian manuscripts. Entirely written in the Latin script, this catalogue broke ground in the
mapping of Mauritanian intellectual history. It listed 2,239 manuscripts, of
which the oldest is by an eleventh-century author.[34] It covered some hundred
libraries and manuscript collections from various regions of Mauritania, as well
as a wide range of subjects classified under the following themes: *ad 'iya* (invocations), *adhkar* (litanies), *fatawa* (legal opinions), *fiqh* (jurisprudence), hadith
(science of traditions), *mawa'iz* (exhortations), *nawazil* (juridical affairs),
Qur'an, *sira* (biography of the Prophet), *tasawwuf* (Sufism), *tawhid* (theology),
usul (sources of law), *adab* (literature), *'arud* (metrics), *bayan* (rhetoric), *lugha*
(language), *mantiq* (logic), *nahw* (grammar), *shi'r* (poetry), political ethics,
astronomy/astrology, geography, mathematics, magic, medicine, and agriculture. This work is more detailed than the *Catalogue provisoire*, featuring as it
does the name of the author, the title of the manuscript, the location of its
digitization, the manuscript's theme, and the date of completion, as well as the
library where it is located.[35]

The third important work in this listing of Mauritanian manuscripts is the
Catalogue de manuscrits arabes of the Institut mauritanien de recherche scientifique (Mauritanian Institute for Scientific Research). Between 1975 and 1990,
the institute collected more than 3,100 manuscripts, some of which were purchased, in order to establish a national manuscript collection.[36] In 1988–1989,
the manuscript collection was computerized in an Arabic/English catalogue
format.[37] The compilers adopted a system of transliteration taking into account
the specificity of Hassaniyya, the Arabic dialect spoken in Mauritania. The total
volume of the catalogued manuscripts (some 1,546 pages of entries, plus 200
pages of index) was first available for consultation at the Mauritanian Institute
for Scientific Research) and at the University of Illinois at Urbana Champaign
in 1990. The themes covered generally reflect those of the Arabic literature of
West Africa: a large number of works on jurisprudence, Sufism, the Arabic
language, Qur'anic studies, literature, science of traditions, and theology. To a
lesser extent they include texts on invocation, history, logic, ethics, mathematics, astronomy/astrology, medicine, esoterism, pedagogy, and geography as
well as encyclopedias.[38] According to Abdel Wedoud Ould Cheikh, former
director of the Mauritanian Center for Scientific Research, the majority of the
manuscripts were initially hosted in collections based in centers of learning in
the towns of Shinqit, Tishit, and Boutlimit. With the subsequent rural exodus
of scholars to the capital city, a significant number of these manuscripts have

been moved to Nouakchott, the capital city of Mauritania.[39] Next to Mauritania, Mali is the region that has received the greatest attention of cataloguers. It is above all thanks to the sponsorship of the Al-Furqan Foundation, based in London, that a detailed cataloguing of a significant number of Malian and other West African manuscripts was made possible.

The Decisive Intervention of the Al-Furqan Foundation

Established at the beginning of the 1990s by Sheikh Ahmad Zaki Yamani, former Saudi oil minister, the Al-Furqan li-Ihya al-Turath al-Islami Foundation states as its main mission the preserving of the Islamic written heritage "principally through ... surveying, imaging, cataloguing, editing and publishing Islamic manuscripts."[40] The foundation estimates that three million Islamic manuscripts are scattered in collections throughout the world.[41] It sponsored a *World Survey of Islamic Manuscripts,*[42] which identified public and private collections of "Islamic manuscripts" in the languages of Muslim people worldwide. With several entries on Sudanic African countries, the survey provides the locations and conditions of access, as well as an overview of the number and themes of the manuscripts contained in those collections. Following the publication of the *World Survey* in 1994, the Al-Furqan Foundation sponsored a detailed and rigorous cataloguing of manuscript collections, leading to the publication of seventy-one detailed catalogues by 2012,[43] twenty-five of which covered West African collections, with Mali taking the lion's share. In Mali, the Al-Furqan Foundation partnered with the Timbuktu-based Ahmad Baba Centre for Research and Historical Documentation (CEDRAB), created in 1973 by the Malian Government, following the recommendation of a UNESCO conference on African history held in Timbuktu in 1967. CEDRAB was renamed Institut des Hautes Études et de Recherches Islamiques Ahmad Baba (IHERI AB).[44] This institute and the Al-Furqan collaborated to produce five catalogues in Arabic between 1995 and 1998, featuring nine thousand manuscripts of the collection. The first volume listing 1,500 manuscripts was compiled by Sidi Amar Ould Eli and edited by Julian Johansen.[45] The second, third, and fourth volumes, each listing 1,500 manuscripts and published in 1996, 1997, and 1998, respectively, were compiled by a team of librarians of CEDRAB and edited by 'Abd Al-Muhsin Al-'Abbas of the Al-Furqan Foundation.[46] The fifth volume, which is larger than the others, was compiled and edited by a team of CEDRAB librarians and features three thousand manuscripts.[47] Each of these catalogues was published with several indices—of titles of manuscripts, names of authors, themes, and names of copyists—so that the contents of the work can be rapidly accessed and consulted.

The collaboration between Al-Furqan and the Mamma Haidara Commemorative Library of Timbuktu has also enabled the publication, in four volumes, of the manuscripts contained in this five-centuries-old library. The Al-Furqan Foundation provided training to the overseer of the collection, Abdelkader Mamma Haidara, in the rigorous cataloguing of manuscripts, and Haidara catalogued a total of four thousand manuscripts from his own library.[48] The Mamma Haidara collection includes texts on literature (*adab*), jurisprudence (*fiqh*), Sufism (*tasawwuf*) and the Qur'anic sciences (*'ulum al-Qur'an*), *ijaza* (authorizations to transmit exoteric or initiation knowledge), ethics (*akhlaq*), invocations (*ad'iya*), sources of religion (*usul al-din*), theory of law (*usul al-fiqh*), genealogies (*ansab*), history (*tarikh*), Qur'anic exegesis (*tafsir*), theology (*tawhid* and *'aqida*), science of traditions (hadith), mathematics (*hisab*), politics (*siyasa*), biographies (*tarajim*), the biography of the Prophet (*sira nabawiyya*), morphology and syntax (*nahw, sarf*), medicine (*tibb*), metrics (*'arud*), astronomy (*falak*), chemistry (*kimiya*), logic (*mantiq*), and exhortations (*wa'z wa irshad*). The length of these texts varies from a few pages to several hundred pages. In addition, a number of smaller documents and marginal notes in existing manuscripts record various events or commercial transactions that open a window into the social and economic life of the Bilad al-Sudan.

Besides the Al-Furqan Foundation, the government of South Africa has become a major sponsor of the rehabilitation of the Malian manuscripts. In November 2001, the former South African president Thabo Mbeki undertook an official visit to Mali, where he was received by the president of Mali, Alpha Oumar Konaré, and First Lady Adama Ba Konaré, who both hold doctorates in history and were eager to find sponsors for the rehabilitation of the Malian intellectual heritage. The Malian hosts managed to include a trip to northern Mali in the agenda of President Mbeki's visit.[49] In Timbuktu, the South African president was moved by the discovery of ancient manuscripts that were threatened by destruction due to the poor conditions of conservation. He pledged South African support for the adequate preservation of the Malian intellectual heritage, and immediately after his Malian visit, a delegation from the Department of Arts and Culture of South Africa was sent to Mali to make an assessment of the archival, conservation, and research situation at the Ahmad Baba Institute.[50] This was the start of the South Africa–Mali Timbuktu

Manuscripts Project. South Africa pushed for the adoption of the Timbuktu Manuscripts Project as the first cultural project of the New Partnership for African Development (NEPAD). The premises of CEDRAB were initially built with financial support from Kuwait. A new institute was built with the assistance of South Africa, which provided specialized training to the CEDRAB librarians as well sophisticated technology for the adequate preservation and digitizing of the ancient manuscripts. South African historian Shamil Jeppie from the University of Cape Town, who was the scientific advisor to the South African government for the Malian project, played a critical role in raising awareness in South Africa concerning the Malian manuscripts. In addition to training graduate students in Timbuktu studies,[51] he organized several scientific events, including a major conference at the University of Cape Town in 2004, which brought together the world's leading scholars in the field of Timbuktu studies as well as traditional Islamic scholars. Composed of twenty-five chapters, the proceedings of the conference are a state-of-the-art review of the research on the Islamic intellectual tradition in Africa.[52]

The large number of manuscripts found in Mali is the legacy of the great intellectual centers of northern Mali, and of Timbuktu in particular. Timbuktu scholars wrote in the seventeenth century the two most cited chronicles on the history of the region: *Tarikh al-Fattash* and *Tarikh al-Sudan*. Translated in 1913 by Octave Houdas and Maurice Delafosse into French[53] and by Weise[54] in 2012 into English, the *Tarikh al-Fattash fi akhbar al-buldan wa al-juyush wa akabir al-nas* (The Researcher's Chronicle, Serving the History of the Towns, the Armies, and the Principal Personalities) is a basic source for the history of the medieval states of the western Sudan.[55] In the latter work, *Tarikh al-Sudan*, which is by Abdarrahman al-Sa'di, the author used the term Al-Sudan to refer to sub-Saharan Africa and more particularly to the region of the Middle Niger. The book is a monumental account of the history of Timbuktu and Djenné, and describes in detail the origin of the Sonni dynasty as well as that of the Askia, which succeeded it. The *Tarikh al-Sudan* also contains a fascinating analysis of the decline of the Songhay Empire in the aftermath of the Moroccan invasion. After being translated into French by Octave Houdas and Maurice Delafosse at the beginning of the twentieth century,[56] it was translated into English by John Hunwick.[57] Hunwick's annotated translation is accompanied by notes and concludes with the collapse of the Songhay Empire in 1613, two decades after the Moroccan invasion. In an appendix to Hunwick's work, there are some important documents that have also been translated, including the description of West Africa by Hasan b. Muhammad al-Wazzan al-Zayyati (more often known as Leo Africanus), correspondence between the Moroccan sovereign Al-Mansur and the Songhay rulers, and personal accounts of the Moroccan invasion of the Songhay Empire. A third important document that might have been written by a Timbuktu scholar is *Tedzkiret en-nisyan fi akhbar muluk es-Sudan* (Reminder for Forgetfulness Regarding What Is Related about Rulers of the Sudan). Unlike the *Tarikh al-Sudan* and the *Tarikh al-Fattash*, it is less a historical than a biographical dictionary of the pasha of Timbuktu, beginning with Jawdar in 1590 and ending at 1750.[58]

In Niger, the Department of Arabic and Ajami manuscripts of the Institut de Recherche en Sciences Humaines (IRSH) hosts the largest collection of Islamic manuscripts. Boubou Hama, the Nigerien historian and former president of the National Assembly, must be credited for initiating the efforts to collect local manuscripts from various sources. Although not an Arabist himself, Boubou Hama was keen to preserve the local archives. He traveled in Niger and beyond to obtain copies of Arabic manuscripts, which he donated to IRSH. In Timbuktu, he solicited the assistance of Ahmad Boularaf, a historian, encyclopedist, archivist, and trader of Moroccan origin who supplied the bulk of the information for his work.[59] Building on the initial donation of Boubou Hama, researchers of the Department of Manuscripts of IRSH collected some four thousand Arabic and Ajami manuscripts, which are now preserved at the center. With the assistance of the London-based Al-Furqan Foundation, the Department of Arabic Manuscripts of IRSH, led by Moulaye Hassane, made a comprehensive and detailed catalogue of eight volumes in Arabic with a detailed presentation of the Nigerien manuscripts.[60]

Senegal is another country with a vigorous Islamic intellectual tradition thanks to the legacy of precolonial colleges. French colonial scholars did some compilation and translation of Senegalese Arabic and Ajami writings in the early twentieth century. Notable early colonial works include the publication of a chronicle of Fuuta based on two texts written by the genealogist Siré Abbas Soh and edited and translated by Maurice Delafosse (1870–1926) and Henry Gaden (1867–1939).[61] Henry Gaden undertook the other major translation work of the early twentieth century, that of a poem in Ajami Pulaar by Mohammadou Aliou Tyam narrating the biography of the reformer al-Hajj 'Umar Tall.[62] The creation of an Islamic studies department at the Institut français d'Afrique Noire (French Institute for Black Africa: IFAN) also contributed to the effort to collect and translate Arabic sources for West African history. One of its directors, French Islamicist Vincent Monteil, brought to IFAN talented young scholars in the late 1960s. Many of them became leading historians: Brazilian scholar Paulo Moraes de Farias is now an emeritus professor of history at the University of Birmingham and the highest authority on Arabic epigraphic writings in the Bilad al-Sudan; Abdoulaye Bathily is a politician and senior historian at the Université Cheikh Anta Diop; the late Moukhtar Ould Hamidoun was considered the doyen of contemporary Mauritanian historians; Boubacar Barry is a world-renowned historian of Senegambia; Amar Samb was a leading expert of the Arabic literary tradition in Senegambia; Ravane Mbaye translated and edited the most important texts of the Tijaniyya in the three decades of his scholarly career; and, finally, Vincent Monteil drew up a provisional list of Arab-African manuscripts, published in 1965, part of which deals with Senegalese manuscripts.[63]

After independence, IFAN was renamed Institut Fondamental d'Afrique Noire (Fundamental Institute for Black Africa) and is now affiliated with the University of Dakar. A great effort to collect and catalogue Arabic and Ajami manuscripts has been pursued by the IFAN researchers, who in 1966 published the *Catalogue des manuscrits de l'IFAN*, listing the Vieillard, Gaden, Brévié, Figaret, Shaykh Musa Kamara, and Cremer collections. These collections contain manuscripts in Arabic, Fulfulde, and Gur languages.[64] Among IFAN researchers and/or contributors to the *IFAN Bulletin*, three deserve mention for the translation work of Arabic sources they carried out: Amar Samb, Claudine Gerresch, and El Hadji Ravane Mbaye. Claudine Gerresch translated several Arabic works, including important writings by Madiakhate Kala,[65] Umar Tall,[66] and Tall's opponent, Ahmad al-Bakkay.[67] Amar Samb authored the first monograph devoted to the contribution of Senegal to Arabic literature. He reviewed a good dozen of what he called literary schools established by Senegalese scholars who had taught the Arabic language to thousands of disciples and made a significant contribution to Arabic literature. He cited the schools of Dakar, Thiès, Kaolack, Saint-Louis, Touba, Louga, Ziguinchor, and others.[68] John Hunwick and myself completed his work, listing, from Senegambia alone, more than a hundred authors and their mostly Arabic works.[69] El-hadji Ravane Mbaye, who spent most of his career studying the Arabic literature of Senegal, was the coauthor, with Babacar Mbaye, of a supplement to the catalogue of IFAN manuscripts.[70]

Thierno Kâ and Khadim Mbacké produced the most recently published catalogue of IFAN manuscripts, which lists recently collected materials and focuses on Senegambian authors.[71] In addition to publishing this catalogue, Khadim Mbacké has translated into French a hagiography of Ahmadu Bamba entitled *Minan al-baqi al-qadim fi sirat Shaykh al-khadim* (Gifts of the Everlasting in the Narration of the Biography of Ahmadu Bamba), written by his son, Bachirou Mbacké.[72] Thierno Kâ has documented in two monographs the history of two major Islamic centers of learning in Senegal, the first one established in the seventeenth century and the second in the late nineteenth century.[73] Finally, the Al-Furqan Foundation, in 1997, sponsored a detailed cataloguing of three private libraries belonging to leading Islamic clerical families.[74]

Notable among Senegalese Arabophones is the erudite Shaykh Musa Kamara (1864–1945).[75] He authored various texts in Arabic and Pulaar on such different fields as history, geography, the hydrology of the Senegal River from Guinea to Saint-Louis, literature, sociology, anthropology, jurisprudence, traditional medicine, and Sufism. IFAN scholars produced annotated translations of several of his works, most of them by Amar Samb.[76] Moustapha Ndiaye produced an annotated translation of Musa Kamara's history of Ségou.[77] Later in the 1990s, a group of researchers from the Centre National de la Recherche Scientifique (CNRS), IFAN, and the Université Cheikh Anta Diop translated and edited Shaykh Musa Kamara's magnum opus, entitled *Zuhur al-basatin fi tarikh al-sawadin* (Flowers from the Gardens in the History of the Black People), an alternative title of which is *Intisar al-mawtur fi tarikh bilad Futa Tur* (Triumph of the Oppressed through the Study of the History of Futa Tur). The first volume of this work (with three others still to appear) was coordinated by J. Schmitz and published in 1999.[78] Like other great historical works, such as *Tarikh al-Sudan* and *Tarikh al-Fattash,* the *Zuhur al-basatin* is very long (1,700 pages) and is written partly in Arabic and partly in Ajami. It constitutes a major source of information on economic and social life in the valley of the Senegal River and gives firsthand accounts of political organization and land tenure in the Middle Valley of the river, particularly in the nineteenth and twentieth centuries.

Another major work in Pulaar Ajami that deserves mention is the didactic poem written by Tierno Mouhammadou Samba Mombeya (1765–1850) in the nineteenth century. Entitled "Oogirde Malal" (Vein of Eternal Happiness), it is, according its translator, Alpha Ibrahim Sow, the most famous and erudite treatise of Islamic jurisprudence in the Pulaar language of Futa Djallon.[79] Inspired by the Arabic meter *rajaz,* it is a poem of 552 verses organized around three main themes—the faith, the law, and the path—citing the Qur'an and

referencing classical works of Maliki jurisprudence. Like similar works produced elsewhere in Ajami by Muslim scholars of West Africa, it targeted and
sought to explain complex notions of Islamic theology and jurisprudence to a
larger audience of Muslims who did not know Arabic.

In Northern Nigeria, some colonial administrators were also interested in
historical sources and made a considerable attempt to collect and translate
them. At the beginning of the twentieth century, H. R. Palmer published a
translation of two important works: the Kano Chronicle,[80] which is our principal source of information on the development of Islam in Hausaland,[81] and a
chronicle of the rule of Mai Idris Aloma of Borno.[82] In the same period and for
the first time, J. A. Arnett introduced to a Western audience sections of the
magnum opus of Muhammad Bello, *Infaq al-Maysur fi Tarikh Bilad al-Takrur*,
which narrates the biography of Uthman Dan Fodio and the nineteenth-
century Sokoto jihad.[83] According to Professor Murray Last, neither Palmer
nor Arnett was a good Arabist. Palmer knew some Arabic, but he probably had
an Arabist translate the Kano Chronicle. Likewise, Arnett translated the *Infaq*
from a Hausa translation that was provided for him.[84]

In the 1950s and 1960s, Nigerian-based British scholars were involved in the
collection of Arabic materials. Notable among them is W. E. N. Kensdale from
University College Ibadan, who catalogued the collection of the college,[85] and
A. D. H. Bivar of the Department of Antiquities of Jos.[86] Such collection and
translation work accelerated after Nigerian independence. Several institutions
contributed to that effort. Notable among them are the Center for Arabic
Documentation, the Jama'at Nasr al-Islam (JNI), Arewa House, and the
Northern History Research Scheme. At the University of Ibadan, historian
John Hunwick (d. 2015) initiated a project called The Center for Arabic
Documentation at the University of Ibadan in 1965, with the goal of publishing
a biobibliographic volume of Arabic writings in West Africa.[87] As he researched,
he found new writings, and his project, as will be discussed later, led to the
production of the largest reference work on Arabic writings in Africa. Named
after the former Nigerian premier, Ahmadu Bello University, the first university of Northern Nigeria, emerged in the late 1960s as a leading institution in
the study of the Islamic scholarly tradition of West Africa. Historian Murray
Last collected over ten thousand manuscripts—mostly in Arabic but also one
hundred in Fulfulde from Adamawa—to establish the Northern History
Research Scheme at Ahmadu Bello University Zaria in 1966.[88] Jama'at Nasr
al-Islam was founded by Premier Ahmadu Bello (d. 1966) to promote the unity

of Muslims in Northern Nigeria on the basis of their common heritage of the jihad of the nineteenth century. Through JNI, Bello sponsored the translation, publication, and dissemination of writings of nineteenth-century jihadist intellectuals.[89] In addition, Bello also established Arewa House, Kaduna, and appointed historian Abdullahi Smith as the first director for the same purpose. Under the leadership of Abdullahi Smith, former professor of history at the University of Ibadan, then at the Ahmadu Bello University, a new generation of historians, mainly Nigerians, attempted to depart from colonial historiography through an extensive use of Arabic sources to rewrite nineteenth-century West African history. Smith argued that the assumption of a growing European influence in the nineteenth century was problematic and had strongly informed the writing of nineteenth-century West African historiography. According to Smith, "the real conflict between African and European institutions was hardly felt anywhere in West Africa more than 200 miles from the Atlantic Coast before the 1880s." This left "700,000 square miles southward of the latitude of Lake Chad unaccounted for during the greater part of the 19th century in so far as the 'European type' of influence theme is concerned."[90] In that area, firearms sold by Europeans at the coast, for instance, were not used in any significant way in the nineteenth-century Islamic jihads, with the exception of that of Al-Hajj Umar Tall.[91] As shown by the costly expeditions to Borno, to Sokoto, and south of Timbuktu, Europe did have commercial interests in Africa, which Smith deliberately omitted. However, Smith's objection to the Eurocentric historiography of colonial Africa is a valid point.

Prominent among students of Abdullahi Smith were Murray Last (whose *Sokoto Caliphate* was the first work to have used the correspondence of the Sokoto bureaucracy as a historical source), Yusufu Bala Usman, Abdullahi Mahadi, and Mahmud Tukur.[92] The Northern History Research Scheme of the Ahmadu Bello University of Zaria participated in the effort to promote the sources in non-Western languages of the history of Nigeria. In addition to Last, who supplied the initial sources, and Graham Connah, who worked on Borno and Adamawa, Sudanese scholars Fathi al-Masri and Ahmad Muhammad Kani made a significant contribution to this effort.[93] Masri translated the magnum opus *Bayan Wujub al-hijra*.[94] Ahmad Kani's *Intellectual Origins of the Sokoto Jihad* provides an account of the nineteenth-century Sokoto jihad and the intellectual influences on Uthman Dan Fodio's political thought. Monographs by Shehu Umar Abdullahi,[95] Sidi Mohamed Mahibou,[96] and Sani Zahradeen[97] analyzed the political thought of Abdullahi Dan Fodio, another leader of the jihad. The well-disseminated material on the jihad is only the tip of the iceberg. The once-neglected field of jihad studies (in the words of Smith) had become very crowded three decades after independence.[98] Meanwhile, historians and Arabophones in Nigeria produced significant numbers of unpublished academic works. The Centre of Islamic Studies of the Usmanu Danfodiyo University of Sokoto in 1988 listed some three hundred dissertations and theses on Islam in Nigeria,[99] a significant number of which deal with the nineteenth-century jihad. Written in English, Hausa, and Arabic, they include biographies of some Islamic personalities, in particular the Fodiawa (disciples and descendants of Uthman Dan Fodio) as well as commentaries and critical analyses of the religious thought of leading Fodiawa, such as Uthman Dan Fodio, Abdullahi Dan Fodio, and Muhammad Bello. Finally, the work of two authors, Ali Abu Bakr and Kabiru Galadanci, should be noted among the contributions on Nigeria. Their syntheses analyze works in Arabic and list their authors.[100]

Another pioneer in the study of the Islamic writings in Northern Nigeria is the late Mervyn Hiskett, a colonial administrator and scholar who taught in Nigerian universities and at the School of Oriental and African Studies (SOAS) in London and trained leading Nigerian scholars of Islamic and Hausa studies. Mervyn Hiskett devotes significant attention to the Fodiawa, producing bibliographic and biographical materials on Uthman Dan Fodio.[101] He identified the precolonial core curriculum among the Fulbe,[102] and his contribution to the study of Ajami and Hausa is second to none. Hiskett's *History of Hausa Islamic Verse* is the first work of this kind in a European language.[103] Hiskett is also the author of an anthology of political verses that reviews and analyzes six poems that teach us much about political life in Northern Nigeria.[104] Among them figure the works of Mudi Spikin, born in 1930, a founding member of the Northern Elements Progressive Union of Northern Nigeria. Written in the early 1950s, the Hausa poem by Spikin entitled *Arewa Jumhuriyya kawai* in Hausa (The North Can Only Be a Republic) was in response to a poem entitled *Arewa Jumhuriyya ko mulkiyya* (The North, a Republic or a Monarchy?) by a member of his party, Saad Zungur, who was also inspired by the confrontation between politicians from the north and the south on the future of Nigeria at the time of the Constitutional Conference held in Ibadan in 1950.[105]

Abdulkadir Dangambo, a student of Mervyn Hiskett, produced an important work on Hausa Islamic poetry. In two volumes of almost eight hundred pages, his doctoral thesis was defended at the School of Oriental and African Studies at London University in 1980 and is devoted to *wakokin waazi* (sermons in verse). Like the panegyrics (*wakokin yaboo*), these sermons in verse constitute one of the main literary categories in Hausa. The material discussed in the thesis covers the period from 1800 to 1970 and constitutes a critical study of the form, content, language, and style of the poems belonging to the sermon category. Also from the "Hiskett school" and worthy of mention is the thesis defended by Abdullahi Bayero Yahaya at the Department of Nigerian Languages and Culture of Bayero University in 1983, a work dedicated to a Hausa poet called al-Hajj Bello Yahaya, who was trained both in English and Arabic and Islamic studies. Inspired by the beggars who recited the poems of Uthman Dan Fodio in Arabic and Hausa, Bello Yahaya composed poems in Hausa on numerous subjects. He wrote political poems in support of the Northern People's Congress, a party dominated by Northern Nigeria in the 1950s and 1960s. The sociological and psychological impact of the economic and technological transformations during the colonial period reflected in these poems makes fascinating reading. His poem *Wakar Reluwe* (Song of the Railway) is constructed in the Arabic meter *mutaqarab* and opens as follows:

Ina gode Allahu mai yau da gobe
[Praise be to God to whom today and tomorrow belong]
Das sanya Hausa cikin reluwe
[For including the Hausa among the users of the train]

Technological progress, far from shaking people's faith, has reinforced it insofar as they consider this progress to be a blessing that God has bestowed upon them. Al-hajj Bello Yahaya is also the author of many poems about the transformation of social relationships in the colonial era and the emergence of waged labor, as well as praise for the Prophet Muhammad and sermons in verse.

International Journals, Encyclopedias, and Online Databases: The Zenith of Timbuktu Studies

Prominent African and European scholars have been laboring in the field of Timbuktu studies since the independence of West African former colonies by collecting and editing manuscripts and translating important works from Arabic or Ajami to European languages. Published in multidisciplinary journals such as the *Bulletin of the School of Oriental and African Languages, African*

Language Studies, the *Bulletin de l'Institut Fondamental d'Afrique Noire,* and *Kano Studies,* their works have had very little visibility until the 1980s, when the creation of international journals in European languages devoted to the study of Islam in Africa gave greater visibility to Timbuktu studies. The first one, *Islam et Sociétés au Sud du Sahara,* was started following an international conference on "Religious Agents South of the Sahara"[106] held in 1982 by the Laboratoire Islam Tropical of the Maison des Sciences de L'Homme. Convened by French historian of Africa Jean-Louis Triaud, the conference brought together dozens of scholars from Africa, Europe, and the United States. Starting with the publication of some of the proceedings, the journal *Islam et Sociétés* has produced over twenty issues and created a space for exchanges between Africans, Americans, Europeans, and Asians researching African Islam and has become a valuable tool for Timbuktu studies. Each issue features many critical studies of Arabic sources and Islamic scholars of West Africa and presents a bibliography of unpublished BA, MA, and PhD theses presented on African Islam throughout the world.

The second journal, *Sudanic Africa: A Journal of Historical Sources,* was created in 1990 by John Hunwick and Sean O'Fahey (and later renamed *Islamic Africa*) as a vehicle by which to publish original documents in Arabic or African languages on the history and culture of Saharan and sub-Saharan Africa. Like *Islam et Sociétés, Sudanic Africa* has published numerous biographies of Islamic scholars. Building on the journal and John Hunwick's manuscript collections at the Center of Arabic Documentation of the University of Ibadan previously mentioned, its founders, Sean O'Fahey and John Hunwick, have initiated the most comprehensive compilation of the Arabic Literature of Africa Project to date. With the collaboration of scholars in Africa and elsewhere, they undertook the ambitious project of listing all the authors belonging to the Islamic intellectual tradition of Africa, as well as their works (in Arabic, Pulaar, Swahili, Hausa, etc.). The complete encyclopedic *Arabic Literature of Africa* will include seven volumes, six of which have already been published,[107] covering, respectively, the Nilotic Sudan until 1900 (Vol. 1), the central Sudan (Vol. 2), northeastern Africa (Vol. 3), the western Sudan (Vol. 4), and Mauritania and the western Sahara (Vol. 5); the last compiles 300 years of literary production, in excess of 10,000 titles by over 1800 authors. One more volume dealing with the Nilotic Sudan in the twentieth will complete the series. As a didactic tool modeled on the *Geschichte der Arabishen*

Litteratur of Carl Brockelmann, *Arabic Literature of Africa* features authors, their writings, and the scholarly tradition to which they belong. As a continuation of this work, in 1999, J. Hunwick and S. O'Fahey founded the Institute for the Study of Islamic Thought in Africa (ISITA), based at Northwestern University, Evanston, Illinois, which strives to mobilize a community of researchers around programs for pre- and postdoctoral fellowships, conferences, and publications—a major step for an analysis of the Islamic library of Africa.[108]

Two notable endeavors will end this survey of the historical library. The first is the publication by the Mauritanian legal anthropologist Yahya Ould el-Bara of a compendium of fatwas of the magnitude of the *Mi'yar* (The Standard) of Al-Wansharisi. But unlike the *Mi'yar,* which focused on Andalusia and the Maghreb, excluding the Bilad al-Sudan, Yahya Ould el-Bara's compilation also covers the south and southwestern Sahara, thus bringing large sections of the Bilad al-Sudan legacy of fatwas to its larger context of the Islamic West.[109] The second is the creation by Charles Stewart of the University of Illinois of an online bilingual catalogue of more than twenty thousand Islamic manuscripts of West African writers that builds on his earlier work on Mauritanian manuscripts.[110] With the sponsorship of the Al-Furqan Foundation, the database will include all the catalogued manuscripts of West African countries already published by the Al-Furqan Foundation.[111]

Finally, newly created Islamic universities and colleges in West and East Africa are providing fora for graduates of Middle Eastern or Islamic universities for academic study of the Islamic scholarly output in Africa. One such forum is the Hawliyyat al-jami'a al-islamiyya bi 'l-Nijer (*Annals of the Islamic University of Niger*), which parallels in scope the two leading international journals *Islam et Sociétés au Sud du Sahara* and *Islamic Africa,* and addresses themes very similar to those of Western language journals yet is produced by African academics writing in Arabic.

This chapter outlines the great amount of work and cataloguing that has been done in recent years. Yet there is still a vast amount of material, particularly in Ajami, stored in private collections and elsewhere that has not made it into academic circles. There are countries in West Africa not listed that have great Arabic archives and have just not received as much work. Likewise some North African countries are developing an interest in the study of the Islamic intellectual tradition of West Africa. Notable among them is Morocco which established a leading institute of African Studies at the Université Mohamed V de Rabat in the 1980s.

One note of caution to close this overview: the discovery of this intellectual tradition created such a great fascination that the word *manuscript* came to have magical qualities.[112] Exaggeration and misrepresentation of the African manuscripts have become commonplace in the past few years. As noted by Shamil Jeppie, manuscripts were sometime misdescribed as "ancient scrolls" or as holding "the secrets" to "the African past"—as if the putative "secrets" would solve our problems or there was one Africa with a single past."[113] The exaggeration did not just come from the media. One scholar of Timbuktu claimed that, had it not been for the environmental degradation caused by "humidity, rain, fire termites, insect and drought," "economic conditions, wars, displacements, negligence ignorance and other human factors," the estimated number of manuscripts would probably amount to several million in Timbuktu and surrounding areas.[114] This figure itself is no doubt an exaggeration.

My note of caution notwithstanding, I hope that this overview disproves Hegel's claim that "Africa Proper" was outside history. Islamic scholarship in West Africa has now been well researched, and the available sources enable us to document its history, starting with the growth and political economy of scholarship, which will be the topic of Chapter 2.

The Growth and Political Economy of Islamic Scholarship in the Bilad al-Sudan

> A debate is taking place about postcolonial literature
> and society in Africa in which writing in English about
> writing in English or French is pursued without any
> acknowledgement that a whole world of debate has been
> going on vigorously and at length in African languages.
> —*Graham Furniss*[1]

T HE ARABIC TERM *Bilad al-Sudan* or *Ard al-Sudan* (The Land of Black People) refers to the land that lies south of North Africa and stretches from the Atlantic Ocean to the Red Sea.[2] Medieval Arab writers coined the term as an "instrument of authorization" over the darker-skinned inhabitants of the regions of Africa penetrated by Islam. In the seventeenth century, Arabized Africans appropriated the term *Bilad al-Sudan* as a badge of greatness,[3] in much the same way as has happened to the term "negro." Originally used derogatively by white people to designate blacks, it was later appropriated by prominent African intellectuals such as Aimé Césaire (1913–2008) and Senegalese former president and poet Leopold Sedar Senghor (1906–2001) in their agenda of political liberation and intellectual emancipation of Africans vis-à-vis white colonial supremacy.

Modern historians have subdivided the Bilad al-Sudan into either two parts (eastern Sudan and western Sudan) or three (the western Sudan stretching from the Atlantic Coast to the Niger Bend, the central Sudan from the Niger Bend to Darfur, and the eastern or Nilotic Sudan from Darfur to the Red Sea). The Bilad al-Sudan straddles the ecological regions of the Sahara and the Sahel. The former is now characterized by high temperatures and low rainfall, whereas the latter is somewhat cooler and therefore more human and animal friendly.

There is a large consensus among historians of Africa that, historically, the Sahara has not been a barrier separating people from North Africa from those of Saharan and sub-Saharan Africa, but rather a bridge. The history of migration and identity formation and transformation induced partly by ecological conditions (drought, diseases, extension of the desert, war, and state formation) is such that rigid binaries inherited from the colonial library—North African/sub-Saharan, Arab/Negro Africans, white/black—which have been so resilient in the Western and African academy, are not helpful in understanding the history of the region. Thus, the term "Sudanic" and the expression "Bilad al-Sudan" are not used in any essentialist sense, since it is the interactions of Arabs, Berbers, and blacks that shaped the contours of this region.

As I have shown in the preceding chapter mapping the geopolitics of the sources, research in the late twentieth and early twenty-first centuries has brought to light the existence of a wealth of documents in non-Western languages relevant to understanding the history of ideas in the region. From the National Archives of Zanzibar in East Africa[4] and the many Timbuktu libraries in the western Bilad al-Sudan to the National Records Office in Khartoum[5] and the Kaduna Archives in Nigeria[6] lies a critical mass of documents, a large part of which has not been adequately studied by most historians of Africa operating within what Mudimbe called the Western epistemological order.[7] For sure, a large number of these manuscripts were written in the Maghreb or the Mashreq, but a significant number were written, copied, or commented upon by scholars of the Bilad al-Sudan, who contributed to the production, reproduction, and dissemination of what can be called Islamic knowledge—and whose works deserve to be studied. Of course, not all the manuscripts found in African libraries and private collections deal with religious topics per se. But, as Ghislaine Lydon rightly argues, since this documentation "was usually framed in the language, perspective, and calendar of Islam, [it] can be qualified as Islamic in nature."[8]

The material unearthed by experts of Islam and Muslim societies in sub-Saharan Africa puts us in a position to provide a synthesis of the Islamic scholarly tradition in its historical and geographical depth. From the introduction of paper in the Bilad al-Sudan, and the book trade across the Sahara and along the Atlantic Coast, to the production of ink and pens and the emergence of a distinct Sudanic calligraphic style in writing Arabic and Ajami, as well as the formation and transformation of the educational system during and after colonialism, enough information is available to enable us to bring the Islamic scholarly tradition in the history of the Bilad al-Sudan to the contemporary debate on the production of knowledge in and on Africa and to the study of Islamic ideas.

Origins of Islamic Scholarship in the Bilad al-Sudan

As suggested by accounts of medieval historians and geographers, copies of the Qur'an had circulated as soon as Muslim communities emerged in the region. One of the main sources for the study of the medieval western Bilad al-Sudan, the eleventh-century Arab author Abd Allah Abd al-Aziz Al-Bakri[9] (d. 1094) mentions in his *Kitab al-Masalik wa 'l-mamalik* (Book of Routes and Realms) the existence of a Muslim community in the medieval West African state of Ghana in the eleventh century: "The City of Ghana consists of two towns situated on a plain. One of these towns, which is inhabited by Muslims, is large and possesses twelve mosques, in one of which they assemble for the Friday prayer[10] . . . There are salaried imams and muezzins, as well as jurists and scholars."[11] According to another later account by the famous North African traveler Ibn Battuta, who visited the region in the fourteenth century, "the people in Walata memorized the Qur'an and studied religious law."[12]

We know that among the early Muslim communities in the Bilad al-Sudan, some were literate in Arabic and knew Islamic theology. Less clear to us is the moment at which they started to produce their own texts. In East Africa (Kenya, Uganda, and Tanzania), the damp and humid conditions along the coast seem to have destroyed medieval local writings.[13] Although the Swahili literary tradition has been long established and is very rich, the earliest documents found in the area consequently date from only the late seventeenth century. With the notable exception of Ishaq Ibrahim b. Ya'qub al-Kanami al-Aswad, no other author of the Bilad al-Sudan is known by name before the beginning of the sixteenth century.[14] The writings of al-Kanami have not been preserved, but medieval Arab writers mention him as a fine poet and teacher. For example, in his biographical dictionary titled *Wafayat al-a'yan wa anba abna al-zaman,* the thirteenth-century Arab biographer Ahmad b. Muhammad Ibn Khallikan reports that the black poet al-Kanami recited the following verses in honor of the Almohad ruler of Ya'qub al-Mansur:

> He removed his veil but my eyes, out of awe,
> saw him through a veil;
> His favor drew me near but being near, out of awe, I
> found myself distant.[15]

As the name indicates, al-Kanami originates from Kanem in the Lake Chad region, which was exposed to Islamic influence as early as the seventh century.

Indeed, Islam was introduced in Kanem in the year 46 of the Muslim calendar when the Muslim general 'Uqba b. Nafi' and his troops penetrated the neighboring regions of Fezzan and Kawar.[16] Kanem is one of the first regions of Sudanic Africa to witness the development of Islamic learning. For several centuries, and to this day, Kanem-Borno in modern Chad and Nigeria has been a major center of Islamic learning and has maintained close intellectual relations with North Africa. In the mid-thirteenth century, a school (Madrasat Ibn Rashiq) had already been established in Cairo[17] for the benefit of Borno students through an endowment given by Borno merchants/pilgrims to the qadi 'Alam al-Din Ibn Rashiq, named after the school.[18] Most probably the first West African foundation in the Middle East,[19] it received Borno students until the eighteenth century.[20] In addition, Mai Dunoma Dabalemi, the then king of Borno, is believed to have offered a hostel named Riwaq al-Barnawi (Borno students'/pilgrims' hostel) in Cairo in 1258, precisely the same year that Baghdad fell to the hordes of the Mongols.[21] It still exists as part of Al-Azhar University. Al-Azhar hosted shaykhs and students from many nationalities, who lived each in their own space (*riwaq*) within the mosque of Al-Azhar.[22] Each riwaq was headed by a leader (*shaykh al-riwaq*), selected most of the time by the riwaq community among their members on the basis of seniority, piety, and knowledge. The shaykh of the riwaq was responsible for providing community leadership. He welcomed and advised newcomers, supervised them, and raised funds to feed them from the Islamic endowments (*awqaf*).[23]

The development of Islamic scholarship was a process that paralleled the spread of Islam. The earliest populations to be exposed to Islam in the Bilad al-Sudan were Sudani merchants who traded with Arabs and Berbers. They were attracted to the way of life of Muslims who helped them understand the religion. Archeological evidence such as "glazed pottery, glass vessels, glass beads and brass metalwork"[24] found in various sites of the Bilad al-Sudan suggest increased commercial interactions between the Bilad al-Sudan and North Africa from the tenth century. Being Muslim seems to have been an advantage for those who wished to join the commercial networks controlled by Arabo-Berber Muslims.[25]

Next to convert were African kings. By the early eleventh century, a few kings had become Muslim,[26] including, in 1040, the king of Takrur (a medieval state located in the middle valley of the Senegal River); in 1050, the king of Manding;[27] his eastern neighbor, the king of Songhay, in 1009; and, further east, the Sayfawa ruler of the kingdom of Kanem in 1085.[28] Although illiterate, most of these rulers surrounded themselves with Muslim clerics on whose expertise they relied for various services, including recording trade agreements, chronicling history, and providing protective talismans and charms. It was common for non-Muslim kings to solicit the services of Muslim clerics as secretaries, including the king of medieval Ghana,[29] the king of Asante, in present-day Ghana, and the king of Oyo in western Nigeria in the fourteenth century.[30] There were also some literate rulers. The medieval Arab geographer Abu 'l-Qasim Muhammad al-Nusaybi, known as Ibn Hawqal (d. 988), reported in his geographical work *Surat al-ard* (Picture of the World),[31] the first comprehensive account of the Saharan Trade routes, that the Banu Tanamak rulers of mixed black and Berber ancestry of Tadmakkat were learned: "They combined leadership with learning, jurisprudence, and political skill, as well as some knowledge of biographies and they are versed in tradition and history."[32] Epigraphic evidence dating from the eleventh century found in royal tombstones in Essuk, Gao, and other areas of the Niger Bend are the earliest traces of Arab writings found thus far in sub-Saharan Africa.[33] The marble and the calligraphic styles of writing in Gao tombs suggest that they were imported through the desert from Almeria, Spain. Other stones have been manufactured locally, but even they imitate the style of the imported ones.[34] In all likelihood, those literate in Arabic have been present in the region since the eleventh century, and some of them knew Islamic law, which was considered the "queen of the Islamic sciences" in classical Islam.[35]

Medieval colleges in the Middle East were endowed primarily for the teaching of Islamic law, all other Islamic sciences being taught as ancillaries.[36] The Arabic term for *school* (madrasa) was synonymous with *school of law*, and the professor (*mudarris*) was a law professor.[37] In North Africa, several colleges (madrasa; plural: *madaris*) had already been established by the early eleventh century. Notable among them was the College of Qayrawan, the oldest in the world, established in 859 CE and devoted to the teaching of law according to the school of jurisprudence named after Malik b. Anas. It was in this college that the famous Almoravid odyssey began, a landmark in the development of Islamic scholarship in the Bilad al-Sudan. Returning from the pilgrimage to Mecca, Yahya b. Ibrahim, the chief of the territory of the Gudala, a branch of Sanhaja Berbers dwelling on the southern fringes of the Sahara, requested of the renowned Maliki scholar Abu 'Imran al-Fasi based at Qayrawan that he supply his people with a scholar who would teach them the correct Islamic faith. Al-Fasi directed him to the jurist Wajjaj b. Zalwi al-Lamti, who was teaching in Malkus in the Moroccan Sus. Wajjaj asked his student Abdallah b. Yasin to accompany him. The Almoravid movement grew from the efforts deployed by Yasin to reform the practices of religion according to Maliki juris-prudence.[38] Although a rival Berber group killed Yasin in 1055, the Almoravid movement, which started in the present-day Mauritanian region of Adrar, spread rapidly.[39] When it reached its peak in the eleventh century, the Almoravid state covered Andalusia, Morocco, and a large part of the western Sahara. It also had a profound economic, political, and intellectual impact on West Africa. Almoravid missionaries attempted to impose a rigorous Maliki Islam on their domains, and their rule led to the eradication of Kharijite Islam, which had been the dominant theological persuasion of Muslim communities in the southern and western Sahara.[40] Even after the fall of the Almoravid state, post-Almoravid Sanhaja Berbers became the most active propagators of Malikism in sub-Saharan Africa, where they taught Maliki texts (discussed in Chapter 4) that became part of the curriculum in most Saharan and sub-Saharan centers of learning.

Political Economy of Scholarship

What economic activity supported scholarship in West Africa? The answer to this question varies greatly according to the scholarly communities and periods. A broad generalization is that trade (gold, slaves, and salt in particular) essen-tially provided the economic basis for scholarship in the time of the great empires of Ghana, Mali, and Songhay (eleventh to sixteenth centuries).[41] From the seventeenth century on, as the message of Islam started to reach rural areas, farming became an important dimension of the political economy of scholar-ship. Although scholarship continued to flourish in some commercial towns in the post-imperial period, a large number of new scholarly rural enclaves were being created in which the community lived essentially from farming yet devoted time to learning.[42]

In all periods, Islamic scholarship consisted of various styles, each of which could be combined to a certain degree with another job, either in farming or trade. In a continuum, three ideal types can be identified. The first one is exem-plified by the finest scholars, who ranked among the best and possessed an advanced knowledge of all the branches of medieval learning, from the Qur'an to the law to geography (and even Greek philosophy), and who spoke classical Arabic fluently. Scholars or clerics who possessed a conventional knowledge of the Qur'an and key texts in theology and jurisprudence formed the second type; and scholars whose sole expertise was to teach memorization of the Qur'an and writing in the Arabic script without even understanding it represented the third type. We see an illustration of this diversity in the Djula scholarly lineages studied by Ivor Wilks,[43] who argued that orientation to scholarship and business varies greatly according to individual members. There is one category of members who are full-fledged scholars. Full-time merchants or farmers produced most of the wealth that sustained those involved in scholarly activities. Between these two, a third group combined trade with scholarship or other clerical functions such as being an imam or a qadi.

Historians of Africa seem to agree that trade is what really prompted the expansion of the Islamic faith in Africa south of the Sahara. They diverge, however, on how trade supported Islamic expansion. Broadly, there are two dominant schools of thought. The first argues that Muslims from North Africa conducted both trade and teaching and proselytizing. Mauritanian legal anthropologist Yahya Ould el-Bara illustrates this school of thought. He argues that the spread of Islam was linked to trade in West Africa to the extent that it is difficult to distinguish the trader from the preacher/scholar—often the same person played both roles. This is particularly true for the Ibadites, who traded on a large scale with the Bilad al-Sudan until the eighth century.[44] Nehemia Levtzion exemplifies the other school of thought. According to him, clerics were not primarily interested in trade, but in Islamization. Merchants opened new roads that clerics followed to reach and proselytize among non-Islamized populations.[45] Commercial caravans typically included at least one cleric who would lead other Muslims in prayer, pray for the success of the risky enterprise, provide charms to protect the business venture, choose the propitious days for traveling or resting, etc. Often, the cleric left the caravans when a local chief asked him to remain in his city and provide religious services.[46] I think that these two interpretations need not be mutually exclusive. There probably were some scholars who combined trade and proselytizing, and others who took advantage of business expeditions to spread and teach the Islamic faith.

In any case, the prosperous trade was critical to the development of scholarship. Because they produced great wealth, commercial towns located in the main trade axes attracted various kinds of people, including scholars. The standard of living in commercial centers was higher than elsewhere. People in such centers could rely on a regular supply of all that is needed for physical survival, such as food and drugs, but also the needed pedagogical material, such as paper, books,[47] ink, leather, and wood. Last but not least, trade routes and trading cities were relatively safe in this period of the growth of literacy (twelfth to fifteenth centuries) despite the major political upheavals that took place in North Africa and the Bilad al-Sudan, including the replacement of the Almoravid state by that of the Almohad, the post-Almohad disintegration of political authority in the Maghreb,[48] the decline of the Fatimids and the rise of the Mamluks in Egypt, and the demise of the Mali Empire, which paved the way for the hegemony of Songhay in the western Bilad al-Sudan. This relative security contrasted markedly with the situation of Islamic Asia in the thirteenth century, for example, which witnessed the spread of the Mongol hordes.

Learned scholars in Islamic jurisprudence were much needed in commercial cities to arbitrate trade disputes and record trade agreements. Trade was a valued profession among Muslims, not least because the Prophet Muhammad had himself been a merchant and Muslims value following his example. Some of the most famous scholarly communities in West Africa made a living from trade. Elias N. Saad argues in his *Social History of Timbuktu* that, "in Timbuktu, especially in the earliest period, scholars were unquestionably drawn from the wealthier merchant families."[49] This remains true even of the later period.[50]

The development of scholarship rested largely on the ability of scholars to devote substantial time to pursuing scholarly endeavors and to delegating the task of producing goods and wealth to others, who could have been family members, disciples, students, or slaves.[51] The attitude of scholarly enclaves toward slavery was ambivalent. On the one hand, they were opposed to enslaving Muslims, and they did indeed welcome runaway Muslim slaves. They were in favor of manumission to a certain extent, as Islam considers manumitting slaves a very virtuous act (which has led some to argue that manumission in fact strengthens slavery). Yet, on the other hand, Muslim scholars were not committed to abolition, not least because scholarship relied on the free labor provided largely by slaves (and unpaid students).

In stratified West African societies based on the existence of castes (free, artisans, and slaves), it was among the free born that specialization in scholarship was found. Very rarely did artisan communities specialize in scholarship. The main reason was that endogamy, professional specialization, and heredity tended to be features of the caste system. Scholarly enclaves, however, relied also on the artisan castes to provide some of the raw materials that they needed.[52]

Pedagogical Support for Learning

The most sophisticated and cosmopolitan scholars in major urban centers had a great need of paper and new books, and Qur'anic schools relied almost exclusively on local logistical support. Qur'anic masters taught the memorization of the Qur'an and the art of writing in the Arabic script. Advanced students wrote down their assigned verses of the Qur'an to memorize. The main tools needed for learning were the wooden tablet, on which students daily wrote these verses to commit to memory, along with ink and pens. After memorizing their verses, they washed away the ink from the wooden tablet, to rewrite new sets of verses. The cane stalks of guinea corn and a special grass, *Andropogon guyanus*, were typically used to make pens by cutting the stalk to the right length and carving its edges and tips to the appropriate size.[53] Students were taught at a very young age how to make pens with which to write. Different sizes and styles of pen were made for copying the Qur'an and for decorating manuscripts with calligraphic writing.

Various kinds of ink were used in different regions. The most basic was made from extracting or scraping the accumulated soot from a cooking pot. The soot is washed in water and collected in a jar.[54] To produce a text, the writer or copyist puts the tip of the pen in the ink jar and then presses it gently on the edge of the jar to collect the right quantity of ink. This type of ink was also used for making talismanic drinks or baths. Other ways of making ink, particularly for drinkable talismanic potions, include burning sugar until it becomes liquid and adding the right volume of water to make the solution thick enough and adding saffron to give a slightly brownish color to the finished product. Alongside locally produced ink, Sudanic chanceries used fine ink imported from the Middle East (as well as fine letter-writing paper) as early as the fifteenth century for the purpose of royal correspondence.[55] Also, for the illumination of the manuscripts of the Qur'an, and especially that of the finest surviving West African manuscripts, calligraphic ink such as orpiment (an arsenic sulfide used in the Maghreb for the yellow color), or vermillion for the red, might have been used.[56]

Books and the Book Trade

From the eleventh to the eighteenth centuries, the main sources for Arabic books, paper, and manuscripts had been through the trans-Saharan trade.

Arabic medieval sources provide a relatively precise description of the main axes of the Saharan trade as well as the distance between them. Unfortunately, they are less precise in describing the kinds of goods traded. Among the authors that provide comprehensive accounts of the trans-Saharan trade routes, three deserve special mention. The first is Ibn Hawqal, whose *Description of the Earth* was produced in the late tenth century.[57] A second, more detailed description of trans-Saharan trade routes appears in Al-Bakri's *Book of the Routes and Realms,* written one century later,[58] and which Al-Idrisi revised in his *Book of Roger.*[59] Yet none of them mentions the book trade. The first author to do so is Leo Africanus, who wrote that "many book manuscripts coming from Berberlands were sold. More profits are realized on this sale than any other merchandise."[60] However, manuscripts dating back to the eleventh century are found in the Saharan libraries. One such example is a manuscript of exegesis of the Qur'an written in 1087–1088 and found in a library of Shinqit,[61] which could have been among goods from the trans-Saharan trade or bought by returning pilgrims or travelers.

The arrival of large quantities of books is closely associated with travel, either the hajj or the *rihla,* both travels in quest of knowledge. Often, pilgrims en route to or coming from the Holy Lands stopped in major cities to study and trade,[62] and thus brought back books to the Bilad al-Sudan. As will be discussed further in Chapter 3, students travelled widely to study with masters from whom they would secure texts.

West African Muslims have often been called people of Takrur or Takruri in the Hijaz and Egypt,[63] because Takrur was one of the first Islamized West African medieval states (mid-eleventh century).[64] With the decline of the Almoravids and of the empire of Ghana in the twelfth century, the kingdom of Takrur emerged as a major economic and political power in the western Sudan. At its apogee in the eleventh century, Takrur controlled a number of important cities in the trans-Saharan trade axis, including Ala, Sila, and Brisa.[65] Well integrated into the trans-Saharan trade network, Takrur was a destination of merchants from the Maghreb who traded wool, cooper, and beads in exchange for gold and slaves with the Bilad al-Sudan.[66] The commercial contacts with North Africa, for which caravans left annually for the pilgrimage, must have made it possible in the twelfth century for Muslims from Takrur to perform the pilgrimage and bring back Arabic texts.

It was the royal pilgrimage, however, which most affected the growth of literacy by bringing Middle Eastern scholars and more texts to the western

Sudan. The first recorded royal pilgrimage from West Africa is that of the Kanem ruler Mai Dunama b. Umme, who, according to the *Diwan of the Sultans of Borno*, written by Ahmad Ibn Furtuwa,[67] made the pilgrimage twice between the end of the eleventh century and the middle of the twelfth and then died while on a third pilgrimage.[68] A few Arab authors from the fourteenth and fifteenth centuries have commented on the royal West African pilgrimages. The most famous among them include Egyptian historian Al-Maqrizi (1364–1442), who wrote about them in his book *Al-tibr al-masbuk fi man hajja min al-muluk* (Moulded Gold on Those Kings Who Made the Pilgrimage) and Ibn Khaldun, in his *Kitab al-'ibar* (Book of Examples).[69] Both Ibn Khaldun and Al-Maqrizi claimed that the first monarch to perform the pilgrimage to Mecca was Barmandana. More recent works, however, have identified Mansa Wali, the son of Sunjata, as the first Malian king to perform the pilgrimage, in 1260. Sakura is yet another king of Mali to go to the Holy Lands, at the end of the thirteenth century, but he died near Tripoli on his return journey.[70]

The most famous recorded pilgrimage of a West African king to Mecca is that of Mansa Musa, who reigned from 1312 to 1337. The sources diverge on how large his entourage was and how much gold he carried with him. But tales of his pilgrimage, and more particularly his visit to Cairo in 1324, were so widespread that his picture was featured in a late fourteenth-century European map of West Africa.[71] According to Mervyn Hiskett, his entourage included sixty thousand followers, eighty camels, and five hundred slaves laden with gold.[72] We recall that during the fourteenth century, West Africa was a global supplier of gold to the major economies in the world, from the Maghreb through the Mashreq to central Asia, the Indian Ocean, and China.[73] Mansa Musa's pilgrimage was a landmark in the arrival of books and Muslim scholars in Sudanic Africa.[74] He brought with him books of Islamic jurisprudence, among them some from the Maliki school.[75]

With conversion to Islam, the number of Muslims in West Africa increased gradually, and traffic to the Holy Lands intensified as a result. Sudani pilgrimage to Mecca became institutionalized in the thirteenth century, as Egypt was an emergent political and intellectual center in the Muslim world—en route to the pilgrimage, Sudani Muslims typically stopped in Egypt to trade and study. Following the lavish royal Sudani pilgrimage of the fourteenth century, Egyptians in their turn developed a great interest in trading with the Bilad al-Sudan, which provided a welcome alternative source of gold supply just as the Nubian gold reserves were becoming depleted.[76] By the late fourteenth century, strong commercial and intellectual relations linked Egyptians and Sudani Muslims. This process had a significant impact on the growth of literacy. More and more Sudanis went to Egypt to study with Egyptian ulama, and, correspondingly, Egyptian ulama were invited to settle in the Sudan to teach. They came with their books to establish schools and to serve as qadi and advisers to the kings, for which they were generously rewarded.[77]

Diplomacy may also have been an early source of supply of books in the Bilad al-Sudan. The traveler Ibn Battuta, who visited the region in 1353, reported that the king of Mali sent local scholars to study in Fez and maintained diplomatic relations with Abu Hasan, the Marinid ruler.[78] It is very likely that returning Malian ulama or Moroccan chancery officers brought to Mali some of the texts that would later become the core curriculum of Islamic studies in the region.

Paper Supply and Bookmaking

In addition to finished books imported from the Middle East, Sudani Muslims also made their own. Based on the surviving manuscripts in the libraries of Sudanic Africa and Timbuktu in particular, paper seems to have been used for literary composition in the Bilad al-Sudan. Papyrus, which had been invented and used in ancient Egypt, and parchment, which was used until the fifteenth century in some parts of North Africa,[79] are rarely found among the surviving West African manuscripts. Only a handful of Timbuktu manuscripts were written on parchment.[80]

Paper and papermaking technology, as we know, spread from China to the countries of the Fertile Crescent (Iraq, Syria, and Egypt) and on to the Maghreb before reaching western Europe.[81] According to a fourteenth-century writer, the city of Fez in present-day Morocco had 472 paper mills by the end of the twelfth century.[82] The papermaking industry declined considerably in North Africa with the rise of western European competition. By the fifteenth century, the Europeans, who learned the technology of papermaking from the Arabs, had surpassed them and had become their main supplier of paper.

When the Bilad al-Sudan witnessed the rise of a class of literates and thus an increase in its demand for paper in the fifteenth century, the papermaking industry in the Maghreb and Egypt had already been eclipsed by Western competition, and Muslims relied completely on Western paper. Sudani Muslims, therefore, did not learn papermaking from their North African coreligionists, "who might once have taught them the technology."[83] Thus, Muslims in the entire African continent relied on European, and especially Italian, paper watermarked with three crescents[84] from the fifteenth century on. From this, Bloom concludes that "in the Bilad al-Sudan paper remained for centuries an expensive, imported luxury item rather than the engine of intellectual and cultural transformation it was elsewhere in the Islamic lands." This conclusion is not uncontroversial. Paper might have been an expensive item because it was imported and the transport increased its cost, but the main trading and intellectual centers of the Bilad al-Sudan were wealthy and prosperous enough to afford paper for their scholarly needs. In those areas, an intellectual life prospered.

Paper and books were supplied to the Bilad al-Sudan from two main sources from the sixteenth to the eighteenth century. Through Timbuktu, the western Bilad al-Sudan relied essentially on Morocco, whereas the central and eastern Bilad al-Sudan were oriented toward Tripoli and Cairo.[85] The rise of European naval supremacy led to the diversification of the sources of paper and also to its greater affordability. By the late eighteenth century, European ships had started supplying the main trading centers of the Atlantic Coast with paper, including Saint-Louis in Senegal and Bathurst in the Gambia.[86] As a result, paper had become affordable and was imported in relatively large quantities. From Tripoli alone, the central Sudan imported two thousand reams of paper in 1767. Each ream comprised five hundred sheets, and from each sheet, four pages were cut, which is the equivalent of four million folios in total.[87] Since Tripoli was only one of two main sources of supply for paper, the total quantity of imported paper in the nineteenth century in the whole Bilad al-Sudan from west to east, including from Asia to the Red Sea, must have been significantly larger.

Of course, paper was not used exclusively for writing. The local garment industry also used some of the imported paper to wrap expensive clothes destined for export.[88] But by the nineteenth century, students or scholars who needed to copy or author a text could afford paper.[89] With regard to the price, a ream cost twenty thousand cowries in the early nineteenth century in Sansanding in the Niger Bend. By the mid-nineteenth century, it cost twelve thousand cowries in Tripoli, but twenty-four thousand cowries in Kano because of the added cost of transport.[90]

Unlike other parts of the Islamic world, the Bilad al-Sudan did not witness an elaborate craft of bookbinding. A shared feature of locally produced manuscripts of the Bilad al-Sudan is that finished books were not sewn.[91] Many manuscripts were made of loose leaves, typically conserved in a goatskin wallet wrapped around the text block. To preserve the most precious manuscripts, an additional precaution consisted of inserting the wallet into a leather satchel with shoulder straps to enable portability. Since texts were not attached in the wallet, leaves of paper were often lost. The implication is that a large number of manuscripts in Sudanic Africa are fragmentary. When owners of the manuscripts died, the manuscripts sometimes ended up in the care of illiterate people who disturbed the original arrangement of the pages. Another cause of manuscript fragmentation was inheritance. Sometimes, book manuscripts were divided as part of an inheritance settlement.[92] This would not be a problem for copies of the Holy Qur'an, for it is often subdivided into parts that are sold separately. Yet it is problematic for scholarly compositions of which only one copy existed.

The lack of numbering of pages reveals another peculiarity of West African manuscripts. Typically, copyists did not number page manuscripts in the Bilad al-Sudan. To link two folios together and provide some direction to the reader, copyists typically wrote on a separate line at the bottom of each folio the first few words of the following page, and the ending words of the preceding folio at the beginning of each folio. This method of headers and footers was used for texts written in Arabic and for texts written in African languages with the Arabic script known as Ajami.

The Development of Ajami

The word *Ajami* derives from the Arabic root *'ujma,* which etymologically alludes to deficiency in speech and / or pronunciation as opposed to eloquence (*fasaha*).[93] Unsurprisingly, pre-Islamic Arabs used the pair of terms (deficiency / eloquence in language) to contrast the presumed eloquence of their language with the assumed incomprehensible languages of their immediate neighbors, notably the Persians. Such a contrast is illustrated in the Qur'an, which refutes charges made by opponents of the Prophet that the Qur'anic revelation was being taught to him in a foreign language (*lisan 'ajami*), when in fact, according to the Qur'an, it was revealed in eloquent Arabic.[94] The Qur'an also uses the plural (*A'jamiyyin*) to refer to non-Arab people. After the Islamic expansion, the term *'ajam* referred to a larger number of people with whom the Arabs came in contact, including the Berbers in Africa. *Ajami* would later acquire a less pejorative connotation when the Arabic script started to be used to transcribe languages of non-Arab Muslims. Learned people in the Islamized world appropriated the Arabic script to promote their own languages. There is virtually no region that has historically been under Islamic influence that has not adopted the Arabic alphabet for transcribing non-Arabic languages. The languages transcribed in Ajami are varied and include some Slavic languages, Spanish, Persian, Turkish, Urdu, Swahili, Hebrew, Berber, Malay, and Afrikaans. In addition to consonants known in Arabic, Ajami has, by appending additional dots to Arabic letters, created new consonants to render sounds unknown in classical Arabic. Current research on the manuscript heritage shows that the use of Ajami was widespread in sub-Saharan Africa. A workshop held in Timbuktu in 2009 revealed that as many as twenty-nine African languages have an Ajami literature of some sort. Many of the precolonial Ajami manuscripts have been lost or damaged due to poor conservation conditions.[95] In extant manuscripts in African languages as diverse as Wolof, Hausa, Fulani, Mande, Songhay, and particularly Swahili, writings in Ajami revealed that it was not used only as the medium of correspondence but also as a medium of learning in which treatises and poems were written.[96]

More recent research suggests a wide use of the Arabic script temporarily and spatially in the African continent. There is attested usage of the Arabic script in eighty languages and in all parts of Africa—northern, western, eastern, central, and southern Africa.[97] In West Africa, Ajami literature is attested in twenty-nine languages. In alphabetical order, they are Akan (Ashanti), Balanta-Ganja, Bamannkan (Bambara, Wasulanka), Dagbani (Dagomba), Fulah (Fulfulde, Pulaar, Fulani), Ga, Gonja, Guang, Hausa, Jakhanka, Jula, Kakaabe, Kanuri, Kuranko, Mampruli, Mandingo (Malinke, Wangara), Mandinka, Mixifore, Nupe, Serer-Sine, Songhay, Soninke, Susu, Tamashek, Tem, Wolof, Yoruba, Zarma (Djerma, Zerma), and Zenaga.[98]

According to historian Hamu al-Arawani Sudani, converts to Islam might have started to transcribe their language with the Arabic script as early as the twelfth century, when they began to preach their religion among their kin.[99] The use might have been very limited, however. There is consensus that its more widespread use began in the eighteenth century, which coincides with the formation of a critical mass of Muslim clerics. Among them, those intellectuals originating from the countryside[100] led movements of religious reform and captured political power in various regions of the west and central Sudan and established Islamic States in the eighteenth and nineteenth centuries.[101] In Hausaland, where the largest volume of Ajami writings is found (essentially poetry), the oldest writing in Ajami is believed to be *Riwayar Nabi Musa* (Story of the Prophet Moses), written by Abdullahi Suka in the mid-seventeenth century.[102] In his *History of Hausa Islamic Verses,* Hiskett (1975), a specialist in the Hausa language, classifies the themes of the Ajami verse literature into the following eight categories:[103]

1. Preaching (*waazi*); writings on asceticism (*zuhudi*); writings about death and resurrection, specifically the interrogations that the dead undergo in the grave; reward and punishment; the day of judgment.
2. Panegyrics (*madihi*), which are writings praising the Prophet Muhammad and other saints.
3. Theology (*tawhidi*), which includes didactic explanations on the attributes of God and some basic principles of Muslim theology.
4. Jurisprudence (*fikihi*), which deals with the precepts of Islamic law and concerns personal behavior, particularly prayer, ablutions, and successions
5. Hagiography (*sira*), which concerns the miraculous biography of the Prophet Muhammad and his companions.
6. History (*tarikhi*), which includes chronicles concerning the history of the region.
7. Astrology (*ilmin nujumi*) and numerology (*hisabi*), which deal with the evaluation of auspicious days for undertaking projects. (There is abundant literature on this subject, showing how popular it is, not only in Nigeria but in West Africa as a whole.)
8. Essentially secular, texts of a political nature and occasionally invocations.[104]

Script and Calligraphy

As revealed by the manuscript heritage, Muslims from the Bilad al-Sudan developed various scripts and calligraphic styles, perhaps as early as the sixteenth century.[105] In a seminal article on the Arabic script of the western Islamic world[106] published in 1886, the French Orientalist Octave Houdas distinguished four sub-types of script,[107] which he considered to be "Maghribi" based on shared features that set them apart from the script of the eastern Islamic world. These features include different alphanumerics, a specific way of pointing some Arabic consonants, and a difference in the ways calligraphers pen their stroke. The first "smooth and even script" is named Qayrawani after the city of Qayrawan (Kairouan) in present day Tunisia. A second, "small, compact and jerky script" is called Andalusi, from Andalusia in Muslim Spain. A third, "large, round and elegant" script is called Fasi and comes from Fez, in southern Morocco. Finally, a fourth, "thicker and blacker script" is called Sudani from the Bilad al-Sudan. Sheila Blair[108] revisited this classification in a recent paper to make two important points. The first is that the subtypes, while distinct, cannot be assigned to a geographic origin, as two subtypes of script can be found in the same texts. In addition, the geographic mobility of scholars and books in the Maghreb ensured that the different subtypes would be found in different areas in the Maghreb. The second point is that the Bilad al-Sudan stretches from the Atlantic Ocean to the Red Sea, and there exist regional variations within the Bilad al-Sudan not only in script, but also in decoration, format, and mode of reading of the holy Qur'an. This point is confirmed by the research of a contemporary Timbuktu scholar on the Arabic writings in the West African Sahel,[109] who argues that available manuscripts in the Sahelian collections reveal the use of scripts from the entire world of Islam by Sahelian scribes and that the type of script provides no conclusive evidence of the place where the manuscript was copied or written. Various Sahelian regions have developed their own specific script, but in all likelihood these have used those scripts in combination with all others and they also have exported calligraphic writings outside the Bilad al-Sudan.

Other scripts that developed in the region include the Saharan script (*al-khatt al-sahrawi*),[110] used largely but not exclusively by western Sahara Muslim communities in present-day Mauritania and also by some of the Songhay-speaking people. There is also a *Suqi* script associated with Tuareg populations identified with the ancient town of Suq, most probably ancient Tadmakkat.[111] Further research has shown that even the so-called Sudani script, associated mainly with the Hausa, the Fulbe, the Wolof, and the Songhay, had itself evolved to produce other subtypes with their own specific features. For example, the region of Kano in Northern Nigeria, which historically was under the intellectual influence of Borno and then initially adopted the Borno variant of the Sudani script (*barnawi*), in time developed its own calligraphic style, called *kanawi*.[112]

The art of calligraphy in the Bilad al-Sudan never paralleled in fame and sophistication that of the Maghreb or the Mashreq. Based on the examination of a few nineteenth-century Qur'anic manuscripts, art historian Sheila Blair comments that "ink and pigment for text and illumination are . . . local and . . . there is no use of gold, a hallmark of fancier manuscripts produced elsewhere in the Maghreb ... the pages are not ruled, and the number of lines varies within a single manuscript. Marginal notes are added in various directions and places. There is no indication of a division of labour between scribe and illuminator."[113] Yet some well-executed manuscripts, particularly copies of the holy Qur'an, were produced in the Bilad al-Sudan and exported to North Africa from the early nineteenth century and sold for the modern equivalent of between fifty and sixty dollars.[114] Most of them came from Borno, which, as previously mentioned, specialized in Qur'anic studies, and where copyists could make a decent living producing fine copies of the Qur'an using three or more colors. Fine copies of the Qur'an from Borno were sold in the Tripoli market in the nineteenth century.[115]

As will be discussed in greater detail in Chapters 6 to 8, twentieth-century technological change (print capitalism, computer literacy, etc.) and geopolitical change (decolonization and attendance of Middle Eastern universities by large numbers of students from the Sudan) led to a wider use of scripts that originated outside the region. For example, graduates from North African colleges and other Middle Eastern universities preferred to use Oriental scripts in their writings. Likewise, print capitalism led to an outpouring of books written in non-Sudani scripts. Yet this did not lead to the disappearance or even the decline of the local script. Large segments of the literate populations from neo-traditional Islamic schools to Sufi communities are still uncomfortable with reading the foreign script. Their demand for books in local script stimulated the industrial production of thousands of small booklets originally written in the local script and printed in large numbers using modern technologies of bookmaking. Part of a long genealogy of devotional or polemical literature, these booklets are found in bookstores in Kano, Niamey, Dakar, and elsewhere. They reveal that in spite of the availability of the typesetting machine, people still maintain old calligraphic styles in traditional centers of Islamic learning.

Available historical evidence about conversion to Islam suggests that people of the Bilad al-Sudan had been exposed to the epistemology of the new religion from the eighth century on. Converts had been taught the Qur'an and the essentials of Islamic worship. Thus, the belief in God, the prophets, the Day of Judgment, angels, and reward and punishments became the ingredients through which they understood their universe. The process of Islamic knowledge transmission, then, started as early as the eighth century in the Bilad al-Sudan. We can also conclude from the work of Abu Ishaq al-Kanami, who flourished in the early thirteenth century, that the history of local composition in the Bilad al-Sudan spans a period of at least eight hundred years. Although no text produced by a Sudanese Muslim earlier than the sixteenth century has been found thus far, with the exception of those of al-Kanami, the presence of students of Kanem Borno in Cairo in the thirteenth century suggests that some Muslims from the central Sudan received the best Islamic education available in the medieval period and that it is therefore not unreasonable to assume that they may have produced texts in Arabic just like al-Kanami. A letter from Borno dated to the fourteenth century is further evidence of Arabic erudition in Borno at the time.[116]

Writing in the mid-nineteenth century before the European scramble for Africa, A. Cherbonneau argued that the Islamic education of the Bilad al-Sudan rivaled in sophistication that of universities in Cairo, Tunis, Fez, and Tlemsen.[117] The colophon of some Timbuktu manuscripts suggests that a scribal tradition existed in the western Bilad al-Sudan by the turn of the fifteenth century.[118] Available testimonies prove that in the sixteenth and seventeenth centuries, Sudani Muslims wrote many important documents in Arabic, including the famous Timbuktu chronicles. The expensive nature of the paper notwithstanding, scholars or their sponsors were wealthy enough to afford the paper they needed.

But the intellectual transformation occurred in the late eighteenth and early nineteenth centuries, by which time paper had become affordable. It was in this period that a critical mass of scholars and clerics emerged, that an abundant intellectual production in Arabic—and to a lesser extent Ajami—was made, and that the expansion of Sufi orders, along with the Tijaniyya and Qadiriyya rivalry, considerably fueled literary production. Finally, it was in the eighteenth and nineteenth centuries that the Islamic intellectual tradition in Africa culminated with the Islamic Revolutions, led mainly by Muslim clerics who established states in which Arabic was the language of instruction and administration. From Borno (as early in the fifteenth century) through the Sokoto Caliphate, the Dina of Masina to the 'Umarian State, Arabic was the official language of administration and instruction long before French, English, and Portuguese were being used. Although local African languages were used for everyday communication, classical Arabic was the language of communication for the elites[119] who taught Islamic religion and Arabic language.

Chapter 3

The Rise of Clerical Lineages in the Sahara and the Bilad al-Sudan

> Masters of talismanic knowledge are either members of the Kunta Clans or Fulbe.
> —*A Mauritanian saying*[1]

THE CENSUS of independent African states inherited the colonial system of ethno-racial classification. For the purpose of administration, the colonial state divided native peoples into "tribes" and "ethnic" groups, assuming that these were primordial sources of self-identification for them. In Nigeria, for example, the dominant groups are classified as ethnic Hausa (sometimes Hausa/Fulani), Yoruba, and Igbo. In Senegal, they are named Wolof, Sereer, Joola, Tukulor, Mandingo, etc. Often based on linguistic criteria, such a system of classification differed from the more flexible precolonial notions of communal belonging. The colonial census was to a large extent the legacy of nineteenth-century Western epistemologies deeply influenced by the European rise to global supremacy and ambition for imperial hegemony. To dominate the rest of the world, imperial Europe developed race theory as an epistemological tool. Based on physical attributes such as skin color or hair types, people were classified into racial groups. Classification implied hierarchy and, thus, superiority and its corollary, inferiority. By showing that some "races" are superior to others in terms of aesthetic and intellectual sophistication, or that some nations were more refined than others, race theory provided an intellectual justification for colonization as a civilizing mission.

Likewise, ethnology, the science of ethnic groups, was invented in the late eighteenth century, the heyday of European imperialism. Its conceptual apparatus included terms such as tribes, clans, natives, indigenes, customary law, bush, and vernacular languages or dialects—terms that typically were not used in the anthropological study of European societies. In his *Citizen and Subject*, Mahmood Mamdani argues that the colonial state in Africa, regardless of its nationality (French, Portuguese, English, Dutch) or underlying colonial philosophy (assimilation, indirect rule, apartheid) or location (East, West, southern Africa), had a generic form that Mamdani dubbed "decentralized despotism." It also had a similar modus operandi in the entire continent. It was a bifurcated state that mediated racial and imperial domination using different categories for whites and native peoples. Mamdani argues that:

> What we have before us is a bifurcated world, no longer simply racially organized but a world in which the dividing line between those human and the rest less human is a line between those who labor on the land and those who do not. This divided world is inhabited by subjects on one side and citizens on the other; their life is regulated by customary law on one side and modern law on the other; their beliefs are dismissed as pagan on this side and bear the status of religion on the other; the stylized moments in their day-to-day lives are considered ritual on this side and culture on the other; their creative activities are considered crafts on this side and glorified as arts on the other; their verbal communication is demeaned as vernacular chatter on this side but elevated as linguistic discourse on the other; in sum, the world of the "savages" [is] barricaded, in deed as in word, from the world of the "civilized."[2]

The colonial state, however, did not invent a racist discourse or racial prejudice against black people. Regarding the Muslim Sahel, Bruce Hall has argued that contemporary constructions of race owed a great deal to ideas of racial classifications developed in the region before the arrival of European colonial forces at the end of the nineteenth century.[3] Focusing on Morocco, Chouki El-Hamel's work has shown that the encounter between black Africans and Arabo-Berbers from the Sahara and northern Africa has benefitted the latter to the detriment of the blacks, against whom strong racial prejudices have existed and continue to exist.[4] Islam, according to Hamel, was surely a powerful social dynamic, but "other cultural and ethnic factors figured prominently into how Islam was engendered in particular social settings." Blackness was often associated with unbelief and even slavery in North Africa. As will be discussed in Chapter 5, there is strong evidence that enslaving free-born black Muslims in blatant violation of Islamic law was commonplace.[5] However, precolonial identities remained fluid, and assimilation to another ethno-cultural identity was possible and did happen. The institution of concubinage, or sexual relations with slave girls, produced racially mixed Muslim societies in many parts of the Sahel. In addition, interethnic and interracial marriages, which incidentally were not completely free from racial stereotyping, were common for the merchant families in trading towns in particular and less so for peasant families living in agricultural villages.[6] In the following discussion of the teachers and messengers of Islam in the precolonial Bilad al-Sudan, I will highlight the relative fluidity of precolonial racial and ethnic identities compared to the post-colonial ones.

Our knowledge of the intellectual life of the Sahara is limited for the period from the demise of the Almoravid state in the twelfth century to the sixteenth century. According to Ould el-Bara, the main reason is the absence of any state control in large parts of the Sahara, which created a favorable ground for war, famine, and insecurity. All this induced several waves of migration from the north to the south of the Sahara.[7] This post-Almoravid period witnessed the Arabization of major Berber tribes. The Sanhaja, who were the backbone of the Almoravid movement, were the first to adopt the Arabic language and create new genealogies tracing their origins to the Arab world.[8] In addition to the Berbers, several other groups participated in this process of ethno-racial transformation and genealogical "sophistication." Scholarship and clericalism (religious service as imam, qadi, and Qur'anic teacher) attracted a variety of groups, including dark-skinned Africans from the Atlantic Coast, the Sahara, the Sahel and the Savannah; Saharan and sub-Saharan Tuaregs; and nomadic Arabs who came to the Bilad al-Sudan from North Africa, Egypt, and the Swahili Coast.[9] Some of them intermarried and/or coalesced, forming new racial/tribal configurations.[10]

Of the greatest medieval cities of Islamic learning, Shinqit and Walata, both in present-day Mauritania, figure prominently. Each of them has witnessed a process of miscegenation and reconfiguration of identities. The etymology of the name Shinqit is *Sun giti*, which means "sources of horses"[11] in an old Soninke dialect and suggests that the first inhabitants of that city were Sudani (blacks). Located at the periphery of the Ghana Empire, and peopled by Mande agriculturalists, Walata was originally named Biru, a Malinke name meaning "roofs made of straw supported by a wooden stick."[12] Its name was changed subsequently to Iwalatan during the Mali and Songhay periods. By the sixteenth century, the name was Arabized as Walata,[13] which also comes from the Malinke word *wala*, meaning a "shady spot." Timothy Cleaveland has shown that Timbuktu and Walata grew as prosperous trade and intellectual centers in the medieval period and as melting pots in which Arabs, Berbers, and darker-skinned Africans merged, thereby producing new Arabo-Islamic identities. In the process, some Soninke families were assimilated into dominant

Arab(ized) clans.[14] An eloquent illustration is the Lemhajib clan. Pre-eighteenth-century historical sources for this region, such as the Timbuktu seventeenth-century chronicles[15] and Ahmad Baba's biographic dictionary *Nayl al-Ibtihaj* (Gaining happiness), which is a very important bibliographical resource for the study of Islamic scholarship in the Islamic West,[16] do not mention this clan. Post-eighteenth-century sources, however, such as the *Fath al-Shakur* by a-Burtuli[17] and the *Bilad al-Takrur*, mention several scholars associated with the tribe of Lemhajib. By the time this tribe came into full existence in the eighteenth century, some black Soninke families of Iwalatan had disappeared. In all likelihood, Cleaveland concludes, they were assimilated into the Lemhajib Arabized clan.[18]

Bachir Diagne notes in his discussion of the Islamization of the Mande that "conversion is not only entering a new religion with its creed, dogmas, and rituals. As the Latin etymology indicates, to convert is to get totally turned around. That means a new self-reappraisal following the adoption of the new cosmology. One visible aspect of conversion has been a radical change in the discourse of identity."[19] Similar ethnic identity change has been documented in many areas of the precolonial Bilad al-Sudan, including in Timbuktu, where some prominent families (Anda Ali, Baba Misru, Ali Sila) were of mixed Arab and Soninke ancestry.[20] The Fulani scholar Shaykh Musa Camara documented the fluidity of ethnic boundaries in the region of the Senegal River valley during the precolonial period.[21]

Being Muslim was a marker of status in urban centers located in the axes of the trans-Saharan trade prior to the arrival of Europeans. Merchants trading with Arabs built strong relationships based on trust, gained by belonging to the same religion. Other sources of prestige associated with being Muslim include the pilgrimage to Mecca. Now the Holy Lands are just a few hours of flight away, but imagine those who performed the pilgrimage several centuries ago, when it took years to reach the Holy Lands, and many candidates either never made it to Mecca or did not return.[22]

Like pilgrimage, literacy was also a source of great prestige. Regardless of their religion, rulers in Sudanic Africa have traditionally surrounded them-selves with literate Muslim clerics. This clerisy performed various administrative tasks for rulers before the rise of self-designated Islamic polities in the eighteenth century. Literacy became a greater source for emancipation in Sudani societies in the nineteenth-century period of Islamic reform and state building. In the present-day Senegal River valley, for example, the nobility is represented by the so-called Torodbe, which means "literates." Originally from a humble social background, the Torodbe rose to the top of the class hierarchy thanks to the prestige of knowledge of Islamic sciences.[23]

Students of African Islam distinguish between two Islamization paradigms, each one associated with an emblematic scholar of the western Sudan. Representative of the first paradigm is al-Hajj Salim Suwari.[24] Very influential among the Jakhanke, Salim Suwari, himself a Jakhanke, held the view that unbelief was the consequence of ignorance and that God's grand design for the world is that some people will remain longer in the "state of ignorance" than others. Conversion will occur in due course according to God's plans. Consequently, both proselytizing and military jihads were unacceptable interference with God's will. Suwari also taught that non-Muslim rule was not only acceptable to Muslims, but should be supported by them insofar as it enabled them to follow the Sunna of the Prophet.[25] Above all, Suwari believed that Muslims should pursue the search for education and provide "unbelievers" with a model that they could emulate until, in due course and according to God's plan, the time of conversion came.[26] Such a worldview enabled the Djula to engage in peaceful trade with non-Muslims for centuries.[27]

The second paradigm is associated with a seventeenth-century Berber scholar, Awbek b. Aschfaghu, known as Imam Nasir al-Din,[28] who belonged to the maraboutic tribe of Banu Dayman. An advocate of military jihad, Nasir al-Din rebelled against the domination of the Banu Hassan, Arabic-speaking warrior peoples whom he portrayed as bad Muslims. The key ideas that influenced Nasir al-Din were the anticipation of the end of time, the arrival of a Muslim eschatological figure known as the awaited Mahdi, and the notion of the Prophet Muhammad as a perfect human being (insan kamil), which provided ideological justification for perfection to be realized through Islamic reform.[29] Nasir al-Din's goal was to set up a unified community that lived according to Islamic Shari'a, under the leadership of an imam, namely Nasir al-Din himself. He recruited Wolof and Fulbe followers in the Senegambian region, who in 1670 succeeded in overthrowing the ruling dynasties in the neighboring Senegambian states of Cajoor, Jolof, Walo, and Futa Toro.[30] The reform movement led by Nasir al-Din is known as Shurbubba, a term that refers to the war of clerics to establish a state governed by Islam. Early efforts for reform were not successful in establishing lasting Islamic entities in the western Sudan, because Nasir al-Din was killed in a battle and the Banu Hassan reasserted their dominance in southwestern Mauritania. Likewise, his followers' domination over Senegambian kingdoms lasted barely ten years; former rulers of these kingdoms garnered support from the French to reconquer their lands. However, the jihadist impulse in the spirit of "Shurbubba" remained alive among some disciples of Nasir al-Din, who strove to communicate their vision of an ideal Islamic society to future generations. It was above all among the Fulbe scholars that the teachings of Nasir al-Din found their realization, with several jihads leading to the establishment of Islamic states in the eighteenth and nineteenth centuries.

In the following sections of this chapter, I will identify the groups that contributed most to the spread of literacy prior to European colonial rule. My classification is based on a mix of ethnic, racial, religious, and genealogical criteria that are not mutually exclusive, as some of these groups have over time moved from one category to another. But each of the terms is analytically useful in that it captures the ways in which these groups might have self-identified at a given historical time. Those overlapping groups are the Ibadi Berbers, the post-Almoravid Sanhaja Berbers, the Zawaya, the Djula Wangara, the Fulbe, and the Wolof of Senegambia.

The Ibadi Berbers

The Ibadis are a subgroup of Kharijites, the first Muslim sect in history. When 'Ali b. Abi Talib, the cousin and son-in-law of Prophet Muhammad, succeeded to the political leadership of the nascent Muslim nation in 656 CE, members of the family of his murdered predecessor, 'Uthman b. 'Affan, disputed his legitimacy. Facing dissent from one of them, Mu'awiya b. Abi Sufyan, the Muslim governor of Syria, Caliph 'Ali marched to Damascus to depose him. At the suggestion of some Muslims who wanted to prevent dissension, 'Ali agreed to submit to arbitration. Following his decision, a group of his supporters withdrew support from him on the grounds that, as a legitimate successor to the caliphate, he should not have accepted any arbitration. Called "those who withdrew" (Kharijites), they are found in Oman and Algeria. According to Ibn al-Saghir, an Arab geographer who wrote in the ninth century, Ibadis dominated the southern Algerian town of Tahert in the early ninth century when Islamic ideas were being introduced in the Sahara and the western Bilad al-Sudan from North Africa. Tahert, a major center in the gold trade, was then linked to the Bilad al-Sudan by a commercial route.[31] Historians agree that the Ibadis were the first groups to spread Islamic teachings in the Sahara, as well as south of the Sahara, including medieval Ghana. The early Muslim communities in Kumbi Saleh, the capital city of Ghana mentioned by Al-Bakri, seem to have practiced Ibadi Islam. Ibadi scholars were also influential in Mali, the successor state of Ghana. In his Kitab tabaqat al-mashayikh (Book of Ranks of Shaykhs), the Ibadi scholar al-Darjini claimed that his great grandfather converted the king of Mali to the Ibadism."[32] According to Yahya Ould el-Bara, there is no region in the Islamic world in which Ibadi influences were as strong as among the Saharan Berbers and in the Bilad al-Sudan.[33] The egalitarian social structures of the native peoples of these regions fit Ibadi beliefs. Ould el-Bara dismisses the charge that Berbers in this region were superficially Islamized and not familiar with Islamic teachings prior to the rise of the Almoravids. This claim might have been informed by the Almoravids' propaganda, which justified their movement of religious reform and state building as an effort to eradicate syncretism and establish a pure Islam among Berbers.

The Post-Almoravid Sanhaja Berbers

After the Ibadis, the post-Almoravid Sanhaja Berbers had the strongest impact on Islam in the medieval Sahara and Bilad al-Sudan. The interactions between Sanhaja Berbers and Sudani people started before Islam and continued with the expansion of the trans-Saharan trade, which brought them into closer contact. At times, Sudani/Berber interactions were peaceful, but at other times, Berbers competed with their Sudani neighbors for land and tended to push them farther south into the savannah.[34] With the rise of the Almoravids, scholarship developed in the Sahara to an unprecedented extent.[35] They unified large parts of the region around Maliki jurisprudence. Through the educational institutions they created, the Almoravids deepened the knowledge of Islam in the region and sent missionaries to teach throughout the Sahara. The theological and political unity resulting from the Almoravid expansion greatly facilitated the movement of commercial caravans and pilgrims.[36] After the fall of the Almoravids and the rise of the successor state of the Almohads, the Sanhaja lost their political and military might, but not their religious zeal. Through intermarriage and various other interactions with Hassaniyya Arabs (Banu Hassan warriors of Mauritania), most of them gradually lost their Sanhaja identity, to become integrated into the larger group of the Zawaya, described later. But regardless of the degree of assimilation to other groups and cultures, some Sanhaja remained attached to their tribal origin and signed their scholarly works with their tribal name—al-Sanhaji. One such scholar is Muhammad al-Busiri al-Sanhaji (d. 1296), who is the author of the much-celebrated poem titled "al-Burda" (The Mantle).[37] Al-Busiri, so the story goes, suffered a stroke and became partially paralyzed. One night, he dreamed of the Prophet Muhammad covering his paralyzed side with a mantle. Awake, he found himself miraculously cured. As a token of his gratitude for the miraculous prophetic intervention, Al-Busiri composed this poem, which is chanted to this day at festivals in West Africa celebrating the birth of the Prophet. In some regions, the poem is collectively recited every day during the entire month in which the Prophet Muhammad was born.

Ardent proselytizers, the post-Almoravid Sanhaja Berbers contributed for several centuries to the dissemination of Islam and Maliki jurisprudence throughout West Africa. Many sources point to the intellectual influence of the Sanhaja Berbers in the medieval Saharan towns of Walata, Takedda, and Timbuktu.[38] The intellectual development of Timbuktu, and notably the establishment of the famous Sankoré College, is credited to post-Almoravid Sanhaja scholars.

The Djula Wangara

Another group known for its contribution to the spread of Islamic scholarship in the Bilad al-Sudan is the Wangara. African historians have long debated its origin, as well as its trading and religious activities in various West African contexts (medieval Ghana, Mali, Songhay, Hausaland, and the Voltaic Bassin).[39] The name Wangara (Land of Gold) was mentioned under different spellings in early historical sources to refer to either a people or a country. As the land of gold, Leo Africanus locates Wangara in Hausaland.[40] Modern historians believe that what Arab geographers referred to as Wangara were the Bambuk Bure goldfields. McIntosh suggested an alternative location in the inland Niger delta.[41] As a linguistic group, the Wangara name is spelled Gangara by Al-Bakri,[42] Guangara by Leo Africanus,[43] Wangara by al-Idrisi,[44] and Wanjarata by Ibn Battuta.[45] The seventeenth-century Timbuktu chronicles (*Tarikh al-Fattash, Tarikh al-Sudan,* and *Tadhkirat al-Nisyan*) used several variant spellings: Wakoré, Wankori, Ouankori, and Wangarbe,[46] based on the name given to them in different languages spoken in medieval Mali (Soninke, Songhay, and Fulani). They are called Jakhanke in Senegambia (probably after the famous city of Dia or Diakha),[47] and in Hausaland they are called "Wangarawa," with the Hausa suffix *wa* as a plural marker added to their name. Historically, the Wangara have been active in the entire West African region, from the Senegal River basin to present-day Northern Nigeria.

In 1963, Mallam Nasiru Kabara, a prominent scholar and Sufi leader from Kano, supplied the late historian Muhammad al-Hajj from the Republic of Sudan with the only known copy of a local but anonymous seventeenth-century chronicle retracing the origins and missionary activities of Wangarawa in Hausaland.[48] Unlike the Kano Chronicle,[49] which dates the arrival of the Wangara in Kano to the rule of Sarkin Yaji between 1349 and 1385, the anonymous chronicle dates their arrival to that of Emir Muhamad Rumfa (1463–1499).[50] The Wangara introduced two key Maliki texts[51] in the region: the *Mukhtasar* (Concise Handbook) of Khalil Ibn Ishaq and the *Mudawwana* (Compendium of Legal Opinions) of Sahnun, which Shaykh Zagaiti, the leader of the Wangara missionaries to Hausaland, committed to memory.

Historians diverge over the main common denominators of the Wangara. In a comprehensive article analyzing from both a historical and a geographical perspective the dispersion of the Wangara in the medieval states of Ghana, Mali, and Songhay—and later in Hausaland and the Volta Region—Andreas W. Massing has shown that the Wangara have retained two main characteristics: trade and scholarship. Lamin Sanneh, whose study focuses on the Senegambian branch of the Wangara known as Jakhanke, argues that Wangara might have welcomed traders in their communities, but they were essentially a clerical group that lived predominantly from subsistence agriculture. Sanneh thus refuted earlier arguments about the centrality of trade in the political economy of Jakhanke communities.[52] M. A. al-Hajj suggested that the factors that precipitated their movement varied according to periods and Wangara groups and that "commercial and missionary motives were often mixed."[53] Sometimes they migrated for mainly political reasons—for example, fleeing insecurity due to state collapse—sometimes in search of economic opportunities, and sometimes their migration was primarily for missionary motives.[54]

Originally Soninke speakers, the Wangara who moved westward became linguistically assimilated into their receiving communities, such as the Songhay, Hausa, and Fulani, among others. Massing believes that they adopted the Songhay language between the turn of the fifteenth century and the late sixteenth century, which coincides broadly with the rule of the Askya dynasty in the Songhay Empire.[55] In Hausaland, where their missionary zeal was notable, they have been linguistically assimilated as well. Those Wangara or Jakhanke who remained in Senegambia where Soninke is widely spoken, however, have used the Soninke language in their teaching of Islam (particularly the exegesis of the Qur'an) alongside other Senegambian languages, such as Fulani or Wolof, to communicate with other populations.[56]

The Zawaya

The origins of the Zawaya can be traced partly to the Banu Hilal and the Banu Sulaym, two Arab tribes that invaded the Maghreb from Egypt in the eleventh century. In the aftermath of their invasion, the overwhelming majority of the people of the Maghreb adopted the Arabic language and culture.[57] From the Maghreb, some of these Arabs migrated southward to the Sahara and/or intermarried with post-Almoravid Sanhaja to form the Zawaya. In the western Sahara, from the seventeenth century on, the Zawaya specialized in the production, reproduction, and dissemination of Islamic knowledge,[58] in contrast with the warrior groups of the Sahara known as Hassan. This dual pattern of specialization is also found among other Muslims in West Africa, including the Fulbe of the Senegal River valley, for example, where the subgroup of Torodbe specialized in learning, unlike the warrior groups of the *sebbe* (singular: *ceddo*), and the Djula-speaking people among whom the subgroup of Mori specialized in learning in contrast with the warrior clans of Tun Tigi.[59]

From the eighteenth century on, the contribution of the Zawaya to the spread of Islamic knowledge was second to none[60] in West Africa. In addition to their scholarly works, which make up the bulk of the manuscripts preserved in the collections of the region, their intellectual influence on the western Sudan is also reflected in the high demand for Zawaya teachers in Islamic centers of learning all over the western Sudan. The Zawaya were reputed to teach correct pronunciation of the classical Arabic language to Sudani Muslims, an art that many Muslim scholars among native speakers of the Niger Congo languages did not master. Another aspect of the intellectual influence of the Zawaya is their introduction of Sufism, which later became the dominant expression of Islam in West Africa. The two most influential Zawaya tribes of what is present-day Mauritania (the Kunta and the Idaw 'Ali) initiated Sudani Africans into the two dominant Sufi orders of sub-Saharan Africa, the Qadiriyya and the Tijaniyya.

From the twelfth century on, the Qadiriyya tariqa, which was founded in Baghdad by 'Abd al-Qadir al-Jaylani, spread throughout Asia, the Balkaans, and North Africa. The famous North African scholar 'Abd al-Karim al-Maghili, whose teachings had long-lasting influence in the medieval and modern Bilad al-Sudan, is believed to have introduced it in the region.[61] Al-Maghili arrived in Kano in 1491, during the rule of Muhammad Rumfa.[62] He sojourned several years in Kano during the rule of Muhammad Rumfa and wrote his famous *Crown of Religion: On the Obligation of Princes,* advising the latter on how to rule according to Islamic principles.[63] He also stayed in Songhay, where he issued a series of fatwas in response to questions of Emperor Askya Muhammad of Songhay,[64] to whom he provided similar advice. In the early sixteenth century, Al-Maghili initiated Sidi Ahmad al-Bakka'i of the Kunta tribe, whose descendants became the flag bearers of the Qadiriyya in the Sahara and the Bilad al-Sudan in subsequent centuries.

One of the wealthiest Arab clans in Sudanic Africa in the eighteenth and nineteenth centuries,[65] by the end of the nineteenth century, the Kunta[66] were well established throughout the region, from the shores of the Atlantic to Borno in the central Sudan[67] and from Tuat in southern Morocco to Tagant in Mauritania.[68] They are also one of the most intellectually prolific families of the region.[69] Kunta scholars produced juridical verdicts (fatwas), chronicles (*tarikh*), and advice to princes. They recorded trade documents and arbitrated disputes among traders. They also wrote an abundance of devotional literature in praise of the Prophet Muhammad, Sufi saints, and simply friends. The two most famous Kunta scholars are Sidi Mukhtar al-Kunti al-Kabir (1729–1811 CE) and his son Sidi Muhammad (d. 1826 CE). It was under their leadership that the Kunta became the most influential clerical group of the Bilad al-Sudan. The hegemony of the Kunta rested on their versatility. They were very learned scholars in the exoteric sciences, and notably in Islamic jurisprudence. The Kunta also had a great mastery of talismanic sciences. Finally, they were very wealthy. This multipositional type of leadership enabled the Kunta to provide a range of services that no other single group could deliver: from knowledge of the Islamic sciences and the Arabic language to the teaching of esoteric sciences, from the initiation to Sufism to the mediation of political conflicts between various racial and ethnic groups, including Tuaregs, Armas, Berbers, and black people in the western and southwestern Sahara.

The other Zawaya tribe, of Idaw A'li, played an equally important role in spreading exoteric knowledge and Sufism. They were the flag bearers of the Tijaniyya,[70] a Sufi order founded by Ahmad al-Tijani in the nineteenth century, which spread throughout the entire world, but more specifically in sub-Saharan Africa, where tens of millions of people joined the order. Most chains of transmission of the Tijaniyya go back to Muhammad al-Hafiz (1759/1760–1830) of the Idaw A'li tribe.

The Tijaniyya claimed to be the synthesis of all Sufi teachings and to abrogate all pre-existing orders. This claim appealed to large segments of the population of West Africa, which joined the new order and included former adherents of the Qadiriyya over the course of the nineteenth and twentieth centuries. Through various institutions (mosques, Sufi lodges, schools), the Zawaya spread Islam, Sufi orders, and talismanic knowledge throughout the Bilad al-Sudan.[71]

The Fulbe

Called Fulani in Northern Nigeria, Peul by the French, and Fellata in Borno and the Nilotic Sudan,[72] the Fulbe are speakers of the fourth most spoken African language after Arabic, Kiswahili, and Hausa. Originating in the Senegal River valley, they spread throughout the West African savannah between the eleventh and nineteenth centuries.[73] They are now present from Senegal to the Nilotic Sudan, with strong concentrations in Northern Nigeria. Although they converted to Islam after the Wangara, they became no less ardent messengers and teachers of Islam. From the eighteenth century on, many Fulbe specialized in scholarship,[74] and Pulaar became an important language for the transmission of Islamic learning, second only to Arabic in the western Sudan. This was so much the case that many aspirants to clerical status among the Wolof, Soninke, and other ethnic groups of the Senegal River valley assimilated to the Haal Pulaar ethnicity in order to become scholars. In the process, some of them adopted Haal Pulaar patronyms.[75] But it is in Hausaland that their teaching had the strongest impact in the late eighteenth and early nineteenth centuries. Under the leadership of Uthman Dan Fodio, a community of scholars was founded that toppled all the Hausa states and founded the Sokoto Caliphate. Known as Fodiawa, the community of Uthman Dan Fodio produced scholarly works at a scale comparable to that of the Kunta Zawaya. In the formative stage of the Fodio community,[76] Uthman Dan Fodio (d. 1817), Abdullahi Dan Fodio (d. 1829), and Sultan Muhammad Bello (d. 1837) produced over three hundred scholarly works in Arabic, Hausa, and Fulfulde. Beverly Mack and Jean Boyd have documented the role played by women in the intellectual and political life of the Sokoto Caliphate. Uthman Dan Fodio himself belonged to a clan in which women received religious instruction. His mother and grandmother were learned scholars,[77] and his daughter Nana

Asma'u[78] (d. 1864) wrote nine poems in Arabic, forty-two in Fulfulde, and twenty-six in Hausa.[79] Like her father,[80] Nana Asma'u was strongly committed to educating the larger community, and particularly Fulbe women. She produced more work in Ajami than in Arabic. Her many achievements in the field of education include the establishment of a literary circle of educated women, known as Yan Taru, in the mid-nineteenth century to promote the Fulbe.[81] We do not know much about the level of erudition and intellectual production of the Yan Taru in general, but we do know that some of Asma'u's sisters had solid intellectual credentials. Her sister Khadija translated the *Mukhtasar of Khalil* from Arabic into Fulfulde in the late nineteenth century.[82] Her other sisters—Habsatu, Fadima, Safiya, and Maryam—also composed various writings.[83]

From Senegambia to Mali—including in the Islamic theocracy in Futa Djallon,[84] in Futa Toro,[85] and among the Dina in Masina—the Fulbe also contributed decisively to state building in nineteenth-century western Bilad al-Sudan.[86] Particularly remarkable among them was Umar Tall.[87] Initiated into the Tijaniyya in his homeland of northern Senegal, Tall travelled to Mecca, where he spent three years studying. He was appointed representative of the Tijaniyya in the Bilad al-Sudan by the Tijani shaykh Muhammad al-Ghali. On his way back to his native Futa, he sojourned seven years in Sokoto as the guest of Sultan Muhammad Bello and produced one of the most important texts of the Tijaniyya order.[88] When he returned to his native land, Umar Tall led a jihad to Islamize his country and succeeded in establishing a state that was brought down by French colonial rule in the late nineteenth century.

By the end of the nineteenth century, states established by the Fulbe Muslim scholars had, on an unprecedented scale, promoted Islamic institutions, including Qur'anic and higher Islamic studies schools and Sufi lodges. Just like other groups, some Fulbe clerical families also became assimilated to other ethnic groups. In Senegambia, for example, though some families such as the Tall kept their identity as Fulbe, other Fulani clerical families such as the Sy of Tivawane were assimilated into the Wolof in the twentieth century while they recruited a predominantly Wolof following.

The Wolof of Senegambia

Senegambia refers to an area of West Africa straddling Mauritania, Senegal, Gambia, Guinea, and Mali, most of which was colonized by the French at the turn of the twentieth century. Modern Senegambian culture is the product of centuries of cultural, economic, and political interactions between Arabs, Europeans, and black Africans. Wolof speakers, who are among the dominant ethnic groups of Senegambia, are among the teachers and messengers of Islam. They have contributed to spreading and teaching Islam, often in collaboration with rulers. We have seen that West Africans kings had a long tradition of collaboration with Muslim clerics, to whom they gave privileges in exchange for spiritual protection. Senegambia was a notable illustration of this situation. Typically, *serin* (Muslim scholars) were given a land grant to pursue agricultural and educational activities under the military protection of a king. Serin reciprocated by offering a variety of services to the kings—among others, praying and providing talismans for the protection of the ruler, his kingdom, and his general population from natural disasters, diseases, and external or internal aggression. There were instances of ambitious serin who sought political power and attacked kingdoms. In such cases, kings retaliated against clerical communities. But the dominant pattern was one of collaboration to the mutual benefit of the serin and the rulers. Serin contributed not only to the Islamic education of Senegambia, but also to rural colonization. After successfully completing their Islamic education, many scholars would seek to establish their own school. To do so, many serin established new villages with their students to devote their time to agriculture and education. More than any other occupational group, it was the serin who created new settlements in Senegambia, particularly in the nineteenth and twentieth centuries.[89] In central Senegal, a major center of Islamic education that attracted students from Senegambia and beyond was created in the seventeenth century at Pir Saniokhor.[90] More recently, the Sufi order of the Murids, founded by Ahmadu Bamba in the late nineteenth century, has created dozens of religious enclaves. The most impressive among them is Touba, the capital of the Murids. Touba was a hamlet at the beginning of the twentieth century. Within a few decades, it rose to prominence and became the second-largest city of Senegal.[91]

The claim to be of Arabic or prophetic descent has been an important marker of status among Muslims from the Bilad al-Sudan and elsewhere in the wider Muslim world.[92] The overwhelming majority of groups that acquire the reputation of knowledge, holiness, and piety claim to be sharif (plural: *ashraf* or *shurafa*). This is particularly true of teachers and messengers of Islam discussed in this chapter, most of whom claimed sharifian descent and produced genealogies linking them to the Prophet or the Arabs. Those genealogies do not withstand analytical scrutiny. As rightly noted by David Robinson:

It was simply not possible for most of the Arabs to be descendants of Muhammad, the Quraysh or early companions, and it was even less likely that Persian, Turkish, Berber, Swahili, or Mandinka would have genealogical ties to the Hijaz. But that was not the point. Those who made the claims and who had quality of personal command, learning, or military leadership to reinforce the claims, came to be believed and their descendants in turn drew upon these genealogical credentials to build their career.[93]

Indeed, the belief in such claims produced powerful social effects. The legitimacy of shurafa is largely based on the assumption that their sharifian origin gives them supernatural powers to harm their adversaries, to cure the sick, to predict the future, and to bestow good luck and happiness on those who venerate them. This has made such claims pervasive in the Bilad al-Sudan.

The early twentieth-century debate on race relations between Arabs and blacks in countries such as the prepartition Republic of Sudan and Mauritania suggests radical otherness between the two "racial groups." In these two countries, so-called Arabs are accused of having continued the centuries-old practices of enslaving and oppressing so-called black people. Even if the demands for social justice and social emancipation for subordinate groups are well founded, they should not blind us to the fact that neither in the past nor in the present have these groups been separated by a color line of any kind. On the contrary, they have maintained sustained interactions at various levels.

Ibadi Berbers, post-Almoravid Sanhaja, Zawaya, Djula, Fulbe, and Wolof have above all been the main teachers and messengers of Islam. The Islamic archive available in the libraries and private collections bears testimony to their intellectual contributions. They taught classical Maliki texts and abridged some of them to make them more easily understood to their students. They issued juridical verdicts to arbitrate trade disputes. They mastered talismanic knowledge, which they could use to heal various diseases, bring luck, and provide protection against real and presumed enemies. The Mauritanian proverb at the beginning of the chapter, which states that masters of talismanic knowledge are either the Kunta Zawaya clans or the Fulbe (*al-hikmatu kuntiyyatun aw futi-yyatun*), shows how two of these groups contributed to the creation of precolonial Islamic epistemologies. I will further highlight their contribution to the production of Islamic knowledge in Chapters 4 and 5 when I look at the historical core curriculum and analyze some of the main debates documented by the Islamic archive.

Chapter 4

Curriculum and Knowledge Transmission

Before, only God existed. When he wanted other beings to
come to existence, he manifested himself in himself. From the
being that was his manifestation, God created the Muhammadan
Reality. From the Muhammadan Reality, God created the
sea. From the sea, God created foam. The sea cannot be quiet,
because it was created from a living being and reflects the
manifestation of God . . . Of all creatures, the sea is the one that
resembles God most in richness, wideness, and generosity. In the
sea, we find fish and jewels; boats can circulate without harming
the sea in any way. From foam, God created earth. From earth, he
created Adam and Eve. That is why Shaykh Ibrahim said
that "only God existed before anything else exists, and even now
that other beings seem to exist, in fact, only God exists." If you
return each person to his parents, and their parents to their
parents, ultimately you will go back to Adam and Eve. If you
return Adam and Eve to the earth, the earth to the sea, the sea to
Muhammadan Reality, Muhammadan Reality to God, then you
realize that nothing else exists except God. If you ask a human
being to show you himself, he would show you a part of his body
but will not show you himself. The truth is that God is present in
all human beings regardless of their awareness or lack thereof.
Proximity is a veil. When something is too close to you, you
cannot see it. The Prophet said: "I originate from the light
of God; human beings originate from my light."

—*Shaykh Hadi Niasse* [1]

THE PROPHET MUHAMMAD is known as the messenger of God to the
Arabs. But for Sufis in the Akbarian tradition, the Prophet was created as
light (*nur*) [2] and a reality (*haqiqa*) [3] before any being. The notion of Muhammadan
Reality put forward by Sufis is important for an understanding of devotional
Sufi poetry learned and taught to the students of higher Islamic studies and
through lectures to the masses. [4] The above abstract could have been taken from
a Sufi treatise in Arabic, but it was delivered in Wolof to a public of devotees.

Attenders took no notes, but many would be able to transmit this cosmology in any language to larger audiences. Scholars used texts, but most knowledge transmission was oral. Many scholars were learned in Arabic, but most of their commentary was conducted in African languages. The oral and the written, African languages and Arabic, were two faces of the same coin in this system of knowledge transmission.

From the secondary literature as well as in the autobiographies of West African Muslim scholars, we get a good idea of the texts that circulated most in the precolonial Bilad al-Sudan.[5] Bruce Hall and Charles Stewart must be credited for the first serious effort to develop a rigorous methodology toward identifying the historic core curriculum in the larger West African Sahel. On the strength of an online database containing more than twenty-one thousand West African Islamic manuscripts preserved in collections of manuscripts in the west and central Sudan and focusing on the period from roughly 1625 to 1925, they identify six disciplines: Qur'an, the Prophet Muhammad, Jurisprudence, Arabic language, theology, and Sufism. Drawing on that literature and especially on Stewart and Hall, this chapter attempts to identify what subjects / texts were taught and how. It identifies the following as central in Islamic education: the Qur'an and related sciences; legal studies; hadith, sira, and devotional poetry; theology; Sufism; Arabic language; talismanic sciences; and, last but not least, African language lexicology. In the sections that follow, I will discuss these subjects as well as the most widely circulating texts in written and oral form in Muslim West Africa.

The Qur'an and Related Sciences

Prominent among subjects studied in West Africa was the Qur'an and derived sciences such as memorization (*hifz*), exegesis (*tafsir*), and the art of its psalmody (*tajwid*). Arabic has always been used as the language for the most important Islamic rituals, including the five daily prayers, the Friday congregational prayer, and the annual festivals celebrating the end of the month of Ramadan (*'id al-fitr*) and commemorating Abraham's commitment to sacrifice his son (*'id al-adha*). With the notable exception of early Kemalist Turkey, where attempts failed to replace Arabic with Turkish as the liturgical language for the call to prayer, nowhere in the Muslim world has any language except Arabic ever been used for canonical prayer (*salat*)—different from supplication (*du'a*), which can be said in any language. Regardless of language and nationality, Muslims must commit at least some parts of the Qur'an to memory.

The overwhelming majority of Muslims are able to recite from memory some *surats* of the Qur'an, and being able to commit the entire Qur'an to memory (*hifz*) has remained a feat and a claim to authority throughout history.

Huffaz (those who have memorized the entire Qur'an) are highly venerated in Muslim societies. Various virtues are attributed to ensuring that one's child commits the Qur'an to memory. These include the belief that the parents of a *hafiz* (pl. huffaz) will be rewarded in the hereafter and redeemed for the fact that their child had memorized the Qur'an. The embodiment of the word of God is also believed to bless the hafiz, so that learning any science would be made easy by the blessing of the word of God. Debates about the centrality of memorizing the Qur'an are held in web forums and blogs visited by millions of Muslims worldwide; the following saying of the Prophet Muhammad, transmitted by a narrator named Hakim, is an example in this ongoing conversation:

> Whoever reads the Quran, memorizes it, and acts upon it, on the Day of Judgment he will be clad (by angels) with a crown of light, its light is like the sunlight and his parents will be clad with two garments better than the whole world and whatever it contains. So they would amazingly ask: "What action did we do to deserve this?" They will be told: "Because your son memorized the Quran."[6]

The art of the psalmody of the Qur'an (*tajwid*) is another important Qur'anic science. From the Arabic verb *jawwada* meaning "to embellish or to beautify," the substantive *tajwid* does not appear in the Qur'an, but a word of similar meaning, *tartil,* does (Qur'an LXXIII, 4) and was interpreted by the fourth caliph, 'Ali b. Abi Talib, to mean "an excellent rendering of the consonant sounds and knowledge of the pauses."[7] Tajwid deals essentially with the skills of oral recitation. As an act of performance, it has become an important dimension of piety because of the sacredness of the word of God.[8] Teachers carefully ensure that pupils do not mispronounce God's word. This is particularly true for non-Arabic speakers who may find it difficult to pronounce some Arabic consonants. An eloquent illustration in a West African context is found in the celebrated autobiography of Senegalese novelist Cheikh Hamidou Kane, where the author narrates the rigor of Qur'anic studies and the physical punishment that the master made him endure whenever he mispronounced the word of God.

> That day, Thierno had beaten him again. And yet Samba Diallo knew his sacred verse . . . It was only that he had made a slip of the tongue. Thierno had jumped up as if he had stepped on one of the white-hot paving stones of the gehenna promised to evil-doers. He had seized Samba Diallo by the

fleshy part of his thigh and, between his thumb and index finger, had given him a long hard pinch. The child had gasped with pain and begun to shake all over. Threatened by sobs which were strangling him in the chest and throat, he had had the strength to master his suffering; in a weak voice, broken and stammering, but he had repeated the verse from the holy Book which he had spoken badly in the first place.[9]

The right pronunciation was important, because mispronouncing might result in distorting the word of God, which Muslims—and particularly school-masters—believed is a great sin. In many supplications closing the recita-tion of the entire Qur'an, known as *khatm*, reciters ask forgiveness for any pos-sible mispronunciation of Qur'an, such as wrongly geminating a consonant or elongating a vowel or pausing where no pause is allowed. Stewart and Hall showed that several copies of various tajwid manuals are found in collections of manuscripts of the region and have been cited as part of the curriculum studied by Abdullahi Dan Fodio and Al-Bartili,[10] including the *Al-durar al-lawami'* (The Shining Pearls) by Ibn al-Barri (d. 1330), the poem "Hirz al-amani wa wajh al-tahani" (Preserving Aspirations and Purpose of Congratulating) by al-Shatibi (d. 1194), and the *Muqaddima* (Introduction) by Ibn al-Jazari (d. 1429). Tajwid is particularly important in the Bilad al-Sudan, where speakers of some African languages might find it difficult to pronounce Arabic consonants that do not exist in their mother tongue. For example, Pulaar-speaking people typically ren-dered the consonant *q* as *g;* Wolof speakers tended to pronounce as *s* consonants such as *dh, d,* and *z;* and Hausa speakers tended to pronounce *f* as *h* or *p*.

A second important subfield of Qur'anic studies is exegesis (*tafsir*). The exe-gesis of the Qur'an has become an established field in Islamic sciences, not least because the Qur'an is not entirely understandable even to native speakers of Arabic. In that respect, Qur'an 3–6 states that some of its verses are entirely clear (*muhkamat*), while others are ambiguous (*mutashabihat*). The *Jami 'al-bayan 'an ta'wil ayat al-Qur'an* (Compiler of Evidence in the Exegesis of the Qur'an), completed in the tenth century by Abu Ja'far al-Tabari (d. 311/923), was a landmark in the formation of the field in the classical period. To arbitrate between rival meanings of the Qur'an in the process of exegesis, Tabari's work makes extensive use of the traditions of the Prophet and relies on grammatical analysis.[11] Although his work was known in the region, it was not used nearly as much as the *Tafsir al-Jalalayn* (Exegesis of the Two Jalals), authored by Jalal al-Din al-Mahalli (d. 864/1459) and Jalal al-Din al-Suyuti (d. 911/1505). This text has been used for the study of tafsir in the region for centuries and still is. Al-Suyuti was among the most reputed Egyptian scholars of his time and was very well known in West Africa for several reasons. First, when Askya Muhammad Ture the Great (1443–1538), emperor of Songhay, celebrated in the Timbuktu chronicles for promoting Islam and supporting Timbuktu scholars, stopped in Egypt on his pilgrimage to Mecca in 1496, he met Al-Suyuti in Cairo. Al-Suyuti introduced him to the Abbasid caliph al-Mutawakkil, who invested Askya Muhammad with the title of Caliph of the Sudan (Black People).[12]

Second, West African Muslims performing the pilgrimage to Mecca typically spent time in Egypt to study with Egyptian ulama. Many of the contemporaries of Al-Suyuti studied with him, including grandparents of 'Abd al-Rahman al-Sa'di, the author of the *Tarikh al-Sudan*.[13] It was these pilgrims/students who introduced the *Tafsir al-Jalalayn* and other works of Al-Suyuti to the Bilad al-Sudan.

Third, Timbuktu scholars also consulted Al-Suyuti on two important issues: the use of amulets and coexistence with non-Muslims. On both issues, he showed some flexibility—allowing the use of amulets and some form of association with non-Muslims. His advice was favored by Timbuktu scholars over that of 'Abd al-Karim Al-Maghili, an Algerian scholar who was prone to preach jihad against infidels and whose thought would be more influential among later generations of Sudani scholars,[14] particularly the jihadists of the eighteenth and nineteenth centuries. From the nineteenth century on, the *Tafsir al-Jalalayn* was often taught in combination with another derived text written by Ahmad Al-Sawi (d. 1825), a leading Maliki scholar in colonial India.[15] Typically published in the margins of the *Tafsir al-Jalalayn*, it is titled *Hashiyat al-Sawi 'ala tafsir al-Jalalayn* (The Commentary by Al-Sawi on the Margins of the Exegesis of the Two Jalals).

Mauritanian scholar Muhammad Yadali al-Daymani, also known as Al-Wali Al-Yadali al-Daymani, produced another important work on Qur'anic exegesis. Titled *Al-dhahabl al-Ibriz ila kitab Allah al-'aziz* (The Pure Gold in [Interpreting] the Noble Book of God), it is found in many collections of manuscripts,[16] suggesting its wide use, particularly among Muslim communities in Senegambia that maintained close ties with Mauritanian scholars. In addition to texts produced by native Arabic-speaking scholars, there are also important contributions to the exegetical literature by Sudani scholars—not just in Arabic, but also in African languages. In Senegambia, shaykhs taught exegesis throughout the year to a limited circle of students. In addition, they offered daily exegesis sessions to larger groups of Muslims in African languages and managed to cover the entire Qur'an during the month of Ramadan. The exegesis of earlier generations of scholars has been lost due to poor conservation, but echoes of their methodology can be found in the exegetical work of subsequent generations whose scholarly production has been recorded and published in hard copy and electronic media. To cite just one example, Shaykh Ibrahim Niasse (d. 1975) belongs to a renowned family of Senegambian clerics; he learned exegesis with his father, who, in turn, was taught by his father. Unlike that of his father and grandfather, Shaykh Niasse's exegesis sessions were transcribed and published after his death. During the month of Ramadan in particular, Shaykh Niasse typically gave two sessions of exegesis. The first, entirely in classical Arabic, was for his most erudite disciples, who included many Arabic-speaking scholars from Mauritania who spent the month of Ramadan in his *zawiya* of Madina Kaolack. The second consisted of reading only the Qur'anic verse in Arabic but delivering an intertextual commentary in Wolof to the larger audience of Wolof-speaking people. Both exegeses were recorded in the 1950s and published recently. The Arabic-only exegesis was transcribed and edited in six volumes by a Mauritanian disciple,[17] whereas the Arabic-to-Wolof exegesis was published in electronic form, initially in sixty cassettes with one as introduction.[18] Since a few Sudani shaykhs had disciples from a wide variety of linguistic and ethnic backgrounds, whom they taught, we can reasonably assume that some also held oral sessions of exegesis in classical Arabic and African languages that were never recorded. Thus, it was not just the Arabs who taught the Sudani—Sudani shaykhs also taught both blacks and native Arabic speakers.

As noted by the entry *tafsir* in the *Encyclopaedia of Islam*, different exegetes "have different concerns and goals, and this is reflected in the relative weight they put upon elements such as history, grammar, semantics, law, theology, or folklore. All commentators are concerned with the process of analyzing the text in light of the 'external world,' however that be defined for the individual author, with the aim of resolving any apparent conflict and making the text 'clear.'" This leads to the discussion of different methods in the teaching of Qur'anic exegesis in Senegambia. Exegesis can be taught as a discipline of its own. In this case, it consists of reading and commenting one after the other on all verses of the Qur'an, starting from those of the opening surah of the Qur'an, known as the Fatiha, through those of the second surah (the Cow) and all the way to the last verse of Qur'an 114, known as surah of "Mankind." Qur'anic exegesis can also be taught in other contexts with different goals. Sufi shaykhs may introduce their own disciples to subtleties typically not found in general exegetical texts destined for the wider public. The Sufi methodology in Qur'anic exegesis, for example, rests on the assumption that the Qur'an has an apparent and a hidden meaning, as demonstrated in the following interpretation of Qur'an 83: 14–15 by Senegalese Sufi shaykh, Ibrahim Niasse, in a lecture on the importance of following the Sufi path to spiritual fulfillment.

> When an aspirant seeks from an able shaykh guidance to reach the Almighty God, the shaykh will ask him first to perform the remembrance of the Almighty God until he reaches the presence of the Almighty God when he became extinguished in his essence. Unless the aspirant is extinguished in the essence of the Almighty God, his faith is not perfected. As long as the veil persists, the slave of God experiences punishment of some sort. The Almighty God said, "verily, from (the Light of) their Lord, that Day, will they be veiled. Further, they will enter the Fire of Hell." Qur'an 83: 14–15[19]

A literalist interpretation of these two verses in most texts of Qur'anic exegesis identifies "the veiled ones" as infidels who, because they did not accept the teachings of the Prophet Muhammad, will be separated from the sight of God by hellfire on the Day of Judgment. This understanding is based on the repertoire of the apparent *zahir*. It exists simultaneously with another understanding revealed in the commentary of Shaykh Niasse, which belongs to the repertoire of *batin* (the hidden). The veil refers, in Sufi parlance, to the lack of experience of the unicity of God. Those who do not have that experience of extinction in the essence of God, regardless of their religion (Muslims or not Muslims), are veiled *mahjub* and cannot access the ultimate truth (*haqiqa*). Living in such a state, Shaykh Ibrahim argues, is tantamount to experiencing punishment like infidels in hellfire. Joseph Hill rightly argues that "the discursive dualism of *zahir* and *batin* does not reflect two coherent realms, forces, and principles but instead a kind of pragmatic and spiritual pluralism. These terms are invoked in particular when truth claims collide ... These paradoxes and multiple truths must not be understood as linguistic tricks or as conundrums to be solved, but rather as approaches to facilitating multiple imperatives and mutually irreducible repertoires of epistemic and practical principles."[20] Sufi-inspired exegesis of the Qur'an introduced by Shaykh Niasse has had wide appeal in sub-Saharan Africa. In Northern Nigeria, tafsir used to be practiced by a few families that specialized in that field, until the first part of the twentieth century. Starting in the second part of the century, Tijani scholars affiliated with

Shaykh Niasse created vast networks of scholars who introduced Sufi exegesis of the Qur'an and offered it to large audiences of disciples.[21]

Legal Studies

The notion of Shari'a, as historically theorized and practiced in precolonial Muslim societies, is very different from the modern understanding of law.[22] Modern law is produced and implemented by state institutions and applies to all citizens. In contrast, the state had virtually no involvement in the elaboration, interpretation, or implementation of Islamic Shari'a, simply because the state as we know it now did not exist in the Islamic world, or for that matter in any part of the world during the formative period of the Shari'a. Where states existed, they might have appointed judges and defined their areas of jurisdiction. But the law itself was produced by jurisconsults in the precolonial times, in the form of juridical opinions through which jurisconsults answered queries emanating either from judges or private individuals. In their verdicts, jurisconsults stated what, in a specific context, was in conformity with the teachings of the Qur'an and the tradition of the Prophet Muhammad. A central feature of the Shari'a is legal pluralism. Even within the same school of law (*madhhab*), a variety of opinions may coexist on the same legal issue. In addition, the juridical verdicts given by jurisconsults (*mufti*) were not binding to individuals or judges, although they were often followed. The absence of impersonal law to be implemented on all individuals created great flexibility. The judge (*qadi*) enjoyed considerable autonomy to adjudicate disputes on a case-by-case basis.

We have seen that the study of law was at the heart of medieval learning in the Muslim world. The reason is that Shari'a provides guidance on all aspects of life, from rituals (such as purification, prayer, fasting, performing pilgrimage) to commercial transactions, family law (marriage, divorce, child custody), criminal law, and law governing the administration of state or the conduct of war. Understandably, the study of law was central to the medieval curriculum everywhere in the Muslim world. As one of the oldest branches of learning, Islamic Shari'a grew to become a complex field subdivided into many subfields and including the study of sources (known as *usul al-fiqh*), schools (*madhahib*), didactic texts, legal maxims (*qawa'id*), and legal cases / opinions (*fatawa* and *nawazil*).[23]

In quantity, legal documents found in the Bilad al-Sudan significantly dwarf manuscripts dealing with other disciplines. As part of the western Islamic world (*al-gharb al-islami*), historically including Andalusia and large parts of North Africa,[24] West Africa had been governed by Maliki jurisprudence since the rise of the Almoravids. It was only in the late twentieth century that rival schools of law (such as the Hanbali school, followed by Wahhabis[25] or Shiites) started to make inroads.

Beginners were taught elementary didactic Maliki texts, whereas the foundational texts and other advanced manuals were used for advanced juridical training. The most used didactic *fiqh* texts in West Africa are the *Mukhtasar fi-l-'ibada* (Abridged Treatise on Worship) by Abdarrahman al-Akhdari (d. 1585) and the *Muqaddima* (Introduction) by the sixteenth-century scholar 'Abd al-Bari al-Rifa'i al-'Ishmawi. Typically, they are referred to, respectively, by the names of their authors—i.e., *Al-Akhdari* and *Al-'Ishmawi*. Copies are found in many collections, and they are available in Islamic schools in the whole West African region still today.

For advanced legal studies, students were taught foundational texts dating from the formative period of the Maliki jurisprudence, such as the *Muwatta* (The Well-Trodden Path), written by the founder of the School Malik b. Anas. Copies of the *Muwatta* are found in most library collections. The Timbuktu scholar Ahmad Baba mentions it as one book that he studied with Bagayogo Wangari in the sixteenth century.[26] We also know that the *Muwatta* has, for centuries, been one of the three key texts used in the training of the Jakhanke clerics. A second important foundational text of Maliki jurisprudence in the Sahel was the *Mudawwana* of Sahnun (d. 864). Although less used, the *Mudawwana* was complementary to the *Muwatta*.[27] In addition to these foundational texts, later-generation manuals of jurisprudence were also taught in the Bilad al-Sudan. These include the *Risala* (Epistle) by Ibn Abi Zayd al-Qayrawani (d. 966); the *Mukhtasar* (Concise Treatise) of Khalil b. Ishaq (d. 1374), a text so dense that it was typically taught with the aid of a commentary;[28] the *Tuhfat al-Hukkam* (A Gift for the Judges) by Ibn 'Asim (d. 1427); and the *Irshad al-Salik ila Ashraf al-Masalik 'ala Madhhab Imam Malik* (Guiding the Aspirant in the Most Noble Paths of the School of Imam Malik) by 'Abd al-Rahman b. 'Askar al-Baghdadi (d. 1332).

A last category of advanced legal texts with which Sudani scholars might have been familiar is the compilation of legal cases/opinions (*fatawa/nawazil*). For centuries, the most comprehensive such text in the Islamic west was the *Mi'yar* (Standard) of Al-Wansharisi (d. 1508), which is a large compilation of legal opinions produced between the ninth and the fifteenth centuries. Only two copies of the *Mi'yar* are found in the Mauritanian collections. Stewart and Hall conclude that it might not have been used often. Ahmed Baba states that he read the entire *Mi'yar*. Likewise, Uthman Dan Fodio, making the case for the obligation to emigrate from the land of infidels, backs his claim by appealing to the *Mi'yar*, among other sources.[29] This suggests that the *Mi'yar*, as an advanced text, was taught in the Bilad al-Sudan, and zealous students would have known with whom to study it.

Jurisprudence was important for religious life, because devout Muslims wanted to perfect religion and whenever confronted with a precedent would approach jurists to guide them to the right path. Jurisprudence was also important for economic life, because Muslim merchants, particularly in major commercial towns such as Timbuktu, Kano, Shinqit, and Walata, were not just driven by the search for profit. In principle, at least, they wanted to make lawful gain (*kasb al-halal*). As to the issue of slavery, there were rules that governed enslavement and ownership of slaves.[30] Jurists and judges would arbitrate between conflicting claims. Jurisprudence was also important in political life, and some rulers sought advice from leading Muslim scholars on how to deal with important issues related to statecraft.[31]

Hadith, Sira, and Madh

Given the role of the Prophet in the redefinition of the notion of knowledge[32] in Islam, there is no field of knowledge in which his life or actions are not invoked as a source. But some disciplines relate more specifically to him than others. Those that are more closely linked to the Prophet include sciences of tradition (hadith), biographies of the Prophet (*sira*), and devotional poetry (*madh*). After the death of the Prophet and the end of the Revelation, Muslims have searched for sources of guidance. The Prophet's words and deeds (known as the hadith)—as narrated and recorded by his companions, family members, and later generations of Muslims—became the secondary source of authority in Islam after the Qur'an. Since hadiths were reported in a context of competing claims for authority, many were of doubtful credibility. In order to determine which hadith were reliable, scholars of hadith developed a methodology based on two dominant criteria. The first is the authenticity of the chain of transmitters (*isnad*), each mentioning the person from whom they heard the hadith until mentioning the originator. The second criterion is the content (*matn*) of the hadith, which must not contradict any fundamental teaching of

Islam. Based on these two principles, traditionalists classified hadith into four categories: sound (*sahih*), good (*hasan*), weak (*da'if*), and infirm (*saqim*).[33] Six collections of the soundest traditions established themselves among Sunni Muslims as authoritative. The most authoritative among the Sunni are those of al-Bukhari and Muslim (d. 261/875), followed in importance by the collection of Abu Dawud, al-Tirmidhi (d. 279/892), al-Nasa'i (d. 303/915), and Ibn Maja (d. 273/886). Of all the collections of hadith, the most widespread worldwide are those of al-Bukhari and Muslim, which had become authoritative by the tenth century. They are found in most collections of manuscripts and are mentioned by many Sudani as part of their hadith studies. Hadith studies did not just consist of knowing these collections; they consisted also of mastering the methodology known as sciences of hadith (*'ulum al-hadith*). As noted by Robson, the sciences of hadith "cover a wide range of subjects, dealing with classes of traditions and transmitters . . . methods of learning and transmitting traditions, . . . rules about details of writing traditions and methods of making necessary corrections in one's manuscript, even with the ages at which it is appropriate to begin and to stop transmitting."[34]

Devotional poetry praising the Prophet Muhammad (and other Sufi saints) is one of the most common genres found in the intellectual production of the Bilad al-Sudan. This genre appeared in the Muslim world as early as the seventh century with the poem "Banat Su'ad" (Su'ad Has Departed), composed by Ka'b b. Zuhayr.[35] Other well-known classics in panegyric literature include the *'Ishriniyyat* by Al-Fazazi (d. 1230), a collection of poems of twenty verses each. Two other much-recited panegyrics of the Prophet in the Bilad al-Sudan and beyond are the "al-Burda"[36] (Mantle) in Arabic by Al-Busiri, and the "Dala'il al-khayrat"[37] (A Guide to Goodness) by al-Jazuli of (d. 1465). Both poems are believed to have talismanic attributes.

In addition to these classics, Sudani authors have produced a huge number of panegyrics of the Prophet. The Senegalese Sufi saint Shaykh Ahmad Bamba Mbacké (d. 1927), who founded the Muridiyya order, is one of the most prolix of such panegyrists. Nicknamed khadim al-rasul (the Servant of the Prophet), Ahmad Bamba composed thousands of lines of poetry praising the Prophet.[38] These poems (*qasa'id*) are learned and recited by his disciples, the Murids, who have a strong faith in their talismanic properties.[39] Authors of panegyrics of the Prophet have also composed collections of poems praising their hero saints. In praise of Ahmad al-Tijani and 'Abd al-Qadir al-Jilani (the founders of the Tijaniyya and the Qadiriyya, respectively), West African Sufi shaykhs have produced a huge literature of devotional poetry. Although competing groups denouncing the veneration of the Prophet and Sufi saints made inroads in urban West Africa in the late twentieth century and produced a huge oral and written anti-Sufi literature,[40] their preaching has not diminished in any significant way the appeal of this genre, which rests on the powerful cosmology of the Prophet as a perfect human being (*insan kamil*).

The sira (biography) of the Prophet has also been widely taught. It seems to have been a continuation of an earlier pre-Islamic historical genre known as *Ayyam al-'Arab* (history of the Arabs),[41] which narrates the genealogy and way of life of Arab Bedouins, as well as their values, such as generosity, bravery, and courage. Among the reasons for its emergence and focus on the Prophet Muhammad, the most important was to extol him as a messenger of God, a claim disputed by polytheist Arabs as well as Christians and Jews.[42] Although the Qur'an refutes the notion of the Prophet as miracle worker (insisting that the Qur'an is sufficient proof of his prophetic mission), the dominant wisdom in the Near East that a prophet must perform miracles has influenced sira as a genre. Stories of the military expeditions of the Prophet (known as *Maghazi*), conducted with the help of supernatural agents, form large sections of the sira literature. The sira also provided a context for understanding the nature of the revelation of Qur'anic verses. In that sense, it overlaps with the exegesis of the Qur'an (tafsir) which attempted to reconstruct the chronology of Qur'anic revelation by identifying the reasons for the revelation (*sabab al-nuzul*).[43]

Last but not least, as a source of inspiration and a model of behavior for Muslims, sira literature forms the foundation of Muslim ethics. The famous hadith reported by Malik b. Anas attributes to the Prophet this saying: "I was sent to perfect good character."[44] The most common sira manual taught in West Africa seems to have been *Kitab al-Shifa bi Ta'rif Huquq al-Mustafa* (Healing by the Recognition of the Rights of the Chosen One) by the Andalusian Maliki scholar al-Qadi 'Iyad (d. 1149). Many scholars of the Bilad al-Sudan of the past centuries mention having studied it, and dozens of copies are found among West African collections of manuscripts. It is also one of the three main texts one is required to know in order to graduate as an accomplished scholar among the Djula.[45] Next to the Shifa, the sira text found in most other collections of manuscripts, suggesting its wise use in the nineteenth and twentieth centuries, is the *Nafh al-Tib fi al-salat 'ala al-nabi al-habib* (The Perfumed Fragrance in the Salutations to the Beloved Prophet), written by the Zawaya scholar Sidi Mukhtar al-Kunti (d. 1811).

The sira genre illustrates eloquently the interactions between oral and written devotional poetry in West Africa. During the festival celebrating the birth of the Prophet, which is organized in all cities and major towns in West Africa and among its Muslim diaspora, Muslim shaykhs spend the night narrating to people biographies of the Prophet Muhammad along the lines of the miraculous sira genre. Here is an illustration of sira oral recitation in the celebration of the *mawlid* (birth of the Prophet) by Tijani members in New York City:

> The Prophet was born in 570 after the birth of the Prophet Isa [Jesus]. When his mother was two months pregnant, his father passed away. His father did not live long. His mother Amina said: "I did not have any idea that I was pregnant. Every night, one prophet came to me [no precision as to whether in dream or reality] and told me, 'Honorable woman, it gives me pleasure to greet you and to announce to you the good news that you have a baby in your belly; no woman has ever held in her stomach a baby like him. This baby is the Lord of all prophets. Whatever God created was derived from him.'" The Prophet's mother would always wonder, "What are they talking about?" because she did not understand the message that the other prophets were trying to convey. She told the story to the Prophet's grandfather, 'Abd al-Mutallib, who recommended that she not tell the story to anybody. She acquiesced. At the month of the delivery, the Prophet Abraham appeared to tell her, "I am pleased to tell you that you will deliver a baby that no woman before you has ever delivered. He will restore a godly order on earth. He will come with the last book that God will reveal. He is the lord of all prophets. After him, no other prophet will be sent." In the first week of the month of giving birth, a group of women appeared to her. Amina narrated that they were gorgeous, as tall as date trees, and shining like light; they were angels, they were *houris* of Paradise. The women introduced themselves. One of them said she was Asiya the wife of the pharoah (who reared the Prophet Moses). Another woman said, "I am Mary, the mother of Prophet 'Isa [Jesus]." The other women were houris of Paradise. The women told Amina, "God has sent us to help you deliver your baby." She responded, "But I don't feel pregnant!"[46] Her clothes were not tight, her body's temperature was not high, she did not have nausea … They told her that she was pregnant and that the pregnancy had reached maturity and that she would deliver that day. The women kept her company. At some point, she needed something in another room. While she was going to the other room, her right breast opened up and the Prophet Peace Be Upon Him appeared. The Prophet Peace Be Upon Him was not born like other babies. When babies are born, their heads appear first, but the Prophet jumped and appeared on his feet. He was already bathed, fed, etc., and he prostrated himself and prayed to God.[47]

This miraculous narrative of pregnancy and birth is typical of sira narrated still today in West Africa. It is not unreasonable to assume that it was transmitted as such from generation to generation for centuries. It is quite different from the more sober historical accounts of the life of the Prophet Muhammad, such as that of Ibn Hisham (d. 835), of which only one copy has been found in documents in the West African Islamic manuscript database that Hall and Stewart analyzed.

Theology

Central to Islamic theology is the notion of monotheism, or the "oneness" of God, known in Arabic as *tawhid.* Treatises of theology discuss what believers must know about God, his attributes, the meaning of prophecy, the apostleship of the Prophet Muhammad, and the hereafter. The most studied texts of tawhid in the western Islamic world and beyond are the treaties of the Algerian mystic Abu 'Abdallah Mahammad b. Yusuf b. 'Umar b. Shu'ayb Al-Sanusi (1435–1490). A renowned exponent of the Ash'ari theology, Al-Sanusi produced three treatises of tawhid, taught at the three levels of learning and so titled. The most advanced is titled *Kubra,* followed by the intermediary, *Wusta,* and then the elementary, *Sughra.* These treatises were taught in colleges in the Maghreb as well as in Egypt and Mecca. The elementary one (*Sughra*) is a text about ten pages long, called *Umm al-Barahin* (Mother of Proofs). It is one of the most taught theology texts in the Bilad al-Sudan. Ahmad Baba mentions the *Sughra* as part of the texts he studied with Bagayogo al-Wangari in the late sixteenth century.[48] Scholars from the Bilad al-Sudan have commented on Al-Sunusi's treatises, including in African languages.[49] Several Fulfulde adaptations of Sanusi theological treatises have been taught in West Africa since the seventeenth century. One of them is known as *Kabbe tawhidi,* which is the translation of the Arabic expression "People of Unicity." Taught orally[50] to gradually initiate Fulfulde speakers into Islamic theology, the teachings of the Kabbe commentary were inspired by Sanusi's pedagogical approach to the topic. Fulfulde clerics broke down the theological discussion into three parts, taught at the elementary, intermediate, and advanced levels. Subsequently, the seventeenth-century Fulani scholar Muhammad al-Wali b. Abdallah al-Fulani produced a commentary in Arabic of the Kabbe, itself based on the *Sughra.*[51]

Another version of Sanusi's theological treatise in Fulfulde is called *Maddin,* from the Arabic "What Is Religion?" It was taught from the early twentieth century in Mali. Like the Kabbe, its method is gradual, starting with the basic elements of the Islamic creed and the accomplishment of rituals such as purification and prayer, which are accessible to most students. The *Maddin* ends with the study of esoteric sciences such as numerology, important for only the most advanced students. Brenner hypothesized that these formulations of Islamic theology were a means for Muslim clerics to teach Islam to the grassroots and/or the youngest to the Islamic faith in a context where Islam was a minority religion. Through the oral explanation of some fundamentals of the faith, clerics could teach in African languages masses who typically did not attend Islamic schools, which were reserved for the elites.[52] This was notably the case in the nineteenth-century Sokoto Caliphate, during which Fodiawa, as previously mentioned, adopted the same methods. Members of the Yan Taru memorized poems composed by Nana Asma'u in Fulfulde and taught them to other women. This intertextual process of translation and commentary from Arabic to African languages and sometime vice versa mediated by Sudani scholars helped bridge the gap between two epistemological universes and contributed to the production of an Islamic space of meaning in the Bilad al-Sudan.

Sufism

Sufi orders played a decisive role in the Islamization of West Africa, particularly from the eighteenth century on. Most Zawaya and the Fulbe claimed membership in the Sufi orders of the Qadiriyya and the Tijaniyya. As such, their worldviews were deeply influenced by Sufi concepts and shaped by Sufi practices. Sufi influences, therefore, could be found in the study of tafsir as discussed earlier, and of course in the huge corpus of devotional poetry praising and seeking the intercession of the Prophet and other saints. Thus, the practice of Sufism has been central in many facets of the life of the Sudani Muslims, particularly in the nineteenth and twentieth centuries. Yet not many Sufi manuals were part of what Hall and Stewart called the "historical core curriculum." Hall and Stewart have found very few copies of works of towering figures of Sufism, such as Ibn 'Arabi, in the West African collections of manuscripts that served as the basis of their database. They have hypothesized that West African Sufis probably did not have firsthand knowledge of works of Sufis such as Ibn 'Arabi,[53] but instead were exposed to the thought of Ibn 'Arabi through the works of later Sufi authors. This seems true for Umar Tall, who does not directly cite Ibn 'Arabi in his magnum opus *Rimah Hizb al-Rahim 'ala Nuhur Hizb al-Rajim* (Spears of the Party of the Merciful Thrown at the Throats of the Party of the Accursed),[54] the second most important treatise of the Tijaniyya tariqa. In fifty-five chapters of varying length, Tall addresses some broader issues of Islamic mysticism and makes the case that the Tijaniyya is superior to and abrogates all others just as Islam abrogates all other religions. Topics covered in his *Kitab al-Rimah* include broader mystical themes such as the relationship between the aspirant and the master, spiritual retreat (*khalwa*), friendship with God (*walaya*), matters concerning Islamic law, and the notion of the Muhammadan path (*tariqa muhammadiyya*),[55] as well as the merits of the Tijaniyya.[56] Umar Tall makes over 600 quotations from 125 different sources dealing predominantly with mysticism (370 citations), but also logic, jurisprudence, theology, exegesis, hadith, *adab,* grammar, and panegyric of the Prophet. Two-thirds of the citations of Sufi sources draw from the works of only three Sufi authors, primarily 'Abd al-Wahhab al-Sha'rani (d. 1565),[57] who gets the lion's share with 98 citations from fifteen of his books, followed by 'Ali Harazim Barrada,[58] whose *Jawahir al-Ma'ani* is cited 84 times. The third most cited source is the one titled *Al-Ibriz* by Ahmad al-Mubarak al-Lamati (d. 1742).[59] Other influential authors cited by Umar Tall include Ahmad Zarruq[60] (d. 1493) and the Egyptian Ibn 'Ata Allah al-Iskandari (d. 1309).

Arabic Language

The scientific study of Arabic-language literature, including the pre-Islamic poetry genres, became very important in Islamic studies. The most important legacy of pre-Islamic poetry included the *Suspended Poems* (*al-Mu'allaqat*). Composed by famous poets, they told stories of love and separation from the beloved. Found in large numbers in West African manuscript collections,[61] the *Suspended Poems* were committed to memory by all accomplished Islamic scholars as part of their studies and thus helped develop a sound vocabulary in the Arabic language.

Also important was the study of Arabic grammar, morphology, and syntax. At the introductory level, the two key texts studied are the *Al-Ajurrumiyya* by 'Abdallah b. Muhammad al-Sanhaji, known as Ibn Ajurrum (d. 1323), and the *Alifyya* (a poem of one thousand stanzas), which summarizes the most important rules of Arabic syntax and is authored by Jamal-al-din Muhammad b. 'Abdallah al-Ta'i al-Jayyani, known as Ibn Malik (d. 1273). Commentaries on this latter poem by authors from the Bilad al-Sudan were also used in teaching.

Notable among them is the *Ihmirar* (Reddening) by Mukhtar b. Buna (d. 1805 or 1806), a Mauritanian scholar. In the study of Arabic morphology, another much-used title is *Lamiyat al-afʿal,* also authored by Ibn Malik as a complement to his one-thousand-stanza didactic poem on syntax.[62]

Although the field of lexicology was taught, it is not clear that large encyclopedic dictionaries were available. We have no evidence that the *Lisan al-ʿArab* (The Arab Tongue) by Ibn Manzur al-Ifriqi (1233–1312) was used. The best-known encyclopedic dictionary in West Africa, according to Stewart and Hall, is the *Qamus al-Muhit* (Comprehensive Dictionary) by Al-Firuzabadi (d. 1415). It is mentioned in the *Tarikh al-Fattash,* attributed to Mahmud Kaʿti. It must also have been known in Hausaland, since Uthman Dan Fodio traveled to Tafadek, north of Agades in the Air Mountains, with his supply of paper to find and make a copy of this dictionary.[63]

Talismanic Sciences

The morning I went to the École Georges Clemenceau for the first time, I (and my brothers and sisters) ate a special meal made of mouton for breakfast. Included in the meal was water collected from the washing of verses of the Qur'an. We were given the same meal every first day of a new academic year. Called *kiis,* it was destined to open our brains and make us intelligent. One verse that appears in such a talismanic recipe is Qur'an 87:6: *Sa nuqri'uka fa la tansa,* "By degrees shall We teach thee to declare (the Message), so thou shalt not forget." We were not the only ones given kiis. At the time of national exams, our house was always full of visitors from families from the lower to the upper class, soliciting petitionary prayers or recipes for their children. Most seekers of the recipes were parents of children who attended Western schools. My mother offered these recipes, which for generations had been transmitted in her scholarly lineage. West African scholars have taught these sciences to their students and their families for centuries. Thus, any attempt to comprehend the curriculum through the sole study of the main texts circulating in region will miss a central subject.

From Al-Bakri's story of the conversion of the King of Mali[64] to the most recent narratives of Islamization, many a history of conversion to Islam in the Bilad al-Sudan has been attributed to the power of Muslim clerics to perform miracles. We have seen that chiefs, including non-Muslim ones, surrounded themselves with Muslim clerics to accomplish many tasks—above all to produce talismans and charms to protect them and their kingdoms. Those talismans draw both from the Qur'an and from other local magical concepts and practices.[65] During the millennium of slow Islamization of the Bilad al-Sudan, survival and freedom were real challenges to most people, who had to face daily adversities such as disease, drought, slave raiding, and more. In this context, for Islam to survive and flourish, its messengers had to manage more or less successfully the misfortunes and hopes of the people. There was no reputable Muslim cleric who did not receive an initiation into the art of talisman making. Established scholarly families each possess their own book of talismanic recipes (*kunnash* or *mujarabbat* in Arabic). These are transmitted from generation to generation within the same family or from a shaykh to highly esteemed disciples or friends. Possessors of talismanic secrets shared them only with people who paid them a lot of money or who had served them devotedly for years. For this reason, it would be hard to find them in public libraries or collections open to researchers. This points to the fact that some types of knowledge were earned in this context and not open and free as in the world of modern scholarship.

Talismanic sciences in West Africa draw from many sources, including the abundant literature known as *Fada'il al-Qur'an* (Virtues of the Qur'an) or *al-tibb al-nabawi* (Prophetic Medicine), which deals with the health virtues of some food, such as honey and dates, but also the talismanic use of the Holy Qur'an. The most important source for the study of talismanic sciences in West Africa is the *Shams al-Ma'arif wa Lata'if al-'Awarif* (The Book of the Sun of Gnosis and the Subtleties of Elevated Things), attributed to al-Buni (d. around 1225), on which West African Muslims have built to develop their own expertise in the field. Talismanic sciences also draw on the use of plants, minerals, animals, and even, in some extreme cases, human remains. In addition to letters and written texts, talismans may include numbers, usually contained in magic squares. One of the most remarkable achievements of medieval Arab mathematics has been the construction of magic squares, known as *waqf al-'adad* in Arabic. The science of the magic squares, which dates back to the ninth century, consists of arranging a set of numbers in square formation so that the total of each row, column, and diagonal is the same. A very common magic square in Islamic talismanic sciences is known as the magic square of Al-Ghazali (*al-muthallath al-ghazali*), although there is no credible evidence linking it to the famous Muslim thinker Abu Hamid al-Ghazali (d. 1111). In this case, the total of each column, row, and main diagonal is fifteen:

4	9	2
3	5	7
8	1	6

The Mauritanian saying that those who master talismanic knowledge are either Zawaya of the Kunta clan or their Pulaar-speaking neighbors of Fuuta in northern Senegal suggests a strong interest developed by these scholars in the talismanic sciences in general and in the magic squares in particular. Shaykh Sidi Mukhtar al-Kunti is credited with having developed a magic square named after him (*al-muthallath al-kunti*).

African Language Lexicology

Last but not least, Islamic studies contributed to a considerable enrichment of African languages. First of all, it transcribed many of those languages that were not written down prior to the Islamization of their speakers. But Islamic studies did more: it led to a considerable development of the vocabulary of those languages. To understand this process, a parallel can be drawn with the ways in which engineering and other sciences contribute to the creation of new terms to capture new scientific discoveries. Because the educational system was bilingual among Non-Arabic speakers, whatever they learned in Arabic, they had to figure out how to translate into their mother tongue. Thus, an exegesis of the Qur'an in Hausa or a lecture on Sufism in Pulaar entailed the development of technical language in the respective African target language. As a result, Islamic studies, far from eradicating or relegating the African language to a lesser status, in fact did much to enrich and expand those languages. The more learned the scholar in Islamic studies, the more distinctively he could express himself in his native language. We see a particular benefit of this centuries-long development of native languages in recent years in West Africa: emphasis has been put on the promotion of African languages. Journalists, in particular, are required to master African languages and provide a version of all broadcast news not only in European but also African languages. It is interesting that, in the process of searching for an adequate vocabulary to translate complex phenomena into

African languages, journalists rely heavily on the expertise of Arabophone scholars who have been doing this for centuries. Most linguists operating in the modern academy do the same. The acquisition of a refined vocabulary in African languages was, however, not a discipline taught as such. It was woven into the process of transmission of Islamic knowledge by the bilingual nature of the latter.

We see how the Islamization of the Bilad al-Sudan paved the way for the development of a complex educational system that integrated the Bilad al-Sudan into the Islamic epistemological order. Different forms of mobility—such as trade, pilgrimage, and travel in search of knowledge—ensured that the Bilad al-Sudan received a regular supply of some of the most important texts known in the region and the world. Sudani Muslim clerics built on those texts in order to establish a curriculum that varied regionally based on the availability of the teachers and interpreters. The *Tarikh al-Fattash* narrates that Sidi 'Abd al-Rahman al-Tamimi from Hijaz, who visited Timbuktu in the first half of the fourteenth century, acknowledged that scholars of Timbuktu surpassed him in the knowledge of Islamic jurisprudence, suggesting that being widely read was a fairly common occurrence there.[66] Yet Sudani scholars were not only consumers of imported literature, but also producers. They authored many commentaries on Maliki texts, proving their full integration in the discursive space of the Islamic west (*al-gharb al-Islami*). We have traces of the involvement of Sudani scholars in major debates among medieval jurists and theologians. Slavery is one such debate in which Sudani scholars such as Makhluf al-Balbali and Ahmad Baba issued authoritative fatwas.[67] Another much more controversial debate is about tobacco, on which Ahmad Baba issued an equally authoritative fatwa.[68] Finally, further evidence of the active participation of Sudani scholars in shaping the Maliki discursive space is the fact that the updated dictionary of Maliki authors by Ahmad Baba included authors from the Bilad al-Sudan.

In addition to the literature just discussed, we can find many tales of travels across the Sahara in both directions. From the beginning of the royal pilgrimages to the twenty-first century, Arab scholars have gone to the Bilad al-Sudan to teach and learn. Sudani scholars have headed in the opposite direction. Some have traveled, studied, and taught in Mecca and Egypt before colonialism. Notable among them is Kashinawi, who taught in Al-Azhar in the eighteenth century. But even after colonialism, this movement continued. As noted in Naqar's study of the pilgrimage tradition in West African, there were Muslims who left for the Holy Lands because they did not want to live in a land governed by infidels.[69] Chanfi Ahmed has effectively documented that West Africans who settled in Saudi Arabia were actively involved in proselytizing and thus "helped the regime of King Ibn Sa'ud at its beginning in the field of teaching and spreading the Salafi-Wahhabi's Islam both inside and outside Saudi Arabia."[70] Others have not traveled beyond their native homeland but were nonetheless fully integrated into the Islamic epistemological universe to which they contributed and by which they have expanded the knowledge base of the Bilad al-Sudan. Chapter 5 will analyze the Islamic archive with a focus on the main debates addressed in the writings of scholars in the Bilad al-Sudan in the period from the seventeenth to the late nineteenth century.

Chapter 5

Shaping an Islamic Space of Meaning

The Discursive Tradition

To write about a tradition is to be in a certain narrative relation
to it, a relation that will vary according to whether one supports
or opposes the tradition, or regards it as morally neutral.
The coherence that each party finds, or fails to find, in that
tradition will depend on their particular historical position. In
other words, there clearly is not, nor can there be, such a thing as a
universally acceptable account of a living tradition. Any representation of tradition is contestable. What shape that contestation
takes, if it occurs, will be determined not only by the powers and
knowledges each side deploys, but by the collective life to which
they aspire or to whose survival they are quite indifferent.

—*Talal Asad*[1]

A S PEOPLE GRADUALLY CONVERTED to Islam, a Muslim clerisy emerged
to consolidate the Islamic religion and expand its space of meaning in
the Bilad al-Sudan. In the process, scholars produced a literature inspired by
classical Islamic writings but addressing their particular contemporary concerns. John Hunwick[2] has suggested that Islamic writings in Africa fall broadly
into four categories: historical, pedagogical, devotional, and polemical. I will
add a fifth category, which I describe as political writings. These five overlapping genres form the bulk of the Islamic library in West Africa. In the main,
they are written in Arabic, but among the political writings in particular, a
portion is written in Ajami.

The first category of historical writings includes, in addition to chronicles
that provide much of our knowledge of the precolonial West African states, a
number of documents describing the customs of the people of the region, relations between merchants and scholars at different periods, and the relations
between the peoples of sub-Saharan Africa, the Sahara, and North Africa. They

also include a number of *ijazas* (authorization to transmit knowledge) and fatwas (formal legal opinions).

The second category is made up of pedagogical writings. Although classical Islamic texts produced outside West Africa have been circulating in the region for centuries, Sudani shaykhs produced their own commentaries and textbooks. They often wrote versified commentaries of classical texts to make them easier for their students to learn. This is true of the great intellectual centers in present-day Senegal and Mali as well as those of remote regions where Muslim communities were isolated from the major trade networks and where copies of books were difficult to obtain. Commentaries have been disparaged by some scholars as mere scholasticism with little claim to originality. This is clearly not true of all commentaries. Some of them provide opportunities for learned scholars to bring other works to bear on the issues raised in the commented text. In this sense, they are informed by deep scholarly engagement, rooted in a vast scholarly knowledge, and represent a substantial intellectual contribution. In a reevaluation of the intellectual production of the Islamic world in the so-called period of "decadence," Muhsin al-Musawi has persuasively argued that "compilers and writers of commentaries are not to be regarded merely as knowledge intermediaries; they wielded authority through their selection and choice of material, not to mention their proclaimed goal of resurrecting the dead through their own words and those of others."[3]

The third category, devotional writings, is found in most collections of West African Islamic manuscripts. They consist essentially of poetry written in Arabic, but also in African languages such as Fulfulde, Hausa, and Wolof. Most Sufi scholars wrote poems or collections of poems in praise of the Prophet Muhammad, and these poems are often recited during Sufi rituals and festivals. There are also a number of poems in praise of Sufi saints.

The fourth category, polemical writings, was produced abundantly from the beginning of the nineteenth century, when it was mainly a feature of the rivalry between the Qadiriyya and the Tijaniyya. Starting in the second half of the twentieth century, as the Wahhabi impact on West Africa increased, polemical writings consisted mainly of attacks on and defenses of Sufism. In the late twentieth century, from Senegal to Kenya, there was no African country with a Muslim population that had been left untouched by the polemics in regard to Sufism and its opponents.

The last and final category is that of political writings. In the nineteenth century, scholars wrote in Ajami and Arabic to protest against rulers. This is particularly true of the Fodiawa, the community of Uthman Dan Fodio. In Hausaland, post-jihadist reformers, after bringing down the Habe kingdoms, restored the very system against which they had fought.[4] This led to the production of writings by opponents who condemned them. As noted by Bobboyi, drastic political change—such as that witnessed in Hausaland under the leadership of Shaykh Uthman Dan Fodio—could come only with huge sacrifices and great expectations. Whenever the leadership failed to meet these expectations, the very instruments used to overthrow the status quo could also be effectively exploited to subvert the new order.[5]

Drawing from this archive of writings, this chapter analyzes the ways in which Muslim scholars endeavored to shape an Islamic space of meaning in the Bilad al-Sudan, but one that was always contested. They did so by defining the Muslim political community, delimiting its boundaries, and determining who within the community gets what, when, and how.[6] They also strove to record the social and intellectual history of the Muslim community for future generations. These two concerns, I argue, have been central in the endeavors of Muslim intellectuals in the period between the seventeenth and the early twentieth centuries.

Defining the Muslim Political Community

The question of who is included in the Muslim community has been and is still debated. It was an important question in the medieval Bilad al-Sudan because of its implication for people's freedom or lack thereof, their social status, and other entitlements. The idea that some individuals could own others was accepted in the precolonial Islamic Sahel and elsewhere. The question then was whether there existed Islamic conventions governing the institution of slavery. More precisely, which category of people could become human commodities and why?

The slave trade has been central in the history, economic development, and state-building processes of most continents of the world, which understandably explains its importance in modern historiography. As the main global supplier of slaves throughout the second millennium, the black continent haunts much of the discussion about slavery. More than any traded commodity, slaves integrated Africa into the world political economy. The institution of slavery existed in Africa prior to the slave trade and Islamization, but the external demand for slaves no doubt considerably intensified it by enlarging the pool of people who potentially could be enslaved.[7] The exportation of enslaved sub-Saharan Africans followed two directions. Lasting over a millennium and continuing well into the twentieth century, the first direction followed the Saharan trade routes to North Africa and/or the Red Sea to Asia. It is referred to as the Oriental or Islamic slave trade. Named the transatlantic slave trade, the second route of supply consisted of passage over the Atlantic Ocean to the Americas. It took place between the sixteenth and the nineteenth centuries, and reached its peak during the seventeenth and eighteenth centuries. Because it was fairly well recorded, the transatlantic slave trade has been thoroughly studied. Slaving companies left historians with a rich archive in Western languages documenting the most crucial aspects of slavery, including statistics, regions of origin and destination, and slave markets. This archive has facilitated historical research on slavery in the Western academy. In addition, the presence of tens of millions of descendants of slaves in the Americas has prompted the rise of what has been called by various names, including black studies, Africana studies, diaspora studies, or African American studies, all of which devote considerable attention to slavery and its impact on the nation-building process of the Americas.

In contrast, the so-called Oriental slave trade[8] has not been studied nearly as thoroughly in modern universities, and this for various reasons. The first is the problem of sources. Due to poor preservation conditions, documents could not be preserved for the entire thousand or so years of the Oriental slave trade in Africa. Thus, much of the written record has been lost. In addition, the bulk of the available documents were written in Arabic, a language not accessible to many Europhone historians. That slavery was a much-debated topic in the African continent in the past several centuries is proven by a wealth of Arabic material, including commercial documents and notably correspondence between commercial agents and their masters;[9] legal treatises by Maliki authors setting general principles about enslavement, slave status, rights, and duties; and juridical verdicts produced to respond to specific instances of slavery.

Of such documents, one of the oldest to have been preserved is a treatise based on fatwas issued by Ahmad Baba in response to questions concerning slavery. This treatise, from which I quote extensively later to highlight Ahmad Baba's views, was translated by John Hunwick and Fatima Harrak as *The Ladder of Ascent: Towards Grasping the Law Concerning Transported Blacks.*[10] One of the very rare Sudani scholars to appear in all major reference works on Islam, including the three editions of the *Encyclopaedia of Islam* and the *Geschichte der Arabishen Litteratur* of Carl Brockelmann, Ahmad Baba (1556–1627) is a much-celebrated scholar of the medieval Bilad al-Sudan. Since the mid-nineteenth century, when his work was first introduced to Western academic audiences,[11] quite a few pieces of writing devoted to his biography and scholarly works have been published.[12]

Ahmad Baba was born on October 26, 1556,[13] and died on October 22, 1627, in Timbuktu.[14] He was a teacher and a bibliophile. His library comprised sixteen hundred books in sixteenth-century Timbuktu. The Arabic Literature of Africa attributed fifty-eight scholarly works to him, including his fatwas on slavery. Ahmad Baba was known not only in the Bilad al-Sudan, but also in North Africa, where he sojourned after the fall of Songhay. As previously mentioned, Al-Mansur, the Moroccan ruler, sent an expeditionary force of four thousand soldiers led by Spaniard Pasha Jawdar to invade Songhay in 1591. Despite heroic resistance, the Arma (army of Moroccan musketeers) conquered Songhay amid huge destruction and for a short while established Moroccan vassal rule there. In the aftermath of the conquest, some prominent Timbuktu scholars, whose libraries the Moroccan invaders confiscated, were exiled in chains to Marrakesh.[15] All of them died in an epidemic of plague except Ahmad Baba, who survived and ultimately returned to Timbuktu.[16] The *Tarikh al-Sudan*, one of the major Timbuktu chronicles written by Ahmad Baba's student ʿAbd al-Rahman al-Saʿdi, poignantly narrates the events leading to their arrest and exile.[17] Ahmad Baba resided in Morocco between May 1594 and February 1608. After two years of house arrest, he was freed but was required to remain in residence in Marrakesh. He was invited to teach in a major Marrakesh college, the Congregational Mosque of the Sherifs, now called the Congregational Mosque of the Mawwasin.[18] He taught and composed several pieces of work in Marrakesh. Some of his students became very influential scholars and helped consolidate his reputation. They include Aḥmad b. Muḥammad al-Maqqari al-Tilimsani (d. 1041/1632); Ibn Abi Nuʿaym al-Ghassani (d. 1032/1623), qadi of Fez; and Ibn al-Qaḍi, qadi of Meknes (d. 1025/1616).[19] A leading authority in Maliki jurisprudence, Ahmad Baba authored a much-cited bibliographic dictionary of Maliki jurists.[20]

Classical Islamic theory of international relations divides the world between the Abode of Islam and the Abode of War, a division largely dictated by real-politik. In the jungle of pre-Islamic Arabia, relations between tribes were either governed by mutual alliance or enmity. When two conflicting tribes confronted each other, the victorious party disposed of the persons and goods of the defeated tribe as it saw fit. This was theorized in Islamic law in a similar way.

According to Maliki jurisprudence, the political leader of the Muslim community (imam) could do one of the following: kill defeated enemies, let them go free, make them pay ransom, make them pay the poll tax and retain their religion, or enslave them.[21]

The trade in human commodities was profitable in the medieval period, and racial prejudices against black people was so deeply entrenched that free-born Muslims, as previously mentioned, were being enslaved by other Muslims, partly because of the color of their skin. But pious Muslims were concerned about not violating Islamic rules governing slavery. Two individuals, named Sa'id Ibrahim al-Jirari and Yusuf b. Ibrahim b. 'Umar Al-Isi, consulted Ahmad Baba on the issue. Broadly speaking, they asked Ahmad Baba three sets of related questions about slavery in the early seventeenth century. The first set was about the timeline of Islamization of the Sudani regions that supplied North Africa with slaves. The second set of questions dealt with the burden of proving the status of slaves captured from lands known to have been Islamized long ago. The third set addressed deeper epistemological justifications of enslaving black people. The language in which the questions were framed suggests that both Al-Jirari and Al-Isi had some knowledge of Islamic rulings about slavery by earlier jurisconsults. But they wanted to take advantage of the reputation of Ahmad Baba as a leading exponent of Maliki jurisprudence and his presumed sound knowledge of the Islamization of the Sudan as a Timbuktu native. Concerning the first set of questions, Al-Jirari asked:

> What do you have to say ... concerning slaves brought from lands whose people have been established to be Muslims, such as the lands of Borno, 'Afnu, Kano, Gao, Katsina, and the like whose adherence to Islam is widely acknowledged among us. Is it permissible to have possession of them and to buy and sell them as we wish or not? ... For it is known that, according to the Shari'a, the reason why it is allowed to own [others] is [their] unbelief. Thus, whoever purchases an unbeliever is allowed to own him, but not in the contrary case. Conversion to Islam subsequent to the existence of the aforementioned condition has no effect on continued ownership. Were those lands which we mentioned, and other similar lands of the Muslims of the Sudan, conquered and [their] people enslaved in a state of unbelief, while their conversion occurred subsequently—hence there is no harm in [owning them] or not? One of the qadis of the Sudan reported that the imam who conquered them whilst they were unbelievers chose to spare them as slaves, since he had the choice ... and that they still remain in a state of slavery, and whenever the sultan needs any of them he brings in as many as he wants.[22]

Ahmed Baba concurred that unbelief was a necessary condition for owning a person, but subject to some limitations. Muslim princes who made a contract of protection with Christians and Jews spared them from enslavement because they lived in the Abode of Truce (*Dar al-Sulh*), an intermediary category in Islamic theory of international relations between the Abode of Islam (*Dar al-Islam*) and the Abode of War (*Dar al-Harb*).[23] Concerning the periodization of conversion of the Islamized Sudani Muslims to Islam, Ahmad Baba stated the following:

> You asked: Were these aforementioned lands belonging to the Muslims of the Sudan conquered and their people enslaved in a state of unbelief, while their conversion to Islam occurred subsequently, so there is no harm [in owning them] or not? The reply is that they converted to Islam without anyone conquering them, like the people of Kano, Katsina, Bornu and Songhay. We never heard that anyone conquered them before their conversion to Islam.[24]

Finally, Ahmad Baba dismissed in the following terms Al-Jirari's comment that a Sudani qadi had ruled that some of these groups were conquered before conversion and, although not captured at the moment of conquest, were spared as potential slaves who could at a subsequent date be called to serve at any time:

> You said: one of the qadis of the Sudan reported that the imam who conquered them whilst they were unbelievers chose to spare them [as slaves]. I say this is something we have never heard of, nor has [any information about it] reached us. So ask this Sudani qadi who this imam was, and at what time he conquered their land, and which land he conquered. Let him specify all this to you. His statement is very close to being devoid of truth. If you investigate now, you will not find anyone who will confirm the truth of what he said. What is based upon what he says, therefore, is not to be given consideration.[25]

As Hunwick and Harrak note, Al-Jirari suggested that "the conquered unbelievers were simply left where they were but were considered slaves who could be taken into service at any time."[26] What was at stake was a definition of who could be enslaved, purchased, or sold. Defining slaves as a social category would have allowed the enslavement of a fairly large population, including free Muslims.[27]

A second set of questions asked by Al-Jirari dealt with the burden of proving slave status of people raided in areas known to have been Islamized. It is well known that at the height of the slave trade, many raiders, regardless of their religion, felt little bound by "ethical" rules governing the capture and sale of slaves. Muslims and non-Muslims alike were raiding lands known to have been Islamized for a long time, and their Muslim inhabitants were enslaved and sold. The practice was sufficiently commonplace to warrant the issuance of several fatwas by Muslim jurists. But Maliki jurists were divided about on whom the burden of proof should fall.[28] While mentioning in a long response a series of conflicting opinions by Maliki jurists on the topic, Ahmad Baba unambiguously ruled in favor of obligating the purchaser to prove slave status and giving the person claiming to be Muslim the benefit of the doubt.

> In the *Nawazil* of Abu Asbagh Ibn Sahl, [we read that] the generally accepted view is that whoever claims to be free and mentions that he is from a land in which free persons are frequently sold, and if the purchaser confirms that he bought him from such a land, then ... the purchaser is charged with proving the person's slave status ... Sidi Mahmud the qadi of Timbuktu ... would accept their word without requiring them to prove that they are from those lands.[29]

The third set of questions relates to deeper philosophical issues about what received wisdom feeds racial stereotypes against black people. Al-Jirari raised the question of the Noah curse, one of the mythological origins of the blackness of the skin.

> What is the meaning of the hadith mentioned by al-Suyuti in *Azhar al-'urush fi akhbar al-Hubush* (The Flowers of the Throne Concerning Information about the Ethiopians) when he said Ibn Mas'ud reported that Noah bathed and saw his son looking at him and said to him; "are you watching me whilst I bathe? May God change your color!" And he became black and he is the ancestor of the Sudan. Ibn Jarir [al-Tabari] said: "Noah prayed for Shem that his descendants should be prophets and messengers, and he cursed Ham, praying that his descendants should be slaves to Shem and Japhet."[30]

Drawing from authoritative sources, Ahmad Baba dismissed in unequivocal terms these stereotypes:

> As regards the hadith which you cited from Jalal al-Din al-Suyuti's *Azhar al-'urush fi akhbar al-Hubush,* coming from the hadith of al-Hakim, on the authority of Ibn Mas'ud, that Noah was bathing and saw his son looking at him and said him: "Are you watching me bathe? May God change your color!" And he became black and he is the ancestor of the Sudan—I came across it myself in his book entitled *Raf' Sha'n al-Hubshan* (The Raising of the Status of the Ethiopians), and the actual words are: "As for the blackness

of their skins, Ibn al-Jawzi said: "it is evident that they were created as they are without any apparent reason." However, we narrate [the following account]: the children of Noah divided up the earth and the children of Shem settled at the center of the earth and they had among them both darkness of skin and whiteness. The sons of Japhet settled in a northerly and easterly direction and they had amongst them both redness of skin and whiteness. The sons of Ham settled in the south and in the west and their color changed. He [Ibn al-Jawzi] said: "As for what is related about Noah's nakedness being exposed and Ham not covering it and being cursed, this is something not proven and is not correct."[31]

This intellectual exchange is enlightening about discourses on and practices of slavery in seventeenth-century North and West Africa. Ahmad Baba knew Islamic rulings very well and was able to back his juridical verdicts with teachings of the highest authorities in the fields of hadith and *fiqh*. This exchange was not the first fatwa produced by Ahmad Baba on slavery. We know from another set of replies by Ahmad Baba that, while in residence in Morocco,[32] he was invited by a man named Al-Isi to update him through a fatwa about the religious distribution of the population and timeline of the Islamization of the Bilad al-Sudan, which provides clues to knowing who could and could not be owned according to Islamic law. Al-Isi's knowledge of Islam in the Bilad al-Sudan relied on a previous fatwa issued by Sidi Makhluf al-Balbali:

> Sidi Makhluf al-Balbali mentioned in his reply that those among them who are Muslims ... it is not lawful to own them. Similarly all of the Fulani, though they dispute with one another and some raid others, making predatory incursions, unjustly and aggressively, like the Arabs who attack free Muslims and sell them unjustly. It is not lawful to possess any of them ... Then we wish you to give clarification of this question, since Islam may have entered some of these lands after his death, or [in other cases] it may have disappeared, and [people] may have returned to unbelief. We also wish to have your reply about what we shall mention concerning what we heard about the names of some tribes, and what you know about the lands and tribes we have not heard ... So that we could discover the truth regarding all those who are lawful to be owned and those who are to be avoided.[33]

In his replies, Ahmad Baba provided an exhaustive discussion of the religious composition of the population of the Bilad al-Sudan in the early seventeenth century—which groups had been Muslims for a while, which were partially Muslim, and which groups did not convert to Islam in the west and central Bilad al-Sudan:

Those whom we have ascertained to be Muslim are all the people of Songhay and its kingdom [stretching for a distance of] some two months in length. Similarly all of Kano are Muslim since ancient times, likewise Katsina, Zakzak, and Gobir. However, close to them are unbelieving people who the Muslims may raid because of their extreme proximity, so we have heard, and they bring them to their place as unbelievers and slaves. As regard to these people, if it is established among you that a slave woman is from these unbelievers and was merely raised in the city of Kano or Katsina or Zakzak or Kabbi, and subsequently converted to Islam, then there is no harm in buying them, since she was taken captive while an unbeliever . . . Similarly, all the people of Borno are Muslims, but close to them also are unbelievers whom the people of Borno raid. The ruling is as before . . . The People of the Rock are of different groups: some are Muslims . . . if anyone of them is made captive, then beware and keep clear of him, for he is a free Muslim. Then there are people . . . forming part of another populace which only their creator can count. These groups are unbelievers until [the] present day. Whomever of them you get hold of, buy him for he was made captive as unbeliever.[34]

Ahmad Baba's reply to Al-Jirari and Al-Isi discussed extensively the status of Islamization of the west and central Sudan, including blacks and some Arabized Berbers. He obviously was not totally opposed to slavery or the enslavement of black people, but he did object to the practice of enslaving Muslims, which was commonplace in the Maghreb, as he was able to witness during his years of exile in Morocco. We do not know how widely this specific fatwa circulated in the Bilad al-Sudan or to what extent it affected practices of slavery. But we do know that defining who is Muslim remained a major debate in the seventeenth and eighteenth centuries, during which time the slave trade peaked. The demand for slaves contributed to fatally undermining the moral foundations of West African societies. Both Islamized and non-Islamized societies violated rules about enslavement. While Ahmad Baba and other seventeenth-century intellectuals were essentially pacifist, subsequent generations of scholars had a stronger commitment to political struggle. Indeed, from the eighteenth century on, clerical classes rose in various parts of the Bilad al-Sudan to challenge the moral bankruptcy of West African societies, of which slavery and political oppression by ruling classes were the most visible manifestations. The drawing of the boundaries of the Muslim community and the qualifications to exercise religious and political authority became even more important in this context. It determined patterns of alliance and conflicts not just between Muslims and non-Muslims, but also among self-designated Muslims, specifically between idealists longing for an ideal Islamic social order and realists of the Suwarian tradition. In many areas, very learned and assertive scholars used sophisticated Islamic legal reasoning to justify emigration and / or military action against those who stood in their way. In the process, they clashed with "pagans" and with self-designated Muslims who would not embrace their project. Many such instances are well documented in the nineteenth century.

In what follows, I spotlight two of the most telling illustrations. The first one is the Fodiawa justification for attacking Hausa states and Borno in the nineteenth century. The second is Umar Tall's elaborate explanation for attacking the Islamic state of Masina. These examples are particularly important because they illustrate the rise to political prominence of the two most impactful clerical groups in the west and central Sudan. The Fodiawa ruled the most powerful economic and political system in nineteenth-century central Sudan, while Umar Tall succeeded in establishing his authority for a short period of time in more than 150,000 square kilometers of the western Sudan. Never before and never again has such a large territory been submitted to an Islamic authority in the western Sudan.[35]

Takfir: The Justification for Waging War against Fellow Muslims

Contemporary Islamic jihadi organizations have justified war against Muslim governments on the grounds that they have not ruled according to Allah's revelation. These Islamists claim to have been inspired by Abu 'l A'la Maududi or Sayyid Qutb, who argued that sovereignty belonged only to God and that any ruler who does not rule according to what Allah has revealed is an apostate whose unbelief demands holy war. This debate on modern Islamism is, however, often conducted without reference to earlier intellectual discussion on a similar topic. I have argued elsewhere that a look at nineteenth-century revivalist movements reveals striking similarities between new and old Islamism.[36] I will further illustrate this contention here by referring to pamphlets produced by Uthman Dan Fodio in Hausaland at the turn of the nineteenth century.

In his biography of Uthman Dan Fodio, Mervyn Hiskett argued that he was "a scholastic and his intellectual assumptions were those of an old world."[37] In a rejoinder, Sudanese historian M. A. Al-Hajj hypothesized that the intellectual work of Uthman Dan Fodio was produced in response to specific historical events. To back up his claim, Al-Hajj subdivided Dan Fodio's forty-year career as a writer into three main phases in relation to his political project.[38] First, he treated the pre-jihad phase (1774–1804), in which Dan Fodio, in his writings, teachings, and preaching, emphasized clarifying belief and unbelief, promoting education and literacy, and denouncing those local customs and traditions deemed incompatible with Islam. This phase was characterized by relative moderation, because Uthman Dan Fodio believed that he could peacefully promote the Islamic order, for which he longed, through preaching and teaching. The second phase (1804–1808) coincides with the jihad period. At this juncture, Dan Fodio had lost any illusion of a peaceful Islamization from below because of Hausa rulers' determination to prevent Muslims from practicing their religion as they saw fit. To galvanize the energy of his followers, he understandably focused on drawing on his writings and preaching the boundaries between belief and unbelief, friends and foes. His approach was very Manichaean: one is either a friend who allies with the jihad and, thus, a Muslim, or one is an opponent and becomes an unbeliever regardless of one's knowledge of and commitment to Islam. A third, post-jihad period (1808–1817) focused on the consolidation of the caliphate. At this juncture, the community had already toppled all Hausa states and established its rule in what became the Sokoto Caliphate. As a consequence of the routinization of charisma, the concern of Dan Fodio shifted from identifying and combating opponents to a preoccupation with state building and community preservation. He became more moderate in his views.

Uthman Dan Fodio began his preaching career in 1774, when he was twenty years old.[39] A decade later, his following, known as Jama'a, centered in Degel, a town that was part of the city-state of Gobir and had grown considerably. In 1788, Dan Fodio exacted from the then sultan of Gobir Bawa the commitment not to interfere with his plans to promote Islam. Per that request, the sultan pledged to allow him to preach in Gobir and to let people who so wished to join him. The sultan further agreed that all men wearing a turban (meaning scholars) be treated with respect, that all those held prisoner be freed, and, finally, that citizens of Gobir not be burdened by taxes.[40] It was in that spirit that Dan Fodio completed his magnum opus sometime before 1793.[41] Titled *The Revival of the Sunna and the Destruction of Innovation*,[42] this erudite work of thirty-five chapters drew on dozens of sources,[43] reviewing a wide range of creeds and rituals, and comparing and contrasting what conforms to the tradition of the Prophet Muhammad and what falls within the realm of "Satanic innovations." In jurisprudence, he draws from the most authoritative in Maliki texts, including the *Muwatta* of Malik b. Anas, the *Mudawwana* of Sahnun, the *Mukhtasar* of Khalil, and the *Risala* of Ibn Abi Zayd al-Qayrawani. In theology, he draws from Al-Sanusi's treatises and on al-Laqani's *Jawharat al-Tawhid* (The Gem of Islamic Theology). He uses the main treatises of hadith, such as Muslim and Bukhari. Writing on Sufism, he uses the famous *Ihya 'Ulum al-Din* (Revival of Religious Sciences) of Al-Ghazzali and the *Hikam* of Ibn 'Ata Allah al-Iskandari, along with the *'Umdat al-Murid al-Sadiq* (The Reliance of the Sincere Disciple) of Zarruq. Writing about sira, he uses the *Shifa* of qadi Iyad. In matters related to legal rulings, Dan Fodio draws from the *Mi'yar* of al-Wansharisi. In political theory, he cites the *Siraj al-Muluk* (Lamp of Kings) of Tartushi, which is a classic in the Islamic "mirror of princes" genre. Themes covered in his work include faith, prayer, and fasting; rules governing the building and attendance of mosques, relieving oneself, performing major and minor ablutions, alms giving, pilgrimage, commerce, inheritance, food and drink; and seeking remedies from sickness, spiritual purification, closing, visions and dreams, circumcision, funerals, marriage, oaths, and slaughtering animals.

This book of his makes clear Dan Fodio's project of creating a new Muslim moral subject living in a society governed by the Sunna of Prophet Muhammad in Gobir. The text established his reputation not just as a scholar, but as a community leader with a vision to bring about fundamental reforms toward a real Islamic order. His community kept increasing in subsequent years. Not long after the completion of *The Revival of the Sunna and the Destruction of Innovation,* the relations between his community and the sultan of Gobir started to deteriorate. The growing following of Dan Fodio worried the sultan of Gobir, who feared that he was creating a state within a state. Nafata, who became sultan of Gobir in 1794, decided to reverse Bawa's accommodationist policies toward Dan Fodio and his community. He ruled toward the end of the last decade of the nineteenth century that nobody except Dan Fodio be allowed to preach. He further banned Muslims from wearing the turban and veil and ordered that converts whose parents were not Muslim return to their former religion.[44] As documented in the Sokoto jihad literature, the community not long after this confronted the troops of Gobir, then ruled by Yunfa, the son of Nafata who became sultan in 1802. In a strong requisitory, Dan Fodio had unambiguously shifted the focus of his critique to Hausa rulers, whom he wanted to disqualify to mobilize the crowd for jihad. In a very erudite writing of the jihad period titled "On the Obligation to Emigrate," Dan Fodio revisited Ahmad Baba's fatwa to argue that Hausaland did not qualify as a Muslim country.

> Another class is those lands where Islam predominates and unbelief is rare such as Borno, Kano, Katsina, Songhay, and Mali according to the examples given by Ahmad Baba ... These ... are [also] lands of unbelief without any doubt, since the spread of Islam there is [only] among the masses but as for their sultans, they are unbelievers ... even though they profess Islam ... It is undisputed that the status of the land is that of its ruler—if the ruler be a Muslim, the land is a land of Islam and if he be an unbeliever, the land is a land of unbelief, from which flight is obligatory.[45]

During the first decade of the nineteenth century, Dan Fodio's followers conquered most of Hausaland. It was in this period that Dan Fodio authored the work *The Book of Difference between the Governments of the Muslims and the Governments of the Unbelievers,*[46] destined for his followers who conquered Hausa states. Unlike in *The Revival of Sunna and the Destruction of Innovation*, he does not content himself with making general criticisms of the social and political order. He provides a detailed critique of the Hausa kingdoms, entirely refuting the notion that they are Islamic and explaining to his followers how the ideal Islamic government differed from the governments of pre-jihad Hausa kingdoms:

> Indeed, the intention of the unbelievers in their governments is only the fulfilling of their lust for they are like the beast ... One of the ways of their government is succession to the emirate by hereditary right and by force to the exclusion of consultation ... one of the ways of their government is the building of their sovereignty upon three things: the people's persons, their honor, and their possessions; and whomsoever they wish to kill or exile/or violate his honor or devour his wealth they do so in pursuit of their lusts, without any right in the Shari'a. One of the ways of their government is their imposing on the people monies not laid down by the Shari'a ... One of the ways of their governments is their intentionally eating whatever food they wish, whether it is religiously permitted or forbidden, and wearing whatever clothes they wish, whether religiously permitted or forbidden, and drinking what beverages (*ta'am*), they wish ... and taking what women they wish without marriage contract, and living in decorated palaces, whether religiously permitted or forbidden, and spreading soft (decorated) carpets as they wish, whether religiously permitted or forbidden. One of the ways of their government which is well-known, is that they bring presents which they call gaisuwa. One of the ways of their governments is the devouring of

the alms of women who are subject to their authority. One of the ways of their governments is to place many women in their houses, until the number of women of some of them amounts to one thousand or more. One of the ways of their government is to delay in the paying of a debt, and this is injustice. One of the ways of their government is that the superintendent of the market takes from all the parties to a sale, and the meat which he takes on each market day from the butchers ... One of the ways of their governments is the taking of people's beasts of burden without their permission to carry the sultan's (food) to him ... One of the ways of their government is to change the laws of God, and an example of that is that the Shari'a decrees that the adulterer shall be flogged if he is not married, and stoned if he is married, and that the thief shall have his hand cut off, and that he who kills a person deliberately shall be killed, or if the killing was unintentional, shall be ordered to pay the blood money, which shall be divided among the heirs of the slain man ... One of the ways of their government which is also well-known is that whoever dies in their country, they take his property, and they call it "inheritance," and they know that it is without doubt injustice. One of the ways of their government is to impose tax on merchants, and other travelers. One of the ways of their government, which is also well-known, is that one may not pass by their farms, nor cross them without (suffering) bad treatment from their slaves. One of the ways of their government is that if the people's animals go among their animals, they do not come out again unless they give a proportion of them, and if the sultan's animals stray, and are found spoiling the cultivated land and other things, they are not driven off. One of the ways of their governments is to compel the people to serve in their armies, even though they are Muslims ... and whosoever does not go, they impose upon him a money payment, not imposed by the Shari'a. One of the ways of their government which is also well known, is that if you have an adversary (in law) and he precedes you to them, and gives them some money, then your word will not be accepted by them, even though they know for a certainty of your truthfulness, unless you give them more than your adversary gave. One of the ways of their governments is to shut the door in the face of the needy. One of the ways of their governments is their forbidding to the worshippers of God part of that which is legal for them, such as the veiling of women, which is incumbent upon them, and turbans for men, which is Sunna for them ... One of the ways of their government is that they ... will not abandon the custom which they found their forebears practicing, even though it is evil. One of the ways of their government is the putting of dust upon their heads when giving a greeting, and it is an evil custom ... One of the ways of their government is their being occupied with doing vain things (continuously) by night or by day, without legal purpose, such as beating drums, and lutes, and kettle-drums ... One of the ways of their governments is the giving of a gift to one who conducts them before the ruler. One of the ways of their governments is lying and treachery and pride, and you cannot see one of them who does not give himself airs, and anyone who shows the least lack of respect (for them), they punish him for that; and these characteristics which have been mentioned, all of them are according to the way of the unbelievers in their governments, and everyone who follows their way in his emirship then he has in truth followed the way of Hell fire.[47]

After conquering the Hausa kingdoms of Northern Nigeria denounced as non-Muslim, the community of Fodio attacked Borno in 1805, which they likewise charged as being non-Muslim. They defeated the army of the king of Borno, but they were later driven out by a coalition led by Muhammad Al-Kanami (1776–1837), a very learned scholar and political leader of Borno. Al-Kanami exchanged letters with Muhammad Bello, refuting the argument of the Fodiawa that attacking Borno was lawful.[48]

As Muslim clerics fought to establish states in West Africa in the nineteenth century, they often clashed with other Muslims. The typical justification for attacking other Muslim states was that their rulers apostacized by befriending non-Muslims or allying themselves with non-Muslims against Muslims. A number of contemporary jihadi organizations justified waging war against Muslim governments on the grounds that they were allies or puppets of Western regimes. A close look at the nineteenth-century polemical Islamic literature in West Africa reveals historical antecedents to such patterns of proclaiming other Muslims "infidels."

Another important illustration is the jihad of Umar Tall, a towering figure of nineteenth-century West African Islam who succeeded in establishing a huge empire centered around Segou in the mid-nineteenth century. Umar Tall had sojourned in Sokoto following his pilgrimage to Mecca. During his seven-year stay, not only was he exposed to the jihad literature of the central Sudan, which provided a model for the region in the nineteenth century, but his proximity to Sultan Muhammad Bello enabled him to learn the art of statecraft. Umar left Sokoto after the death of Bello with the intention of waging jihad in the western Sudan. He initially sought to extend the Islamic zone of influence by targeting and conquering non-Muslim Bambara states. But he also ultimately clashed with another Muslim state, the Diina, established by Ahmad Lobbo, a former disciple of Dan Fodio.[49] In his work titled "Sword of Truth concerning What Happened between Umar and Ahmad b. Ahmad,"[50] Umar explained why he attacked the Diina. His text drew inspiration from a pamphlet with a similar title attributed to Uthman Dan Fodio, in which Dan Fodio claimed to have had a vision of the Prophet Muhammad and 'Abd al-Qadir al-Jilani girding him with a sword of truth to wage war against false Muslims and to establish an Islamic state in Hausaland. The arguments, methodology, and canonical sources from which Umar Tall drew for his demonstration are very similar to Uthman Dan Fodio's requisitory against Hausa states and Borno, as exposed in Dan Fodio's works mentioned earlier.

A crucial notion in the demonstration of Umar Tall, which is also found in the Fodiawa's arguments against Borno, is the notion of befriending (*muwalat*) unbelievers against fellow Muslims. Umar Tall discusses five different types of muwalat. First is the muwalat in the sense of natural love that one might feel toward a partner or a family member, which is permissible. Second is the love or spirit of good understanding that one displays in public toward infidels out of fear. This is an attitude that necessity might dictate to pious Muslims and for which they cannot be blamed. Third is the muwalat toward infidels aimed at procuring goods that they possess. This is forbidden according to Umar. Fourth is the assistance provided to infidels protected by a truce in conformity with the Shari'a against forms of injustice threatening them. This is lawful. Fifth is the muwalat consisting of providing assistance to infidels in a way that contradicts the Shari'a and contributes to undermining and destroying Islamic religion. This is the case when Muslims provide assistance to "People of War" (non-Muslims) and help them commit acts contrary to the Shari'a. This, according to Umar Tall, is an "act of infidelity."[51] In the last paragraph of his work, Umar proclaims his adversary Ahmad. b. Ahmad an infidel in the following terms:

> From this, it is clear that he [Ahmad] has provided a testimony against his own self that he is not a part of the Islamic nation (*milla*). On the contrary, he has joined those who commit hypocrisy, those who believe neither in God, nor in his Messenger, and who try to prevent the fulfillment of the will of the Almighty God. This is evidenced by his claim that the Pagans did convert to Islam, and by his misleading of his followers whom he convinced that he and his pagans are following the path of the truth and that he and his followers are better guided than we are in the path of the truth. In addition he claims that we erred to the extent of allowing and even forcing pagans to fight against us, to shed our blood, and legitimizing the seizure of our property and the violation of our honor. He therefore had joined the party of the hypocrites among the People of the Book.[52]

After the many successful jihads of the nineteenth century, jihad leaders faced a daunting task: to build "genuine Islamic institutions" in the ruins of those states that they denounced and brought down. Such a radical transformation was far from easy, because the leaders had a very diverse following. In Hausaland, for example, the number of idealists with a firm commitment to an Islamic state were not that many. After the jihad, quite a few combatants were tempted to enjoy the privileges of the Hausa royal system—and in fact succeeded in restoring it by the mid-nineteenth century.[53] The vision of the Islamic state and how to promote it was an important debate throughout the nineteenth century.

Constructing Political Authority

The work of Abdullahi Dan Fodio[54] opens an interesting window into this debate within the community of the Fodiawa. To relate Abdullahi's intellectual production to its political context, Sidi Mohamed Mahibou suggested that it can be periodized into four phases. The first is the period from 1777 to 1804, in which he is a disciple and the spokesperson of his brother, Uthman Dan Fodio. Abdullahi produced much of his poetry in that period. The second period is the early jihad, from 1804 to 1807. Toward the end of this period, Abdullahi was disenchanted with the conduct of the jihad to the point of withdrawing from the community and attempting to go to Mecca for the pilgrimage. During the third period (1807–1812), he formed a separate group of committed believers and produced most of his political writings. The fourth period starts in 1812, when Uthman Dan Fodio divided the Sokoto Caliphate into two parts, both under his supervision. In one part, he appointed his son Muhammad Bello, and in the other, his brother Abdullahi, to enable each to devise his own vision of the Islamic state. Abdullahi wrote his commentaries of the Qur'an and most of his works on Sufism during this last period.

A distinguished feature of Abdullahi's political works is that all three contain the word *enlightening*—*diya* in Arabic—in their titles,[55] suggesting an intellectual effort to enlighten people about an important issue. Written in Kano at the request of its inhabitants in 1806, the first is titled "Enlightening Rulers concerning Their Rights and Duties." This treaty was the opportunity to express disagreements over a number of issues regarding the organization of the jihad and the state in Sokoto. In five chapters, this text covers the themes of emigration (*hijra*); the appointment, rights, and duties of the imam and his administration;

and the politics based on Shari'a (*siyasa shar'iyya*). It concludes with the discussion of pilgrimage and pious visits to the shrine of the Prophet.[56] On the issue of hijra, Abdullahi supported the view that Muslims should emigrate from any land where the practice of religion is not possible. But he does not proclaim infidels those Muslims who failed to emigrate. The first chapter dealing with the appointment of the imam and the rights and duties of the imam and his administration is particularly interesting. Abdullahi argues that the institution of the imam, which is interchangeable with that of caliph, is a permanent institution in Islam. But he acknowledges that the institution has often degenerated to kingship in the past. This was particularly the case for Muslim rulers who did not procure and redistribute wealth according to the Shari'a.

The imam, according to Abdullahi, must first and foremost be just. Other qualifications include knowledge, integrity, maturity, competence, and male gender. He also discusses two criteria that are controversial among scholars: that the imam must be a member of the tribe of the Quraysh and the sole leader of all the Muslim community. If the imam is just and fulfills all other criteria, Muslims must obey him. Concerning the duties of the imam, Abdullahi argues that he must be pious and concerned about community matters. He must be convinced that he is the representative of God and successor of the Prophet. He must abide by the law to provide a model for his subjects. He appoints able and just functionaries to staff the administration of the state (notably viziers, emirs, and judges). Through periodic meetings, he must maintain communication with subjects in order to be updated about their concerns and remedy them to the best of his capacity. He must collect taxes and redistribute state income in conformity with the Shari'a. Finally, he must decline any form of gifts, because accepting them can lead to the corruption of the state apparatus and its mores.[57]

In the post-jihad period, Abdullahi had expressed disagreements with his brother Uthman's views on a number of issues regarding the organization of the state, including the use of musical instruments; the use of the title of king; the wearing of clothes ornamented by gold and silver; and the related question of the magnificent appearance of state authorities such as imams, judges, and governors.[58] In his early writings (such as *On the Obligation to Emigrate*), Uthman Dan Fodio condemns the use of musical instruments on the basis of their rejection by many Muslim jurists. But in his *Najm al-ikhwan* (Star of the Brothers), Uthman Dan Fodio argues that they should not be systematically rejected, whereas Abdullahi had consistently opposed the use of any musical instrument, basing his opinion on the majority of Muslim jurists. Regarding the magnificent appearance of state officials, Uthman Dan Fodio condoned it in his *Najm al-ikhwan,* on the grounds that, unlike believers during the lifetime of the Prophet, later generations of Muslims tended to respect people of authority merely for their majestic appearance. Abdullahi disagreed and argued instead that piety is all that is required from an imam. On the issue of ornamentation of clothes with gold and silver, Uthman Dan Fodio suggested that the occasional wearing of such was a way of expressing gratitude for God's favor and a way of raising the morale of Muslims and humiliating unbelievers. Abdullahi totally rejected that opinion, on the grounds that no Maliki scholars allowed it. Finally, Uthman Dan Fodio argued in his *Najm al-ikhwan* that names like *khilafa* (caliphate), *imara* (emirate) *Wilaya* (principality), *Saltana* (sultanate), and *Mulk* (kingdom) are acceptable. Abdullahi had expressed disagreement with such an opinion in both the *Diya al-Sultan* (Enlightening the Ruler) and *Diya Ulu al-amr* (Enlightening Those Charged with Authority).

Chronicling History

A second set of writings in the Islamic archive that attempted to consolidate Islamic identity deals with the chronicling of social and intellectual history. Most of these writings are chronicles and hagiographies. Several chronicles were composed to describe the political history of the whole or parts of the Bilad al-Sudan. They focused on the rulers and the major events during their rule. Some chronicles, such as the *Tarikh al-Sudan* by Al-Sa'di, provide biographical accounts of scholars and holy men of Jenne and Timbuktu,[59] but it was really the biographical dictionaries that specialized in mapping the intellectual landscape. Biographical dictionaries primarily are of two types. The first category is sect specific. The *Nayl al-ibtihaj,* or its revised form, *Kifayat al-Muhtaj,* by Ahmad Baba falls within this category. It complements the *Dibaj al-mudhahhab* by Ibn Farhun with a few more biographies, including eighteen from the Bilad al-Sudan. The second category covers the ulama of a specific region, regardless of religious affiliation. The eighteenth-century work titled *Fath al-Shakur* by al-Bartili[60] belongs to this category. This genre remained active until the twentieth century. The *Al-Wasit fi tarajim udaba Shinqit,* which specifically covers present-day Mauritania,[61] is an important illustration.

Historians of West Africa have diverged in their interpretation of the motivations of the chronicle writers.[62] In an analysis of the ideological background of the Timbuktu chronicles, Jean Pierre Olivier de Sardan and Djibril Tamsir Niane have seen the chronicles as a celebration of the social hierarchy of Songhay prior to the Moroccan invasion—that is, the alliance between the Askya dynasty and the learned class of urban traders to dominate the large population of slaves. In a critique of such an interpretation, Paulo F. de Moraes Farias raised a number of important and valid points. While recognizing that the seventeenth-century chronicles are useful historical sources for the study of the region, Moraes Farias argued that the chronicles are not always factually true. Using epigraphic evidence in royal tombstones of Gao, he showed, for example, that the title of Askya was used at least two centuries before the time mentioned in the chronicles—the arrival of the Askya Mohammad Ture's dynasty in Songhay. Moraes Farias showed that the authors of the seventeenth-century chronicles built on earlier reliable writings, but that sometimes they also borrowed from the local folklore and myths. Above all, their motivation was to reconcile the ruling Moroccan Arma with the surviving Askya elites. To do so, they constructed the notion that three great empires succeeded one another in the Sahel (Ghana, followed by Mali, followed by Songhay), a construction that informed the modern historical reconstruction of the Sahel. Moraes Farias contrasted such imperial claims for Songhay with the more modest description of Songhay as a mere sultanate by Ahmad Baba a few decades earlier. The authors of the seventeenth-century Timbuktu chronicles, Moraes Farias argued, provided a unified narrative of the Sahel from time immemorial to the moment of their writing, in order to present preinvasion Songhay as a successor empire to Ghana and Mali, which could rival in scope the Moroccan state. Moraes Farias further argued that the attempt to reconcile elites was the raison d'être of the seventeenth-century chronicles as a genre. This endeavor was not successful, because the Arma and Songhay elites were divided. After the failure of this attempt, the seventeenth-century chronicle died as a genre.[63]

A third school of thought, which resonates with my own position, envisions the chronicles in the *longue durée* in the genealogy of the *tarjama* or the *tabaqat*.[64] In his introduction to the annotated translation of the *Fath al-Shakur*, Chouki El-Hamel argues that the *Fath al-Shakur* belongs to the same intellectual genealogy as the Timbuktu chronicles and the biographical dictionaries written by Ahmad Baba. It was written with the goal of updating and completing them by putting emphasis on reputed ulama of the Bilad al-Takrur and their contribution to Islamic knowledge and particularly Islamic law. By producing biographical dictionaries of ulama of their region, Muslim scholars in the Bilad al-Sudan hoped to make their intellectual contribution better known, and to be rewarded for doing so.[65] The selection of whom to include in such a compilation was of course arbitrary. Most compilers cited and praised scholars that they admired. Al-Bartili[66] draws from earlier compilations of works such as the *Tarikh al-Sudan* of Al-Sa'di. Of the 210 authors listed in the *Fath al-Shakur*, he composed 167 pieces and reproduced the remaining 43 from earlier works such as *Tarikh al-Sudan*. The overwhelming majority (125) of scholars listed in Al-Bartili's dictionaries claimed Arab origin; 38 are of Berber origin, and only 15 of black Sudani ethnicity. Al-Bartili includes many scholars from North Africa, such as Ibn Battuta, who only visited the Sudan briefly. He even includes scholars from North Africa and elsewhere who never sojourned in the Bilad al-Sudan. El-Hamel argued that Al-Bartili was trying to prove that the Takrur, understood as the western Sahara, was actually part of the Arab world. To be fair to Al-Bartili, his goal was simply to cover the most prominent intellectuals (*a'yan 'ulama*). By doing so, one could argue, he aimed to provide a picture of the Bilad al-Sudan as fully integrated in a unified Islamic epistemological universe to which he believed it belonged.

While Al-Bartili was writing from Walata in the eighteenth century, his fellow countryman Muhammad al-Amin Al-Shinqiti, who wrote in Egypt in the early twentieth century,[67] shared the same goal: to make the contribution of pious and learned Muslim scholars better known. When Al-Shinqiti informed a learned Egyptian scholar about his project, the latter was surprised, because he believed that only peoples of the East had contributed to Islamic knowledge. Authors of chronicles and biographies emphasized the importance of piety. Their chronicles and biographies conveyed an Islamic vision of history according to which God is always on the side of believers and in which the best people of God's creation are the ulama or the *awliya*. The miracles of the saints are narrated on several occasions in such works, as is the punishment of all enemies of God who ventured to harm them. In this sense, the Timbuktu chronicles were a genre alive and well in Sahelian history before and after the seventeenth century.

It is clear from our survey that Maliki jurisprudence provided the larger discursive space for learning, teaching, and writings in the Islamic west in the post-Almoravid period. When clerical classes reached a critical mass and had enough confidence to pursue the Almoravid project of implementing a strict Islam—i.e., in the eighteenth and nineteenth centuries—they drew extensively on major Maliki texts to state their political project of creating a new Muslim subject and promoting an Islamic political dispensation in the Bilad al-Sudan. While the language of scholars is rooted in theology, their texts addressed real-world concerns. They delimited the boundaries of the political community to determine who should get what as well as when and how. Like Muslims elsewhere, Sudani scholars shared in what Talal Asad describes as the Islamic discursive tradition, that is "a tradition of Muslim discourse that addresses itself to conceptions of the Islamic past and future, with reference to a particular Islamic practice in the present."[68]

In Chapter 6, I will shift my attention to the study of the response of Muslim intellectuals to European colonial rule. As I will show, the colonial state had a very ambivalent relationship with the Arabic language and Muslim scholars. The presence of an educational system and literates in Arabic was clearly an asset in the process of consolidation of the colonial state. Their link to the precolonial Islamic state and jihadi and anticolonial credentials was perceived as a threat, however. Thus, the colonial state simultaneously strove to build on this Islamic education system while attempting to sever it from its Islamic roots in order to promote a modern European colonial subject.

Chapter 6

Islamic Education and the
Colonial Encounter

Zalamuna wa rabbina zalamuna
Absat al-haqq fi'l-dunya haramuna

They have oppressed us, O God, they have oppressed us
Of the most elementary right they have deprived us.
—*Cheikh Tidiane Gaye*[1]

A S OF THE WRITING of this book (2015), the Qur'anic school my mother
started more than six decades ago has been radically transformed. From a
school without a classroom, in the yard of my family's house in Dakar, it has
become a network of schools serving different purposes to different clienteles in
different linguistic combinations. The largest school of the network, Keur Sultan,
is based in a centrally located neighborhood at the entrance to the capital city of
Dakar. More than 20,000 students have attended the school in the past two
decades. Its student population now exceeds 1,500 students. Keur Sultan was
built on a plot of land of 3,500 square meters granted to my mother by the
Senegalese state, then ruled by President Abdou Diouf, as part of the state's
commitment to support the modernization of Islamic education and promote
gender equality. Foreign donors, including late Prince Sultan Bin 'Abd al-'Aziz
of Saudi Arabia, after whom that specific school was named, donated most of
the funding for the buildings. Keur Sultan started an integrated curriculum
model, which became very widespread in the Muslim world from the 1980s on.
This consisted of offering all courses as in the public school system in a European
language (French in this case). In addition, students receive a few hours of initiation into the Qur'an, Islamic theology, and the Arabic language. Unlike in the
traditional Qur'anic schools that focus on the memorization of the Qur'an—
schools such as the one I attended, which still exist—most pupils in this integrated curriculum configuration are taught in both French and Arabic. This
entails a slightly heavier workload, but nothing like the ordeal I experienced as

a child. Not least among the differences is that students can rest on weekends and in the evenings. In parallel to the bilingual system (predominantly French, with some Arabic), Keur Sultan is also offering, simultaneously, a modern curriculum entirely in Arabic, taught chiefly by Arabophone graduates of the school and dozens of instructors sent and paid for by Arabic-speaking countries such as Mauritania and Egypt. But my mother's school is more than just Keur Sultan in its modernized bilingual version or all-Arabic system. In three other venues in Dakar, including the family house where I grew up, Qur'anic education that foregrounds memorization is still the norm. Hundreds of students continue to come—some from Senegal, others from neighboring countries—to learn to memorize the Qur'an and still graduate as *huffaz* (memorizers of the Qur'an). Some parents still believe that the memorization of the Qur'an provides great blessing to the child. They send their children to Qur'anic school only; and when they graduate, such children typically become self-employed, but with the blessing of having memorized the Qur'an. Other parents send their children to the Qur'anic school first and then to the French school only after they have memorized the Qur'an. Arguably, pupils trained to store huge amounts of information would have an edge over those who were not. The following sections of this chapter look at how the colonial encounter affected the system of Islamic education in West Africa, leading to a hybrid system with different linguistic configurations, of which my mother's school system is very representative.

The debate about defining community, constructing authority, and defending the *Dar al-Islam* remained important in the nineteenth-century period of Islamic reform and state building. As Europe established its imperial domination and quashed all attempts at resistance at the turn of the twentieth century, a gradual shift to accommodation became perceptible in the writings and attitudes of Muslim scholars of the Bilad al-Sudan.[2] Many Muslim clerics exerted considerable intellectual effort to rethink the notion of the *Dar al-Islam* and how to defend it. By the early twentieth century, the dominant school of thought understood the defense of the *Dar al-Islam* as the defense of the practice of Islam and accepted the idea that non-Muslims might rule Muslims.[3] This shift in the position of Muslim clerics, which could be legitimized by the claim that it was Allah's will to allow colonialism, paved the way for the emergence of a mutually beneficial cooperation between Muslim notables and the colonial state in most of West Africa.

After the establishment of colonial rule in Africa, European colonial authorities became preoccupied with the "native question"[4] or how to rule the huge continent that was now under their direct control. Technological supremacy enabled colonial armies to easily subdue the resistance of native Africans, but it did not provide ready-made solutions for territorial control and for the implementation of the colonial project of exploiting the colonies. European imperial powers quickly realized that direct rule required logistical resources beyond what they could reasonably afford to invest. Among the challenges of colonial rule, two were paramount at the beginning of the twentieth century: "the lack of personnel" and the "extreme difficulty in communicating over long distance."[5] The lack of personnel was a notable fact in the West and Central African colonies of France, Great Britain, Portugal, and Belgium—the four main colonial powers. Overall, the ratio between European officials and the native population in their largest colonies before World War II was roughly 1 European to 5,777 Africans. Yet there were great subregional disparities:[6] in British Nigeria, 1,315 European officials were in charge of 20,000,000 inhabitants; in the Congo, 2,384 Belgian officers controlled 9,400,000 Africans;[7] in French Equatorial Africa and French West Africa, there were, respectively, 887 and 3,660 French colonial officials for populations numbering 3,200,000 and 15,000,000.[8]

In addition to the lack of adequate road and rail infrastructure and the desert environment in much of West Africa, tropical diseases decimated European residents on African soil. Under such circumstances, direct territorial control was an option only when colonial authority was threatened by rebellion or dissent. Therefore, colonial powers devised a philosophy of rule based on the carrot and the stick and enforced this in general. On the one hand, no serious threat to European imperial hegemony would be tolerated. Thus, the French and the British strove to isolate Muslims from sub-Saharan Africa from those of North Africa to prevent the building or maintaining of strong trans-Saharan Islamic solidarity. They feared in particular religious movements with translocal membership such as the Sanusiyya[9] and the Mahdiyya.[10] On the other hand, "docile" Muslims enjoyed considerable religious freedom to practice their religion as they saw fit, without the colonial state interfering in their religious affairs in any significant way. The French and the British were so committed to protecting Islamic religion that they prevented Christian missions from proselytizing in some predominantly Muslim regions. They co-opted the Muslim clerisy and political authorities in the colonial administration, and even sponsored the pilgrimage to Mecca. In addition, colonial authorities granted the highest state distinction to Muslim elites, namely as knights in Nigeria and the

Gambia, and as members of the légion d'honneur in Senegal. They also created religious titles in favor of loyal Muslim leaders, such as "Caliph général."[11]

Clearly, the notion that the French always practiced assimilation and the British always indirect rule does not stand analytical scrutiny.[12] The French, like the British, exercised indirect rule where they found reliable African collaborators. In Senegal, for example, maraboutic enclaves were given considerable autonomy for self-rule and benefitted greatly from the colonial political economy to develop peanut production and acquire economic and political clout. Likewise, Muslim emirs of Northern Nigeria, who were the heirs of the Sokoto Caliphate, headed the Native Authorities under the supervision of a British resident. But in all cases, Islamic authorities enjoined disciples and subjects to pay taxes and abide by colonial laws. To staff the colonial bureaucracy, the colonial state recruited Africans for low clerical jobs. As they consolidated their rule, they needed to train more native people. For that purpose, they devised a colonial educational policy that provoked a fundamental transformation of the existing system of the Bilad al-Sudan.

The Colonial Restructuring of Knowledge Transmission

Before the scramble for Africa, Western education in Africa was limited to the coastal enclaves controlled by Europeans. We have already seen that Fourah Bay College was one school pioneering Western education. It was established by the Church Missionary Society in 1826 in Freetown, Sierra Leone, for "the purpose of training the children of freed African slaves as schoolmasters, catechists and clergymen."[13] After the colonial conquest, the colonial state and Christian missions played a decisive role in promoting Western education. A notable consequence of the European imperial hegemony was the rise to prominence of colonial languages such as French, English, Portuguese, German, Italian, and Spanish, which put an end to centuries of the quasi monopoly of Arabic as the language of schooling, administration, and diplomacy. Correlated with the introduction of Western-type schooling in the Muslim world were the promotion of the Latin script and the relative marginalization of the Arabic script. This was not just true for colonies of Europe. In Turkey, for example, which had never been colonized, the Muslim leader Mustafa Kemal Attaturk, in his attempt to modernize his country, decreed that the Turkish language should no longer be transcribed with the Arabic script but with the Latin. This led to the abandonment of a system of transcription that had dominated one of the most powerful empires in world history. Indeed, the Ottoman Empire lasted several centuries, included virtually all of the Arab world and the Balkans in addition to Anatolia in its sphere of domination, and left a legacy of tens of millions of Turkish-language documents written in the Arabic script as its historical archive.

In West Africa, the colonial state, particularly in English-speaking countries, also tried to promote the Latin script to transcribe indigenous languages. In Northern Nigeria, for example, the British favored the use of the Latin script to transcribe Hausa. Hausa was the language of the army in the sense that commands were given in Hausa. To get a promotion, all British administrators had to speak Hausa and pass an exam. As a result, Hausa has now been taught for decades using the Latin script. Educated Nigerian Hausa speakers have developed the ability to write elaborate academic literature in the Hausa language with the Latin script. Newspapers, magazines, and academic books in Hausa, printed in the Latin script, have been and are quite common in Nigeria.

As part of the colonial restructuring of knowledge transmission, major transformations affected the material culture of learning in the Bilad al-Sudan. First, the wooden tablet and the locally manufactured inks used for centuries became restricted to traditional Qur'anic schools. Instead, pupils in Western-type schools used exercise books and pens or pencils, and instructors used chalk to write on the blackboard. Introduced in large numbers in Western schools, printed books in Western languages were widely disseminated and available to students in areas where books had hitherto existed essentially in manuscript form. Likewise, a number of Arabic texts printed by the Egyptian printing press Bulaq (also known as El-Amiriyya Press) were being imported in West Africa and circulated in Arabophone circles starting in the 1920s. The organization of learning was also transformed. In the two-tier Islamic system of education, schools did not always have their own premises, and students typically shared the same space regardless of their level of learning or age. Western-type schools dedicated classroom space for each age grade. In primary, middle, and high school, students in each grade were of the same age or had very little age difference. The recruitment of students also differed in the two systems. We have already seen that in the Islamic system, parents typically surrender their child to a Qur'anic schoolmaster, who might be a nomad or a sedentary from the same area or from a distant locale or country. Islamic higher education students traveled far away to study a specific text with a shaykh. At best, they might bring in their bags a recommendation from a respected shaykh, testifying to their piety or morality, but there was no formal registration process. In contrast, in Western-type schools, clear guidelines determined school enrollments. Factors such as age, nationality, residential location, sound physical and mental health, and intellectual qualification governed the recruitment of students, which was impersonal. Parents had to submit an application showing that their child fulfilled all of these requirements. Transfer students took necessary tests to evaluate their qualifications prior to enrollment.

The certification of education was also different. Unlike in a madrasa, where a shaykh delivered an *ijaza* (written or oral) to a student to certify his completion of a specific text and authorize him to teach it, Western-type schools organized exams and delivered degrees with the label of the school, certifying a general qualification based on the study of a variety of subjects. In other words, the (general certificate of education) in English-speaking countries (or the *baccalauréat du premier* cycle) in the French system, for example, as indicated by its name, is a certification by the state department of education of the successful completion of high school studies, not an authorization to teach a specific book of, say, Aristotle or Avicenna or even philosophy in general. In the Islamic system, instructors taught orally in mosques or in studies inside their own homes. Students in their inner circles served as their assistants and could access their masters' libraries. There was no formal school administration or school library in the Bilad al-Sudan. By contrast, Western-type schools had their own premises with offices for members of the administration and also library holdings.

In the Islamic system, the teacher is typically self-employed. Students provided agricultural labor in rural areas to help feed the community. But the labor of a student, it must be noted, was part of the educational process and not simply a form of compensation for the master. Occasionally, parents offered grain, meat, or cash to the master. But this hardly covered the needs of the school or of the master. Thus, teachers devised various ways of supporting the school, including sending students to appeal for community solidarity (begging); offering (for a fee) various religious services, such as marriage, naming, and funeral ceremonies; and providing talismans or propitiatory prayer for people into a new house. In contrast, teachers in Western-type schools received a regular salary. Their career was governed by an impersonal system that included evaluation of performance, provision of pedagogical training destined to improve teaching skills, career advancement, and, of course, salary increases based on seniority and/or performance. Within this system, a bureaucracy exercised disciplinary power over students and instructors. It defined clearly what would or would not be allowed. In the Islamic school system, by contrast, the schoolmaster exercised his personal rule. Although Islamic ethics provided an overall foundation for the transmission of knowledge, and a good reputation helped in raising demand in school enrollments, nobody monitored the schoolmaster to evaluate his performance. As noted by a well-known Arabic saying, the basic rule was the stick for disobedient students (*al-'asa li man 'asa*). In contrast, physical punishment tended to be banned in the Western school system (although the ban was not always effective).

The colonial educational system brought a much larger corpus of books to pupils than had the historical core curriculum. Compared with a corpus limited to religious texts, readers now had access to a larger variety of texts dealing with more topics. A similar transformation has been documented in the West in the eighteenth century following the invention of printing and the Protestant Reformation.[14] Before the reading revolution, readers had access to a limited number of texts, which "were read, reread, memorized and recited, deeply understood and possessed, and transmitted from one generation to another."[15] Religious texts for the most part, they were imbued with sacrality[16] and venerated. In contrast with this intensive method of reading, a new method of more extensive reading was implemented that included a larger number of texts for which readers had no particular veneration and which they submitted to analytical scrutiny and methodological doubt.[17]

Above all, the epistemological framework of the Islamic school rested on the notion that knowledge must be based on religion and that it helps the believers live a life in conformity with God's commands. Hence, schooling starts with the study of the Qur'an, followed by subjects aimed at deepening the understanding of the law based on the Qur'an. In contrast, the Western-type school emphasized the study of subjects not directly related to religion, such as math, physics, chemistry, history, geography, etc. Even in the Christian mission schools, which did provide some religious instruction to Christian students, general nonreligious subjects formed the core curriculum. The Western-type schools introduced a parallel secular framework that would compete with the previously dominant religious one.

The response of Muslims to the colonial reorganization of schooling has been of three kinds. A first group opted to send their children to public schools offering instruction in European languages, where they received an education certified by the award of a degree. Among these, the majority arranged for their children to receive some parallel Islamic education. They might either send them to the Qur'anic schools to study a few hours during the weekend or hire a private tutor to initiate them in Qur'anic studies at home. A second group adopted a learning method inspired largely by Western pedagogy, as described earlier, while using either exclusively Arabic or both Arabic and the colonial language as the media of instruction. This trend led to the rise of hybrid schools called by various names (Islamiyya schools in Northern Nigeria, Franco-Arabic schools in Senegal, and *médersa* in Mali and Mauritania). A third group of Muslims opted to preserve the traditional system and offer only Arabic-based education. This is particularly the case in clerical enclaves that resisted Westernization. The different types of schools coincided with different needs, however. Therefore, they have maintained complex patterns of interactions, and none of these three types of schooling has completely precluded any or all of the others.

Education in Western Languages: The Rise of Europhone Intellectuals

In most schools established by colonial states or Christian missions, colonial languages (and their underlying secular epistemology) were typically the medium of instruction. Students could study Arabic as a "foreign language,"[18] but the teaching of religion was not typically allowed in public schools. Some renowned schools, such as Barewa College in Katsina, Nigeria, or the Lycée William Ponty in Dakar, trained elite students who were subsequently appointed to the colonial bureaucracy. An even smaller elite among them was admitted to colleges or universities created toward the end of European colonial rule. One such college in Nigeria was University College Ibadan, which was affiliated with the University of London. In French-speaking West Africa, a few institutions of tertiary learning were in existence in the first decades of the twentieth century, including a medical school and a research institute (IFAN), established in Dakar in 1918 and 1938, respectively. Some of those schools were merged in 1957 to create the University of Dakar, which was then affiliated with the Universities of Bordeaux and Paris. Graduates from these colonial schools could attend French and British universities for further training. This educated elite had a good command of the colonial languages, but in general, with the notable exception of some Hausa-speaking intellectuals in Northern Nigeria, very few of them had an academic mastery of their own native African language. Typically, it was students in the Islamic system who had such a command.

Novelists and other writers in the Western tradition have made a lasting contribution to African literature and postcolonial studies in English and French. The Nigerian Nobel laureate Wole Soyinka and his countryman Chinua Achebe; the Ivorian Ahmadou Kourouma; and the Senegalese Léopold Senghor, Abdoulaye Sadji, and Ousmane Socé Diop—to cite just a few—are among the most prominent. These intellectuals were nationalists and strongly committed to Pan-Africanism and African independence and development. They wrote well-received and widely cited novels. A few of them and others— such as the Senegalese thinker Cheikh Anta Diop and the Kenyan novelist Ngugi wa Thiong'o—mastered, wrote in, and strove to promote intellectual production in native languages. The overwhelming majority, however, wrote in European languages. In West Africa and elsewhere, students who spoke their mother tongues on the premises of public schools received humiliating punishments. A typical punishment consisted of forcing the offender to wear a "symbol," which could be a metal plate or a necklace made of bones, empty cans, horns, and all kinds of strange materials; the student was forced to wear this at school and sometimes to take it home until he or she caught another student speaking an African language.[19] Kenyan novelist Ngugi Wa Thiog'o describes a similar punishment in the colonial school in Kenya: "one of the most humiliating experiences was to be caught speaking Gikuyu in the vicinity of the school. The culprit was given corporal punishment—three to five strokes of the cane on bare buttocks—or was made to carry a metal plate around the neck with inscriptions such as I AM STUPID or I AM A DONKEY."[20]

As a result, Western-educated intellectuals in French colonies could not speak their native languages without using a high percentage of French words. Worse than physical punishment was the contempt that French-educated intellectuals had for African languages. Fluency in African languages was construed as a lack of sophistication. I attended primary and secondary school in the 1960s and early 1970s in Dakar, Senegal, and rural students of my generation, who spoke their mother tongue fluently (that is, with a minimum of words from the French language), were ridiculed and dismissed as "bush people" by their classmates.

As eloquently illustrated by Senegalese novelist Cheikh Hamidou Kane,[21] Islam was not absent from the intellectual universe of Muslim Europhone intellectuals. The acquisition of Western culture generated profound existential interrogations among some Muslim intellectuals. Many of them became pre-occupied with the question of how to reconcile Western and Islamic values. (For example, former Senegalese prime minister Mamadou Dia, 1909–2007), whose life spanned almost a hundred years evenly divided between the colonial and the post-independence eras, wrote a series of books dealing with Islam and modernity.[22]) But their Islamic consciousness notwithstanding, the colonial language of schooling had transmitted to these intellectuals a conceptual appa-ratus rooted in what Mudimbe called a Western epistemological order.[23]

After independence from European colonial rule, African states promoted Western types of schools in which education was provided in Western lan-guages and rested on Western philosophical principles. Subsequently, when private entrepreneurs joined the teaching industry, they copied the same model, with the effect of producing intellectuals whose framework of reference was above all Western. The overwhelming majority of such intellectuals had no clue of the existence of an archive of learning in any non-Western language. And yet all the while, most Muslim families were sending their children, on nonschool days or in the evenings, to Qur'anic schools, where they would receive rudi-mentary Islamic education for the purpose of worship.

Bilingual Islamic Schooling

A second type of school started during colonial rule consisted of bilingual instruction in Arabic and one colonial language, which combined Islamic reli-gious studies such as of the Qur'an, *tawhid*, and hadith, and general subjects such as math, history, and geography. Initiated by the colonial state with the objective of training clerical personnel to staff the colonial bureaucracy, this model was later copied by Muslim activists to promote their own agendas and, in the process, challenge colonial authority. One of the most renowned bilin-gual modern Islamic schools in Northern Nigeria was the Northern Province Law School, established in 1934 by the emir of Kano, Abdullahi Bayero. Later renamed the School for Arabic Studies, it trained a large number of Muslim elites, including those who occupied important administrative and political positions in the northern region of Nigeria after independence; Shaykh Abubakar Mahmud Gumi (d. 1992), the former grand qadi of independent Northern Nigeria, graduated from this school.

The French also developed a model of bilingual French and Arabic schooling, then named médersa (from the Arabic word *madrasa*) in Algeria, which they colonized as early as 1832.[24] The médersa system was later transposed into French colonial West Africa to train Muslim judges, interpreters, secretaries, and teachers. Of course, in creating such schools, the French neither intended to support Islamic education nor raise the level of Arabic education. Rather, their underlying goal was to expose the youth, and particularly children of notables who were targeted in school enrollment, to the so-called French civilizing mission.[25] By so doing, they also hoped to undermine the then very influential Sufi orders in their colonies. The first médersa was created in Jenne, Mali, in 1906; this was followed by a second one in Saint-Louis, the former capital of French colonial West Africa, in 1908, and a third in Timbuktu in 1910.[26] Later, in the 1930s, a few more médersa were established in Boutilimit (1930), Timbédrea (1933), and Atar (1936)—all in Mauritania.[27] On the occasion of the opening of a French médersa in Timbuktu in 1910, the French governor of the French Soudan (meaning here Mali) stated the objectives of the médersa as follows:

1. To exercise an indirect control over the activities of the indigenous educators of Timbuktu.
2. To attract to French culture the young persons of a milieu which is closed to the influence of France using the lure of their own traditional culture.
3. To domesticate these young people, and even the entire population, and familiarize them with the institution of French education.[28]

At this particular period of colonial rule, the Black Islam paradigm informed colonial policy. In other words, the French colonials assumed black Africans to be superficially Islamized. As such, they supposedly did not pose an Islamic threat of any significance to the colonial state. In Mali, for example, those populations assumed to be deeply Islamized—such as Arabs, Berbers, and Tuaregs (sons of chiefs and notables among them, in particular)—were targeted for recruitment because it was they who colonial authorities believed needed to have French values inculcated in them. As it turned out, the colonial state failed to achieve such recruitment objectives. The targeted population did not trust colonial schools in any shape or form—neither those offering instruction exclusively in French nor the bilingual ones. They suspected, and rightly so, that the goal of the colonial schools was to undermine Islamic culture.[29] As Brenner notes, the médersa in northern Mali recruited predominantly black Africans of nonaristocratic origin[30] until the 1930s. The colonial schools opened avenues for social mobility to children of low social class and from among the Christianized African populations. As a result, Christians figured prominently among the political, administrative, and commercial elites of post-colonial West Africa.[31]

The médersa system introduced by the French inspired the creation of schools based on a similar pedagogy among Muslims. Unlike the colonial version of the system, the médersa sponsored by Muslims were private schools. Young Muslims managed these schools, which competed on the one hand with the colonial médersa and on the other with the old Islamic schools teaching the historical curriculum discussed in Chapter 4. In Northern Nigeria, the Islamiyya schools were introduced in the 1950s as an intermediary model between the schools offering instruction exclusively in colonial languages and the traditional Qur'anic schools.[32] The Islamiyya schools were based on a very similar pedagogy as that of Western schools. Students learned the Qur'an and other Islamic subjects, together with English, arithmetic, and Hausa in the Latin script, for instance. Toward the end of colonial rule, Islamiyya schools became hotbeds for contesting colonial and Native Authorities. As a result, Native Authorities suppressed dozens of them. But the Islamiyya provided a model to be copied later. After independence, the predominantly Muslim population of the northern region outnumbered the rest of the federation. The South, however, where Christian missions were allowed to operate, had more Western-educated people than did the North. As a result, southerners occupied the most senior positions in the federal and regional administrations, including in the northern region. Bridging the gap between the North and the South in the field of education became a major policy concern for the northern elites. They created a number of schools that provided English-language instruction, but these did not nearly fill the gap, partly because some Muslim communities were still reluctant to send their children to modern schools. To remedy such resistance, the Department of Education of the northern region of Nigeria developed various strategies to modernize traditional Qur'anic schools. It approached a number of traditional schools and offered various forms of subsidy, including building classrooms and recruiting and paying instructors to cover non-Qur'anic subjects such as English and math. Northern colleges also created remedial programs to which graduates from Islamiyya schools were admitted to follow coursework that led to the award of certificates as a stepping-stone to a proper college education.

In addition to these state-sponsored programs, various individuals and Islamic organizations were involved in creating modern schools to educate the

Muslim youth and provide them with marketable skills. In the post-colonial period, in that respect the work of new Muslim organizations such as Fityan al-Islam and the Yan Izala movement in Nigeria, and Al-Falah and Ibadourahmane in Senegal were particularly remarkable. Providing modern Islamic education became critical for recruiting and retaining religious constituencies. Sufi orders joined the bandwagon by creating their own modern schools, including bilingual ones that offered education in the colonial language and Arabic. In the same vein, some Muslim private organizations and individuals opened modern schools to teach exclusively in Arabic but inspired by the pedagogy and organization of learning in Western-type schools. Since the end of colonial rule, there have been thousands of such schools in existence.

Modernized Islamic schools faced three main challenges in contemporary West Africa. The first was credible certification. Students in schools dominated by the Arabic language for the most part were not prepared to take national tests (the General Certificate of Education in the British system and the baccalauréat in French-speaking countries). Those schools delivered degrees of their own not recognized by the state. In addition, many such post-colonial Arabic schools cut deals with foreign Islamic institutions of learning that provided degrees with their names. Notable among them is Al-Azhar University in Cairo. But even with such names, Arabophones tended to be disadvantaged compared with Europhone counterparts, because French, English, and Portuguese remained the languages of business and administration in West Africa.

The second major challenge was employment. In the 1960s and 1970s, states were the major provider of employment. A high school or a college degree, combined with competence in the colonial language, guaranteed employment at least until the unemployment crisis of the 1980s in most of West Africa. Because they had no adequate proficiency in a Western language, however, most graduates of Arabic schools were denied that opportunity.

The third challenge was postsecondary education. Local Arabic schools provided sound primary and secondary education. But until the 1980s, there was no full-fledged university offering instruction in Arabic in sub-Saharan Africa, with the exception of the University of Omdurman in the Sudan. Conventional universities operated departments of Arabic and Islamic studies. But in French-speaking universities, admission was offered only to those students who had successfully completed the national baccalauréat exam, which in Senegal until the 1980s was administered by the Université de of Bordeaux and required proficiency in French, which most graduates of Arabic schools did not have. Thus, the only option for the overwhelming majority of Arabophones to pursue higher education was to seek admission to universities in countries where Arabic was the official language of instruction—essentially Egypt, Morocco, Tunisia, Libya, the Sudan, and, from the 1980s on, Saudi Arabia and other Gulf countries.

West African Students in the Arab World

Since the independence of West Africa in the early 1960, thousands of Muslim students from the Bilad al-Sudan have in this way pursued higher education in the Arab world. Whereas in the 1960s and early 1970s most of them attended colleges in North Africa, after the oil boom of the late 1970s large contingents began to attend institutions of higher education in the oil-rich Gulf countries, the majority of them in Saudi Arabia. Of all Arab countries, however, it was Egypt (and Al-Azhar University[33] in particular) that received the largest numbers of Muslims from Africa and also Asia. In the early 1960s, the old college mosque of Al-Azhar underwent radical administrative and pedagogical reforms under the aegis of Egyptian president Abdel Nasser. To a large extent, these reforms reflected Nasser's ambition to provide intellectual and political leadership in the emerging Third World. At the 1955 Afro-Asian Conference of Bandung, which was a landmark in the rise of the spirit of nonalignment, President Nasser[34] emerged as a leading figure of Thirdworldism. His success at nationalizing the Suez Canal a year later—despite the military expedition led by France, Britain, and Israel against Egypt—catapulted the Egyptian president to the pantheon of Third World nationalism. He was deeply committed to anticolonialism, nonalignment, and the promoting of South-South solidarity. In his vision, an important component of this solidarity was to promote Arabo-Islamic culture and strengthen ties with Muslims, 90 percent of whom lived in Africa and Asia. Before the reforms initiated by Naser, Al-Azhar was largely supported by religious endowments, which gave it some autonomy. After the reform, the Egyptian state became the sole purveyor of funds and financial support of the ulama of Al-Azhar.[35]

In addition to restructuring the organization of learning and the methods of knowledge transmission of traditional topics (Arabic and Islamic studies),[36] new departments opened in Al-Azhar, offering degrees in fields such as agronomy, business, medicine, and engineering. The ulama of al-Azhar became civil servants. The mode of designation of the great imam of the mosque (Shaykh al-Azhar) changed. Henceforth he was to be appointed by the

Egyptian president. On the administrative side, the reforms led to the creation of new bodies that implemented President Nasser's cultural policy abroad. To help propagate Islam outside Egypt, a new academy of Islamic research (*Majma' al-Buhuth al-Islamiyya*) was established; it had a council of fifty members, thirty of whom were Egyptians, with the remaining members coming from other Islamic countries.[37] Affiliated with the academy, three newly created bodies shifted the focus of Al-Azhar abroad: an administration of research and publication, which sponsored research and through its monthly journal (*Majallat al-Azhar*) disseminated information about Muslims worldwide; an administration of *da'wa* and instruction, which sent delegations worldwide to teach and preach Islam; and an office of Islamic missions, which supervised international students (*wafidin*) expected to work to spread Islam in their countries after graduation. To replace the former nationality-based houses known as *arwiqa*, the institute of Islamic missions provided training to the majority of young international students admitted to Al-Azhar. As Chanfi Ahmed rightly notes, the whole project was driven not just by the emphasis on propagating Islam, but also to sell the ideals of Arab nationalism and socialism as preached by Nasser as an integral part of Islam itself.

Between the reform of Al-Azhar in 1961 and 2005, a total of 22,571 international students received a master's degree from Al-Azhar University.[38] Of these, 16,827 students (74.55%) came from Asia and 5,447 (24.13%) came from forty-one African countries. More than half of the African students came from three countries (Republic of Sudan [33%], followed by Senegal [10.69%] and Nigeria [10.44%].) If we include students who received only undergraduate education or dropped out or attended other Egyptian institutions of higher learning such as the University of Cairo or 'Ayn al-shams University, the number of African Arabophones who have studied in Egypt is even higher.

After Nasser's death, Al-Azhar continued to be an instrument for Egypt's cultural policy, welcoming thousands of students from the Muslim world and supplying technical assistance, especially teachers, to most Arabic schools in sub-Saharan Africa. The overwhelming majority of African students majored in Arabic and Islamic studies. Out of 6,605 non-Egyptian African students who graduated from Al-Azhar between 1961 and 2005, 4,357 majored in Islamic studies. A small number of students were admitted to Egyptian high schools. After completing a high school education, this minority was then qualified to study scientific subjects at Al-Azhar or other Egyptian institutions such as Cairo University and the Ain Shams University.

Upon graduation, African students suffered a double prejudice. The first was that they had received instruction in a language other than that of the administration and business worlds in West Africa. The second was that their expertise was not highly valued in the job market. In his poem entitled Takwin al-'atilin (training the [future] jobless) mentioned in the epigraph of this chapter, Cheikh Tidiane Gaye expresses the deep frustration of the Arabophones. Competition with graduates from the schools of engineering, business, and even the humanities trained in the French- or English-speaking universities put them at a clear disadvantage in the job market of their home countries. Of the first cohort of graduates in the 1960s and 1970s, the majority had a hard time finding a well-paid job. This unfortunate experience inspired later cohorts of Al-Azhar graduates to devise alternative strategies. From the 1980s on, West African graduates from Arab universities, rather than returning to their home countries, sought to further their education in Europe. France was the favorite destination for citizens of former African French colonies. French higher education was open to non-French-speaking international students, subject to acquisition of proficiency in the French language. Those students would typically study French for a year or so before pursuing a degree program. West African graduates from Arab universities took advantage of this opportunity. In general, they obtained French master's or doctoral degrees without having the same proficiency as students who were the products of English- or French-speaking schools. As African Arabophones did not intend to work in France (or so it was assumed), their dissertation sponsors were not too demanding regarding their command of the French language or even the quality of their graduate work. As a result, many produced academic research of a low standard. Yet upon return to their country of origin (such as Chad, Cameroon, Senegal, Mali, or Niger), these Arabophones who possessed a French degree still had better chances of obtaining professional occupations than did their peers who knew only Arabic.

Next to Egypt, Morocco welcomed the largest number of Arabophones from West Africa. Morocco had political, religious, and cultural ties with the Bilad al-Sudan going back centuries. We have seen that a large part of Songhay had come under the political domination of the Saadia dynasty following the 1591 expedition. But the strongest ties were religious and intellectual. Sufism and Malikism, two dominant features of West African Islam, are the legacy of intense historical interactions between West Africa and North Africa— Morocco in particular. The spread of the Tijaniyya Sufi tariqa, whose main base is in Fez, Morocco, created strong ties between Morocco and the rest of West Africa. All three kings who ruled postcolonial Morocco (Mohamed V, Hassan II, and Muhammad VI) were committed to maintaining those ties. They provided generous assistance to the building or renovation of major mosques in Senegal (for example, those of Kaolack and Tivaouane); invited and offered five-star hospitality to West African Sufi leaders to spend Ramadan in Rabat as guests of the king every year; provided healthcare to all major West African Sufi leaders in the best Moroccan hospitals; and offered grants to West African students to study in Moroccan universities, particularly the ancient Qarawiyyin college. Consequently, since independence, thousands of West African students have studied in Morocco where the best research on Afro-Arab relations is now produced at the Institut d'Etudes Africaines of the Université Mohamed V at Rabat.

Algeria also offered higher education opportunities to West African Arabophones. Some of the first Senegalese Muslim Salafis were trained in Algeria. In the late 1950s, Cheikh Touré, the former leader of the Union Culturelle Musulmane (Muslim Cultural Union) and Alioune Diouf, the first emir of the Ibadourahmane movement, attended the institute created by Ibn Badis in Constantine.[39] After Algerian independence and above all after the oil boom, thousands of scholarships were offered to West African students by Algeria.[40] Unlike in Morocco and Saudi Arabia, where most African students were trained only in religious studies and in Arabic, Algeria received both Arabic and French-speaking West African students and trained them in a greater variety of disciplines, either in French or in Arabic. Those West African students who graduated in French in the scientific disciplines in Algeria had better job opportunities upon their return to their home countries.

Libya welcomed many Arabophones from West Africa throughout the long rule of Colonel Khaddafi. Two institutions created by the former Libyan president offered educational opportunities to African students. Founded in 1972 and 1974, respectively, to promote Libya's cultural influence in the Muslim world, the first is the Jam'iyyat al-Da'wa al-'Alamiyya al-Islamiyya (World Islamic Call Society) and the second, the Kuliyyat al-Da'wa al-Islamiyya (Faculty of the Islamic Call). An excellent propaganda machine, the World Islamic Call Society was well financed and had considerable freedom in transferring funds abroad. It was active in a number of fields, including preaching and training, communication, and financial support, and it operated offices around the world, including in sub-Saharan Africa.[41] It gave scholarships to students from African, Asian, and European countries, as well as from the Americas, to pursue Arabic and Islamic studies in Libyan universities and at the Faculty of Islamic Call. The Association for the Islamic Appeal also provided financial assistance for the construction of mosques and Islamic training centers, as well as medical help for the destitute. It sent out hundreds of African and Asian preachers and organized conferences in Libya and in other African countries. The Faculty of Islamic Call created campuses in Syria, Lebanon, Pakistan, England, and—as I will discuss in Chapter 7—West Africa.

In Tunisia, Arabophones from West Africa typically attended one of two institutions:[42] the Rakada High School and the Faculty of Theology of the University of Zeytuna. The contingents of West African students in Tunisia were much smaller than those in Egypt or Morocco. Most of the students were Senegalese and studied in Tunisia in the 1960s and 1970s when the Rakada High School was a hotbed of Islamist activism. The majority of the Rakada teaching staff were Islamists who introduced students to the ideas of the leading exponents of Islamism, such as Sudanese Hasan Al-Turabi (b. 1932), the Egyptians Hasan Al-Banna (d. 1949) and Sayyid Qutb (d. 1966), the Pakistani Abu 'l A'la Maududi (d. 1979), and the Tunisian Rashid al-Ghannouchi (b. 1941).[43] Unlike in the wider Tunisian society, West African students felt very welcome in the Rakada school community, and this increased considerably the appeal of Islamist thought among them. Consequently, many returned home as convinced Islamists.

Sudan has been another major destination for Arabophones from West Africa. Like Mauritania, Sudan has a large Arabic-speaking population, and Arabic is its official language. Before independence, Sudan received a limited number of West African students from the British colonies of sub-Saharan Africa. After independence, Sudan sought to promote Islam and the Arabic language there. According to Grandin,[44] three main factors explained Sudanese cultural policy in sub-Saharan Africa: the conviction of the Sudanese elite of the low level of training, both in religious field and in the general education of African youth; an old tradition of Islamic proselytizing of neighboring black populations; and, finally, the strong anti-Western and anticolonial attitudes among the Sudanese Arabic-speaking political elite. Most West African students attended the African Islamic Centre, established in Omdurman in 1967 as an institute affiliated with the Ministry of National Education. Closed in 1969 for eight years,[45] the center reopened in 1977 as an institute based on the outskirts of Khartoum and affiliated with the ministry of religious affairs. It offered instruction in Arabic, but also in English and French,[46] so that graduates from English and French-speaking countries would not be disadvantaged in the job market. It also offered basic training in scientific disciplines that enabled graduates to exercise a profession or further their training elsewhere after graduation. On returning to their countries, they then have every chance of obtaining employment, a prerequisite for credibility. Unlike Egyptians, Sudanese believed that providing religious expertise only to African students would not allow them to play a decisive role in the Islamization and development of their country of origin.[47] In 1992, the government of Sudanese president Omar al-Bashir upgraded the institute to the status of university and named it the International University of Africa. Since then, it has expanded its offerings considerably and has become a leading African university. Many students from West Africa and elsewhere in the Muslim world have graduated from this school.[48]

Outside the African continent, it is Saudi Arabia that has contributed most to providing Islamic higher education to West Africans and to promoting the Arabic language in West Africa. We have seen that Muslims from the Bilad al-Sudan have been performing the pilgrimage and studying in Saudi Arabia for centuries. Unlike students of the post-colonial period, preceding generations of pilgrims/students traveled on their own or in caravans to the Holy Lands.[49] After the oil boom of the 1970s, Saudi Arabia generously contributed to Islamic education in Africa through the creation of schools. According to Fouad al-Farsy,[50] Saudi assistance to Third World countries represented 6 percent of its total GDP. Until the early 1980s, 96 percent of this assistance went to Muslim countries in Africa.[51] In addition to the official aid, many Saudi NGOs—including the Muslim World League, the Dar al-Ifta, the World Assembly of Muslim Youth (WAMY), and the International Federation of Arab and Islamic Schools—provided assistance to Muslims in Africa. Through these organizations, funding is given to Muslim associations, schools, and leaders in Africa (and also Asia and America). At the beginning of the 1980s, there were two thousand African students attending Saudi universities,[52] all of them taught in Arabic. Since then, many more have attended Saudi schools of higher learning.

In general, attendance at Arab universities has created two very different attitudes among graduates when they return to their home countries. Some, after witnessing a lesser degree of religiosity in Arab countries than in their own and having suffered from racial prejudice,[53] not only have returned as anti-Arab, but also have abandoned practicing the Islamic religion altogether. Others—those who acquire an in-depth knowledge of Arabic and Islamic studies and have been exposed to Islamist ideas—preach a re-Islamization either of society or the state upon their return to their home countries.

Neo-Traditional Islamic Learning

Did the two-tier system of Islamic education disappear after colonialism? The answer is no. To this day, Qur'anic schools whose teaching method is based on memorization are flourishing, and the texts of the historical core curriculum are still being taught in sub-Saharan Africa. There is great diversity within Qur'anic schools today, and the quality of the learning environment varies considerably according to the level of economic development of the country, its geography, and the social class of the students who attend. In the relatively prosperous country of South Africa, for example, the premises of the madrasas of the upper-middle-class Indian and Malay Muslims of the Cape are well maintained and comfortable, just like those of the best private schools to be found anywhere in the world. In contrast, few Qur'anic schools of such high standards are found in poor Sahelian countries of West Africa such as Senegal, Mauritania, Mali, Niger, and Northern Nigeria. In these countries, Qur'anic schools can be either urban or rural/seminomadic. Rural/seminomadic schools are based in rural areas in the rainy season when the school community produces agricultural goods and stocks up food for future use. During the dry season, these Qur'anic school communities may move to urban areas where Muslim philanthropists offer them shelter. To survive, the teacher often sends students as young as five into the streets to beg for long hours. They are often given leftover food that may not even be safe to eat. They don't receive basic healthcare. To make a living, the master and his students might also provide a variety of religious services, including the manufacture of charms and the recitation of the Qur'an on various occasions. Although some of these schools provide Qur'anic education as a stepping-stone for higher Islamic education, others are specifically devoted to the memorization and talismanic utilization of the Qur'an.

In contrast, some urban areas host higher-quality Qur'anic schools that appeal to affluent urban Muslim communities. Muslims in West Africa have always ensured that their children receive some Islamic education. Unlike rural, semi-nomadic Qur'anic schools, Qur'anic schools in urban middle-class neighborhoods do not send their pupils to beg. They also strive to maintain a higher standard of hygiene. Corporal punishment is also less common at such schools. Most students in this category are predominantly Western educated. They receive a minimal Islamic education consisting essentially of memorizing enough Qur'anic verses for worship purposes. In some cases, they only memorize the verses but cannot read them in Arabic script. A small elite among Muslims who combine sound Western and Qur'anic/Islamic education, send their children to schools at which they will learn to memorize the entire Qur'an before joining the public school system to receive a secular education.

Although a number of formal Arabic or bilingual Arabic/Western language schools have been created to provide primary and secondary education, and even higher education, the traditional madrasa system of higher Islamic education has not disappeared with the modernization of education. Many texts that were used in the precolonial core curriculum, discussed earlier, are taught to students still today in traditional centers of Islamic education such as Timbuktu, Walata, Kaolack, and Kano. Likewise, quite a few Western-educated intellectuals with a little Islamic education are likely at some point to have studied traditional core texts with a shaykh.

Chapter 7

Modern Islamic Institutions of Higher Learning

The various branches of learning in the sciences, law, arts and humanities as well as the social sciences are heavily indebted to the system of inquiry from the West that rejects, condemns, and disregards revelation as a source and means of gaining development and disseminating knowledge in our sensory world. There is now an urgent and imperative need to classify, research, develop, and disseminate knowledge from a comprehensive Islamic methodological framework.

—*Baffa Aliyu Umar*[1]

THE OTTOMAN EMPIRE, which ruled over virtually all Arabic-speaking lands, undertook major administrative, legal, political, military, and educational reforms in the nineteenth century to halt its decline.[2] It was in this context that the organization of higher learning started to change and modernize in the Middle East and North Africa. Remarkable in this respect was the transition of the Al-Azhar institution in Cairo from a medieval type of Islamic college to a university in the modern sense of the word. Started in 1872, these reforms were pursued throughout the twentieth century and culminated in 1961 with reforms imposed by former Egyptian president Nasser.[3]

As previously mentioned, modern Islamic institutions of higher learning were established in West Africa beginning only in the mid-1980s. Prior to that, West Africans who wanted to pursue higher Islamic studies leading to the award of an accredited degree had two options. The first was to join North African universities such as Al-Azhar University, where Arabic is the dominant language of instruction. The other option was to gain admission to the departments of Arabic and Islamic studies in West African universities. Largely inspired by the European Orientalist tradition, it was mostly Western scholars who had started these departments—and provided instruction mainly in

English or French.[4] Most graduates of the Islamic educational system could not qualify because of their lack of proficiency in European languages.

Between 1987 and 2013, several modern Islamic institutions of higher learning were established in sub-Saharan Africa. They enabled increasing numbers of Arabophones to pursue higher education in their own countries. These schools are playing an important development role, first by providing educational opportunities to many hitherto excluded groups, and second by bridging the gap between purely religious education and more general education in the arts, sciences, and technology. This chapter will situate their emergence in a post-colonial context marked by two paradigm shifts that led to the Islamization of knowledge and the liberalization of education.

The Islamization of Knowledge

In Chapter 6, I analyzed how European colonial rule transformed the educational system in Africa. Far from being specific to Africa, those transformations affected the entire Third World, in which the majority of Muslims lived. By the early twentieth century, virtually all Muslims in the world—from South and Southeast Asia to the Middle East and North Africa, and on to Saharan and sub-Saharan Africa—had become colonial subjects. Notable exceptions of noncolonized Muslim countries include Turkey, the successor state to the Ottoman Empire, and some former Ottoman provinces of the Najd and the Hijaz, which became the kingdom of Saudi Arabia. After independence from European rule, Muslims have been engaged in debates on how to develop a modern system of education rooted in Islamic ethics and values, and we saw in Chapter 6 how some individual African countries such as Nigeria and Senegal have tackled the issue. In addition, African Muslims have also been involved in the global debate about post-colonial education and the place of Arabic and Islamic studies in the educational system.

The World Conferences on Muslim Education are the highest-profile fora to take up the global debate on post-colonial education in the Muslim world. Seven conferences so named have already been convened in various parts of the world, bringing together thousands of experts in the field of education. The first conference was held at the King Saud University in Mecca from March 31 to April 8, 1977. A large consensus emerged among the 350 participants that the educational system imposed by Western colonization has created disharmony in the Muslim world. The participants felt that, on the one hand, it has separated religious from nonreligious education. As a result, many graduates of secular schools have had no proper religious education, whereas graduates of Islamic schools have limited marketable skills. On the other hand, conference participants felt that the epistemological foundations of knowledge in colonial-inspired schools are flawed because they are based on a Western methodology, which many devout Muslims such as the Nigerian Muslim scholar Aliyu Baffa believe, "separates reason from revelation thereby undercutting the very essence of Islamic knowledge."[5]

Six follow-up conferences were organized to continue the conversation and provide appropriate policy recommendations. Held in Islamabad from March 15 to March 20, 1980, the university of King Saud of Mecca and the Quaid Azam University of Islamabad cosponsored the second conference. The Institute for the Study and Research on Islamic Education and Research convened a third conference from March 5 to March 11, 1981 in Dakka, Bangladesh, on the theme of "Islamic Teaching Methods." The fourth conference was organized in Jakarta, Indonesia from August 23 to August 28 1982. The fifth World Conference on Muslim Education was held in Cairo from March 8 to March 13 1987. In addition to participants from the Muslim world, several delegations representing Muslim communities based in the West attended this conference. In the late 1980s, tens of millions of Muslims settled in the West—an unprecedented development in history—and, just like their coreligionists elsewhere, they were grappling with the issue of how to educate their children. Some ten years later, a Sixth World Conference on Muslim Education was held in Cape Town, South Africa from September 20 to September 25, 1996. This was the first time that a world conference on Muslim education was organized in a minority Muslim country. Only about 2 percent of the South African population is Muslim. The added significance of the increased attendance of Muslim communities from the West and convening such a conference in Cape Town was that the debate had become truly global. A seventh World Conference on Muslim Education was held in Shah Alam, Malaysia, from December 21 to December 23, 2009. A major recommendation of these conferences was to bridge the divide between secular and religious education through the development of an Islamic approach to knowledge based on the premise that "knowledge as a universal truth emanates from Allah and that man is expected to use the knowledge, in his capacity as a trustee, to worship Allah."[6] Of course, not all Muslims shared this premise, and numerous decision makers in the Muslim world had no issue with secular education. Furthermore, many Muslims sent their children to Christian schools, which enjoyed a good reputation for the quality of their instruction and discipline, religious instruction being in principle offered only to Christians in such schools.

The number of advocates of Islamic education increased noticeably from the 1970s, when the Muslim world saw the rise of civil society organizations advocating a greater public role for Islam. The ultimate goal of those Muslim revivalists was to establish an Islamic sociopolitical order, but they diverged considerably on the strategies they used to attain that goal and the speed with which they thought society ought to be re-Islamized. On the one hand, gradualists believed that Islamization is a long process, to be started first with the training of a vanguard of dedicated and well-educated Muslims in all fields of activity. These would be doctors, engineers, teachers, scientists, and artists who would pervade all economic, political, and social activities and usher in a truly Islamic order.[7] A good example is Abu 'l A'la Maududi, an influential twentieth-century Islamic thinker who advocated gradualism and established the Jamaati Islami, one of the most influential Islamic militant organizations in the twentieth century.[8] At the other end of the spectrum, some activists believed that the attainment of political power would be the most effective way to promote an Islamic order—and the sooner, the better. Some organized politically to capture political power either through elections, through alliances with the military, or by assassinating rulers and replacing them.

Contemporary Islamist organizations have made a great contribution to the Islamization of education, and particularly to the creation of schools, including primary and secondary schools with an integrated curriculum that combined general and religious education. Arabic language was the main language of instruction in some schools, French or English in others. The main goal of all of the schools was to prepare graduates for the job market while providing them with a solid Islamic education. As many students in these secondary schools were close to graduating, World Conferences on Muslim Education recommended the creation of Islamic universities to provide them higher education opportunities and help them continue to forge their Muslim personalities at a critical stage of their lives and training. In response to these recommendations, the number of Islamic institutions of higher learning increased considerably. Some started with a focus on Islamic and Arabic studies, with a plan to gradually broaden their offerings. Others offered from the outset most of the disciplines in the arts and the sciences taught in conventional universities. Both types endeavored to create an Islamic environment and promote an

Islamic perspective on knowledge. The central epistemological premise that undergirded these endeavors is what has been referred to as the Islamization of knowledge, a project initiated at the World Conferences on Muslim Education and now carried out in a variety of settings, including in conventional universities, by Muslim public intellectuals and other Islamic NGOs and Muslim think tanks.[9] In several universities of predominantly Muslim Northern Nigeria— such as Bayero University Kano, Ahmadu Bello University Zaria, Usmanu Danfodiyo University Sokoto, and the University of Maiduguri—Muslim scholars are strongly committed to promoting an Islamic perspective of knowledge in their teaching and research. The International Institute for Islamic Thought (IIIT), established in 1981 in the United States, with offices in Africa and Europe, has been the major think tank committed to the Islamization of knowledge. In the past three decades, IIIT has strived to provoke an educational paradigm shift through sustained research and publications. Thirty years after its creation, IIIT has published more than four hundred books in English, Arabic, and other languages.[10] Its Nigerian branch—based at Bayero University, Kano—has been particularly active. Through its journal titled *Al-Ijtihad: The Journal of the Islamization of Knowledge and Contemporary Issues,* as well as many other publications, IIIT Nigeria has mobilized a very diverse group of scholars / public intellectuals to address from an Islamic perspective a whole range of contemporary social, economic, and political issues, including gender theory, monetary and fiscal policies, education, international relations, and globalization. Thus, Islamic activists provided the intellectual leadership for the Islamization of knowledge project so that when African states embraced the idea of the liberalization of education, advocates of Islamic universities were ready to seize the opportunity to create them. This leads us to the discussion of the second paradigm shift that gave rise to the prominence of private higher education.

Liberalization of Higher Education

In the first three decades following the independence of African countries, the state was assigned a primary role in African development. It was the main provider of education and employment. From the 1980s on, African countries experienced a severe economic crisis, which led to defaults in repaying their loans. Throughout the 1980s and the 1990s, international development circles were preoccupied with identifying the root causes of the crisis and providing policy prescriptions. The most accepted wisdom within international financing agencies and among Western donors was that state intervention had not been positive.[11] The views and disciplinary power of the donors provoked a paradigm shift in development thinking, from the conviction that the state was a key player in development—a premise most development economists shared in the postwar period of reconstruction—to the opposite (not uncontroversial) conviction that state intervention was harmful to the economy. This shift ushered in what some have called the triumph of neoliberalism. A number of policy prescriptions were imposed on African countries that requested a rescheduling of their debts from various donors. State disengagement became the buzzword for the new developmental paradigm. Central aspects of such disengagement included the dismantling of state-led industrialization, the privatization of the economy, and also the reform of education in the direction of greater liberalization. Higher education, which was the reserved domain of the state, became liberalized, and a number of private entrepreneurs started to invest in university education.

Up until the economic crisis of the 1980s, there existed very few private universities in West Africa. In many countries, the creation of institutions of higher learning required the accreditation of state bodies; the accrediting agency varied by country. In Nigeria, it is the National Universities Commission; in Kenya, the Commission of Higher Education; in South Africa, the Department of Education. In French-speaking countries, it is an intergovernmental body in which virtually all Francophone universities are members: Le Conseil Africain et Malgache pour l'Enseignement Supérieur (African and Madagascar Council for Higher Education).

In just three decades, private institutions of higher learning had mushroomed in West Africa. In Nigeria, for example, the National Universities Commission had accredited twenty-nine federal universities, thirty-three state universities, and forty private universities by 2011.[12] Activists in the field of Islamic education took advantage of such an environment to start implementing the recommendations of the World Conferences on Muslim of Education related to higher education. Various players were involved in establishing and supporting Islamic universities in Africa, including international Islamic organizations, such as the Organization of the Islamic Conference (OIC), created in 1969 and renamed the Organization for Islamic Cooperation in 2011; large Islamic NGOs, such as the World Assembly of Muslim Youth, the African Muslim Agency, and the Libyan World Islamic Call Society; and smaller NGOs, mostly with the support of Arab donors. Between 2007 and 2011, I conducted field research on Islamic universities established in Abeokuta, Ilorin, Oshogbo and Katsina (Nigeria); in Nairobi, Mombasa, and Lamu (Kenya); in Say and Niamey (Niger); in Cape Town (South Africa); in Pikine and Pire (Senegal); and in Mbale (Uganda). The following sections of this chapter summarize the findings of my research on these Islamic universities and colleges. The OIC sponsored the first two Islamic universities in sub-Saharan Africa in the mid-1980s, and these provide the model for dozens of Islamic institutions of higher learning established in recent years.

The OIC-Sponsored Pioneering Islamic Universities of Say and Mbale

The OIC Summit of Heads of State held in Lahore in 1974 recommended the creation of two Islamic universities in Africa—one in a predominantly French-speaking country and another in an English-speaking country. Niger was chosen to host the Islamic university for the francophone countries of West Africa, and Uganda for the Anglophone countries of East Africa. At the time of conception of the Islamic university in Niger, experts envisioned that it would ultimately be made of six units: a school of Arabic and Islamic studies; a school of engineering; a school of pharmacy and dental surgery; a school of economics, law, and sociology; a school of language, Arts, literature, and education; and a school of sciences.[13] The OIC and the government of Niger agreed on a gradual implementation of the project based on the availability of funding. Representatives of the OIC held meetings with education officials of the Republic of Niger to address the logistics of implementation. In addition to granting a huge tract of land in the city of Say located fifty kilometers away from Niamey, the capital city of Niger, the Nigerian government, led by President Seyni Kounche, committed to provide free water and electricity, as well as a tax exemption for all donations to the university.[14] In 1986, the Islamic Solidarity Fund, controlled by the Saudi kingdom, provided the funding for the building of the Faculty of Islamic and Arabic Studies, a few administrative buildings, a limited number of student hostels, and housing for faculty members. In February 1986, the board of trustees of the university held a meeting and appointed two Saudis to the most strategic positions: ʿAbdallah ʿAbd al-Muhsin al-Turki, then rector of the Jamiʿat al-Imam Muhammad b. Saʿud al-islamiyya (Imam Muhammad Ibn Saud Islamic University) of Riyad, was appointed president of the board of trustees, and Mohammad Jamil Khayyat, former dean of the Faculty of Education of the University Umm al-Qura of Mecca, was appointed rector. The Université islamique de Say was officially inaugurated on January the 15th, 1987, in the presence of the then president of the Republic of Niger, Seyni Kounche, and World Muslim League secretary general, 'Abdallah 'Umar Nasif. This was the second university established in this Sahelian country. The first was the Université Abdou Moumouni in Niamey, under the tutelage of the Ministry of Higher Education of Niger. Like other universities of French-speaking countries, the Université Abdou Moumouni was accredited by the Conseil Africain et Malgache pour l'Enseignement Supérieur, whose secretariat is based in Ouagadougou. In the Université islamique de Say, by contrast, only one faculty operated—that of Islamic and Arabic studies (later split into two units: the Faculty of Arabic Studies and the Faculty of Islamic Law). Arabic was the only language of instruction in those faculties. Since its creation, the university has had no annual budget and essentially depends on donations, the disbursement of which is monitored by the president of the board of trustees based in Saudi Arabia. In 2010, the library of the university owned over forty thousand Arabic titles, making it the largest Arabic library of sub-Saharan Africa. Virtually all books were donated from the Middle East, either by Islamic NGOs or retired scholars or the families of deceased scholars from the Middle East. A doctoral student working on any aspect of Islamic religious sciences such as Shari'a, hadith, or Qur'anic studies, can find in one place all the reference works needed to write a dissertation. However, I could not find in the history section of the university library a single history book written by Nigerien historians such as Djibo Hamani, Andre Salifou, Kimba Idrissa, and others who have published well-received books on the history of Islam in the central Sudan in European languages. Those books, it must be emphasized, are available for sale in the bookstores of Niamey, the capital city of Niger. One former rector of the Université islamique de Say confided to me that "the rector has no executive powers" and that the president of the board of trustees of the university ordered him while he was rector to allow no book coming from anywhere other than the Gulf to be shelved in the library. As a result, books donated by the Iranians and Libyans had not been allowed into the library.

Like similar colleges created later in West and East Africa, the curriculum is largely copied from Islamic studies colleges. The weekend is Thursdays and Fridays, unlike in other private and public institutions of learning in Niger, where Saturdays and Sundays are the days of rest. Students come from twenty-one African countries, including Niger, Nigeria, Benin, the Sudan, Algeria, Chad, the Gambia, Sierra Leone, the Comoros Islands, Togo, Mauritania, Guinea, Senegal, Côte d'Ivoire, Mali, Ghana, Cameroon, and Burkina Faso. The majority of students come from French-speaking countries, including 30 percent from Niger alone. In 2010, 1,250 students were enrolled, two-thirds of whom were males and one-third female. Education is free, and all students receive a stipend to cover living expenses. Recently there have been some changes that have raised the standards of the university. The teaching staff at the Université islamique de Say must have received at least a master's degree, but in 2010, most held a PhD, in contrast with instructors in smaller colleges of Islamic education, most of whom have only bachelor's degrees. Students, instructors, and staff of the university are all Muslim. Up until 2010, the university offered only Arabic and Islamic studies. In 2010, it opened a second faculty of management offering education entirely in French.

The first cohorts of graduates of the Islamic Université islamique de Say faced the typical problem of Arabophones in French-speaking countries. Trained in Islamic and Arabic studies, most would either become self-employed teachers or teach in public and private schools. A few found clerical jobs in embassies of Arabic countries or in branches of Islamic NGOs, which proliferated in the 1990s in Africa. Others joined the foreign service to work as diplomats in Arab countries. A good many, however, found no employment because of their lack of proficiency in European languages or their lack of degrees recognized by bodies accrediting Europhone universities. From the mid-1990s forward, the university therefore set up a professional training program funded by IQRA (a Saudi NGO very active in Africa) to provide training in technical fields such as auto mechanics, electricity, and cooling systems so that students who so wished could be self-employed after graduation. Such professional training had been offered to African students in Arabic and Islamic studies in Libya, whereas students trained in accredited universities offering instruction in European languages had not set up any kind of similar program. Finally, the Université islamique de Say, which, when it began, admitted students on the basis of having memorized the Qur'an but without the requirement of any further studies whatsoever, in the meantime has become much more selective. Now all those admitted have completed secondary school, and the majority are bilingual (Arabic and French).

The second Islamic university was established in Mbale, Uganda. Although sponsored by the OIC, the trajectory of the Islamic University in Uganda

Mbale was slightly different to that of Say. At its inauguration in 1988, it had only two faculties or departments—the Faculty of Education and the Faculty of Islamic Studies and Arabic Language—both based at the Mbale campus, 250 kilometers away from the capital city of Kampala, with a total of eighty students from East Africa. It expanded very quickly to become a leading institution of higher learning in Uganda. As of 2012, it accommodates over seven thousand students in four campuses scattered throughout Uganda. It operates fifty-six academic programs in its seven academic schools: the Faculties of Islamic Studies and Arabic Language, Arts and Social Sciences, Management Studies, Education, Sciences, and Law, as well as the School of Nursing. By 2010, it had already held nineteen graduation ceremonies and produced ten thousand graduates with certificates and diplomas, and bachelor's, master's, and doctoral degrees.[15]

In contrast with the Université islamique de Say in Niger, the Islamic University in Uganda offers instruction predominantly in English. It is only in the Faculty of Islamic Studies and Arabic Language that instruction is offered in Arabic. Unlike the Université islamique de Say, students are neither exempted from paying fees nor automatically entitled to a stipend; fees vary between schools and can be very high. Also unlike the sister institution in Say, enrollment has been open to students regardless of religious affiliation, and many non-Muslim students have attended the university. Likewise, the teaching and administrative staffs include non-Muslims. The university preserves its Islamic character, however, by imposing certain rules, such as an Islamic dress code, which apply to all students regardless of religious affiliation. Female Christian students must wear a headscarf just like Muslim students. Alcohol is not allowed on the campus, and the schedule of courses must not conflict with the Muslim daily prayers.[16]

Like the Université islamique de Say, the Islamic University in Uganda relied heavily on external funding, particularly from Saudi Arabia, in its first years of operation. In the aftermath of September 11, 2001, and the restriction on the transfer of "Islamic funds," the Islamic University in Uganda, like similar institutions that depended on Arab funding, faced serious financial problems. The university subsequently, and gradually, reduced its external dependence to 15 percent from 100 percent, by charging higher tuition fees to students and diversifying its sources of funding. It now receives assistance from African countries, including Nigeria, which supplied qualified teaching staff from its program of technical assistance serving many African countries. As a result, the teaching environment is as sophisticated as in Makerere, the other public Ugandan university based in Kampala. Unlike the Université islamique de Say in Niger, the libraries of the Islamic University in Uganda have a budget to purchase books and offer diverse documentary sources to the students. Likewise, the university produces high-caliber English-language journals in different fields, including law. In contrast, the Université islamique de Say only produces one journal, that is published in Arabic. Graduates of the Islamic University in Uganda serve various professional fields in Uganda and elsewhere in the world. Graduates of the sister institution in Niger, in comparison, have more limited job opportunities.

From the 1990s to 2010, following the creation of the two OIC-sponsored Islamic universities, institutions of higher learning claiming the label "Islamic" have proliferated in sub-Saharan Africa. Most are modeled on the Université islamique de Say and could be described, at least in the first decade of the twenty-first century, as colleges of Islamic studies; a smaller number modeled on the Islamic University in Uganda resemble what in the United States are called liberal arts colleges.

The Colleges of Islamic Studies

Colleges of Islamic studies that offer a BA have proliferated in the late twentieth and early twenty-first centuries. In Kenya, a country with a minority Muslim population, three such colleges have been established by Kenyan Muslims with the assistance of local benefactors and/or Islamic NGOs. The first is the Faculty of Islamic Studies in Kisuani Mombasa, created in 1982 as an Islamic seminary by South Asian Muslims in Kenya and later upgraded to the rank of college of Islamic studies. The second was the College for Sharia and Islamic Studies at Thika, located on the outskirts of Nairobi. Both colleges have a Salafi orientation in their teaching. They attracted high school graduates from many parts of East Africa, including from the Riyad, a school created by Habib Saleh, a Kenyan of Arabic Yemeni descent who had become the most venerated Alawi saint on the island of Lamu in Kenya.[17] Throughout the twentieth century, the Riyad trained countless East African Muslims,[18] many of whom established their own schools. But because Riyad did not offer college education, many of its graduates joined the two other Salafi-oriented colleges. In the process, some of them deserted Sufism to become Salafi. In response, the Riyad administration envisioned the establishment of a college of Islamic studies in

Lamu to offer a Sufi-friendly undergraduate training leading to the award of a BA in Islamic studies.[19]

Of all Kenyan Islamic institutions of higher learning, the College of Sharia and Islamic Studies in Thika is the most advanced. Supported by the African Muslim Agency since its creation, it has a very qualified teaching staff. Instructors have at least master's degrees, and most have a PhD. Unlike most other schools of Islamic studies in Africa, the college set up mechanisms for the promotion of faculty members through affiliation with the International University of Africa in the Republic of Sudan. It is also the first and only Islamic college in Kenya to have received accreditation from the Kenyan Commission for Higher Education. To fulfill the requirements of the commission, the college had to expand its premises, build new classrooms, and open other units. In addition to Arabic and Islamic studies, the college is also offering a bachelor's degree in management; a bachelor's degree in computer sciences is awaiting accreditation. As soon as it is accredited, the Thika college will fulfill all the requirements of the Commission for Higher Education to become a full-fledged university and will be known as the Umma University of Kenya.[20]

Another important player in Islamic higher education in Africa is Libya. The Faculty of Islamic Call of Libya has several branches in the Islamic world, including in Lebanon, Syria, Senegal, Chad, Niger, and Britain. These campuses offer the same training as the mother faculty in Tripoli: Islamic call and Islamic civilization, the Qur'an and Qur'anic sciences, and Arabic language and literature. Unlike the main branch in Tripoli, the smaller campuses do not offer a graduate program. Most instructors on its many campuses are graduates of the mother institution in Tripoli. The administration of the six campuses is very centralized: for example, exam questions are similar for all centers, all final exams in the six centers are held at the same time, and exams are sealed and sent to the mother institution in Libya for grading.[21] Graduates of these centers receive a degree with institution name of Faculty of Islamic Call and may attend the mother school in Tripoli for graduate studies.

A Libyan registrar managed the Senegalese campus of the faculty based in Pire. Just like the Université islamique de Say in Niger, the Pire instructors have little involvement in the management of the campus or in setting the intellectual agenda of the college. Most instructors have a master's degree, and a few have a PhD, but they mostly teach on an adjunct basis. There is no mechanism for promoting faculty, nor is there a serious research agenda. Research opportunities are very limited. Every year, the campus organizes a cultural week, and faculty members and others present papers, which typically are considered for publication in Libyan journals such as the *Journal of the Faculty of Islamic Call*, published in Tripoli. Unlike other Salafi-oriented colleges of Islamic studies, this college has a very tolerant approach, and faculty members enjoy some freedom in organizing their teaching. As a matter of policy, however, the school does not shelve books donated by the Iranian embassy on the grounds that Shiite theological literature tends to be fanatical and critical of venerated Islamic figures such as the first three caliphs.[22] Just like the Islamic colleges of Niger, Senegal, and Kenya, education is free, and students who originate from various West African countries receive a stipend to support them.

A third important player in Islamic higher education in Africa is the Islamic Republic of Iran. Prior to the Islamic Revolution of 1979, West Africa was exclusively Sunni and Maliki. Members of the Levantine community from Lebanon and Syria, whose settlement was facilitated by colonial powers in the twentieth century, represented a small Shiite presence in this Maliki world. In general, Levantine Shiites had few interactions with local Africans beyond business partnerships. For the most part, they were not interested in proselytizing and gaining converts. Three decades after the Islamic Revolution, Shiism has made inroads in Africa. The first converts were young Islamic activists who sojourned in Iran after the revolution and returned to their country to spread Khomeini's vision of an Islamic state.[23] Initially, these young people were not doctrinal Shiites but rather enthusiastic supporters of the Islamic Revolution who saw in Khomeini's revolution a model for African Muslim countries. It was in Nigeria that such a trend—under the leadership of Ibrahim El-Zakzaky— was most powerful. Gradually, many of these young people embraced the doctrines of Shiism and spread it to the grass roots. Large segments of the population started to celebrate Shiite rituals such as 'Ashura. In other West African countries such as Senegal, Shiism is also making inroads[24] among local populations as a result of sustained Iranian campaigns in Africa. In addition to sponsoring young Africans to study in Iranian theological seminaries (*hauza*), several Iranian activists have created theological schools in Africa to train people locally. A major theological seminary operating in Iran has been at the forefront in spreading Iranian Shiism in the world. Supported by pious followers of leading religious leaders (*marja'*) such as Ali al-Sistani (b. 1930), Fazel Lankrani (b. 1931), Naser Makarem Shirazi (b. 1926), and Ali Khamenei (b. 1939), it provided traditional training in Islamic studies.[25] In 2008, it was renamed the Al-Mustafa Open University and now offers university degrees at the bachelor's, master's, and doctoral levels. It established campuses in many countries, including Senegal, Benin, Niger, Togo, Mali, Guinea, Burkina Faso, and Chad, as well as Ghana, where the largest branch is based—the Islamic University of Ghana.

The Nigerien branch, which I visited in 2010, is named Madrasat al-Rasul al-Akram and is based in Niamey. Like the Université islamique de Say in Niger, it received a land grant from the Nigerien government in Niamey to build the school premises; the government also waived tax duties on school supplies. Like other branches of the Al-Mustafa Open University in Africa, it is fully supported by the mother university (Jami'a al-Mustafa al-'alamiya). Every year, it submits a request for an operating budget, including salaries for instructors and administrators, and stipends for students. To apply for admission, students must possess a high school certificate (baccalauréat). Education is free, and all students are eligible for a stipend to cover living expenses. Affiliation to Shiism is not a prerequisite for joining the university. The school does not have many full-time instructors. It relies on instructors teaching at the Université islamique de Say. All tests are produced and graded locally now, but in due course graduating students will receive a degree carrying the name of the Al-Mustafa Open University.

The "Islamic Liberal Arts Colleges"

A new category of schools claiming the label of Islamic university, or perceived as such, has been created in Nigeria in the first decade of the twenty-first century. Modeled on the Islamic University in Uganda, these schools (Fountain University, Crescent University, Al-Hikma University, and Katsina Islamic University) require a fee, are largely self-funded, and are private. Unlike the Islamic studies type of colleges, these schools are not focused on religious studies but instead offer general education in the arts and sciences and were created partly in response to the crisis of higher education in Nigeria. Nigeria, it must be recalled, invested a large part of its 1970s oil wealth in higher education and became an attractive place to live and teach. Dozens of federal and state universities were created, and these attracted scholars from Africa, South Asia, Europe, and America. As a consequence of structural adjustment policies implemented by the Nigerian government in the 1980s, the national currency was devaluated and the standard of living deteriorated. The state-funded public school system followed suit. Poorly paid instructors deserted public universities. In addition, crime, insecurity, and cultism became notable features of Nigerian campuses. As a result, many people were reluctant to send their children there. After the liberalization of higher education, private universities proliferated. Christian churches created most of these. Unlike public universities, these new schools imposed high morality on campus, banning drug consumption and cultism.

Because most of those private universities were Christian, Muslim communities endeavored to create their own private "Islamic universities." Like the Islamic University in Uganda Mbale, these new Islamic universities are open to non-Muslims, and indeed many students are not Muslims. To affirm their Islamic character, however, the schools enforce an Islamic moral code. All female student and staff, regardless of their religion, must wear a headscarf. The drinking of alcohol is banned on campus. Dance parties and the mixing of male and female students outside common areas such as the library, restaurants, and classrooms are prohibited. The National Universities Commission of Nigeria accredits all these universities. Their academic standards are more than decent. Wireless Internet access is available throughout their campuses. Here laboratories are better equipped than those of public universities.

Notable is the fact that one of the schools, Fountain University,[26] offered no major in Islamic studies five years after its opening. It started to operate in January 2008 with two colleges—namely, the College of Natural and Applied Sciences and the College of Management and Social Sciences. The library is small but well equipped, with the best textbooks in the disciplines taught at the university. The university library has a policy of purchasing 50 percent of its books and journals from local sources, and the remaining 50 percent from international sources. The most recent issues of the top journals in the fields taught at the university are available in the library, including the *Harvard Business Review,* the *Journal of Financial Economics,* the *British Journal of Sociology,* the *British Journal of Political Science,* the *Journal of Biochemistry,* the *Journal of Microbiology,* the *International Journal of Biotechnology and Biochemistry,* and the *Journal of Parasitology.* With its own server, the library has access to many online journal databases, including JSTOR and African Journal Online. The entire campus is wireless. In addition to the hard copies available on the library shelves, many books and journals are purchased in the form of access kits that enable students to read books in the e-room as well as elsewhere on campus.[27] From a beginning enrollment of 185 in 2008, the number of students had risen by 2011 to 700 students, 20 percent of whom are Christian.

The university plans to open a faculty of humanities, which will have a department of Islamic studies in due course. However, the vice chancellor has expressed concern[28] that most students interested in Arabic and Islamic studies come from local Islamic schools that may not meet the high standards set by the National Universities Commission to join a university, including obtaining the General Certificate of Education of West Africa and passing the Joint Academic Matriculation Board exams. All in all, these schools seem more like liberal arts colleges than traditional colleges of Islamic studies.

Main Features of the Islamic Institutions of Higher Learning

What are the main features of Islamic higher education in sub-Saharan Africa? First, there is a strong reliance on Middle Eastern donors, who, among other things, dictate the terms of the recruitment of students and faculty, determine the curriculum, and continue to provide postgraduate training in Arab universities for West African students. Second, there is a heavy teaching load and limited research opportunities, along with a focus on classics in the teaching and research that devotes little attention to local Islamic dynamics. Third, there is little networking between Islamic institutions of higher learning. Finally, employment opportunities for graduates remain limited.

As to heavy reliance on foreign donors, with the notable exception of the liberal arts type of colleges, Islamic institutions of higher learning essentially rely on foreign financial and logistical support. The main donors are based in the Gulf countries—Saudi Arabia in particular. The Islamic Development Bank and the Organization of the Islamic Conference make an important contribution. Other important NGOs include the Africa Muslim Agency, which is based in Kuwait, is active in twenty-four African countries, and supports the Université islamique de Say and the Islamic College of Thika in Nairobi. Another is the World Assembly of Muslim Youth, which partnered with a Nigerian Muslim to build the Al-Hikma University. Other important donors include the Foundation IQRA in Mecca, the Faculty of Islamic Call in Libya, and the Iranian Al-Mustafa Open University. With regard to staffing, the Egyptian university of Al-Azhar has remained the main provider of teachers in Islamic studies in Africa. Donors decide from which nationalities Islamic universities and colleges recruit, and they impose recruitment quotas. In general, the Islamic institutions of higher learning have a big population of international students. Large and well-established universities, such as the Université islamique de Say in Niger, recruit students of some twenty-one nationalities, whereas smaller colleges such as the College of Islamic Studies in Lamu, recruit from about five nationalities, mainly in East Africa.

Most Islamic institutions of higher learning do not yet have graduate programs. After more than twenty years of operation, in 2011, the Université de Say in Niger graduated two master's degree candidates in Islamic studies. The Islamic University in Uganda does have a PhD program in Islamic studies from which a few students have graduated. But their dissertations were cosupervised by a local professor and a full university professor based in the Arab world because none of the members of the Faculty of Islamic Studies at the Islamic University in Uganda has reached the rank of senior lecturer or above, which is a requirement to supervise a doctoral dissertation in Uganda.

As mentioned earlier, another feature is limited research opportunities. Most Islamic institutions of higher learning focus on teaching and show little commitment to supporting and rewarding research. In general, their full-time members have conducted solid academic research to receive master's degrees or doctorates, but most of them have not conducted any serious research beyond their degrees. Some of the reasons for this neglect of research include the fact that scholars do not seem to be aware of international publication outlets. Journals created by the universities to provide publication opportunities to the faculty, where these exist, are limited in relation to the demand. For example, in twenty-four years, the *Annales de l'Université islamique de Say* has published only eight issues, and the *Journal of the Islamic University in Uganda* only three issues, which is insignificant compared with the demand emanating from faculty members. In addition, the teaching load is so heavy that faculty members have little time to do research. At the Islamic University in Uganda, for example, where the standards tend to be higher, fifteen hours a week is the statutory teaching load for faculty members, but most teach at least an additional five to seven hours to make ends meet.[29] Finally, most universities do not have a promotion policy based on research. In other words, faculty members receive salary increases every once in a while, but they cannot be promoted from one professorial rank to another, so there is no great incentive to do research.

As to the focus on classics, the curriculum is modeled on that of Islamic colleges in Arab countries. With slight variations, it is the same in most colleges. Consequently, research of faculty members, where it does exist, deals with Qur'anic studies, hadith, and *fiqh*, and is typically published in Middle Eastern academic journals, which may not even be available in their universities.[30]

For example, the College of Islamic Studies of Thika, Kenya, is one of the rare Islamic institutions of higher learning in sub-Saharan Africa where some mechanisms are in place to promote faculty based on performance in teaching and publication. This college is affiliated with the International University of Africa based in Khartoum, which evaluated all the promotion cases prior to the accreditation of the college by the Kenyan Commission for Higher Education. The research of those faculty members of the College of Islamic Studies at Thika who have been promoted from one professorial rank to another has generally been published in Middle Eastern journals. Very few faculty have done research on Kenyan or East African Islam, which therefore remains poorly researched. Noteworthy is the fact, however, that hundreds of students who graduated from African Islamic institutions of higher learning have been encouraged to write honors theses or master's theses in Arabic dealing with various aspects of local Islam. Some of these provide useful information on the Islamization in their countries and on the works of influential Muslim scholars, as well as on Islamic social movements. Similar theses are also available in departments of Arabic and Islamic studies in accredited Europhone universities, but they are typically written in European languages. When Islamic institutions of higher learning eventually establish effective graduate studies programs, it is possible that greater research attention will be devoted to the study of the impact of Islam on local African societies.

Finally, there is a lack of networking. Unlike accredited universities operating under the supervision of national bodies such as the National Universities Commission in Nigeria or supranational bodies such as the Conseil Africain et Malgache pour l'Enseignement Supérieur in French-speaking countries, the Islamic institutions of higher learning in Africa do not network or share experiences and resources. In November 2011 when I visited the Université islamique de Say in Niger and informed its secretary general that I was conducting research on Islamic institutions of higher learning in Africa, he told me that there were only two such institutions in Africa:[31] the Université islamique de Say in Niger and the Islamic University in Uganda. I disagreed and argued that there are a few more, including in Burkina Faso. Doubting the claim, he immediately phoned a colleague based in Burkina Faso, who told him that there were indeed three such universities in Burkina Faso (two in Ouagadougou and one in Bobodioulasso). When I asked him if the Université islamique de Say collaborates with the sister university in Uganda (both were established by the Organization of the Islamic Conference), his answer was no. Colleagues at the

Islamic University in Uganda confirmed that there is no collaboration between them. Although the Organization of the Islamic Conference has established a Federation of Universities of the Islamic World, of which both the Université islamique dey Say and the Islamic University in Uganda Mbale are members,[32] they still do not collaborate. Thus, the main publications of the university in Niger were not known to the colleagues teaching Islamic studies in Uganda when I visited the Mbale campus in 2011, and the *Annales de l'Université islamique de Say* was not even available at the main library of the Islamic University in Uganda. In contrast, the network of accredited universities in French-speaking countries of Africa and Madagascar collaborate very closely through the creation of joint research teams as well as visiting professorships. They also collaborate with teaching and research institutions in France and elsewhere that share the same intellectual mission.

Employment and the Predicament of Graduates from Islamic Universities

Most of these Islamic universities have no office of alumni relations and have not kept track of their graduates. Students are typically recruited from several countries, to which they return after graduation. Thus, it has not been possible so far to obtain accurate information on the trajectory of graduates beyond anecdotal evidence. According to most people I interviewed, graduates of Islamic studies are typically employed as teachers in government or private Islamic schools. Others serve as imams or administrators in local or international Islamic NGOs. Some work as judges or chaplains in the army, and others have set up their own companies.

As discussed in Chapter 6, the two major hurdles that Arabophones faced are the lack of proficiency in colonial languages and of expertise in a field in high demand in the job market. Various strategies were devised to address this predicament. Individual solutions consisted of African graduates from Arab universities seeking postgraduate training in European universities. Institutional strategies favored in the Republic of Sudan include providing training other than just Arabic and Islamic studies to African students and also offering courses in European languages so that graduates gain proficiency in those languages in addition to Arabic, which is the main language of instruction. Another strategy adopted by the Université islamique de Say in Niger and the

Faculty of Islamic Call in Libya has been to set up parallel programs for professional training in refrigeration, electronics, and computer hardware maintenance so that all graduates of Islamic studies have an additional marketable expertise. Thanks to this parallel expertise, a few graduates of those universities have set up companies in their countries of origin upon graduation.

What is the likely trajectory of Islamic universities and colleges in Africa in the years ahead? In all likelihood, old and better-established universities will transition to conventional universities in terms of their offerings. The Islamic University in Uganda Mbale has very quickly moved away from a focus on Islamic studies and reliance on foreign donors to become a full-fledged university. The Université islamique de Say has taken more time but is now in the process of establishing new departments similar to those of conventional Francophone universities in Africa. It is also planning to join the Conseil Africain et Malgache pour l'Enseignement Supérieur. In the years ahead, more such schools are likely to be established, and other Islamic colleges such Kisuani in Mombasa and Thika in Nairobi (both in Kenya) are following that same path. Yet the old model of Islamic colleges is unlikely to disappear. The dean of the International Peace Varsity in South Africa[33] told me that IPSA does not seek to compete with universities specializing in general education. It views the provision of Islamic education as a mission, a service to the community. Its research is oriented toward addressing the needs and concerns of the Muslim community in South Africa. Other colleges that share these views include the College of Islamic Education in Pikine, Senegal, and the College of Islamic Education in Lamu, Kenya.[34]

By reviewing how Arabic and Islamic studies scholars are trained in the Middle East and in various African countries, I have demonstrated how the Islamic intellectual tradition gained vitality in post-colonial Africa. The thousands of graduates of Arabic and Islamic studies programs have worked hard to extend the Islamic space of meaning in the post-colonial period. In the process, they used modern forms of legal, social, and political organization—as well as media outlets such as newspaper, radio, TV, and the Internet—to reach the wider society, including Europhone elites. They strive to undermine the dominant epistemological framework that colonialism and secular and Westernized African elites imposed in the twentieth century, a process that I discuss in Chapter 8.

Chapter 8

Islam in the Post-colonial Public Sphere

Any attempt to impose secularism on Nigeria or on any other
country having a predominantly Muslim population is nothing
short of injustice. This is because it is a Christian dogma, a
Christian concept, and a Christian worldview.

—*Aliyu Dawuda*[1]

IN CHAPTER 5, we saw how Arabic-educated intellectuals in West Africa
managed to topple illiterate rulers and establish Islamic states in which
Arabic was the language of administration until the advent of European colonial rule at the beginning of the twentieth century. During the first half of the
twentieth century, colonial languages gradually rose to prominence, in the process undermining the centrality of Arabic. This was so much the case that when
West African countries became independent, French, English, and Portuguese
had already imposed themselves as languages of administration and, to some
extent, also business. The top African political elites who inherited political
power and provided leadership in the post-colonial quest for development and
political and intellectual emancipation were Western educated and viewed
secularism (separation between religion and state) as a panacea to rule their
multireligious countries.

Despite the vitality of the Islamic intellectual tradition throughout colonial
rule, its graduates have remained outside of decision-making circles. Only a
few of them were co-opted into circles of power as advisors in Arab or Islamic
affairs to heads of state or diplomats. Due to a lack of adequate knowledge of,
and degrees in, European languages, the voices of Arabophones were not heard
in public debates. But they did speak. In fact, Arabophones were preoccupied
with issues very similar to those of their Europhone compatriots and had pursued intellectual conversation in their own ghettoized forums. As a result, two
sets of debates were taking place among educated West African intellectuals.
Considered the real intellectuals, Europhones took advantage of their control
of hegemonic languages and access to media to weigh in on major debates.

Pure Arabophones created their own narrow space to address a variety of issues related to nation building. There was little awareness of such endeavors by Arabic-speaking intellectuals, because very few bilingual (Arabic and Europhone) actors could navigate between these two worlds and raise awareness about the complexity of the intellectual field.

In the study of Islam in Africa, I was able to appreciate fully the compartmentalization of knowledge production when I visited for the first time the Université islamique de Say in Niger in 2007. I discovered the *Annales de Université de Say*, published in Arabic, to which faculty members of the departments of Arabic and Islamic studies of that university were the main contributors. In the editorial of the first issue of the journal, the then rector of the university, Abdul 'Ali al-Wadghiri,[2] stated that the study of Islam and Muslim societies in sub-Saharan Africa was central to the intellectual mission of the university. Indeed, between the date of publication of the first issue of the journal and 2007, nine issues totaling some 2,500 pages carried several dozen scholarly articles of a respectable academic standard, a number of which dealt with the history and sociology of Muslim societies in Africa. I was gratified to make that discovery in particular, since I myself have served in the preceding two decades as assistant editor or editorial board member of a similar journal striving to shape the field of Islamic studies in sub-Saharan Africa. Titled *Islam et sociétés au sud du Sahara*, this journal was created by French historian Jean-Louis Triaud[3] and published articles dealing with themes very similar to the ones addressed by the publication of the Université islamique de Say, but in English and French and written by scholars from Europe, Africa, and the United States. For a couple of years, I handled correspondence with contributors and also worked with the marketing department of the Maison des Sciences de L'Homme to promote *Islam et sociétés*. Yet in all that time, I never heard that a similar journal existed in Africa. After further investigation, I found that scholars involved in each of these two journals, including those with linguistic competence in both European languages and Arabic, like myself, did not know about the existence and efforts of the other—and therefore did not cite the other publication.

In French West Africa, the official media gave voice essentially to debates in European languages, which they assumed to be intellectually sophisticated simply on the basis of the language in which they took place. They looked down upon Arabophones, who, they believed, belonged to a premodern world. In response to their marginalization, Arabophones attempted to resist Europhone intellectual hegemony in different ways. Aware of the centrality of Arabic language and expertise in Islamic studies in an Islamic order, many sought through peaceful means to promote such an order. In the process, they participated in the vibrant Islamic associational life generated by the expansion of modern education in post-colonial West Africa. Some Arabophones strove to gain fluency in European languages to participate fully in public debates without neglecting the Arabic language. They created their own media outlets to state their views in public debates—not just in their home countries but also in the diaspora.

Like the Western-educated students in France, Great Britain, and the United States, West African Arabophones in Arab universities created a multitude of nationality-based student societies to debate matters of concern to them. Echoes of the debates of African students in Cairo can be overheard in their newsletters. In perusing issues of the newsletters of *Al-Ittihad* (The Union), published by the Association of Students from Cameroon in Egypt, and *Sawt al-Rabita* (Voice of the League), by the National League of Senegalese Students in Egypt, I realized that they were engaged in debates very similar to those of African students in France. In the late 1970s and 1980s, I was a student in France, and, like other Africans of my generation attending French institutions of higher learning, I was affiliated with two student associations: a nationality-based association—in my case the Association des Étudiants et Stagiaires Sénégalais de France (AESEF)—and a Pan-African organization called Fédération des Étudiants d'Afrique Noire en France (FEANF). Sponsored by French leftist organizations and most notably the French Communist Party, the FEANF was created in 1950, just ten years before West African French colonies became independent, and it was dissolved by French authorities in 1980.

In general, African student associations in France were engaged in two types of debate. On the one hand, they addressed the conditions of immigrants in general and students in particular in the host society. Although education was very affordable in France (and in Egypt also) and most students enrolled in French universities without paying high tuition fees, many did not have a scholarship to cover their living expenses. Under such conditions, survival was a struggle. How to pool resources necessary to provide material support to all African students was a major preoccupation of student associations. International student associations lobbied their home governments but also networked with larger proimmigrant coalitions such as leftist political parties and trade unions, human rights groups, or charitable religious associations to facilitate the admittance of students and to protect them against intolerance from xenophobic segments of the host society. But student associations were also concerned with the conditions of their home countries and more generally the entire African continent. In the three decades of its existence, the FEANF provided a high-profile forum for discussion about anti-imperialism, national independence, and neocolonialism. In association meetings—typically held during weekends on university campuses—African students either in the FEANF or in the nationality-based associations held long discussions on matters relating to nation building in the continent. They vehemently denounced apartheid in South Africa. They criticized widespread authoritarianism and criminalization of political opposition in Africa. They spoke against neocolonial domination, of which puppet African rulers were accomplices. And, of course, they celebrated Pan-African heroes such as Ghanaian Kwame Nkrumah, Senegalese Cheikh Anta Diop, Burkinabe Thomas Sankara, and South Africa's most famous prisoner and later president Nelson Mandela.

Similar questions and issues were being debated by Arabophones in Cairo and elsewhere. In the opening of an article titled "What Is a Negro?"[4] a student from Cameroon cited former South African prime minister Peter Botha's argument that black people are inferior to white. While condemning such racist statements, the Cameroonian argues that not all African problems can be blamed on imperialism—that African ruling elites have a great share of responsibility in the persistence of problems on the continent, such as illiteracy, malnutrition, pandemics such as AIDS, malaria, cholera, and the unavailability of potable water.

In the 1992 issue of the *Voice of the League,* the newsletter of the association of Senegalese students in Egypt, Mouhamed Diouf, a Senegalese graduate of a business school, reflected on the causes of underdevelopment of the Third World:

> Why are we backward and others developed? This question preoccupies everybody, including scholars and researchers, and various answers have been provided. Some attributed underdevelopment to natural causes, others to imperialism, others to the social environment (attachment to traditions), others to religious beliefs ... others offer a racial explanation of global inequality, arguing that the white race is superior to other colored races in intelligence, entrepreneurship, and ability to innovate. To support this claim, they state that the population of developed countries is white, with the exception of Japan, whereas the majority of the Third World is colored. The truth is that none of these theories is founded.[5]

For a decade, I taught a course titled "Political Development in the Third World" at the School of International and Public Affairs (SIPA) of Columbia University. Half of our students were American, and the other half came from a hundred other countries, most of them in the Third World, to study development at SIPA. The material I used in my teaching addressed the very same controversial explanations of global patterns of inequality.[6]

At the end of his article, Diouf wrote:

> I must emphasize that national development will not come from scratch or void slogans; it makes no sense and cannot be achieved without hard work and discipline ... I would also like to draw attention to the fact that we are like all educated Senegalese. There is no difference between us. People must not think that we are less capable than anybody else or that we have no role to play in nation building. If we have proven our determination and courage outside the country by fulfilling all requirements to obtain accredited knowledge and culture; we must prove this upon our return to our country by contributing to production and nation building.[7]

Although they faced some of the same problems as students in foreign countries, the referenced returning graduates had different trajectories. Europhone graduates had greater recognition and stronger chances of getting jobs than Arabophones—at least when their countries' economies were booming in the 1960s and 1970s. It was from among Europhones that ruling parties recruited top political and administrative leaders; it was the same for managers of state-owned companies that promoted industrialization. Once co-opted into the circles of power, quite a few of these students gradually deserted their dreams for revolution. The story was a bit different for Arabophone intellectuals. After graduation, Arabophones returned home to continue their struggle for recognition. Starting in the 1990s, greater civil liberties were granted to citizens by most West African countries as a part of political liberalization, among them a great variety of societal initiatives that included those promoted by activists in the field of Islamic call.[8]

In Francophone countries such as Senegal, Arabophones produced magazines and journals, created radio and TV stations, and used both Arabic, French, and African languages to reach larger audiences, including Europhone intellectuals, and promote their ideas about Islam and the centrality of the Arabic language in Muslim societies. In Northern Nigeria, Arabophones produced Islamic literature in English and wrote in Hausa in both Latin and Arabic script to reach a wide audience. Drawing on developments in the Anglophone and Francophone countries of West Africa, this chapter will address the post-colonial Islamic public sphere—understood as "a space separate from pre-existing religious authorities and political authorities and the space of household and kins"[9]—in which Arabic and Islamic scholarship will acquire greater public visibility. I will likewise address new associational groups, for the most part led by Arabophones, which will challenge the hegemony of Western-educated intellectuals.

The Rise of an Islamic Associational Life

Central to the rise of an Islamic civil society in post-colonial West Africa has been the expansion of modern education. Compared to the colonial period, when education was the reserve of a privileged elite, the postindependence period witnessed mass literacy. African rulers rightly believed that the greatest development challenge was to provide education. In virtually all countries, education received the lion's share of state resources. In oil exporting counties such as Nigeria where the boom of the 1970s provided unexpected additional resources, the investment in modern education was the greatest. In 1976, Nigeria launched a universal primary education program. According to official sources, nine million children enrolled in primary schools—more than the population of any other single West African country at the time.[10] Although the enrollment figures might have been inflated by member states of the Nigerian federation competing for federally allocated resources, there is little doubt that enrollment ran into the millions. In addition to primary schools, the federal government and member states of the federation invested huge amounts in secondary and tertiary education. High schools, teachers' colleges, centers for vocational training, polytechnics, colleges, and universities all mushroomed beginning in the 1970s.

The expansion of education created a fertile ground for students in general and Arabophones in particular to organize and promote their agenda. Students and academic staff members created a variety of organizations that brought together people on the basis of common interest or communal belonging. Leftist organizations inspired by Marxism and/or Pan-Africanism dominated campus life in the 1970s, a period of intense intellectual decolonization. Starting in the early 1980s, these groups had to compete with new religious organizations. Unlike in the traditional churches and Muslim communities that hitherto had dominated the religious landscape of West Africa and to which many

people belonged by virtue of birth, affiliation with the new religious organizations was voluntary. Prominent among Christians were Pentecostal and
charismatic organizations from Britain and North America, which attracted
significant numbers of Christian youth.[11] In Nigeria, they were started in the
southwestern region of the country and gradually expanded to the rest of the
federation.

The Muslim youth were often attracted by new patterns of Islamic militancy. The Muslim Students' Society of Nigeria (MSS) was among the most
prominent of such movements in West Africa. Created in 1954 by Yoruba
Muslims attending Christian schools and striving to protect their Islamic identity, the MSS rose to prominence with the expansion of education. There was
no high school, college, or university in the Nigerian federation that did not
have a chapter of the Muslim Students' Society. The MSS became the platform
of Islamic activism in university campuses and beyond. Some of its members
went to train in Iran, Libya, Saudi Arabia, and other countries propagating
Islamist ideologies. They organized rallies to promote the re-Islamization of
society and to weigh in on the deliberations of constituent assemblies entrusted
with drafting the constitution of the second and subsequent republics in
Nigeria from the 1970s. They also clashed with assertive Pentecostal movements representing the interests of Christian minorities, particularly those
based in Northern Nigeria that had resented Muslim ethnoreligious and political domination. In the 1980s, the MSS often clashed with the Fellowship of
Christian Students, a major Pentecostal movement in Nigeria on university
campuses. Often, their clashes were exported to the larger communities and led
to deadly confrontations between opposing Muslim and Christian communities.[12] Graduating Muslim students created various professional associations,
some religiously based (such as the Islamic Propagation Center, the Islamic
Trust of Nigeria, and the Islamic Foundation) and others based on religion and
gender, such as the Federation of Muslim Women's Associations in Nigeria.
The proliferation of religious organizations in Nigeria was partly the consequence of prolonged military rule during which political parties were banned,
creating a vacuum that other organizations of civil society filled. In those associations, people could congregate, debate, and organize for political activism to
influence society and the state.

Graduates of Islamic and Arabic schools were also involved in creating and
promoting those societies. The largest such movement in post-colonial West
Africa is the Society for the Removal of Innovation and Reinstatement of

Tradition (known as Yan Izala),[13] which recruited millions of members and whose worldviews and modes of organization were exported to neighboring Niger, Cameroon, Chad, and Ghana. Created in 1978 by former students of Shaykh Abubakar Mahmud Gumi (1922–1992), who provided its intellectual leadership, the Yan Izala movement preached an abandonment of Sufi practices such as dhikr as well as the reform of many social customs, which, as I argued elsewhere, curtailed aspiration for emancipation of the rising Muslim middle class.[14] Inspired by neo-Salafism, the Yan Izala sent members throughout the Nigerian federation to preach. It became very popular among urban youth, by building its own mosques, taking control of other mosques, and imposing its own understanding of Islam. Before the Yan Izala started to preach in Nigeria, marriages, funerals, and naming ceremonies involved a variety of religious actors and traditional actors and used to be fairly expensive. The Yan Izala movement denounced such celebrations as un-Islamic and offered to celebrate these for free. Another major contribution of the Yan Izala was the education of women. Yan Izala denounced the widespread Hausa custom of secluding and not educating married women and instead created thousands of schools in which it offered instruction for women. Many of their ideas appealed to urban, educated people, particularly students. Religious entrepreneurs, who for the most part were products of the Islamic intellectual tradition, led Yan Izala and similar religious organizations elsewhere in West Africa. Branded Wahhabi by their opponents, these organizations contributed greatly to disseminating Salafi worldviews in West Africa, to the detriment of Sufi orders. Many of them received Islamic literature from oil-rich Muslim countries that also promoted Islamic associational life throughout the Muslim world, including in West Africa. Spurred by the oil wealth, various international Islamic NGOs opened branches in sub-Saharan Africa to deliver development aid in the name of Islamic solidarity. This offer triggered a huge demand for Islamic entrepreneurial vocations. Many an entrepreneur conceived projects and tried to sell them to benefactors from those rich countries.

In addition to individual Muslim benefactors distributing their zakat in poor African countries to please God, there were also states in search of influence that consciously used Islamic solidarity to reach that objective. Libya under the rule of Colonel Khaddafi was one such state. In addition to the World Islamic Call Society, Khaddafi created an "Islamic Legion" in 1972, composed mainly of migrants from sub-Saharan Africa, Bangladesh, and Pakistan who fought in Chad, the Sudan, Uganda, and elsewhere. The Legion attracted many impoverished young Tuareg from Niger in search of job opportunities in the context of the drought of the 1970s. The Legion was disbanded in 1987, but Khaddafi's hegemonic ambitions in Africa led several sub-Saharan African countries to break diplomatic relations with Libya based on credible evidence of his involvement in funding Islamic activism to destabilize those countries.[15] Likewise, Iran, in an attempt to export its Islamic revolution, provided financial support to Muslim activists from various African countries. The oil boom and the rivalry between various countries competing for prominence in Africa became a real blessing for Arabophones in particular. The growing appeal of Islamic activity meant a greater role for them. Many graduates from Saudi universities secured funding to establish schools, orphanages, Islamic centers, magazines, journals, and associations by which to reach larger sectors of society. In Senegal, several Islamic associations became very prominent in public life, including the Cercle d'Étude et de Recherche sur Islam et Développement (CERID), which brought together many intellectuals, including scientists and doctors. New Sunni associations began to make an even bigger impact on society—organizations such as the Jamaatou Ibadourahmane or Al-Falah, which transitioned from being union-like associations in defense of Arabophones searching for social mobility to larger social movements that appealed to all sectors of society, including Western-educated people and the urban middle class. As measured by membership of young males and females in high schools, colleges, the civil service, and the private sector, these associations have had a substantial impact on society.

From the late 1960s to the mid-1970s, I attended high school and the Université de Dakar, renamed Université Cheikh Anta Diop in 1984 to honor the Senegalese philosopher. I do not remember a single classmate wearing the headscarf at that time. But when I was a junior lecturer in the early 1990s in Senegal, no less than 20 percent of young female students were wearing the Muslim headscarf, as a result of the proselytizing of the Jamaatou Ibadourahmane and Al-Falah. The numbers increased to include members of all age groups and Islamic doctrinal persuasions. Indeed, the impact of Sunni proselytizing went beyond the small circle of adherents, and in imitation of them, many other Islamic societies and groups started to promote the wearing of the Islamic headscarf.[16] These groups developed their own strategies of communication, using various media outlets and platforms, including radio, TV, the Internet, journals, preaching tours, cassettes, Islamic summer camps, and visits to prisons. Unlike earlier generations of Islamic leaders, such as Sufi shaykhs who contented themselves with teaching and preaching without challenging the separation between religion and state, some Arabophones used their newly created organization as a forum to influence state policies and promote re-Islamization of the state.[17]

Islam and the Media Revolution

In much the same way as the liberalization of higher education created greater educational opportunities for Arabophones, the emergence of private media contributed to giving them greater public visibility. Before privatization, colonial languages and leftist discourses dominated university campuses and the public sphere in Africa, to the detriment of African languages. Notable exceptions are Kiswahili and Hausa. In their Arabic transcription, these two languages were important repositories of Islamic precolonial writings. After colonialism, they have remained widely taught in the Latin script and have been used for communication alongside English in some English-speaking countries. With one hundred million speakers at the beginning of the twenty-first century, Kiswahili is the second most spoken African language in Africa[18] after Arabic. Adopted in some East African countries such as Tanzania and Kenya as a national language, it is now taught to all pupils there. With sixty million speakers, the second most used language is now Hausa. We saw in Chapter 6 that the British promoted it in the framework of their policy of indirect rule in the north of Nigeria, and it has remained important after independence as well. But the majority of European colonies adopted French, Portuguese, or English as their main language of communication.

After decolonization, African ruling elites claimed that promoting pluralism, both linguistic and political, would undermine efforts at nation building. Given that no native group could claim a colonial language as a mother tongue and that modern schools typically offered instruction in colonial languages, the latter were enthusiastically adopted as the languages of administration. As such, they remained the main languages for communication in the official media until the liberalization of the media. I cannot overemphasize the impact of the liberalization of the media on politics and society, particularly in French-speaking countries. In Senegal, for example, the ruling party had a quasi monopoly on the mass media and controlled virtually all the information broadcast in the country. It was able to rule from independence in 1960 to the year 2000. For four decades, this party was also able to rig elections and easily get away with it.[19] When private media were established and strong enough in Senegal, they provided live coverage of the elections results not just in French, but also in African languages. The correspondents of private media with national coverage reported the results from all voting centers. Twice, they made it extremely difficult for defeated incumbents to hijack the elections. In May 2000, the broadcast results announced a resounding defeat of former president and ruling party candidate Abdou Diouf, who conceded defeat to his opponent, Abdoulaye Wade. In March 2012, broadcast results reflected that incumbent president Wade received barely one-third of the votes at the run-off for the presidential elections. He made a phone call to his opponent to congratulate him on his victory.

Yet greater than its political effect was the impact of the liberalization of the media on society and religion. In 1980, the majority of the population of West Africa did not have a command of European languages. However, most broadcast media transmitted mainly in European languages. A notable exception, of course, was the BBC, whose Hausa service had an audience of sixty million people in West Africa and whose Hausa service developed an elaborate vocabulary in Hausa to report international affairs to its audience. There was nothing similar in the Francophone world. As the liberalization of the media was unfolding, there was a sense, in French-speaking West Africa, of the necessity to rethink communication strategies and give greater attention to African languages in order to reach and educate larger sections of the population. At the time of writing this in 2015 I can say that greater progress has been achieved to decolonize communication. In Senegal, private media are now devoting much more broadcast time to African languages. Although written media are essentially in French, all news broadcast on TV and radio stations is offered in French and in Wolof, the lingua franca. People who are interviewed in French are also asked to summarize the content of their answers in Wolof for the Wolof edition of the news. Several important debates are held in Wolof. Other national languages—such as Pulaar, Sereer, Diola, and Mandinka—are also given broadcast time through radio and TV programs. Given their greater facility with national languages, Arabophones are typically sought out to help develop an adequate language to communicate economic, political, and social issues to non-Western-educated people.

One of the leading Senegalese media networks is the Walfadjri group, founded by Sidi Lamine Niasse, who belonged to a prominent Muslim clerical family of Senegal, the Niassene Tijaniyya. A graduate of a traditional Qur'anic school, he subsequently attended Al-Azhar University in Egypt. Upon his return to Senegal, he created a monthly Islamic magazine in 1984. Named *Walfadrji*, the magazine was very eschatological in its editorial content, as it was critical of aggressive secularism inspired by the French philosophy of rule. Three decades later, his enterprise has grown to become one of the leading media groups in West Africa, publishing newspapers but also running a radio and a TV station with thorough national coverage and a great variety of programs in French, Arabic, and national languages. Through Internet and linkage to various satellites, its television station WALF TV now has global reach.[20] Of its many programs, the one titled *Diine ak Jamano* (Religion and Contemporary Issues) has the largest national audience. Presented in Wolof, it brings various actors from political, economic, and cultural life to address timely issues. There is no issue of national or international importance that has not been debated on the program since it was established in the mid-1990s. Above all, the program has been centered on the discussion of the ethics of good governance and consequently has contributed considerably to giving greater political awareness to the population, including those without knowledge of European languages. Sidi Lamine Niasse and the WALF group are one of the many important actors of civil society to have established themselves in the Senegalese public sphere.

Several other Islamic groups in Senegal have created various forums to impact public life. One neo-Sufi group, the Mustarshidin movement[21] led by a Senegalese shaykh initially trained in Arabic, was a serious threat to the rule of former president Abdou Diouf in the 1990s. It has recently shifted its focus to issues of development and education. In addition to supporting various development activities at the grassroots level, the Mustarshidin movement organizes a "Ramadan University" annually. Inspired by similar programs organized by political parties to educate their members and develop strategies of recruiting and retaining members, the "Ramadan University" of the Mustarshidin consists of inviting prominent national scholars, often university professors, to share their knowledge with the larger public. Attended by thousands of people, the lectures are held throughout the fasting month of Ramadan. They bring together a wide national audience as well as a variety of international personalities based in Dakar, such as Islamic NGOs, representatives of political parties, students, and others. The Ramadan lectures are very well organized. They are held in Wolof and simultaneously translated into French, English, and Arabic for a large and diverse audience. They are also broadcast via satellite to major cities, where crowds gather in public places to watch the lectures in tents equipped with large and sophisticated screens. A remarkable feat of the Ramadan lectures has been to bridge the gap between the academic and wider public audiences. Academics who have tended to be confined to their university ivory towers and have typically lectured exclusively in the French language have, through the Ramadan lectures, taken up the challenge of explaining complex notions in Wolof to larger audiences.

Several religious groups have created their own radio and TV stations, which offer a large variety of religious education programming. Because these groups are above all committed to spreading their own worldviews, they are making a major contribution to the dissemination of writings in Arabic and Ajami. For example, the two Senegalese TV stations owned by the Murids (Lamp Fall and Touba TV) devote significant broadcasting time to the works of Ahmadu Bamba. Some Murid NGOs, such as Matlaboul Fawzayn, have undertaken the translation of the writings of Ahmadu Bamba's prolific intellectual production into European languages, most notably French. Some Murid TV stations are broadcasting these writings via the Internet to the national and international diasporic audiences.

Another program that has created a particularly strong awareness of this intellectual tradition is called *Taalifu mag gni* (Writings of the Ancients). Broadcasts devote particular attention to religious songs (*qasa'id*) written by Senegalese Sufi shaykhs, the singing of which is believed to bless reciters. These songs provide us with research material for the study of the worldviews of the Muslim people of West Africa. They can help document aspects of the biographies of the authors as well as the context in which those biographies are produced.

The emergence of new media has provided fertile ground for the diversification of the musical offerings. Several new musical repertoires are being introduced by new bands created by urban youth. In Muslim areas such as Senegal and Northern Nigeria, Islamic songs in Arabic and African languages such as Hausa and Wolof are now in the majority. Not long ago, with the notable exception of some Qadiri groups that beat drums to accompany the singing of religious songs during their religious festivals, the use of musical instruments was atypical in Islamic religious singing in West Africa. Sacred music and profane music were considered separate repertoires. Muslims would listen to the singing of religious songs in religious functions and to profane songs at home or in nightclubs. The two were not mixed, and the singing of religious songs was rarely accompanied by the use of musical instruments. Then some popular stars such as Youssou Ndour, Cheikh Lo, and Omar Pène occasionally devoted a song or an album to the praise of religious saints, using modern musical instruments, but their music was essentially considered "profane." Now, many musical bands using different genres from *rapp* to *mbalax* and all types of musical instruments are singing poems written by African Sufi shaykhs, praising the Prophet or other saints in Arabic and African languages.[22] And in this way they are disseminating knowledge of the Islamic archive. Through innovation in the use of musical instruments, these bands are reshaping both the musical and religious landscapes and blurring the boundaries between sacred and profane music. The creation of new TV channels seems to have increased the demand for such songs, and groups have been created in response. But it is really the diversification of the sources of supply for the new information technologies that increased demand and democratized access to sacred music. Before China started to tap into the African market, electronics were supplied mostly from Europe and thus were fairly expensive, partly because of the high cost of labor in those industrialized countries. As a result, only the upper classes had access to TV, satellite channels, and other electronic gadgets. Now, these items become relatively affordable.

When I started to teach in Senegal as a lecturer in 1992, a computer with 20 megabytes of storage cost almost US $2,000, and most university instructors did not have computer equipment of their own. Twenty years later, a brand new desktop computer with a 500-gigabyte hard drive costs less than US $200, and thus is available even to the lower middle classes. In 1997, a cell phone cost US $1,000, and service providers charged US $300 for the subscription fee alone for a network restricted to major cities. Fifteen years later, many providers were awarded licenses. With US $20, one can now purchase a good entry-level Samsung cell phone and for $3 can get a SIM card with a pay-as-you-go subscription. Most cell phone service providers now have national coverage. In 1992, the digital divide was striking between the North and the South, and less than 1 percent of the African continent had access to the Internet. Twenty years later, the digital divide has been bridged, and local service providers make wireless Internet connection for computers and cell phones affordable even to the working class. Satellite dishes and receivers, along with MP4 drives, have become accessible and provide cheap access to hundreds of TV channels from any West African country. Despite the fact that power outages are frequent and the irregular supply of electricity makes the operation of these gadgets challenging, there is no question that the development and democratization of the new technologies of information and communication have empowered, in particular, religious entrepreneurs striving to propagate religion. Most religious celebrations in Senegal (mainly Sufi festivals) are disseminated in real time through various media to a national and world audience. The new media have made it possible for traditional religious communities to give greater public visibility to their activities.

The emergence of a modern Islamic public sphere has had two effects on Arabophones. On the one hand, it bridged the gap between some of them and Europhone intellectuals. Large segments of the membership of Islamic organizations created or led by Arabophones are Western educated now. This provided some Arabophones with great social recognition. As a result, they have become more moderate. Other Arabophones have remained intransigent in their demand for de-Westernization. These individuals have built alliances with like-minded groups to question secularism in public debates and in their writings, and, in due course, to take up arms against the state.

Challenging Secularism

When they became independent, virtually all West African countries adopted secularism (meaning here the separation of religion and state) as a philosophy of government. Their constitutions state that sovereignty essentially belongs to the people who exercise it through its representatives or through referendum. Even Mauritania, the only West African country that claimed the label of Islamic republic, did so.[23] Copied from the constitution of the former colonial powers and written for the most part by European experts in constitutional law, the post-colonial West African constitutions did not always reflect the fact that Islamic law in fact governed many aspects of the lives of Muslims. European colonial masters reformed Islamic criminal law by abolishing harsh bodily punishment such as amputation of hands or stoning, which colonial rulers deemed inhumane, but they never sought to abolish Islamic law completely. In matters related to marriage, divorce, inheritance, and child custody, Muslim populations remained governed by Maliki jurisprudence during colonial rule. At the time of independence, West African countries adopted a unified penal code, which applies to all citizens, irrespective of their religion. Even in Northern Nigeria, one of the most deeply Islamized societies in the world, the Muslim elites who negotiated decolonization agreements with the colonial state and other non-Muslim communities took no issue with the adoption of a unified criminal code inspired by European law. Maliki law continued to regulate matters pertaining to personal status. From the second decade following independence onward, West African ruling elites have been committed to modernizing their countries and promoting greater gender justice, and they have initiated further reforms of family law. Not without resistance, new codes were adopted restricting polygamy,[24] prohibiting unilateral repudiation, or creating various provisions such as alimony to correct the strong patriarchal bias of Maliki family law. Like other Muslim societies in Asia and North Africa, West Africa seemed to be progressing toward modernization. Then Islamist movements emerged all of a sudden in the Muslim world to challenge the notion of separation between religion and state. The failure of the post-colonial development project and the resounding defeats of the Arab armies in their war against Israel sounded the death knell of post-colonial secular ideologies in the Muslim world. In this context, the Iranian Revolution of 1979 seemed to bring the promise that self-reliance on Islam would provide an alternative to Western-inspired ideologies such as secularism, nationalism, and socialism, none of which fulfilled their promise to bring prosperity to countries espousing them.[25]

There was considerable consensus among Muslim militant groups worldwide that Islamic law should govern all aspects of the life of Muslims. "Islam only" became the slogan of such groups as the Islamic Salvation Front in Algeria, the then Movement of the Islamic Tendency in Tunisia, the Muslim Brothers in the Sudan, the Muslim Brothers in Nigeria,[26] and the Jamaat Islami in the Indian subcontinent.[27] In their writings, prominent exponents of Islamist thought such as Ayatollah Khomeini,[28] Sayyid Qutb,[29] and Abu 'l A'la Maududi[30] challenged the notion rooted in post-colonial Western-inspired constitutions that sovereignty belongs to anyone other than the Almighty God. According to them, investing sovereignty in the people is tantamount to returning to the *Jahiliyya*[31]—a term used in Islamic theology to describe pre-Islamic Arabian society that was assumed to have erred in ignorance until the Prophet Muhammad brought them the knowledge that there is only one God and that he, Muhammad, is his messenger.[32] Islamists produced pamphlets to challenge the notion of popular sovereignty enshrined in constitutions of West African countries. This debate is abundantly documented in Islamist literature, including *Le Musulman*, a journal published by the Senegalese Sunni movement Jamaatou Ibadourahmane, *Études islamiques* by Cheikh Touré, and the magazine *Walfadjri* in the early 1980s. In Nigeria, the largest country in the world to have almost equal populations of Christians and Muslims,[33] Islamists were even more vocal in their call for Shari'a. When I conducted fieldwork in Nigeria between 1985 and 1991, I witnessed the agitation in northern university campuses over the call for Shari'a. Christians and some Muslims favored separation between religion and state. Islamists, in contrast, challenged that notion. The Muslim Students' Society (MSS) provided leadership in the fight for Shari'a. Starting in the late 1970s, the MSS organized rallies to influence the deliberations of the constituent assemblies for the second, third, and fourth Nigerian republics, demanding a greater recognition of the Shari'a in the Nigerian Federal Constitution, a premise that their opponents refuted on the grounds that it violated the principle of neutrality. Muslim activists, in contrast, disagreed that what was claimed to be secular was indeed neutral. A telling illustration is the vignette opening this chapter in which Aliyu Dawuda, then a young lecturer at Bayero University Kano rejected secularism. Dawuda further argued during his lecture that:

> The principle of secularism, wherever it is practiced, is nothing short of the practicalisation of the Biblical statement which says: "Give unto Caesar what is Caesar's and unto God what is God's"; this is contained in the Bible— Matthew, 22:21 and Mark, 12:17. Therefore, right from the onset, secularism is not religiously neutral, it is a Christian concept, a Biblical dogma, reflecting the parochial nature of the Christian worldview. The principle and practice of secularism, in other words, is Islamically obnoxious, seriously revolting, and totally unacceptable because it is fundamentally based on what our Creator and Lord, Allah (may he be glorified) considers as the greatest crime which He never forgives once a person dies committing it—that is *shirk*. For there is absolutely no doubt about the fact that *shirk* is clearly involved in the statement which says: "Give unto Caesar what is Caesar's and unto God what is God's," because the Authority, Power, Sovereignty of Allah, may he be glorified, have been clearly dichotomised, one half is given to some nonentity called Caesar and the remaining half is left to Allah, may he be glorified. Therefore, even if a so-called secular country does not observe Saturday, which is a Jewish day of rest and religious services in a week, and Sunday, a Christian day of rest and church services in a week, both of which the so-called secular Nigeria religiously and fanatically observes, the fact that secularism itself as a concept is fundamentally based on a Christian dogma, a Christian worldview, as it is clearly enshrined in their Bible, is a clear testimony to the fact that a secular state wherever it is, is in fact, a Christian state, because it is governed by the principles and practices of a Biblical statement: "Give unto Caesar what is Caesar's and unto God what is God's" (Matthew 22:21 and Mark 12:17).[34]

In Francophone African countries, Islamists challenged the prevailing type of secularism, largely inspired by the French model of hostile separation between religion and state. They took issue with the ban on places of worship on university campuses, as is the case in public schools in France. They also took issue with the fact that the Christian holidays of Christmas and Easter received the lion's share of school-day vacations in a predominantly Muslim country. In response to the assertive Islamist movements, West African states are now rethinking their orientation toward religion in the sense of making compromises to advocates of Islamization. One important concession was to upgrade the administrative importance of religious issues from a directorate based in the ministry of the interior (as is the case in secular France and Turkey) to a cabinet-level position. Mauritania was the first to do so in 2007.[35] It was followed in 2010 by Niger, Senegal, and Mali, which have all created a ministry of religious affairs. They thus sent a strong signal that they take religion very seriously. In Senegal, the study of religion was introduced for the first time in public schools in 2007. Then public Qur'anic schools were created and affiliated with the ministry of education. In 2013, the Senegalese government established a baccalauréat entirely in Arabic that was recognized by the state and accredited by the ministry of higher learning. This enabled Arabophones to pursue higher education in Senegalese universities, just as graduates from schools offering instruction in French had long been able to do. This move was tantamount to giving Arabic the status of an official language of instruction, a move that is unprecedented not just in Senegal but also in other Francophone countries.

The ban on having places of worship in public institutions of education—a practice copied from the French system—is now being lifted. Starting with the Université Cheikh Anta Diop de Dakar in the 1980s, university communities in Senegal have built their own mosques, where the faithful congregate and pray. Now the religious clerisy, and Arabophones in particular, are represented in the Senegalese parliament, where they have lobbied for a greater recognition of Islamic religion. One such parliamentarian, named Imam Mbaye Niang, successfully sponsored a bill to stop all debates in parliament early on Friday afternoons so that Muslims can attend the Friday congregational prayer. In recent years, advocates of Islamization have gone a step further and succeeded in many countries with imposing their worldviews through effective implementation of harsh aspects of Islamic criminal law that hitherto were banned in most countries.

Chapter 9

Arabophones Triumphant

Timbuktu under Islamic Rule

Islamism is not a specter haunting West Africa.
—*William Miles*[1]

W HILE I WAS a doctoral student in France between 1985 and 1991, I
visited Northern Nigeria every year to conduct fieldwork. At the time,
there was great intra- and interreligious polarization in the area. Sufi groups
and their opponents, the Yan Izala, engaged in vigorous controversy about what
beliefs or practices conformed to Islamic orthodoxy. Sometimes it was a civil
debate, but at others it was confrontational. At that time, the Muslim group
perceived as the most radical was called the Brothers, or Shiites. Inspired by the
Iranian Revolution, the Brothers championed the idea of the Islamic state. The
most radical among the Brothers preached against attending public schools
and working for the government. But none of these groups challenged the state
monopoly on violence.

Nigeria was also profoundly divided over issues such as the country's full
membership in the Organization of the Islamic Conference[2] and the establishment of a federal Shari'a court of appeals.[3] Interreligious riots pitted Christians
against Muslims and sometimes resulted in a heavy death toll and the destruction of property. Still, no religious group had an army or sought to acquire any
military capability whatsoever.

None of those working on the political sociology of Islam in West Africa
seriously believed that Islamic activists had the power to effectively challenge
the political authority of secular states in West Africa. As exemplified by the
outcome of the insurgency rebellion led by the charismatic teacher Maitatsine
in Kano in 1980, law enforcement agencies have promptly suppressed religious
insurgency and restored order. Religious militants never acquired any substantial

military capabilities to exercise territorial control. Professor William Miles, a leading expert on West African politics, argued the following in the conclusion of a collective volume titled *Political Islam in West Africa,* published in 2007

> Islamism is not a specter haunting West Africa. Despite the politicization of Islam in [Senegal, Mali, Niger, Nigeria, Gambia, and Mauritania] the likelihood of a national theocratic state arising in any of them is virtually nil. Nor are national integrity and identity existentially endangered by Islamist movements that have arisen. Not even in Mali, where Tuareg secessionism has been most violent, is secessionist splintering a likely imminent outcome.[4]

Back in 2007, Professor Miles shared this conviction with many authors, including myself.[5] When last I visited Nigeria in 2011, things had changed dramatically. In the name of religion, new armed groups have been challenging state monopoly on the exercise of violence in Nigeria and other parts of West Africa. I will argue that two interconnected developments explain the new religiopolitical dispensation. The first is the appeal of Islamist ideology, and the second is the militarization and globalization of jihadi groups.

In Chapter 8, I discussed Islamic associational life in the post-colonial period. A study conducted by the Pew Forum on Religion and Public Life in 2010 attempted to capture the transformation of Islamic militancy with quantitative data. Its title, "Tolerance and Tension,"[6] summarizes its main paradoxical findings: a majority of Africans are simultaneously seeking to make their religion central to the organization of state and society and are also committed to pluralism and democracy.[7] With four to five hundred million adherents each, Christianity and Islam constitute two dominant religions on the African continent as a whole.[8] Predominant in the northern half of the continent is Islam, whose expansion stops just north of the equator. The southern half of the continent is predominantly Christian. It was during the twentieth century that both religions experienced their fastest growth. From 11 million in 1900 to 230 million in 2010, Islam multiplied twentyfold in sub-Saharan Africa. The expansion of Christianity was even more spectacular. From about 7 million in 1900, the number of Christians increased seventyfold to 470 million by 2010.[9] Following are the findings most relevant for my analysis.

An overwhelming majority of Muslims (and Christians) believe that religion is very important in their lives and should serve as a basis for making civil laws. More specifically, the survey asked this question of Muslims: "Do you favor making Shari'a or Islamic law the official law of the land?" Overall, substantial majorities of Muslims in the overwhelming majority of sub-Saharan countries support a legislation based on Shari'a.[10] One can of course argue that Shari'a is not new and some aspects of it (like family law) have inspired legislation in these countries since their Islamization, through colonialism to the post-colonial period. But Shari'a was reformed and modernized, and modern conceptions of justice have inspired the organization of criminal law and have led to bodily punishments being banned. Many faithful Muslims seem increasingly to be challenging this ban, which was previously taken for granted.

The report also found some endorsement for the use of violence against civilians in defense of religion as well as support for extremist groups such as Al-Qaida.[11] This leads to the second development explaining the transformation of Islamic militancy in West Africa—the militarization of Islamist radicals that goes back to the Afghan jihad.[12] The anti-Soviet coalition, of which the United States, Pakistan, and Saudi Arabia were prominent members, encouraged a massive migration of militants to Afghanistan in the 1980s. They provided sophisticated military training as well as billions of dollars worth of weapons to these jihadi groups to fight against the Soviet Union. Al-Qaida was created by Osama Bin Laden in this context to drive the Soviets out of Afghanistan. After the defeat of the Soviet Union, these veterans, often called Arab Afghans, returned home and turned against the governments of their home countries and Western allies. They spread in South and western Asia, North Africa and later in West Africa, where they linked up with some advocates of the Islamization of the state. In the following sections, I will illustrate the militarization of Islamic militancy in Nigeria and Mali; there, some Islamist groups built a large coalition of supporters and procured the logistics to successfully challenge the state monopoly of violence and control large tracts of land in West Africa. Not all actors involved in these insurgencies are Arabophones, and not all of them have religious motivations. Yet Arabophones are an important component of the coalition actors, and the challenge to Western epistemological hegemony in the name of Islam and the preeminence of Arabic language is a main item on their agenda.

The Reenactment of Islamic Criminal Law in Nigeria

The consensus on a unified penal code based on common law, a cornerstone of legal modernization, is being successfully challenged in many parts of West Africa. The first warning sign occurred in Nigeria at the turn of the twentieth century. In 1999, Olusegun Obasanjo, a Yoruba Pentecostal, won the presidential election. This was an event of major political importance in a country in which virtually all heads of state in the preceding three decades were Muslims from the North. During the gubernatorial elections held the same year, Sani Yerima was elected governor of the northern state of Zamfara. Right after his election, Yerima reinstated Islamic criminal law as per his preelection commitment and ordered the first amputation of the hand of a man accused of theft.[13] This move was supported by large segments of the Muslim population in Northern Nigeria, partly because of the deep politicization of ethnoreligious schisms. In the following months, popular pressure forced eleven northern states of the Nigerian federation to reintroduce some forms of Shari'a in their criminal legislation.

The country was divided between three schools of thought on this issue. A first group believed that this was a violation of Section 10 of the Nigerian constitution, which states that the "Government of the Federation or of a State shall not adopt any religion as a State religion." A second group, of Muslim advocates of Shari'a law, invoked Section 38 of the same constitution, which states that "Every person shall be entitled to freedom of thought, conscience and religion . . . and freedom to manifest, propagate his religion or belief in worship, teaching, practice and observance."[14] Enthusiastic advocates of Islamic criminal law further argued that the reenactment would apply only to Muslims and thus did not violate Section 10 of the constitution.[15] A third group of Muslims viewed the implementation of Shari'a favorably, convinced that it would promote justice, but expressed disagreement with the literal interpretation, which, they held, flouted the spirit of the Shari'a and targeted vulnerable groups.

Notable among those who disagree is Sanusi Lamido Sanusi, the current emir of Kano, who served as governor of the Nigerian Central Bank until 2013. An economist by training, Sanusi studied the Shari'a at the International University of Africa in Khartum, Sudan. A prominent political commentator and public intellectual, Sanusi delivered lectures and published several op ed pieces to denounce the hijacking of the Shari'a by governors of predominantly Muslim northern states of the Nigerian federation for self-seeking political agendas. Sanusi himself believes that "religion cannot be separated from political life" and that "Muslims should be governed by the law of Allah as revealed to the Prophet."[16] But he took issue with the ways in which powerless groups (chiefly the poor and women) were punished while powerful people were committing crimes of similar or greater magnitude and getting away with them. Unlike Muslims who praised Governor Sani Yerima for ordering the amputation of Buba Jangebe's hand in Zamfara in 1999 for stealing a cow, Sanusi reminded people that according to the spirit of Shari'a, amputation is justified if the motive for stealing is greed, not if it is deprivation.[17] He further reminded people that 'Umar b. al-Khattab, the second caliph of the Prophet Muhammad, had suspended all amputations during a year of starvation, a position that inspired deliberations among Muslim jurists of later generations when dealing with theft. According to Sanusi, the numbers of beggars in the street signals the level of economic deprivation in late twentieth-century Northern Nigeria. He concludes that the governor of Zamfara would truly have followed the spirit of Shari'a had he followed the example of Caliph 'Umar and suspended amputations pending alleviation of widespread poverty.

In the same spirit, Sanusi deplores that corruption among government officials is not even considered an offense in Shari'a states. He also questions the fact that women have been singled out and convicted for the crime of fornication, completely letting men off the hook for their complicity. He refutes that pregnancy, which so far had been the basis for convicting most women, is an irrefutable proof of fornication; after all, rape can also lead to pregnancy. Invoking the authority of Maliki jurists, he also reminded people that pregnancy is not unequivocal evidence of intercourse, since "a woman can be[come] pregnant without coitus if a man's sperm goes through her vagina either by her own design or those of another party.[18] Sanusi's plea echoed the voices of poor, convicted women who complain that Shari'a penal codes target them because they are poor. Daughters of rich parents have so far not been convicted for pregnancy, because their parents fly them out of the country to have an abortion, then return them safely home.[19]

President Obasanjo personally disapproved of the reinstatement of Islamic criminal law, but the federal government abstained from any interference in the affairs of northern Shari'a states. Human rights activists and other international actors lobbied successfully to stop the implementation of the bodily punishments. As a result, although Islamic criminal law is still in place in the twelve northern states, and although Islamic courts have handed down dozens of sentences, a total of three amputations have been implemented and none since 2001.[20]

As the Shari'a agitation was dissipating among the masses in Nigeria, a much more radical group was emerging during the first decade of the twenty-first century. The group is known by the name "Boko Haram," given to it by its opponents in reference to its hostility toward the attendance of government schools. Tracing the etymology of *boko* to the English word *book*, much academic analysis and press coverage has rendered the expression "boko haram" as

"Western education in sinful." In an article published in January 2013, Paul Newman established that *boko* is an indigenous Hausa word meaning deceitful and that it existed long before colonialism.[21] The etymological resemblance between *boko* and *book* is purely coincidental. Rather, the expression should be translated "deceitful knowledge is sinful."[22] Members of the group call themselves either "movement of followers of Sunna for preaching and jihad" (*Jama'at ahl al-Sunna li al-da'wa wa al-jihad*), or "followers of the Sunna who unite upon it in the footsteps of the pious forefathers" (*ahl al-sunna wa'l-jama'a 'ala minhaj al-salaf*), or more simply Yusufiyya.

More than any other "religious" group in West Africa, the Boko Haram has instilled fear and security concerns. Little ethnographic research has been conducted on the group, and scholars based in Nigeria have abstained from publishing or signing with their own name scholarly research on Boko Haram. Although it has been around for more than a decade (2003–2015), it is only in the period between 2012 and 2015 that some literature highlighting the origins, transformations, and objectives of the group has begun to emerge.[23] The origins and doctrinal views of the groups are still debated, and the group is changing constantly, making it very challenging for analysts to offer a coherent account of the group from the beginning to the present day.

Various hypotheses linking Boko Haram to preexisting radical groups in Nigeria, North Africa, and Saudi Arabia have been suggested. As one of its names—Yusufiyya—suggests, Mohamed Yusuf (1970–2009) was instrumental in organizing the group, in the first decade of the twenty-first century. At the time of his execution by the police in 2009, Yusuf lived in Maiduguri in northeastern Nigeria and had four wives and twelve children,[24] a progeny not unusual for a middle-aged Muslim leader in Northern Nigeria. Yusuf's father is believed to have gone to Nigeria from Niger to join the following of Maitatsine[25] who led a millenarian revolt of Qur'anic students in Kano. Yusuf's father was among the victims of the riots of 1980. Could that have prompted Yusuf's aversion to Western education? Possibly. But Yusuf was more learned than the typical student of Qur'anic schools, and he was not against the use of modern technology. Yusuf was a Qur'anic student in Yobe state, but unlike the typical rural Qur'anic student, he did pursue further studies, including schooling in Saudi Arabia, but also among Ahl al-Sunna scholars such as Ja'far Mahmoud Adam.

Yuusuf is also believed to have been affiliated at some point with the pro-Shiite movement of the Brothers under the leadership of Ibrahim El Zakzaky, the Brothers being a group that argued against working for the Nigerian government on the grounds that it was not Islamic. When Abubakar Mujahid, the lieutenant of El Zakzaky, broke away to create the Kano-based Jamaatul Tajdidi Islam (JTI) in the 1990s, Muhammad Yusuf is said to have followed him. Later in the 1990s, he (Yusuf) was appointed the emir (leader) of the JTI group for Borno state.

In the most recent and well-researched articles on the group, there is a substantial consensus that most Boko Haram members, including Muhammad Yusuf himself, have been affiliated with Ahlus Sunna, an organization created by graduates of the University of Madina (Arabophones) and committed to spreading Wahhabi views in Nigeria.[26] Inspired by Shaykh Mahmud Gumi and the Yan Izala movement, it has been very active in reforming Islam in Northern Nigeria. It commands strong support among the urban middle class of Northern Nigeria, particularly in major cities. In Maiduguri, Borno state, which used to be a center of traditional Islamic education dominated by Sufi orders, the group won the hearts and minds of substantial segments of the youth. During the Shari'a agitation, Ahlus Sunna members, including Muhammad Yusuf himself between 1999 and 2002, called for the official implementation of Shari'a.[27] But since 2003, some members of the group have dismissed the Western-inspired philosophy of rule as *taghut*,[28] a term that occurs in the Qur'an to describe ungodliness.

These members of the group withdrew from the mainstream Salafi of the Alhaji Ndimi mosque community of which Yusuf was still a member. Referred to as the "Taliban of Nigeria" or *muhajirun* (those who performed the *hijra*), they left Maiduguri to settle not far from Kanama, Yobe state, close to the border with Niger, in a place they called Afghanistan. Some of them migrated with their families, with the goal of creating their own virtuous communities away from a world they viewed as corrupt. But according to that account, at that point they had no plan to engage in military confrontation. In late 2003 / early 2004, following altercations with the police, muhajirun are said to have attacked police barracks and stolen weapons and munitions in Damaturu, Yobe state. The police killed most of them, but the remaining members returned to Maiduguri to join Yusuf's following. An intellectual source of influence on these radicals, according to another account, were recordings of preaching by a London-based radical preacher named Shaykh Abdullah al-Faisal, originally Trevor William Forrest. Born in 1964 in St. James, Jamaica, he emigrated to the UK in 1981, when he was about 17, and traveled to Saudi Arabia, where he spent about eight years before earning a degree and converting to Islam. He returned to the UK in 1989 and preached radical and intolerant views against non-Muslims. At that time, the muhajirun were in search of a learned scholar to lead them, and they convinced Yusuf, who at that point was moderate and willing to work within the framework of Nigerian laws, to articulate increasingly radical views toward government and Western education.[29]

According to another account,[30] Yusuf's views on education were influenced by the work of a Wahhabi scholar named Bakr b. 'Abdullah b. Abi Zayd (d. 2008), a prolific writer. Zayd wrote dozens of treatises and held prominent positions in academic, judicial, and religious institutions in Saudi Arabia. In a lecture given by Yusuf a year before his death, he quotes extensively from a book by Zayd titled *al-madaris al-'alamiyya al-ajnabiyya al-isti'mariyya wa makhatiruha* (Global, Foreign, and Colonial Schools: Their History and Danger). The main idea is that "European colonialists introduced modern secular education into Islamic societies as an elaborately planned and camouflaged conspiracy to maintain colonialist hegemony over Muslim societies. Their aim was to corrupt the pure Islamic morals with Western liberal norms, especially to replace proper gender roles with permissive sexual mores, and to undermine solid Islamic individual and communal identities built on Salafi notions of piety and righteousness. Abu Zayd also claims that the colonialist conspiracy embedded in modern secular education is more pernicious in perpetuating Western hegemony than outright military conquest and political domination. He maintains that both these are apparent and can be resisted accordingly whereas the educational conspiracy is not so apparent, and hence it is imperative for Muslim religious leaders to wage unrelenting opposition to modern secular education by unmasking the real but hidden colonialist agenda.[31]

According to a third account offered by a moderate Ahl al-Sunna opponent named Muhammed Auwal Albani Zaria, Yusuf was introduced to Algerian jihadis, who provided him and his followers with military and ideological training. He heard sermons by Algerian jihadis fighting against the Algerian government after the democratic process was derailed in the early 1990s. More specifically, Algerian jihadis issued a fatwa prohibiting militants from working for the government or attending government-sponsored schools. Yusuf sought to promote the same views in Nigeria.[32] Thus, the jihad was part of Yusuf's agenda earlier than 2009.

Another hypothesis presented by Brigaglia is that the split between Yusuf and more moderate Salafis in Nigeria mirrors a similar one within Salafism in Saudi Arabia and its global ramifications. Two main schools of thought can be distinguished among Saudi Salafism. The spokesperson of a legitimist trend supported by the regime is Shaykh Rabi' b. Hadi al-Madkhali (b. 1931). There is also a rejectionist branch, which is extremely critical of the Saudi regime. Osama Bin Laden was of course one of the most famous of such rejectionists. But before Bin Laden's rise to prominence, other Wahhabi scholars also expressed criticism against the Saudi regime. One of them is Muhammad Surur Zayn al-'Abidin (b. 1938 in Syria),[33] who settled in Saudi Arabia in 1965 when the kingdom opened its universities to Muslim Brothers. Surur became a very influential teacher but was expelled from the kingdom in 1974 due to his antiestablishment views. Surur then lived in Kuwait for a few years before settling in Birmingham (United Kingdom) until 2004. Since then, he has lived in Jordan. During his time in Britain, Surur created an NGO named Al-Muntada Trust in London to do development work in health and education. But Al-Muntada was also involved in preaching radical Salafi ideas and training jihadis. In the years since September 11, 2001, the Al-Muntada Trust has been charged for recruiting and training jihadis, and in 2004, its offices in Nigeria, Kenya, Chad, and Mozambique were shut down.[34] The muhajirun who attacked the police in northeastern Nigeria on New Year's Eve 2004 might have been trained in Al-Muntada camps. According to such a reading, police repression might have contributed to the radicalization of the group, but the jihad was clearly part of the agenda of the most extremist Salafis who gravitated around the Alhaji Ndimi Mosque. In any case, Yusuf and his followers split from other Ahlus Sunna in late 2003 and in early 2004 settled in the Markas neighborhood of Railway Coast in Maiduguri and built their own mosque, named Masjid Ibn Taymiyyah.

Between 2003 and 2009, people associated with muhajirun or Boko Haram killed several Muslim scholars who condemned extremist views on Western education, including Malam Ja'far Adam.[35] Apart from this, not much was heard from the group, but Yusuf's following continued to grow over the years. Some prominent people, including politicians and businesspeople, appeared to have been supporting the group. Yusuf continued to preach adamantly against the Nigerian federal government and Western education, but there is no evidence that he intended to engage in military jihad against the state.

In 2009, Yusuf and his followers led a much larger insurgency. Echoing community concerns about the group, law enforcement agencies in Borno began imposing restrictions on its preaching. This soured relations between group members and the Maiduguri police. One day in 2009, group members who were riding motorcycles bareheaded refused to abide by the police injunction to wear motorcycle helmets, leading to a confrontation in which seventeen of Yusuf's disciples were wounded. Yusuf wrote a letter of warning to officials that he would retaliate if attacked again. In July 2009, Yusuf claimed that the police had killed forty of his disciples. He apparently instructed his disciples to acquire weapons and get ready for jihad. In several parts of northeastern Nigeria, group members started to confront police forces. The police and federal army intervened to restore order. More than one thousand people were killed in Maiduguri, Damaturu, Potiskum, and Bauci. Many were Boko Haram members, including Yusuf himself, who was killed while in police custody. The majority of the people were killed after the end of the insurgency, and the death toll also included many nonmembers. A video obtained by Al Jazeera showed handicapped Muslims walking on crutches—in short, people who were unlikely to have been involved in the riots—arrested by army officers and asked to lie on the floor, then executed in cold blood by those officers.[36] The disproportionate and indiscriminate use of force by law enforcement agencies contributed to the radicalization of the insurgency and to creating growing sympathy for the group, whose members vowed revenge.

By 2010, people identified as Boko Haram were conducting military operations of a kind that heretofore no religious group had been capable of perpetrating, not just in Nigeria but in the whole of West Africa, in the fifty years since independence. In 2013, the group became the focus of worldwide media attention and the most serious security concern in West Africa. A large gamut of operations were attributed to Boko Haram, including bank holdups; attacking army barracks; stealing weapons and ammunition; taking and ransoming hostages for money, including more than two hundred schoolgirls in 2014; and targeting for violence churches and mosques, government buildings, and international organizations such as the UN. In July 2011, one suicide bomber drove and exploded a loaded car into the headquarters of the UN in Abuja, causing great property destruction and a heavy death toll.[37] Whereas suicide bombing was hitherto unknown in Nigeria, it has now become commonplace. It is not clear whether all of these acts attributed to Boko Haram were indeed conducted by adherents of the movement or even ideologically motivated. Looters and other criminals often take advantage of the confusion and insecurity created by insurgency to steal and settle old scores with their foes. Nor do we know that there is a chain of command that plans the acts claimed by or attributed to Boko Haram members. But this much we do know:

in the summer of 2013, Boko Haram had acquired great fighting experience and sophisticated weapons; the funding is believed to come from rich people in Nigeria, holdups of banks, and foreign sources. Now the group has a huge arsenal—some of which was manufactured by university graduates of sciences trained in the manufacture of explosives and other detonative devices[38]—thousands of fighters, including potential suicide bombers, and dozens of cars. When the rebellion of 2009 broke out, the then Nigerian head of state was Umar Musa Yar'Adua (1951–2010); he was a Muslim, as was the army commander, Salisu Maina, who led the counter insurgency to suppress the rebellion. However, Yar'Adua died before completing his term and was replaced by his vice president, Goodluck Jonathan, a Christian.

The heavy-handedness of the operation and religious polarization contributed to fuel animosity between insurgents and the Nigerian government. To solve this huge security issue, the Nigerian federal government under Goodluck Jonathan has put all options on the table. Through the mediation of Muslim notables, it has sought to negotiate with the purported leader of the group, Abubakar Shekau. But instead of this strategy resulting in improvement, Boko Haram has become more and more daring in its attacks. On May 14, 2013, President Goodluck Jonathan had to declare a state of emergency in Borno, Yobe, and Adamawa states, large parts of which were controlled by Boko Haram members[39] for six months. In August 2013, Lt. Col. Musa Sagir, the spokesperson of the Joint Task Force Operation Restore Order, reported that Abubakar Shekau was wounded in a confrontation between the army and Boko Haram fighters on June 30, 2013, and died between July 25th and August 3rd in neighboring Cameroon, where he had been transferred to receive treatment.[40] But Boko Haram denied this claim. In December 2013, President Jonathan extended the state of emergency, which is still in effect. In March 2015, former Nigerian military head of state Muhammadu Buhari defeated Goodluck Jonathan in the presidential elections largely because of the inability of Jonathan to remedy the prevailing insecurity. That same month, Boko Haram, which pledged its support to Abu Bakr al-Baghdadi, the leader of ISIS, in 2014, renamed itself Islamic State in West Africa. Since January 2015, a coalition of military forces of five countries (Chad, Cameroon, Nigeria, Niger, and Benin) has been conducting a counterinsurgency but has still not defeated Boko Haram.

Unlike Islamist groups that fought the state in the past, Boko Haram draws support not just from Nigeria—where there is allegation of complicity between

Boko Haram fighters and the Nigerian law enforcement agencies—but, since 2011, also from other insurgent groups, and this leads me to discuss the jihadi impact in other parts of the Muslim Sahel, including northern Mali.

Jihadis in Northern Mali and Beyond

Northern Mali has historically been a melting pot for different Saharan and Sudani socioeconomic and cultural groups. Prominent among them are the pastoral nomads on the desert fringes (Sanhaja and other Berber groups since the sixteenth century, Tuareg and Hassaniya Arabs, Fulani in the South); sedentary hunting and agriculturalist populations nearer the river, segments of which engage in interregional trade (Songhay, Wangara, Bambara, Malinke); and populations engaged in fishing and hippopotamus hunting (the Bozo and the Sorko).[41] Each of these groups has exercised political control at some point in history. The Soninke dominated the empire of Ghana, the Malinke the empire of Mali, and the Songhay the empire of Songhay. As already discussed, the Fulbe led most Islamic revolutions in West Africa in the eighteenth and nineteenth centuries and ruled the resulting Islamic emirates until the advent of European colonial rule. Arab clerical lineages such as the Kunta exercised enormous political and economic influences as successful merchants and scholars and mediators in political conflicts between most other groups throughout the entire Western Sahara. Al Tamashek, or speakers of the Tamashek language known as Tuareg, strove to take political control whenever there was a power vacuum.[42] The Bamana ruled the Bambara Empire from circa 1640 to the invasion of Umar Tall in 1861. Through intermarriage and matrimonial slave institutions, these groups had mixed a great deal before colonialism. Colonial divide-and-rule policies contributed to the hardening of ethnic identities and the sowing of seeds of discord between these different groups. The Al Tamashek in particular felt much disenchanted by the colonial and post-colonial political and economic dispensation.

Unlike most other Saharan groups who claimed Arab identity, the Al Tamashek, who had a long history of conflict and dissension in the Arab world, focused on Berber specificity and their Tamashek language.[43] One of their main claims has been a homeland of their own, called Azawad. The twentieth century is replete with instances of Tuareg rebellion in the Niger Bend. The first rebellion occurred in 1916 against the French occupation. Its leaders were associated with the Sanusiyya, a religiopolitical Sufi order that three colonial powers (France, Britain, and Italy) confronted in the Sahara.[44] The French quelled the rebellion mercilessly, executed all leaders, and confiscated lands from the Al Tamashek.[45] After independence, political power was transferred to southern French-educated black African leaders, to the detriment of Saharan groups in Mali and Niger. Not only did those ruling groups have little sympathy for Tuareg nomadic culture, development policies also contributed to undermine the means of livelihood of the Al Tamashek. Inspired by Soviet models of agricultural production, the land reform in post-colonial Mali reduced privileged access of the Al Tamashek to land. The creation of marketing boards that were given a monopoly on the purchase of basic food crops considerably limited the economic autonomy of northern pastoral groups. Economic deprivation and political marginalization generated deep resentment among the Al Tamashek and led to several rebellions. In the first rebellion of postindependence Mali, known as the Alfellagha rebellion of 1962–1964, Tuareg insurgents—who lacked unified leadership, a coherent strategic vision, and above all adequate military equipment—suffered a resounding defeat. Furthermore, the Malian state headed by Modibo Keita placed Tuareg regions under a repressive military administration, forcing many Tuareg communities to migrate to neighboring Niger, Algeria, and Mauritania, where sizeable Tuareg communities lived. The Sahelian drought of the 1970s contributed to further undermine the pastoral economy of Al Tamashek, causing further resentment among Tuareg in the Niger Bend region.

In 1990, ethnic unrest in northern Mali involving Tuareg and other groups prompted Malian president Moussa Traoré to declare a state of emergency. In March 1991, Moussa Traoré was toppled, but the transitional government led by Amadou Toumani Touré negotiated a peace settlement with insurgent Tuareg groups at a special conference held in Mopti in December 1991. Algeria, whose southern region is the home of Tuareg communities, mediated between the Malian government and Tuareg insurgents. In April 1992, a national pact was signed between representatives of the transitional government and various Tuareg groups that formed a coalition named Mouvements et Fronts Unifiés de l'Azawad (MFUA). The National Pact provided comprehensive measures for a full integration of northern Mali people into the Malian economic and political life. New administrative regions were created, including the region of Kidal, providing substantial autonomy for Al Tamashek. Some Tuareg fighters were integrated into the Malian army, and others into civilian sectors. The Ganda Koy self-defense militia of the Songhay people also agreed to demobilize. Most Tuareg groups committed to national reconciliation as agreed in the National

Pact. Most Kel Amghad and Kel Entesar Tuareg have remained loyal to Mali and have served as army officers, deputies, and senior administrators since the pact. In contrast, the Kel Ifoghas have provided most of the leadership of subsequent irredentist movements. Indeed, in spite of the signing of the National Pact, the settlement of the Tuareg question has remained a work in progress. Sporadic revolts and negotiations have followed one after another throughout the last decade of the twentieth century and the first decade of the twenty-first.

In October 2011, two new Tuareg groups emerged in northern Mali to make the same old claims for the independence of Azawad. The first is the Movement National de Liberation de l'Azawad (MNLA). Led by Iyad Ag Ghali, a veteran of the 1990 rebellion, the second group, named Ansar Dine, has as its agenda the creation of an Islamic state in northern Mali. These two groups enlisted the support of heavily armed veterans who fought on the side of Khaddafi during the Libyan revolution and returned to Mali with an impressive arsenal.[46] They also attracted army officers who deserted the Malian army to join them—and not just with their weapons, but with expertise in counterinsurgency. Ironically, some of them were trained in counterinsurgency warfare within the U.S.-sponsored Trans-Saharan Counterterrorism Initiative, which included Mali, Niger, Chad, Algeria, Morocco, Tunisia, Senegal, and Nigeria.

In addition, the financial might of the Groupe Salafi pour la Prédication et le Jihad (GSPC), which later became Al-Qaida in the Islamic Maghreb (AQIM), funded most Tuareg groups[47] and contributed to the shift of the military balance of power in favor of the insurgency. Unlike Ansar Dine and MNLA, whose leadership arguably consists of Al Tamashek Malians, the GSPC / AQIM originated in the derailing of the democratic process in Algeria. From the independence of Algeria in 1962 until 1989, the only authorized political party in Algeria was the Front de Libération Nationale. In 1989, the Algerian government, led by Chadli Benjedid, committed to political liberalization and allowed registration of several political parties. The most prominent of these newly created parties was the Front Islamique du Salut (FIS). It attracted urban youth but also the Bazaar, who all resented the domination of the Front de Libération Nationale.[48] The FIS scored significant victories in mayoral elections in 1990. Then, in the first round of the presidential elections held in 1991, the FIS did very well and seemed to be marching to victory in the runoff elections planned the following week.

At that juncture, the Algerian army intervened to derail the democratic process. Frustrated by this interruption of the electoral process, Algerian Islamists committed to bring down the Algerian government. In 1992, an umbrella group named Groupe Islamique Armé (GIA) became the military wing of the Front Islamique du Salut. It attracted Algerian Afghans and many others committed to waging a merciless war against its enemies. The GIA led a campaign of terror against military targets, but also against intellectuals and journalists. As a result of the indiscriminate targeting of civilians and military, GIA was quickly disavowed by the Front Islamique du Salut, which created a military wing named Armée Islamique du Salut. Very quickly, the conflict between Islamists and the Algerian government turned into a full-blown civil war. The death toll and destruction of property was such that by the mid-1990s, Islamists had lost the sympathy of most Algerians. Forced more or less to reconsider their strategy to conquer power, the Armée Islamique du Salut declared a unilateral ceasefire. Most Islamists committed to the national reconciliation offered by President Abdel Aziz Bouteflika in 1999 to end the civil war.[49] Hardliners among the GIA who continued the jihad became divided over the indiscriminate targeting of civilians and military. Members hostile to attacks against civilians broke away to form the GSPC around 1996–1997. They claimed that four thousand fighters remained committed to bringing down the Algerian government and creating an Islamic state in Algeria, and concentrated their attacks on military targets and also some tourists. After the national reconciliation of Algeria, President Bouteflika granted a pardon to groups that surrendered their weapons. Starting in 2002, he also vowed to strike mercilessly at any rebel group that declined offers of amnesty—notably the GSPC. In light of the military supremacy of the Algerian state, the GSPC redeployed strategically in the Sahara and settled in northern Mali.

About the same time, the GSPC became divided in its strategy. A first group of nationalist jihadis favored fighting against the Algerian government to establish an Islamic state in Algeria, and another group of internationalist jihadis embraced a global jihadi ideology along the lines of Al-Qaida and committed to continue the war. In 2003, Hattab, a nationalist jihadi emir, was deposed and replaced by Nabil Sahrawi, an internationalist. GSPC started to conduct military operations in the Sahara. In June 2004, Sahrawi was gunned down by security forces and replaced by Abdel Malek Droukdel. In September 2007, GSPC had merged with Al-Qaida to become Al-Qaida in the Islamic Maghreb, with the blessing of Osama Bin Laden. During the first decade of the twenty-first century, AQIM successfully settled in northern Mali.[50] Organized around relatively autonomous brigades led by Algerian emirs, including Abou Zeid, killed in 2013 in northern Mali, and Moctar

Belmokhtar,[51] AQIM gained some acceptance from the population and recruited membership and allies from different groups.[52] Apparently, their first allies were Arabo-Berbers from northern Mali, who shared the same culture. Algerian leaders of GSPC / AQIM encountered hostility from some Tamashek, and particularly the Kel Ifoghas, but they were also able to recruit among them. Between 2003 and 2010, GSPC / AQIM was able to procure huge resources. According to a Radio France International (RFI) correspondent in Mali, GSPC / AQIM received an estimated fifty million euros in cash and double that amount in various payments in exchange for the release of a couple dozen European hostages in the decade 2000–2010.[53] In October 2013, four French hostages were released. Although French authorities understandably denied paying any ransom, the press reported that twenty million euros were paid to secure their release. AQIM had also gained the release of members jailed in Mauritania as part of their negotiations to release hostages. As proven by the execution of British citizen Edwin Dyer by AQIM, Western states that refused to submit to the dictates of jihadi groups had to pay a very heavy price. Likewise, when Nigerien and French troops attempted to free two young Frenchmen hijacked by AQIM operatives in Niamey, the intervention ended with the killing of the hostages as well the few Nigerien soldiers and the jihadis.

Through intermarriage and other forms of social and economic engagement, AQIM was able to infiltrate the social fabric of northern Mali, particularly in Timbuktu, where it built its first social and political alliances.[54] It also acquired sophisticated weapons, GPS devices, and cars. Local populations collaborated with AQIM by offering their expertise in navigating the mountainous regions of the Adrar of Ifoghas. AQIM subcontracted criminal activities to members of impoverished groups in northern Mali, who provided information on European targets or possibly hijacked and sold them to AQIM. The control of resources in this impoverished region enabled AQIM to provide a social safety net to some impoverished populations in the absence of a welfare state.

In 2011, a splinter group named Mouvement pour l'Unicité et le Jihad en Afrique de l'Ouest (Movement for Unicity and Jihad in West Africa MUJAO) split from AQIM on the grounds that black Africans were not given any major positions in AQIM and did not receive a fair share of its booty.[55] Led by a black Mauritanian, Hamada Ould Mohamed Kheirou (b. 1970), the MUJAO committed to spread jihad in West Africa and continued to collaborate with AQIM. This was the larger context of the crisis of northern Mali.

In February 2012, a coalition including the Mouvement National de Libération de l'Azawad, Ansar Dine, Al-Qaida in the Islamic Maghreb, and Movement for Unicity and Jihad in West Africa defeated the Malian army garrison in the north part of the country. Two months later, the insurgent groups occupied two-thirds of the Malian territory. Islamists led by Iyad Ag Ghali sidelined the MNLA to proclaim an Islamic state of Azawad. Then some members perpetrated acts of cruelty, justifying them as the implementation of "Islamic penal law." People accused of theft had limbs amputated, and a couple accused of adultery was stoned to death. Moussa Kaka, the correspondent of Radio France International (RFI) in Niger, reported having been invited by a militia to record the implementation of a punishment. A man who put out the eye of another was tried by a Shari'a court, sentenced to death, and slaughtered like an animal in public[56] by the Islamists. Jihadis also destroyed seventeen shrines of Sufi saints in northern Mali, including some that the UNESCO declared part of the World Heritage. This was the first time that a rebellion dominated by Islamists had acquired the military capability to rule such a large region for such a long period. Throughout 2012, the Malian crisis was placed at the heart of the agenda of leading regional African and international bodies: the Economic Community of West African States, the African Union, the European Union, and the United Nations. For ten months, the Islamist coalition ruled in northern Mali. Other jihadis from North Africa, West Africa, and Europe (specifically French nationals) traveled to northern Mali to join the insurgents.

Notable among them have been members of Boko Haram. Based on the testimony of two Boko Haram members arrested in Niger, a delegation of members of AQIM and Boko Haram first met in 2010 and agreed that they were fighting the same enemy, against whom they reserved the right to use any weapon available to them. They agreed to cooperate for the triumph of Shari'a. Although each of the two groups would retain its autonomy, they would continue the discussion about possible unification. Finally, AQIM provided the logistical support necessary to Boko Haram to implement Shari'a in Nigeria. By the end of 2010, twenty Boko Haram fighters had trained in the AQIM camp. In 2011, AQIM members were in Nigeria providing military training and guerrilla warfare strategies. In March 2011, AQIM received two million euros of the thirteen million that AQIM had demanded as ransom for the release of the hostages of Arlit in Niger.[57]

Boosted by the nonchalance of the international community and the possible backup provided by other international jihadis, the Islamist coalition undertook to extend their territorial control to the remaining third of Mali in January 2013. At that stage, Malian interim president Dioncounda Traoré requested assistance from France to halt the jihadis. French president François Hollande ordered a French military intervention to help the Malian army reconquer northern Mali.

Far from being an improvised and last-minute affair, the French intervention in northern Mali had been planned several years in advance.[58] Since the time that AQIM had settled in Mali, the French had perceived it as a major threat to French national security and strategic interests in the Sahel. Some French citizens had been hijacked and then ransomed for millions of euros, others had been killed during attempts to rescue them, and AQIM had recruited French citizens. Moreover, the French uranium plant of Areva in neighboring Niger had been attacked by jihadis. The French had been gathering intelligence and planning to intervene for a while. With the outbreak of the Arab Spring, France participated in the effort to create a no-fly zone in Libya. This delayed the intervention in Mali, because two simultaneous French interventions would have been financially and logistically prohibitive. Then the upcoming presidential elections in France made external military intervention unwise for President Sarkozy. By the time François Hollande was elected in May 2012, all logistical preparations for an intervention were already in place.

But the political instability in Bamako further delayed outside military intervention. The humiliation inflicted on the Malian army in the North created deep resentment among the military. A Malian junior army officer named Amadou Haya Sanogo led a mutiny of soldiers protesting not only the neglect of the Malian army and the corruption of the military elites, who were suspected of having ties with criminal networks, but also unmeritorious military promotion and more generally bad governance in Mali.[59] On March 2013, the junior soldiers announced that they had toppled the regime of Amadou Toumani Touré. Sanogo proclaimed himself the leader of the Comité national pour le redressement de la démocratie et la restauration de l'État (National Committee for Recovering Democracy and Restoring the State: CNRDRE) but would not actually rule for a long time. Under pressure from the international community and above all the African Union and ECOWAS, he officially stepped down in favor of Dioncounda Traoré, who was named interim president on April 12, 2013. But for most of 2013, it was not clear whether it was Dioncounda Traoré or Amadou Sanogo who ruled in Bamako from the military encampment of Kati. The political instability in Mali contributed to delay an intervention from outside. On May 21, 2012, an angry crowd, most likely engineered by the military junta, stormed the presidential palace and seriously wounded interim president Dioncounda Traoré. Traoré went to France for two months to receive treatment, but on his return at the end of July, Captain Sanogo was still running things from behind the scenes. In December 2012, members of the military sent by Sanogo arrested Prime Minister Cheick Modibo Diarra and forced him to resign.

Negotiations between the Malian government and African regional bodies such as ECOWAS were making little progress. One major obstacle was that the junta was not in favor of the presence of international troops in the capital, Bamako. In addition, most countries were very reluctant to commit troops and money to assist Mali. Mauritania and Algeria[60] feared that a military intervention would displace Tuareg and Moorish populations toward regions of their territories inhabited by their own kin, with disastrous economic consequences. The UN Secretary General Ban Ki Moon voiced similar concerns; he warned that a military intervention in northern Mali would lead to a humanitarian tragedy. Other West African states paid lip service to African solidarity but made no logistical contribution to the reconquest of northern Mali. Instead, they preferred a political settlement and, through ECOWAS, entrusted former Burkinabe president Blaise Compaoré with negotiating a political solution. To save face, ECOWAS negotiators created the fiction that MNLA and Ansar Dine were legitimate Malian political organizations with whom negotiation was possible, and only terrorist groups like AQIM and MUJAO that had shed the blood of innocent people should be targeted. Consequently, throughout 2012, jihadis ruled northern Mali. By January 2013, Islamist groups had been largely discredited in Mali and beyond for the campaign of terror and destruction they had wrought on northern Mali. African regional organizations were not capable of solving the problem. A formal request from legitimate president Dioncounda Traoré provided the cover for the French intervention. In less than two weeks, the reconquest was going forward. On January 27, 2013, the French and Malian troops reconquered Timbuktu. On the same day, a journalist from Sky News, embedded with the French troops, reported that twenty-five thousand manuscripts in Timbuktu had been burned or disappeared.

Interviewed from Bamako, the capital city of Mali, located hundreds of miles away, the mayor of Timbuktu, Ousmane Hallé, reported having heard that the largest library in Timbuktu had been torched by fleeing insurgent groups. The news of the destruction of manuscripts spread like wildfire. In reality, 95 percent of manuscripts held in Timbuktu had been smuggled to safety in Bamako during the crisis. The actual number of lost manuscripts was 4,200, but insurgents also stole the hard drives of most of the computers at the Ahmad Baba Institute, in which digital copies of thousands of manuscripts were stored.[61] After they retreated, some of these Islamist fighters melted into the population, and others migrated to neighboring countries or to the Adrar of Ifoghas Mountains. After a vigorous fight to dismantle jihadi camps and arsenals in northern Mali, the French scaled down their military presence. The United Nations committed to the area a peacekeeping force called MINUSMA, of ten thousand troops and under the leadership of a Rwandan general. But the task of peacekeeping remains a major challenge because of the porous Sahelian borders and the transnational mobility of jihadi groups. From the recent French intervention to the time of this writing (2015), jihadis have continued to be engaged in guerilla warfare, including suicide bombing in northern Mali.

During the period of Islamic rule, insurgent Islamists relied largely on local collaborators in their administration of occupied northern Mali. Algerians control only the supreme leadership of AQIM. The membership of AQIM brigades included nationals from various West and North African countries. These people were the most zealous in their implementation of Shari'a. While committed to promoting Islamic rule in the Sahel, the leadership of AQIM in Algeria was in favor of a gradual implementation. A manifesto found in Mali after the military intervention, signed by Abdel Malek Droukdel,[62] the Algeria-based leader of AQIM, provided evidence that AQIM had tried to reorient the initial impulse of the jihad. Droukdel criticized Mokhtar Belmokhtar and other jihadis in northern Mali for sidelining the Armée Nationale de Liberation de l'Azawad, which Droukdel believed was an important ally capable of winning the hearts and minds of the Tuareg. As shown in his comments below, he also disagreed in strong terms with the hasty implementation of Islamic corporal punishments:

> One of the wrong policies that we think you carried out is the extreme speed with which you applied Shariah, not taking into consideration the gradual evolution that should be applied in an environment that is ignorant of religion, and a people which hasn't applied Shariah in centuries. And our

previous experience proved that applying Shariah this way, without taking the environment into consideration, will lead to people rejecting the religion, and engender hatred toward the Mujahidin, and will consequently lead to the failure of our experiment.

We must not go too far or take risks in our decisions or imagine that this project is a stable Islamic state. It is too early for that, God knows. Instead, it is necessary to be cautious in the matter and we must be more realistic and look at it from a broader and more complete perspective to see a historic opportunity that must be exploited to interact with the Azawad people, including all its sectors, with the aim of uniting it and rallying it behind our Islamic project, by adopting its just cause and achieving its legitimate goals, while giving it an authentic Islamist tinge ... It is an important golden opportunity to extend bridges to the various sectors and parts of Azawad society Arab and Tawareg and Zingiya (black) to end the situation of political and social and intellectual separation (or isolation) between the Mujahidin and these sectors, particularly the big tribes, and the main rebel movements with their various ideologies, and the elite of Azawad society, its clerics, its groupings, its individuals and its noble forces.[63]

Under the influence of greater global interconnectedness, West African Muslim societies are going through major paradoxical societal transformations. On the one hand, there is strong support for democracy. In the past two decades, the people have won several victories against authoritarianism. From Traoré's regime in Mali in 1991 to Blaise Compaore's, which fell in October 2014 after twenty-seven years of rule in Burkina Faso, many authoritarian regimes have been defeated. All countries have committed to a charter of good governance, including freedom of the press, freedom of association, respect for human rights, electoral transparency with the presence of international and national observers, and a commitment to term limits for ruling heads of state. Paradoxically, they have also witnessed the emergence of religious groups advocating intolerant conceptions of religion who are prepared to use force to impose their views, as was the case in northern Mali and Nigeria.

In the past two decades, Islamist militants have conducted huge outreach efforts in West Africa, through their mosques, Qur'anic schools, charitable NGOs, and training camps. The spearheads of this movement of Islamization have been the Arabophones. As mediators of Islamic knowledge and experts in the language of the Qur'an, they take center stage in public life. Western-educated intellectuals who are embracing new perspectives on Islamization are cultivating a great interest in learning the Arabic language and acquiring an expertise in Islamic religion. Arabophones have never been as important in modern West Africa as they are now.

"Islamist rule" lasted less than one year in Timbuktu. Judging by the warm welcome that French president François Hollande received when he visited the liberated city of Timbuktu, Islamist rule was resented by many in Timbuktu and other parts of northern Mali. Most of those people were sincere and devout Muslims. For them, shrines of saints in Timbuktu were an integral part of the Islamic legacy. Desecration of centuries-old shrines of the patron saints of the city was a great sacrilege. The people of Timbuktu were in favor of a moral order inspired by Islamic teachings, as had been transmitted to them for centuries. The core of the popular resentment against the insurgents in northern Mali is not Islam, but the narrow-mindedness of the jihadis.

The physical punishment prescribed by Islamic penal law has never disappeared completely in the modern world. Saudi Arabia has enforced it since the establishment of the kingdom in 1932 by Ibn Sa'ud. Other leaders of majority Muslim states have reenacted Islamic penal law and enforced physical punishment in an attempt to appeal to Islamist sympathies. This was the case in Pakistan under the rule of Zia ul Haq, when a referendum on Islamization was approved that introduced physical punishment such as stoning and amputation. Likewise in the Sudan, Ja'far Nimeiri allied with the Muslim Brothers and imposed Shari'a, including physical punishments. A very prominent Muslim thinker named Muhammad Mahmud Taha, the founder of the Republican Brothers, who opposed the implementation of Shari'a, was brought to court in Sudan, tried, and condemned to death for apostasy in 1985. Mauritania, which opted for separation between religion and state at independence, despite its name "Islamic Republic of Mauritania," reintroduced Islamic physical punishments as part of a re-Islamization package under the rule of Colonel Mohamed Khouna Ould Haidallah (head of state from 1978 to 1984) in 1981. The physical punishments based on Shari'a are still part of its criminal legislation.[64] But in all these cases, it was ruling political elites who reintroduced Shari'a, arguably as a political move to build alliances with Islamic sectors of the population or to neutralize opponents. But in Mali, the story is very different, because it was not a state, but a collection of Islamist groups, that defeated law enforcement agencies, took control of its territory, and implemented their vision of Islamic criminal law.

Epilogue

Laysa fi kutubin wa dafatira 'ilmun,
innama 'ilmu fi sudur al-rijal.

Knowledge does not reside in books or
notebooks, but in the chests of [pious] men.
—*Ahmed Skirej*[1]

IN JULY 2012, I left Columbia University to relocate to Cambridge, Massachusetts, as the inaugural holder of the Prince Alwaleed Bin Talal Chair in Contemporary Islamic Religion at Harvard Divinity School. This was one of four chairs that the sponsor committed to endow at Harvard, with $20 million to promote the study of contemporary Islam in the aftermath of September 11. Prince Alwaleed Bin Talal endowed several other centers at the universities of Georgetown and Cambridge in England, as well as the American University of Cairo and the American University of Beirut. Since the oil boom, millions of petrodollars have been given to support the building of mosques and Islamic centers and the teaching of Islam at all levels. Dozens of chairs were established in Western universities by other donors from oil-rich Arab countries of the Gulf to promote Islamic studies in the West.

There is an assumption in both academic and popular perceptions of Islam that money from Saudi private donors, the Saudi religious authorities, and Saudi NGOs was used essentially to promote a global spread of Wahhabism, and fanaticism and violence. One commentator with such an outlook, Dore Gold, lumped together all initiatives from Saudi Arabia, including the endowment of professorships and the building of mosques or Islamic centers, as mainly driven by the spread of Wahhabism.[2] Such a perception is a gross oversimplification. No holder of a professorship funded by Saudi money at Harvard is a Wahhabi, and many are not Muslims.

We have seen that my mother's school was radically transformed forty years after it started. It has indeed received millions of dollars of support in cash, books, and the paid salaries of three dozen teachers, many of whom are university graduates and a few have received a PhD. Paid teachers were sent from Egypt and Mauritania, but most of the cash came from Saudi Arabia, including from Saudi princes, other private donors, and Saudi NGOs such as the Muslim World League and the World Assembly of Muslim Youth.

In the prologue of this book, I alluded to the village founded by my maternal grandfather, Shaykh Ibrahim Niasse, as being a microcosm of West African integration. Arabo-Berbers from Mauritania; Hausa from Niger, Nigeria, and Ghana; and many other West African ethnicities have engaged in spiritual, economic, and matrimonial transactions. Madina Kaolack has changed very much since my childhood years. In the 1960s, it was a village in the suburbs of the commercial city of Kaolack. Huts made of mud significantly outnumbered houses made of concrete. Only the houses of notables had running water and electric power. Now, after the turn of twenty-first century, Madina Kaolack has been radically reconfigured architecturally. Mansions worth hundreds of thousands of dollars have mushroomed there. Those houses are equipped with all the modern amenities, including big-screen TVs, luxury furniture, and satellite connections, and their owners drive expensive cars. They maintain a large clientele that in local parlance is called *hukuma* (government). Members of those clienteles meet daily to share meals, drink tea, perform congregational prayer, and, last but not least, exchange information. A head of hukuma will look after most of the needs of the core members of his clientele, including providing basic survival needs such as food, healthcare, and negotiating matrimonial alliances. He might also subcontract to them petitionary prayers.[3] Most of these "government heads" have no political position and own no formally registered businesses. From where do they derive the resources to maintain such a lavish lifestyle? The prayer market!

Madina Kaolack has attracted people from all over West Africa and beyond for decades. They come for a variety of reasons: some come to study, others for spiritual training. Many come seeking a blessing, professional advancement, prosperity, fertility, or healing and will pay fees in exchange for petitionary prayers. Among the people who solicit prayer services from the divines of Madina Kaolack, there are also non-Muslims. Christian ruling elites of other West African states are known to be among those who solicit the spiritual guides of Madina Kaolack. It is an open secret that the former socialist president and Pan-Africanist leader Nkrumah of Ghana, although a Christian, relied on Shaykh Ibrahim Niasse[4] for spiritual protection. In soliciting a Muslim shaykh for such protection, he was simply continuing a long tradition among ruling elites in Ghana.[5] Kings of precolonial Ashanti in Ghana are known to have surrounded themselves with Muslims and traditional African divines to provide supernatural protection. Other frequent visitors in my family's house in Dakar and Kaolack included Alfred Benedict Tolbert, son and heir of the William Tolbert family that ruled Liberia till the revolution staged by Samuel Doe. After the passing of Shaykh Ibrahim Niasse, his heirs provided spiritual protection to many, including high government officials and other influential people operating in various spheres of economic and political life in West Africa and beyond. Most of the money that transformed Madina Kaolack at the turn of the twentieth century came from oil-rich countries. Nigeria is one of those from which Shaykh Ibrahim Niasse had a large following.[6] During the oil boom, Nigerians poured millions of dollars into the town.

Among other oil-rich countries and persons that contributed to the transformation of Madina Kaolack, special mention must be made of Gulf monarchies such as Saudi Arabia. Given that Salafism is the official religious ideology of Saudi Arabia, one wonders how spiritual guides from Madina Kaolack could attract clients from there. The truth is that before the rise of the third Wahhabi kingdom established by Abdul Aziz Ibn Saud in 1932, divines in Arabia offered a variety of talismanic services to people facing life challenges, such as illness and reversals of fortune.[7] The establishment of a state that banned all those religious practices on the grounds that they undermine the first pillar of Islam, which is the belief in one omnipotent God, created a vacuum that was filled by divines from West Africa, who made huge fortunes offering talismanic services to Arab princes. The master narrative of how Saudi wealth supported the expansion of global Wahhabism is definitely not the entire story.[8] The Saudi wealth equally strengthened the consolidation of alternative Islamic views. I shall even surmise that West African shaykhs providing fee-for-service prayers have made much greater fortunes in Saudi Arabia and other Gulf countries than Salafis, most of whom raised their funds locally to disseminate their religious message in West Africa.

The World Muslim League (WML) is often presented as the main organization committed to spreading global Wahhabism, or even to have sponsored terrorism. The truth is that the WML was created in the context of "the Arab Cold War"[9] by King Faysal of Saudi Arabia in 1962. Its goal was to promote Pan-Islamism as a counterforce to the Pan-Arabism sponsored by Egyptian president Nasser, which Saudi Arabia perceived as a threat. Prominent members of the World Muslim League included Islamists such as Abul 'l A'la

Maududi, but also Sufis such as my grandfather, Shaykh Ibrahim Niasse, who was a founding member and one-time vice president of the League, and former prime minister of Northern Nigeria Ahmadu Bello, who identified with the Sokoto Qadiriyya. In the five decades of its existence, the World Muslim League supported the building of mosques and Islamic centers in the Muslim world and the West, and Wahhabis and non-Wahhabis received financial and logistical support from the organization.

As is well known, Africa's interaction with the outside world has not been completely defined by or limited to the Muslim world, and the colonial encounter with European powers had a great effect on Africa's history, intellectual and otherwise. The colonial powers saw the occupation of Africa as a means of promoting their economic interests while pursuing their so-called humanitarian mission. Major transformations followed during the twentieth century. The colonial state encouraged its subjects to cultivate cash crops needed to support European industrialization. It took control of the extraction of mineral resources. Exportation of primary commodities required building transport infrastructures. Tarred roads and railways soon linked the main centers of agriculture and mining to the coast in order to facilitate the movement of people and goods. European technologies and science were used to engineer other societal transformations. The colonial state introduced a new postal service, new health infrastructures, and new educational opportunities in colonial schools. All those transformations were executed as part of a civilizing mission.

Colonialism, so the claim went, heralded an era of hope for Africa, a new history believed to be the beginning of history. Africans south of the Sahara were taught how to read and write. They were brought into the orbit of "civilization" by imperial Europe. Modernization, which the colonial encounter was believed to be delivering, was supposed to produce the transition from prehistory to history. It is obvious, however, that the colonial encounter, unlike what most advocates of modernization assume, did not produce the linear change from tradition to modernity, from superstition to faith in scientific reason, from non-Europhone to Europhone intellectual traditions, or from the veneration of masters to the assertion of the free individual.

In his study of the transformation of Islamic education in post-colonial Mali, Louis Brenner analyzed the rise of the *médersa* system based on a combination of Western and modern Middle Eastern pedagogy. Brenner argued that the rise of these new schools is provoking an epistemic shift from an esoteric to a rational episteme. The esoteric episteme that governed precolonial Islamic education had features that set it apart from the episteme of modern forms of knowledge. According to Brenner, knowledge in the esoteric episteme was perceived as hierarchical in the sense that "religious knowledge is seen to be superior to 'secular' knowledge." Other features of the esoteric episteme include the stated difference between conspicuous knowledge (*zahir*) and hidden or initiatic knowledge (*batin*) that is not available to all persons but only to initiates who received it from qualified persons sanctioned to transmit it. In such a paradigm, there is also a hierarchy in the pyramidal structure of the possession of knowledge, with a small elite faction at the very top of the hierarchy.[10] In contrast, in the rational episteme represented by the learning environment created by the new schools (Islamic or otherwise), "religious revelation and divine law are retained while accepting rationalist concepts of knowledge and its transmission." Brenner concludes that "in this paradigm, knowledge is theoretically available to everyone. Reflection and explication are based on principles of rational exposition as derived from divine revelation. Religious devotion becomes separate from the process of learning, and the individual's intellectual development is no longer associated with divine intervention."[11]

But Brenner also adds that "it is important not to exaggerate this epistemic shift, which is both limited and uneven. It is probable that the vast majority of Malians, including many products of French schooling, still operate under the influence of the esoteric episteme in many aspects of their lives. It is certainly not unusual for persons to espouse rationalist formulations in public while embracing esoteric ones in private."[12] I would like to build on that point and argue that the relationship between these different forms of traditional Islamic, Western, and hybrid education is indeed very complex, and the limited shift notwithstanding, the majority of Muslims navigate easily between the esoteric and the rational episteme.

In the epigraph that opens this conclusion, I cite Ahmed Skirej (1878–1944), a learned Moroccan scholar and judge and a disciple of the Tijaniyya Sufi order who wrote extensively on many fields of knowledge, but above all in defense of the Tijaniyya against its detractors. Learned as he was in the exoteric sciences, Skirej stated that knowledge does not lie in books or notebooks, but in the chest of [pious] men. This is crucial to understanding classical Islamic epistemology and its resilience. Not all that people want to know lies within books that can be ordered online or purchased in bookstores. Part of what they want to know is acquired through a direct and sustained contact with a teacher, a master, a shaykh. Unlike the modern context in which students learn much from reading books alone in their rooms, in the classical period, the most reliable method of knowledge transmission was students hearing the author of the text (or someone who had been taught the text) teach the lesson.[13]

The versatility of Sufi orders and their ability to reform provide the best illustration of the coexistence of the two paradigms. While preserving the fundamentals of Sufi epistemology rooted in an esoteric episteme, Sufi orders have proven to have a remarkable ability to appropriate modern technology and pedagogy. The number of new Sufi organizations in West Africa and their ability to synthesize the esoteric and exoteric episteme are simply remarkable. The Tijaniyya and the Qadiriyya Sufi orders, which competed for hegemony for over a century in West Africa, united in Northern Nigeria to face the rise of the Salafis. They built new schools based on modern pedagogy, while still operating *zawiya* that provided esoteric knowledge.

Faith in scientific reason and belief in the supernatural and the sacred have continued to coexist.[14] Many of the same people who have a strong belief in the supernatural also expect benefits from the worlds of science and technology. When science and technology fail to meet their expectations, they turn to the sacred and supernatural. All sectors of West African populations (men, women; literate, illiterate; lower, middle, and upper classes) seek refuge in the sacred when confronted with the vicissitudes of life. The huge audiovisual production industry of movies and sketches produced in West Africa in the first decade of the twentieth century most eloquently illustrates this inclination. In the overwhelming majority of such productions, the presence of witchcraft demonstrates its place in the reality of African society. On a regular basis, politicians, elite sportspeople, ill people, and business persons will hire a cleric for petitionary prayer, to be safe from misfortunes, to recover from diseases, to win elections or a sporting tournament, or to settle a score with a foe. This reliance on the sacred has made experts of this field relevant in contemporary West African societies. In the name of rationalism and orthodoxy, some contest the image of the master as someone who guides ordinary believers in navigating existential uncertainties, but the majority of people continue to venerate such masters. Many still believe that knowledge is plural and hierarchical and that there is a realm in which Western science is not efficient. In this tradition, the master is still the holder of a hidden knowledge.

What is true for divines of Madina Kaolack attracting people from different social and religious backgrounds is true for other religious traditions elsewhere in West Africa. Oludamini Ogunnaike's work has shown that Ifa, a divination practice among the Yoruba, is thriving, and every single Yoruba town has its council of Babalawo that serves as advisors of traditional rulers and their communities. Many of the seekers who consult these Babalawo are highly educated, Muslim or Christian, and "virtually all of them seemed confident in the power of Ifa to solve their problems."[15] Oludamini argues persuasively that these priests are widely regarded as being among the foremost traditional intellectuals of Yoruba society and that their counsel and insight are sought on practical and personal matters; affairs of state; and all manner of ritual, mythological, theological, and philosophical questions.[16]

In colonial Mauritania, Arabs never trusted Western education. Most graduates of Western schools were black Africans from among the Wolof, Soninke, and Pulaar. After independence, the Arab-dominated post-colonial state apparatus adopted Arabization of the educational system. A huge number of modern schools that offered instruction in Arabic were created in the capital, Nouakchott, where the drought of the 1970s forced a large rural population to settle. The state-sponsored modern schools attracted a huge number of rural people who had previously attended traditional religious schools offering instruction in Arabic. However, attending and graduating from modern schools did not cut off these students from traditional sources of education and learning. Many still obtain training in the two systems simultaneously. Some go to modern schools in Nouakchott part time and return to the village to study with reputed shaykhs when public schools have holidays. Many use the new technologies of information and communication for distance learning—for example, Skype or the cell phone. In short, one does not have to choose between the two epistemes, and many embrace the coexistence and tension between different paradigms of knowledge.

Large new Sufi organizations have been created in the post-colonial period in West Africa and its diaspora. Among the Murids, groups such as Matlaboul Fawzayn and Hizbou Tarqiya[17] are involved in major development work such as sanitation campaigns for the Holy City of Touba, the creation of hospitals and clinics, and the establishment of modern schools that operate within the rational episteme. They have also created research institutes and television and radio stations devoted to the study of Muridism and the dissemination of the thought of Ahmadu Bamba. Virtually all major Sufi communities in Senegal have created such modern organizations that are adapting to and embracing the simultaneous existence of multiple repertoires of knowledge and truth.

The Groupe de Réflexion Ansarudine is another interesting illustration of the complex patterns of interaction between the tradition and the modern. Created by Western-educated members of the Niasse Tijaniyya, the group is based in Dakar. Members met biweekly in the house of Shaykh Ibrahim Mahmoud Diop (d. 2014) to study fundamental Sufi texts in Wolof. Just like traditional *majalis*, the master reads the text in Arabic and comments in an African language. Lectures are recorded and translated into French by the audience and then disseminated among Western-educated members of the movement. Likewise, Arabophones operating in the modern school sectors as students or teachers join the informal sessions devoted to the classical core curriculum. It is notably the public sessions on the exegesis of the Qur'an that draw the largest crowds. Listeners expect a blessing by attending, which they are not likely to get in more formal school settings.

I have provided frequent anecdotal evidence rooted in my family and personal history in this book. The first goal of bringing such anecdotes into the narrative is to provide microillustrations of macrotrends in the dynamics of Islam in the postcolony, and the second is to make my subject position clear to the reader. Born in a Muslim family, I grew up in Senegal, was socialized in traditional African values, simultaneously attended Qur'anic schools and Senegalese public schools, and graduated in French institutions of higher education, thus embodying the African triple heritage, to use a phrase of the late Ali Mazrui.[18] Mazrui forcefully argued that post-colonial Africa is the product of the interactions between three main sources of civilizational influences: black African, Arab, and Western. The encounter between these civilizations has at times been violent. The study of Africa in the modern academy has generously documented this aspect. But violence is just one part of the story, one that I deliberately avoided by looking at another side of the story of Afro-Arab and intra-African relations. My own personal story, which shaped this narrative of the intellectual history of Islam, is certainly not generalizable, but it is not uncommon in West Africa. Arabic-speaking shaykhs of the Sahara and North Africa have many disciples in West Africa. Likewise, many African shaykhs—including Ahmadu Bamba, the founder of the Muridiyya, Abbas Sall; and Madior Cissé—have disciples among Arabic-speaking Mauritanians and/or Moroccans.

I expect Afrocentrists to construe my narrative as an apology of Pan-Arabism or the negation of endogenous forms of knowledge of "Africa proper." To them I will say that Islam and the Arabic language are no more foreign in Africa than they are in Syria, Lebanon, Palestine, and Iraq. Islam was introduced to the African continent before it spread in Arabia, let alone to the neighboring countries of the Peninsula. The Prophet Muhammad sent dozens of his companions to Ethiopia before the beginning of the Muslim calendar. Africans in the broad sense of the word have made a major contribution to the development of Arabic, and it is worth recalling that the majority of Arabs now live on the African continent and that Arabic is by far the most widely spoken African language. Most countries of the Sahel—Mauritania, Mali, Niger, and Nigeria—have large populations of native Arabic speakers.

Literacy was of course not introduced to Africa by the Arabs. Ethiopia had an established scholarly tradition going back centuries before Islam. Likewise, writing was not unknown in West Africa before the arrival of Muslims. The Yoruba have used writing in practices of divination, and one of their traditional deities, Oluorogbo, is believed to have developed his own form of writing and notation. Tuareg people had an alphabet of their own (the Tfinaagah alphabet). Nor am I denying or disparaging nonwritten forms of indigenous knowledge. African populations have had elaborate forms of knowledge whose transmission did not require the use of writing.[19] The scope of this book is simply to bring to the attention of Europhone intellectuals the authentic lived experience of millions of Muslims in West Africa.

In 1964, Nigerien intellectual Abdou Moumouni, after whom the first university of independent Niger was named, published a state-of-the-art study of education in Africa, identifying its strengths and weaknesses.[20] He argued forcefully that the reform of the educational system of Africa was a priority. Five decades after the publication of Moumouni's work, knowledge production is still fragmented, and the current educational system is still not fully capable of integrating the different intellectual traditions. The problem with this knowledge divide is of course not specific to West Africa. The issue of knowledge divides in the world was the subject of the first of the World Social Science Report (ISSC-UNESCO) 2010.[21] Of the problems posing an obstacle to the accumulation, transmission, and use of knowledge in different societies, the report cites inequalities and asymmetries as the paramount factors. These are no doubt questions confronting West Africa in particular. The divide between Europhones and non-Europhones—and in particular Arabophones—needs to be bridged in order to make the intellectual legacy of the African continent legible and to build a solid foundation for education in the new millennium.

NOTES

GLOSSARY

ACKNOWLEDGMENTS

INDEX

Notes

Prologue

1. Kwame Nkrumah, "Flower of Learning," inaugural address delivered at his installation as chancellor of the University of Ghana, November 25, 1961. Accessed March 13, 2014, http://nkrumahinfobank.org/article.php?id=470&c=46.
2. They were shouting *moom sa reew,* which literally means in Wolof, the lingua franca of Senegal, "owning one's country," thus the end of foreign rule.
3. Kwame Nkrumah, *Ghana: The Autobiography of Kwame Nkrumah* (New York: International Publishers and Co., 1989), 164.
4. See Ruediger Seeseman, *The Divine Flood. Ibrahim Niasse and the Roots of a Twentieth-Century Sufi Revival* (New York: Oxford University Press, 2011), 7.
5. See Mervyn Hiskett, *The Development of Islam in West Africa* (London: Longmans, 1984), 287; *idem,* "The 'Community of Grace' and Its Opponents, the 'Rejecters': A Debate about Theology and Mysticism in Muslim West Africa with Special Reference to Its Hausa Expression," *African Language Studies. Collected Papers in Oriental and African Studies* 17 (1980): 99–140.
6. For the most recent studies, see Zachary Valentine Wright, *Living Knowledge in West Africa Islam. The Sufi Community of Ibrahim Niasse* (Leiden and Boston: Brill, 2015), 2; Joseph Hill, "Divine Knowledge and Islamic Authority: Religious Specialization among Disciples of Baay Ñas," PhD diss. in anthropology, Yale University, 2007; Cheikh Niang, "Le Transnational pour argument socio-anthropologie historique du mouvement confrérique tidiane de Cheikh Ibrahim Niasse," PhD diss. in social anthropology, Université de Toulouse, September 2014; Oludamini Ogunnaike, "Sufism and Ifa: Ways of Knowing in Two West African Intellectual traditions," PhD diss., Department of African and African American Studies, Harvard University, August 2015.
7. John Hunwick and Alida Jay Boyle, *The Hidden Treasures of Timbuktu. Rediscovering Africa's Literary Cultures.* (London: Thames & Hudson, 2008), 82; Elias Saad, *A Social History of Timbuktu: The Role of Muslim Scholars and Notables 1400–1900* (Cambridge: Cambridge University Press, 1983), 17.
8. Hunwick and Boyle, *Hidden Treasures of Timbuktu,* 10.

9. Ralph Austen, *Trans-Saharan Africa in World History* (Oxford: Oxford University Press, 2010), 27.

10. Ibid.

11. Murray Last, "The Book and the Nature of Knowledge in Muslim Northern Nigeria 1457–2007," in Graziano Krätli and Ghislaine Lydon, eds., *The Trans-Saharan Book Trade. Manuscript Culture, Arabic Literacy and Intellectual History in Muslim Africa* (Leiden: E. J. Brill, 2010), 175–211, 180.

12. James L. A. Webb Jr., *Desert Frontier. Ecological and Economic Change along the Western Sahel 1600–1850* (Madison, WI: University of Wisconsin Press, 1995), 15. For the expansion of Arabs from North Africa to south of the Sahara, see H. T. Norris, *The Arab Conquest of the Western Sahara. Studies of the Historical Events, Religious Beliefs and Social Customs Which Made the Remotest Sahara a Part of the Arab World* (Essex and Beirut: Longmans and Librairie du Liban, 1986).

13. Chase Robinson, *Islamic Historiography* (Cambridge: Cambridge University Press), 2003, xx.

14. Sylviane Diouf, *Servants of Allah: African Muslims Enslaved in the Americas* (New York: New York University Press, 1998), 8.

15. Francis Moore, *Travels into the Inland Parts of Africa* (London: Edgar Cave, 1738), 30.

16. René Caillé, *Journal d'un voyage à Tombouctou et à Jenne dans l'Afrique centrale pendant les années 1824–1828,* (Paris 1830) 206, cited in Saad, *Social History of Timbuktu,* 92.

17. This estimate is based on my research on Islamic institutions of higher learning in Africa. In 2010, about two dozen Islamic colleges or universities had been established in sub-Saharan Africa (see Chapter 7).

18. See Pew Forum on Public Life, Global Mapping of the Muslim Population, accessed September 2014, http://www.pewforum.org/2009/10/07/mapping -the-global-muslim-population/.

19. Kwame Anthony Appiah, *In My Father's House: Africa in the Philosophy of Culture* (London: Methuen, 1992), 4.

20. Paul Marty, *Etudes sur l'Islam maure* (Paris: Leroux, 1916); *Etudes sur l'Islam au Sénégal* (Paris: Leroux, 1917); *Etudes sur l'Islam et les tribus du Soudan français* (Paris: Leroux, 1920–1921); *Etude sur l'Islam en Côte d'Ivoire* (Paris: Leroux, 1922); *L'Islam en Guinée: Fouta Diallon* (Paris: Leroux, 1921); and *Etudes sur l'Islam au Dahomey* (Paris: Leroux, 1926).

21. Valentin Mudimbe, *The Invention of Africa: Gnosis, Philosophy, and the Order of Knowledge* (Bloomington: Indiana University Press, 1988), x.

22. Stuart Hall, "Introduction" in Stuart Hall, David Held, Don Hubert, and Thompson Kenneth, *Modernity: An Introduction to Modern Societies* (Cambridge, MA: Blackwell, 1996), 185–227.

23. Ibn Battuta, "Audiences of the Sultan of Mali," in Robert O. Collins, ed., *Documents from the African Past* (Princeton: Markus Wiener, 2009), 15.

24. On the centrality of memorization in the medieval and early modern West, see

Cavallo Guglielmo and Roger Chartier "Introduction" in Guglielmo Cavallo and Roger Chartier, eds., *A History of Reading in the West* (Amherst and Boston: University of Massachusetts Press, 2003), 1–36, 24–25; Mary Caruthers, *The Book of Memory: A Study of Memory in Medieval Culture* (Cambridge: Cambridge University Press, 1992), 18–98.

25. Georges Makdisi, *The Rise of Colleges: Institutions of Learning in Islam and the West* (Edinburgh: Edinburgh University Press, 1981), 102.

26. Rudoph Ware, *The Walking Qur'an: Islamic Education, Embodied Knowledge, and History in West Africa* (Durham: University of North Carolina Press, 2014), 7–8.

27. Talal Asad, *Genealogies of Religion: Discipline and Reasons of Power in Christianity and Islam* (Baltimore: Johns Hopkins University Press, 1993), 82; *idem, Formations of the Secular: Christianity, Islam, Modernity* (Stanford, CA: Stanford University Press, 2003), 2.

28. Michel Foucault, *Ethics, Subjectivity and Truth,* Paul Rabinow, ed., Robert Hurley and others, trans. (New York: New Press, 1997), 225.

29. Makdisi, *Rise of Colleges,* 224.

30. John Hunwick, *Timbuktu and the Songhay Empire: Al-Sa'di's Tarikh al-Sudan down to 1613 and Other Contemporary Documents* (Leiden: Brill, 1999), lix: Makdisi, *Rise of Colleges,* 224.

31. Saad, *Social History of Timbuktu,* 62.

32. Jean-Louis Triaud, "Khalwa and the Career of Sainthood. An Interpretative Essay," in Christian Coulon and Donal Cruise O'Brian, *Charisma and Brotherhood in African Islam* (Oxford: Clarendon Press and New York: Oxford University Press, 1988), 55.

33. See Jean Schmitz, "Le Souffle de la parenté: Mariage et transmission de la baraka chez les clercs musulmans," *L'homme* (2000): 154–155, 241–278.

34. Talal Asad, "The Idea of an Anthropology of Islam," *Qui Parle?* 17, no. 2 (Spring 2009): 1–30.

35. Charles Briggs and Richard Bautnan, "Genre, Intertextuality and Social Power," *Journal of Linguistic Anthropology* 2, no. 2 (1992): 131–172.

36. Briggs and Bautnan, "Genre," 165.

37. Ibid., 149.

38. Wael Hallaq, *Introduction to Islamic Law* (Cambridge: Cambridge University Press, 2009), 27, 165, 169.

39. There is no academic consensus on the use of the term. In the West African context, I use the word *Arabophone* to refer to intellectuals whose language of discourse (not their mother tongue) is Arabic. In French, the term *Arabisant* may be used to designate products of the Islamic intellectual tradition in North and West Africa as opposed to *francisants* schooled exclusively in French. But in the French context, scholars or students engaged in the academic study of Arabic in the Orientalist tradition and whose knowledge of French is outstanding are also called "Arabisants." In English, the two words *Arabists* and *Arabophones* are often used interchangeably.

40. Ali A. Mazrui, *The Africans: A Triple Heritage* (Boston: Little, Brown and Company, 1986).

1. Timbuktu Studies: The Geopolitics of the Sources

1. Georg Wilhelm Friederich Hegel, *The Philosophy of History* (New York: Willey Book Co., 1900), 99.
2. For the English version, see Shaykh al-Islam Ibrahim b. 'Abdallah Niasse, *The Removal of Confusion Concerning the Flood of the Saintly Seal Ahmad al-Tijani: A Translation of Kashif al-ilbas 'an faydat al-khatm abi 'Abbas,* translated by Zachary Wright, Muhtar Holland, and Abdullahi Okene, with forewords by Sayyid Ali Cisse, Shaykh Tijani Cisse, and Shaykh Hassan Cisse (Louisville, KY: Fons Vitae, 2010). For a French version, see Cheikh Al Islam Elhadji Ibrahim Niass, *La Levée des Equivoques concernant la Fayda du Sceau Abil Abbas,* translated by Mouhammadou Lasse Khar Ba and Djim Guèye, (Kaolack: Librairie An-Nahdatou, n.d.)
3. Zachary Wright, "Introduction" in Niasse, *Removal of Confusion,* ix–x.
4. Edward Said, *Orientalism* (New York: Vintage Books, 1994), chapter 1.
5. Carl Brockelmann, *Geschichte der Arabischen Litteratur,* 2nd ed., 2 vols. (Leiden: Brill, 1943–1949); *idem, Geschichte der Arabischen Litteratur* (Leiden: Brill, 1943–1949); *idem, Geschichte der Arabischen Litteratur,* Supplementbände, 3 vols. (Leiden: Brill, 1937–1942).
6. Abdel Kader Haïdara, "An Overview of the Major Manuscript Libraries in Timbuktu," in Graziano Krätli and Ghislaine Lydon, eds., *The Trans-Saharan Book Trade: Manuscript Culture, Arabic Literacy and Intellectual History in Muslim Africa* (Leiden: Brill, 2010), 241–264, 262-263.
7. A notable example is the library of Umar Tall confiscated by the French expedition led by Colonel Archinard, which conquered the Umarian state in 1891. Kept in the French Bibliothèque Nationale since then, it is as recent as 1985 that a rigorous catalogue was produced presenting about five hundred of the four thousand texts of the collection. See Nouredine Ghali, Sidi Mohammed Mahibou, and Louis Brenner, *Inventaire de la bibliothèque umarienne de Ségou conservée à la bibliothèque nationale* (Paris: Editions du CNRS, 1985).
8. Khayr al-din al-Zirikli, *Al-A'lam. Qamus tarajim li-ashhar al-rijal wa 'l-nisa min al-'arab wa 'l-musta'ribin wa 'l-mustashriqin* (Beirut: Dar al-'ilm lil-malayin, 1990).
9. 'Umar Rida Kahhala, *Mu'jam al-mu'allifin* (Beirut: Dar ihya al-turath al-'arabi, 1958), 15 vols.
10. Youssouf Kamal, *Monumenta Carthographica Africae et Aegypti* (Frankfort am Main: Institut für Geschichte der Arabish-Islamischen Wissenschaften an der Johann Wolfgang Goethe-Universität, 1987), 2nd ed., with an introduction by Fuat Sezgin, 6 vols.
11. Fuat Sezgin, "Introduction" in Kamal, *Monumenta.*

12. Ibid.

13. Mauny, "Introduction," in Joseph Cuoq, *Recueil des sources arabes concernant l'Afrique occidentale du VIIIe au XVIe siècle* (Paris: Editions du Centre National de la Recherche Scientifique, 1975), xi–xii.

14. Joseph Cuoq, *Recueil des sources arabes concernant l'Afrique occidentale du VIIIe au XVIe siècle* (Paris: Editions du Centre National de la Recherche Scientifique, 1975).

15. Nehemia Levtzion and J. F. P. Hopkins, eds., *Corpus of Early Arabic Sources for West African History* (Cambridge, London, New York, Melbourne, Sydney: Cambridge University Press, 1981).

16. Levtzion and Hopkins, *Corpus,* ix.

17. Chouki El Hamel, *La vie intellectuelle dans le Sahel ouest-africain, XVI–XIX siècles: une étude sociale de l'enseignement islamique en Mauritanie et au nord du Mali (XVI–XIX siècles) et traduction annotée de Fatḥ ash-shakūr d'al-Bartilī al-Walāti mort en 1805* (Paris: L'Harmattan, 2002).

18. 'Uthman b. Fudi, *Bayan wujub al-hijra 'ala al-'ibad wa bayan wujub al-nasb 'ala al-imam wa iqamat al-jihad,* edited and translated by F. H. Masri (Khartoum: Khartoum University Press and New York: Oxford University Press, 1978).

19. The text was summarized and translated in part by Ismail Balogun, *The Life and Work of 'Uthman Dan Fodio* (Lagos: Islamic Publication Bureau, 1975), 49–81. Subsequently, the full text was translated and published in Sudan as Shehu Uthman Dan Foduye, *Ihya al-Sunna wa Ikhmad al-Bid'a,* English translation by Muhammad Sharif (Sennar Sudan: Sankore, 1998).

20. Sidi Mohamed Mahibou, *Abdullahi Dan Fodio et la théorie du gouvernement is-lamique* (Paris: L'Harmattan, 2010) attempts to provide a synthesis of Abdullahi Dan Fodio's writings through an integrated analysis of the four texts.

21. E. J. Arnett, *The Rise of the Sokoto Fulani,* being a paraphrase and in some parts a translation of *Infaku'l Maisuri of Sultan Bello* (Kano: 1922). For a critical analysis of the work, see Yasir Anjola Qadri, "An Appraisal of Muhammad Bello's *Infaqul-Maysur Fi Tarikhi Biladi Takrur," Journal of Islamic and Religious Studies Ilorin,* 3, 1986, 52–62.

22. Jean Schmitz, *Florilège au jardin de l'histoire des Noirs: Zuhuur al-basaatin/ Shaykh Muusa Kamara,* edited and introduced by Jean Schmitz and translated by Said Bousbina (Paris: CNRS, 1985).

23. Niasse, *Removal of Confusion.*

24. El Hadji Ravane Mbaye, *Le grand savant El Hadji Malick Sy. Pensée et action.* Vie et oeuvre, foreword by Iba Der Thiam, Vol. 1; *Ifham al-munkir al-jani: Réduction du silence du dénégateur,* translated and annotated by El-Hadji Ravane Mbaye with Arabic text, Vol. 2; *Kifayat ar-Raghibin: Ce qu'il faut aux bons croyants,* trans-lated and annotated with Arabic text, Vol. 3 (Beirut: Dar Elbouraq, 2003).

25. Sidi Ali Harazim b. al-'Arabi al-Barrada, *Jawahir al-Ma'ani: Perles des sens et réalisation des vœux dans le flux d'Abu–l-'Abbas at-Tijani,* translation by El Hadji Ravane Mbaye with Arabic text (Beirut: Dar Elbouraq, 2003).

26. Nana Asma'u, *Collected Works of Nana Asma'u, Daughter of Usman dan Fodiyo* (1793–1864), edited by Jean Boyd and Beverly B. Mack (East Lansing: Michigan State University Press, 1997).

27. Fernand Dumont, *La Pensée religieuse d'Ahmadou Bamba* (Dakar: Nouvelles Editions Africaines, 1975).

28. 'Umar Tall, *Bayan ma Waqa'a*, translated from the Arabic, with an introduction by Sidi Mohamed Mahibou and Jean-Louis Triaud, *Voila ce qui est arrivé. Plaidoyer pour une guerre sainte en Afrique de l'Ouest au XIXe siècle* (Paris: Editions du CNRS, 1983).

29. Charles Stewart et al., "Catalogue of Arabic Manuscripts at the Institut mauritanien de recherche scientifique," *Islam et sociétés au sud du Sahara*, 4, 1990, 79–184.

30. Hamel, *Vie intellectuelle*.

31. Ahmad al-Amin al-Shinqiti, *Al-Wasit fi tarajim udaba al-Shinqit* (Cairo and Nouakchott: Maktabat al-khanji and Mu'assasat al-Munir, 1989).

32. Adam Heymouski and Moukhtar Ould Hamidoun, *Catalogue provisoire des manuscrits préservés en Mauritanie* (Nouakchott and Stockholm: 1965–1966).

33. Ulrich Rebstock, *Sammlung arabischer Handschriften aus Mauretanien: Kurzbeschreibungen von 2239 Handschrifteneinheiten mit Indices* (Wiesbaden: O. Harrassowitz, 1989).

34. Abdel Wedoud Ould Cheikh, Review of "Rohkatalog der arabischen handschriften in Mauretanien, *Islam et sociétés au sud du Sahara*, 1, 1987, 109–113, 109.

35. Ibid.

36. Charles Stewart, Sidi Ahmad Ould Ahmed Salim, and Ahmad Ould Muhammad Yahya, "Catalogue of Arabic Manuscripts at the Institut mauritanien de recherche scientifique," *Islam et sociétés au sud du Sahara*, 4, 1990, 179–184, 180.

37. Ibid.

38. Stewart et al., "Catalogue," 183.

39. Ould Cheikh, personal communication, Evanston Illinois, 2001.

40. http://www.al-furqan.com/en/introduction/introduction. Accessed November 2012.

41. http://www.al-furqan.com/en/introduction/introduction.

42. G. J. Roper, ed., *World Survey of Islamic Manuscripts*, 4 vols. (Leiden: E. J. Brill, 1994).

43. http://www.al-furqan.com/en/category/publications/catalogues?page=5

44. http://www.tombouctoumanuscripts.org/fr/libraries/ahmed_baba_institute_of _higher_learning_and_islamic_research_iheri-ab/. Accessed November 15, 2012.

45. Sidi Amar Ould Eli, comp., Julian Johansen, ed., *Handlist of Manuscripts in the Centre de Documentation et de Recherches Historiques Ahmad Baba Timbuktu*, Vol. 1 (London: Al-Furqan, 1995), mss 1–1500.

46. CEDRAB Librarians, comp., 'Abd al-Mushin Al-'Abbas, ed., *Handlist of Manuscripts in the Centre de Documentation et de Recherches Historiques Ahmad Baba Timbuktu*, Vol. 2, mss 1500–3000 (London: Al-Furqan, 1996); *idem*, Vol. 3, mss

3000–4500 (London: Al-Furqan, 1997); *idem*, Vol. 4 , mss 4500–6000 (London: Al-Furqan, 1998).

47. CEDRAB Librarians, comp., *Handlist of Manuscripts in the Centre de documentation et de recherches historiques Ahmad Baba Timbuktu* (London: Al-Furqan, 1998), Vol. 5, mss 6000–9000.

48. Abdelkader Mamma Haidara, comp., Fuad Sayyid Ayman, ed., *Catalogue of manuscripts in Mamma Haidara Library*, Vols. 1, 2, 3, (London: Al-Furqan, 2000); *idem*, Vol. 4, (London: Al-Furqan, 2003),. Haidara subsequently catalogued another private library, that at al-Zeiniyah in Boujbheiha, northern Mali, which was also published by the Al-Furqan Foundation as Abdelkader Mamma Haidara, comp., Fuad Sayyid Ayman, ed., *Catalogue of Islamic MSS in al-Zeiniyya Library Mali* (London: Al-Furqan, 2006).

49. Shamil Jeppie, "Re/Discovering Timbuktu," in Jeppie and Diagne, *Meanings of Timbuktu*, 1–17, 3.

50. Jeppie, "Re/Discovering Timbuktu," 8.

51. The South Africa–Mali Timbuktu Manuscripts Project is hosted at the Institute for Humanities in Africa, based at the University of Cape Town. http://www .tombouctoumanuscripts.org/about/.

52. An English version has been published in 2006 by Shamil Jeppie and Souleymane Bachir Diagne, eds., *The Meanings of Timbuktu* (Cape Town: Human Sciences Research Council, 2008). It was followed by a French version published by Shamil Jeppie and Souleymane Bachir Diagne, eds., *Tombouctou: Pour une histoire de l'érudition en Afrique de l'Ouest,* trans. Ousmane Kane (Dakar and Cape Town: Codesria and Human Sciences Research Council, 2012). An Arabic version is under preparation.

53. Mahmud Ka'ti, *Tarikh al-Fattash fi akhbar al-buldan wa 'l-juyush wa akabir al-nas.,* trans. O. Houdas and M. Delafosse (Paris: 1913; and with Arabic text, Paris: Maisonneuve et Larose, 1964).

54. Christopher Weise, ed., *Tarikh al-Fattash: The Timbuktu Chronicles 1493–1599. English Translation of the Original Works in Arabic by al-hajj Mahmud Ka'ti,* translated by Christopher Weise and Hala Abu Taleb (Trenton NJ: Africa Word Press, 2011).

55. Madina Ly, "Quelques remarques sur le Tarikh el-Fettash," *Bulletin de l'IFAN,* T.XXXIV, B, no. 32 (1972): 471–493, 471. The Tarikh al-Fattash has been attributed to Mahmud Ka'ti for a longtime, but this attribution has been contested by Nehemia Levtzion who argued that the author might have been a grandson of Ka'ti. See Nehemia Levtzion, "A seventeenth-century chronicle by Ibn al-Mukhtar: A critical study of "Tarikh al-Fattash", Bulletin of the School of Oriental and African Studies *34,* (1971), 571–593.

56. Abderrahman ben Abdallah ben 'Imran ben 'Amir es-Sa'di, *Tarikh al-Sudan,* French translation and edited Arabic text by O. Houdas (Paris: Leroux, 1898 and Paris: Libraire d'Amérique et d'Orient, 1964).

57. John Hunwick, *Timbuktu and the Songhay Empire: al-Sa'di's Tarikh al-Sudan down to 1613 and other contemporary documents* (Leiden: Brill, 1999).

58. Anonymous, *Tedzkiret en-nisyan fi akhbar molouk es-Soudan* [followed by the History of Sokoto], French translation and edited Arabic text by O. Houdas (Paris: Libraire d'Amérique et d'Orient, 1966).

59. Boubou Hama, "Contribution à l'étude de l'histoire des Peul" (Paris: 1968), cited in Shamil Jeppie, "History of Timbuktu: Ahmad Bula'raf, Archives and the Place of the Past," paper delivered at the Ifriqiyya Colloquium, (New York: Columbia University, October 2010).

60. Moulaye Hassane, comp., Fuad Ayman Hassan, ed., *Catalogue of Islamic MSS at the Instiut des Recherches en Sciences Humaines* (London: Al-Furqan, 2004–2006), 8 volumes.

61. Maurice Delafosse, *Chroniques du Fouta Sénégalais,* translated from two Arabic manuscripts by Siré Abbas Soh with the collaboration of Henry Gaden (Paris: Ernest Leroux, 1913).

62. Mohammadou Aliou Tyam, *La Vie D'El Hadj Omar: Qacida en Poular,* transcription, translation, notes, and glossary by Henry Gaden (Paris: Institut d'Ethnologie, 1935).

63. Vincent Monteil, "Les manuscrits historiques arabo-africains. Bilan provisoire," *Bulletin de l'Institut Fondamental d'Afrique Noire,* 1965, B, no. 27: 531–542; *idem,* "Les manuscrits historiques arabo-africains. Bilan provisoire," *Bulletin de l'Institut Fondamental d'Afrique Noire* B, no. 28 (1966): 668–675.

64. Thierno Diallo, Mame Bara Mbacké, Mirjana Trifcovic, and Boubacar Barry, "Catalogue des manuscrits de l'IFAN: Fonds Vieillard, Gaden, Brévié Figaret, Shaykh Musa Kamara et Cremer en langues arabe, peule et voltaique" (Dakar: IFAN, 1966).

65. Claudine Gerresch, "Le Livre de Métrique de Mubayyin Ishkal du Cadi Maadiakhaté Kala: Introduction historique, texte arabe, traduction et glossaire," *Bulletin de l'IFAN,* Série B, XXXVI, 4, 1974, 714–832.

66. Claudine Gerresch, "Tadhkirat al-Ghafilin ou un aspect pacifique peu connu de la vie de Al-Hajj Umar Tall."

67. Claudine Gerresch, "Une lettre de Ahmad al-Bakkay de Tombouctou à Al-Hajj Umar," *Bulletin de l'IFAN,* Série B, 38, no. 4 (1976): 890–903.

68. Amar Samb, *Contribution du Sénégal à la littérature d'expression arabe* (Dakar: IFAN, 1972).

69. Ousmane Kane and John Hunwick, "Senegambia II: Other Tijani Writers"; *idem,* "Writers of the Murid Tariqa"; *idem,* "Other Writers of the Senegambian Region"; Ousmane Kane, John Hunwick, and Rudiger Seeseman, "Senegambia I The Niassene Tijani Tradition," in John Hunwick, comp., *Arabic Literature of Africa: The Writings of Western Sudanic Africa* (Leiden: Brill, 2003).

70. El-Hadji Ravane Mbaye and Babacar Mbaye, "Supplément au catalogue des manuscrits de l'IFAN," *Bulletin de l'Institut Fondamental d'Afrique Noire,* Série B, 37, 1975, 878–895.

71. Thierno Ka and Khadim Mbacké, "Nouveau catalogue des manuscrits de l'IFAN," *Islam et sociétés au sud du Sahara*, 8 (1994), 165–199.

72. Khadim Mbacké, *Les Bienfaits de l'éternel ou la biographie de Cheikh Ahmadu Bamba* (Dakar: n.p., 1996).

73. Thierno Ka, *Ecole de Pir-Saniokhor et culture arabo-islamique au Sénégal du XVIIe au XXe siècle* (Dakar: GIA, n.d.); idem, *Ecole de Ndiaye-Ndiaye Wolof: Histoire, enseignement et culture arabo-islamique au Sénégal 1890–1990* (Dakar: IFAN, 2009).

74. Ousmane Kane, *Handlist of Manuscripts in the Libraries of Shaykh Mor Mbaye Cissé, al-H_ājj Malick Sy & Shaykh Ibraahim Niasse* (London: Al-Furqan, 1997).

75. David Robinson, "Un historien et anthropologue sénégalais: Shaikh Musa Kamara," *Cahiers d'Etudes Africaines,* 28, no. 109, 1988, 89–116.

76. Amar Samb (translation and annotation), "La vie d'El hadji Omar par Cheikh Moussa Camara," *Bulletin de l'Institut Fondamental d'Afrique Noire,* B, 32, no. 1, (1970), 44–135; idem, "La vie d'El hadji Omar par Cheikh Moussa Camara suite," *Bulletin de l'Institut Fondamental d'Afrique Noire,* B, 32, no. 2, (1970): 370–411; idem, "La vie d'El hadji Omar par Cheikh Moussa Camara suite et fin," *Bulletin de l'Institut Fondamental d'Afrique Noire,* 32, no. 3, (1970), 770–818; idem, "Condamnation de la guerre sainte de Cheikh Moussa Camara," *Bulletin de l'Institut Fondamental d'Afrique Noire,* B, 38, no. 1, (1976): 158–199.

77. Moustapha Ndiaye (presentation, translation, annotation), "Histoire de Ségou par Cheikh Moussa Camara," *Bulletin de l'Institut Fondamental d'Afrique Noire,* B, 43, no. 3, (1978): 458–488.

78. Schmitz, *Florilège.*

79. Tierno Mouhammadou Samba Mombya, "Oogirde Malal Ma'adinus sa'aadati," *Filon du Bonheur éternel,* Alfa Ibrahim Sow, trans. and ed. (Paris: Armand Collin 1971).

80. H. R. Palmer, trans., with an introduction, "The Kano Chronicle," *Journal of the Royal Anthropological Society* 38 (January–June 1908): 58–98.

81. Nehemiah Levtzion, "Islam in the Bilad al-Sudan," in Nehemia Levtzion and Randall Pouwels, eds., *The History of Islam in Africa* (Athens, OH: Ohio University Press, 2000).

82. Ahmad Ibn Fartuwa, *History of the First Twelve Years of the Reign of Mai Idris Aloma of Borno (1571–1583),* trans. H. R. Palmer (Lagos: Government Printer, 1973).

83. E. J. Arnett, *The Rise of the Sokoto Fulani* (Kano: 1922).

84. Professor Murray Last, personal communication, Cambridge, MA, April 2015.

85. See W. E. N. Kensdale, "The Arabic Manuscript Collection of the Library of the University College of Ibadan, Nigeria," *WA LA News* 2 (June 1955): 21–22. "A Catalogue of the Arabic Manuscripts Preserved in the University Library. Ibadan, Nigeria. Ibadan University Library, 1955–1958," 3 vols.; and "Field Notes on the Arabic Literature of the Western Sudan," *Royal Asiatic Society Journal,* 1955, pt. 3/4: 162–168; 1956, pt. 1/2: 78–80; 1958, pt. 1/2: 53–57. See http://www.loc.gov/rr/amed/afs/NigerianSurveyTour2007/NigerianSurveyTour.html.

86. Bivar, A. D. H. "The Arabic Calligraphy of Nigeria," *African Language Review,* 7, 1968: 3–15; "Arabic documents of Northern Nigeria," *Bulletin of the School of Oriental and Africa Studies,* 22, pt. 2, 1959: 324–349; Bivar and M. Hiskett, "The Arabic Literature of Nigeria to 1804: A Provisional Account," *Bulletin of the School of Oriental and African Studies,* 25, 1962: 104–148.

87. John Hunwick, "The Arabic Literature Project," in Shamil Jeppie and Souleymane Bachir Diagne, eds., *The Meanings of Timbuktu* (Cape Town and Dakar: HSRC and CODESRIA, 2008), 303–313, 303.

88. Professor Murray Last, personal communication, Cambridge, MA, April 2015.

89. John Naber Paden, *Ahmadu Bello, Sardauna of Sokoto: Values and leadership in Nigeria* (Zaria: Hudahuda Publishing Company, 1986), 552.

90. Abdullahi Smith, "A Neglected Theme of West African History: The Islamic Revolutions of the 19th century," in the Abdullahi Smith Centre for Historical Research, *A Little New Light. Selected Historical Writings of Abdullahi Smith* (Zaria: Gaskiya Corporation, 1987), 131–148, 132.

91. Smith, "Neglected Theme," 144.

92. Murray Last, *The Sokoto Caliphate* (London: Longman, 1967); Mahmud Tukur, "The Imposition of British Colonial Domination on the Sokoto Caliphate and Neighbouring States. 1817–1914. A Reinterpretation of Colonial Sources," PhD diss. in history, Ahmadu Bello University, 1979; Abdulahi Mahadi, "The State and the Economy, the Sarauta System and Its Role in Shaping the Society and Economy in Kano with Particular Reference to the Eighteenth and Nineteenth Century," PhD diss. in history, Ahmadu Bello University, 1982; Yusufu Bala Usman, *The Tranformation of Katsina* (Zaria: Ahmadu Bello University Press, 1981).

93. Ahmad Muhammad Kani, *The Intellectual Origin of Sokoto Jihad* (Ibadan: Imam Publications, 1984).

94. Fudi, *Bayan wujub al-hijra.*

95. Shehu Umar Abdullahi, *On the Search for a Viable Political Culture* (Kaduna: NNN Commercial Printing, 1984).

96. Sidi Mohamed Mahibou, *Abdullahi Dan Fodio et la théorie du gouvernement islamique* (Paris: L'Harmattan, 2010).

97. Muhammad Sani Zahradeen, "Abdullahi b. Fodio and his Contribution to the Fulani Jihad," PhD diss., McGill University, 1976.

98. Smith, "Neglected Theme."

99. Abdullahi Muhammad Sifawa, *Research in Islam: A Catalogue of Dissertations on Islam in Nigeria* (Sokoto: Centre for Islamic Studies, University of Sokoto, 1988).

100. Ali Abu Bakr, *Al-thaqafa al-'arabiyya fi Nijeriya* (Beirut: Mu'assassat 'Abd al-Hafid al-Bassat, 1972); Ahmad Said Galandanci, *Harakat al-lugha al-'arabiyya wa adabiha fi Nijeriya* (Cairo: Dar al-ma'arif, 1982).

101. M. Hiskett, *The Sword of Truth: The Life and Times of the Shehu Usman dan Fodio* (New York: Oxford University Press, 1973); *idem,* "Kitab al-Farq: A Work on the

Habe Kingdoms attributed to 'Uthman Dan Fodio," *Bulletin of the School of Oriental and African Studies,* 23, 3, 1960, 558–579.

102. Mervyn Hiskett, "Material Related to the State of Learning among the Fulani before Their Jihad," *Bulletin of the School of Oriental and African Studies,* 19, 3, 1957, 550–578.

103. Mervyn Hiskett, *A History of Hausa Islamic Verse* (London: University of London School of Oriental and African Studies, 1975).

104. Mervyn Hiskett, *An Anthology of Hausa Political Verses* (Hausa texts edited and annotated) (Evanston: Northwestern University Africana Library, 1977), ref. AFRI L893.721.

105. Ibid., 77.

106. Jean-Louis Triaud, "Les agents religieux islamiques en Afrique tropicale: réflexions autour d'un thème," *Canadian Journal of African Studies,* 19, no. 2, 1985, 271–282.

107. R. S. O'Fahey, comp., *Arabic Literature of Africa: The Writings of Eastern Sudanic Africa,* Vol. 1 (Leiden: Brill, 2003); John Hunwick, comp., *Arabic Literature of Africa: The Writings of Central Sudanic Africa,* Vol. 2 (Leiden: Brill, 1995); R. S. O'Fahey, comp., *Arabic Literature of Africa: The Writings of the Muslim People of Northeastern Africa,* Vol. 3; John Hunwick, comp., *Arabic Literature of Africa: The Writings of Western Sudanic Africa,* Vol. 4; and Charles Stewart, comp., Arabic *Literature of Africa: The Writings of Mauritania and the Western Sahara,* Vol. 5 (Leiden: Brill, 2015), 2 vols.

108. http://www.northwestern.edu/african-studies/research-centers/isita.html

109. Yahya Ould el-Bara. *Al-Majmu'a al-kubra al-shamila li fatawa wa nawazil wa ahkam ahl Gharb wa Janub gharb al-Sahra* (Nouakchott: al-maktaba al-wataniyya bi-nuakshut, 2009).

110. For a history of the database formation, see Charles Stewart et al., "Catalogue of Arabic Manuscripts"; Charles Stewart, "A West African Arabic manuscript database," in Jeppie and Diagne, *Meanings of Timbuktu,* 321–329.

111. See http://westafricanmanuscripts.org/. Accessed November 20, 2012.

112. Jeppie, "Rediscovering Timbuktu," 10.

113. Ibid.

114. Haïdara, "An Overview of the Major Manuscript Libraries, 241.

2. The Growth and Political Economy of Islamic Scholarship in the Bilad al-Sudan

1. Graham Furniss, *Poetry, Prose, and Popular Culture in Hausa* (Washington, DC: Smithsonian, 1990), ix.

2. Sheila Blair, "Arabic Calligraphy in West Africa," in Jeppie and Diagne, *Meanings of Timbuktu,* 59–75, 61; Jean-Louis Triaud, "Sudan (Bilad al)," *EI,* ii.

3. This was the case in the chronicles of Timbuktu, which, for the first time in the intellectual history of the region, presented a unified narrative of the different

regions of the Sahel in order to politically promote the descendants of the Askiya after the Moroccan conquest of Songhay. See Paulo F. de Moraes Farias, "Intellectual Innovation and Reinvention of the Sahel: The Seventeenth-Century Timbuktu Chronicles," in Jeppie and Diagne, *Meanings of Timbuktu,* 95–108, 104.

4. Anne K. Bang, "Textual Sources on an Islamic African Past: Arabic Material in Zanzibar's National Archive," in Jeppie and Diagne, *Meanings of Timbuktu,* 349–359.

5. Sean O'Fahey, "Arabic Literature in the Eastern Half of Africa," in Jeppie and Diagne, *Meanings of Timbuktu,* 349–359.

6. Murray Last, "The Book in the Sokoto Caliphate," in Jeppie and Diagne, *Meanings of Timbuktu,* 135–163.

7. Mudimbe, *Invention of Africa,* x.

8. Ghislaine Lydon, "Inkwells of the Sahara: Reflection on the Production of Islamic Knowledge in *Bilad Shinqit,*" in Scott Reese, ed., *The Transmission of Knowledge in Islamic Africa* (Leiden: Brill, 2003), 38–71, 41–42.

9. See "Al-Bakri," in Levtzion and Hopkins, *Corpus,* 62–87. Born in a princely family in Muslim Spain, Al-Bakri had never left Spain, but his informants had sojourned in the Sahara and the Sudan. For a translation of sections of his work on the Maghreb and the Sudan, see Abu ʿUbayd ʿAbd Allah ʿAbd al-Aziz Al-Bakri, *Kitab al-masalik waʾl-mamalik,* ed. Baron MacGukin de Slane, with the Arabic title *Kitab al-mughrib fi dhikr bilad Ifriqiyya waʾl-maghrib* and the French title *Description de l'Afrique Septentrionale* (Algiers: A Jourdan, 1913).

10. Levtzion and Hopkins, *Corpus,* 79.

11. Blair, "Arabic Calligraphy in West Africa," 69.

12. Ibn Battuta, *Travels of Ibn Battuta,* cited in Blair, "Arabic Calligraphy," 69.

13. Sean O'Fahey, "Arabic Literature in the Eastern Half of Africa," in Jeppie and Diagne, *Meanings of Timbuktu,* 333–347.

14. Jonathan Bloom, "Paper in Sudanic Africa," in Jeppie and Diagne, *Meanings of Timbuktu,* 45–57, 52.

15. On al-Kanami, see Levtzion and Hopkins, *Corpus,* 35; Hamidu Bobboyi, "The 'Ulama of Borno': A Study of the Relations between Scholars and State under the Sayfawa, 1470–1808," PhD diss. in history, Northwestern University, 1992, 10; M. Bencherifa, *Ibrahim al-Kanimi, Unmudhaj mubakkar li-l-tawassul al-thaqafi bayn al-Maghrib wa Bilad al-Sudan* (Rabat: Publications de l'Institut d'études africaines, 1991).

16. Bobboyi, "The 'Ulama of Borno," 8.

17. Bloom, "Paper in Sudanic Africa," 52; ʿUmar al-Naqar, *The Pilgrimage Tradition: A Historical Study with Particular Reference to the Nineteenth Century* (Khartoum: Khartoum University Press, 1972), 29.

18. See Taqi al-Din Ahmad al-Maqrizi, "Kitab al-Mawaʿiz wa ʾl-iʿtibar," in Levtzion and Hopkins, *Corpus,* 353.

19. Al-Naqar, *Pilgrimage Tradition,* 29.

20. Levtzion and Pouwels, "Islam in the Bilad al-Sudan," 81.

21. Muhammad Nur Alkali: "Nigeria: Significance of the Visit of Shehu of Borno to Istanbul," *Daily Trust*, November 21, 2011.

22. Malika Zeghal, *Gardiens de l'islam: Les Oulémas d'Al-Azhar dans l'Egypte contemporaine* (Paris: Presses de la Fondation Nationale des Sciences Politiques), 1996, 20, n. 1.

23. Mahmud 'Abbas Ahmad 'Abd al-Rahman, *Al-Azhar wa Afriqiyya. Dirasat wathaiqiyya*, 2003. I thank my colleague Malika Zeghal for drawing my attention to this reference.

24. Timothy Insoll, *The Archaeology of Islam in Sub-Saharan Africa* (Cambridge: Cambridge University Press, 2003), 220.

25. Insoll, *Archaeology of Islam,* 220; Nehemia Levtzion and Randall Pouwels, "Introduction," in Levtzion and Pouwels, *History of Islam in Africa,* 3.

26. See John Hunwick, "Towards a History of the Islamic Intellectual Tradition in West Africa down to the Nineteenth Century," *Journal for Islamic Studies* 17 (1997): 4–27, 5.

27. See al-Naqar, *Pilgrimage Tradition*, 7.

28. See Eric Ross, "Historical Geography of the Trans-Saharan Trade," in Krätli and Lydon, eds., *The Trans-Saharan Book Trade* (Leiden: Brill, 2010), 1–34, 15–16; al-Naqar, *Pilgrimage Tradition*, xxiv.

29. Levtzion and Pouwels, "Islam in the Bilad al-Sudan," 64.

30. John Hunwick, "Les rapports intellectuels entre le Maroc et l'Afrique subsaharienne à travers les âges," (Rabat: Publications de l'Institut des Etudes Africaines, 1990).

31. See Abu l-Qasim Ibn Hawqal al-Nusaybi, *Kitab Surat al-ard,* ed. J. H. Kramers. A French version of the book was published by Kramers as *Configuration de la Terre.* See Levtzion and Hopkins, *Corpus,* 44.

32. See Stefan Reichmuth, "Islamic Education and Scholarship in Sub-Saharan Africa," 422; Letvzion and Hopkins, eds., *Corpus,* 51.

33. See Paulo F. de Moraes Farias, "The Oldest Extant Writing of West Africa: Medieval Epigraphs from Essuk, Saney, and Egef-n-Tawaqqast (Mali)," *Journal des Africanistes,* 60, n. 2, 1990, 65–113 (cited in Reichmuth, *Islamic Education,* 436); Insoll, *The Archeology of Islam,* 216; and John Hunwick, "Gao and the Almoravids: A Hypothesis," in B. Swartz and R. E. Dumett, eds., *West African Culture Dynamics: Archeological and Historical Perspectives* (The Hague: Mouton & Co., 1979), 413–430.

34. See Farias, "Oldest Extant Writing;" John Hunwick, "Les rapports intellectuels," 14; Jean Sauvaget, "Les épitaphes royales de Gao," *BIFAN,* xii, 1940, 418–440.

35. See Makdisi, *Rise of Colleges,* chapter 1, which discusses extensively the ways in which Islamic endowments (*waqf* plural *awqaf*) contributed to the development of colleges.

36. Ibid., 36–37.

37. Ibid., 9.

38. "Al-Bakri," in Hopkins and Levtzion, *Corpus,* 71.

39. Ross, "Historical Geography," 17.

40. Ibid., 3. For more on the early Ibadi influence in the Bilad al-Sudan prior to the rise of the Almoravids, see el-Bara, *al-Majmu'a al-kubra,* 1, 70–75.

41. Nehemia Levtzion, "Merchants vs. Scholars and Clerics in West Africa. Differential and Complementary Roles," in Nehemia Levtzion and Humphrey Fisher, eds., *Rural and Urban Islam in West Africa* (Boulder, CO: L. Rienner, 1987), 21–37, 37.

42. Levtzion and Pouwels, "Introduction," in Levtzion and Pouwels, *History of Islam in Africa,* 11.

43. Ivor Wilks, "The Transmission of Learning in the Western Sudan," in Jack Goody, ed., *Literacy in Traditional Societies* (Cambridge: Cambridge University Press, 1975), 162–197, 170–171.

44. El-Bara, *Al-Majmu'a al-kubra,* 1, 66. Historian I. M. Lewis holds the same view; see *Islam in Tropical Africa* (London: Oxford University Press, 1966), 20.

45. See Levtzion, "Islam in the Bilad al-Sudan," 68; *idem,* "Merchants vs. Scholars and Clerics."

46. Levtzion, "Merchants vs. Scholars and Clerics," 23.

47. On the paper and book trade in the precolonial Bilad al-Sudan, see Bloom, "Paper in Sudanic Africa"; Last, "Book in the Sokoto Caliphate"; *idem,* "The Book and the Nature of Knowledge in Muslim Northern Nigeria 1457–2007," in Krälti and Lydon, *Trans-Saharan Book Trade,* 175–211; Ghislaine Lydon, "A Thirst for Knowledge: Arabic Literacy, Writing Paper and Saharan Bibliophiles in the Southwestern Sahara," in Krälti and Lydon, *Trans-Saharan Book Trade,* 35–72; Terrence Walz, "The Paper Trade in Egypt and the Sudan," in Krälti and Lydon, *Trans-Saharan Book Trade,* 73–107; Graziano Krälti, "Camel to Kilobytes: Preserving the Cultural Heritage of the Trans-Saharan Book Trade," in Krälti and Lydon, *Trans-Saharan Book Trade,* 35–72.

48. Roman Loimeier, *Muslim Societies in Africa: A Historical Anthropological* (Bloomington: Indiana University Press, 2013), 48–53.

49. Saad, *Social History of Timbuktu,* 16.

50. See, for example, the Kunta scholars in Saad, *Social History of Timbuktu,* chapter 2.

51. See Levtzion, "Merchants vs. Scholars and Clerics," 37; Last, *Sokoto Caliphate,* 231; Lamin Sanneh, *The Jakhanke Muslim Clerics: A Religious and Historical Study of Islam in Senegambia* (Landham MD: University Press of America, 1989), 47.

52. Sanneh, *Jakhanke,* 47.

53. Hasan Salah, *Art and Islamic Literacy among the Hausa of Northern Nigeria* (Lewison: Queeston, Lampter, 1982); René Bravmann, *Islam and Tribal Art in West Africa* (Cambridge: Cambridge University Press, 1974); *idem, African Islam* (Washington, DC: Smithsonian, 1983).

54. Salah, *Art and Islamic Literacy.*

55. Last, "Book in the Sokoto Caliphate," 142.

56. Blair, "Arabic Calligraphy," 63.

57. Levtzion and Hopkins, *Corpus*, 43–52.

58. "Al-Bakri," in Levtzion and Hopkins, *Corpus*, 62–87.

59. The full title is *Nuzhat al-mushtaq fi ikhtiraq al-afaq* (The Pleasure of Him Who Longs to Cross the Horizons). It was written for the king of Sicily, Norman Roger II, while Al-Idrisi was in residence there. See Levtzion and Hopkins, *Corpus*, 104.

60. See Lydon, "Inkwells," 52.

61. Ross, "Historical Geography," 18.

62. Hiskett, *Development of Islam*, 45.

63. Ibn Fadl Allah Al-'Umari (1301-1349) mentions in his Masalik al-absar fi mamalik al-amsar (*Pathways of Visions* in the Realm of Metropolises) that Mansa Musa, the king of Mali, was known by the Egyptians as the king of Takrur although in the fourteenth century Takrur was a province of the Empire of Mali. See Al-'Umari, Pathways of Visions in Levtzion and Hopkins, *Corpus*, 261.; Chouki el Hamel shows that the Takrur, which referred to a small kingdom in northern Senegal in the eleventh century, came to encompass almost the entire west and southwestern Sahara in the imagination of eighteenth-century writer Al-Burtuli. See maps of Takrur in, Chouki el Hamel, *La vie intellectuelle dans le Sahel ouest-africain.*, pages 62, 69, and 78.

64. al-Naqar, "Takrur: The History of a Name" *Journal of African History*, X, 3, 1969, 365-74

65. Al-Naqar, *Pilgrimage Tradition*, 4.

66. Ibid.

67. Hunwick, *Arabic Literature of Africa*, II, 568.

68. Al-Naqar, *Pilgrimage Tradition*, 27.

69. See the section "Pilgrimage of the king of Takrur" in Ibn Khaldun's text, the title of which is *Kitab al-'ibar wa Diwan al-mubtada wa 'l-khabar fi ayam al-'arab wa 'l-'ajam wa 'l-Barbar* (Book of Examples and the Registrar of the Subject and Predicate on the Days of the Arabs, the Persians and the Berbers), in Levtzion and Hopkins, *Corpus*, 322–323.

70. Hiskett, *Development of Islam*, 29.

71. Ibid.

72. Ibid., 15.

73. Ross, "Historical Geography," 18.

74. Jean-Louis Triaud, "Bilad al-Sudan," *Encyclopaedia of Islam II* (Leiden: E. J. Brill, 2002).

75. Hunwick and Boyle, *Hidden Treasures of Timbuktu*, 51.

76. Hiskett, *Development of Islam*, 15.

77. Ross, "Historical Geography," 21; Hiskett, *Development of Islam*, 15.

78. Levtzion and Hopkins, *Corpus*; Levtzion, "Islam in the Bilad al-Sudan," in Levtzion and Pouwels, *History of Islam*, 69, 292; Blair, "Arabic Calligraphy," 69.

79. Jonathan Bloom, *Paper before Print: The History and Impact of Paper in the Islamic World* (New Haven and London: Yale University Press, 2001), 85.

80. Bloom, "Paper in Sudanic Africa," 52.
81. Lydon, "Arabic Literacy," 45; Bloom, "Paper in Sudanic Africa," 45; Bloom, *Paper before Print*, 1.
82. Bloom, *Paper before Print*, 86.
83. Bloom, "Paper in Sudanic Africa," 55.
84. Ibid., 52.
85. Last, "Book in the Sokoto Caliphate," 138.
86. Lydon, "Arabic Literacy," 47.
87. Last, "Book in the Sokoto Caliphate," 152.
88. Ibid., 156.
89. Ibid., 141. The two famous nineteenth-century German explorers Heinrich Bart (1821–1865) and Gustav Nachtigal (1934–1895) noted in their travel narratives that paper was affordable and imported in large quantities in nineteenth-century Bilad al-Sudan. See Bloom, "Paper in Sudanic Africa," 53.
90. Last, "Book in the Sokoto Caliphate," 153.
91. Ibid., 155.
92. Ibid., 149.
93. For an analysis of the etymology, see F. Gabrieli, "'Adjam," in *Encyclopaedia of Islam II*.
94. Qur'an 16–103: "And we certainly know that they say, 'It is only a human being who teaches the Prophet. The tongue of the one they refer to is foreign, and this Qur'an is [in] a clear Arabic language."
95. Jan Knappert, "The Transmission of Knowledge: A Note on the Islamic Literatures of Africa" *Sudanic Africa*, 7, 1996, 159-164.; Ousmane Kane, "Senegal," in G. J. Roper, *World Survey of Islamic Manuscripts*.
96. Moulaye Hassane, "Ajami in Africa: The Use of Arabic Script in the Transcription of African Languages," in Jeppie and Diagne, *Meanings of Timbuktu*, 109–121.
97. Meikal Mumin, "The Arabic Script in Africa: Understudied Literacy," in Meikal Mumin and Kees Versteegh, *The Arabic Script in Africa. Studies in the Use of a Writing System* (Boston and Leiden: Brill 2014), 41–76.
98. Mumin, *Arabic Script in Africa*, 64–68.
99. Mahmud Hamu, *Al-kashf 'an al-makhtutat al-arabiyya wa al-maktubat bil-harf al-'arabi fi mintaqat al-sahil al-Ifriqi*, Timbutku, undated and unpublished manuscript. I am grateful to Andrea Brigaglia for supplying me a copy of this manuscript.
100. Levtzion, "Islam in the Bilad al-Sudan," in Levtzion and Pouwels, *History of Islam in Africa*, 11.
101. A huge body of postindependence literature analyzed the jihad. Some good syntheses include Mervyn Hiskett, "The Nineteenth-Century Jihads in West Africa," in John E. Flint, *The Cambridge History of Africa* (Cambridge: Cambridge University Press, 1976), vol. 5, 125-69; Murray Last, "Reform in West Africa: The Jihad Movements of the Nineteenth Century," in J. F. Ade Ajayi and Michael

Crowder, *History of West Africa* (London: Longmans, 1974, vol. 2, 1-29; David Robinson, "Revolutions in the Western Sudan," in Levtzion and Pouwels, *History of Islam in Africa;* Smith, "Neglected Theme."

102. Hamid Bobboyi, "Ajami Literature and the Study of the Sokoto Caliphate," in Jeppie and Diagne, *Meanings of Timbuktu,* 123–133.

103. Knappert, "Transmission of Knowledge," 123–124.

104. For an analysis of such texts, see Bobboyi, "Ajami Literature and the Study of the Sokoto Caliphate."

105. Blair, "Arabic Calligraphy," 69; Adrian Bivar, "The Arabic Calligraphy of West Africa," *African Language Review,* 7, 1968.

106. O. Houdas, "Essai sur l'écriture maghrébine." In *Nouveaux mélanges orientaux* (Paris: Ecole des langues orientales vivantes, 1886).

107. Blair, "Arabic Calligraphy," 61.

108. Ibid.

109. Hamu, *Al-kashf 'an al-makhtutat al-'arabiyya.*

110. Ibid.

111. Hunwick, *Arabic Literature of Africa,* Vol. II, 172.

112. Andrea Brigaglia, "Central Sudanic Arabic Script Part 1. The Popularization of the Kanawi Script." Islamic Africa, Vol. 2, 2, 2011, 51-85.

113. Blair, "Arabic Calligraphy," 70.

114. Last, "Book in the Sokoto Caliphate," 153.

115. Last, "Book and the Nature of Knowledge," 187.

116. Last, *Sokoto Caliphate.*

117. A. Cherbonneau, "Essai sur la littérature arabe au Soudan d'après le Tekmilet ed-Dibaje d'Ahmed Baba le Tombouctien," *Annales de la Société archéologique de Constantine;* ii, 1854-55, 1-42., 3.

118. Blair, "Arabic Calligraphy," 64.

119. Last, "Book in the Sokoto Caliphate," 136.

3. The Rise of Clerical Lineages in the Sahara and the Bilad al-Sudan

1. In Arabic: Al-hikmatu kuntiyatun aw futiyatun.

2. Mahmood Mamdani, *Citizen and Subject: Contemporary Africa and the Legacy of Late Colonialism* (Princeton: Princeton University Press, 1996), 61.

3. Bruce S. Hall, *A History of Race in Muslim West Africa, 1600–1960* (Cambridge: Cambridge University Press, 2011).

4. Chouki El Hamel, *Black Morocco. A History of Slavery, Race and Islam* (Cambridge: Cambridge University Press, 2013), 9.

5. See Timothy Cleaveland, "Ahmed Baba and His Islamic Critique of Slavery in the Maghreb," *Journal of North African Studies* 20, no. 1 (2015): 42–64.

6. Ibid., 45.

7. El-Bara, *Al-Majmu'a al-kubra,* 1, 90.

8. Ibid.

9. Hiskett, *Development of Islam,* 44.
10. For intermarriage between Fulanis and Berbers in eighteenth-century Central Sudan, for example, see Hiskett, *Development of Islam,* 49, 51.
11. See my article on "Shinqit" in the *Encyclopaedia of Islam,* 2nd ed.
12. Information on Walata in this paragraph relies on Timothy Cleaveland, *Becoming Walata: A History of Saharan Social Formation and Transformation* (Portsmouth, NH: Heinemann, 2002), chapter 5, and, *idem,* "Timbuktu and Walata: Lineages and Higher Education," in Jeppie and Diagne, eds., *Meanings of Timbuktu,* 77–91.
13. Cleaveland, "Timbuktu and Walata," 79.
14. Ibid.
15. Ibid., 86.
16. See John Hunwick, "Review of Al-Timbukti's *Nayl al-Ibtihaj,*" *Sudanic Africa,* 3, 1992, 182–185, 182.
17. El Hamel, *La vie intellectuelle dans le Sahel ouest-africain.*
18. Cleaveland, "Timbuktu and Walata," 86–89.
19. Souleymane Bachir Diagne, "Toward an Intellectual History of West Africa: The Meanings of Timbuktu," in Jeppie and Diagne, *Meanings of Timbuktu,* 19–27, 21.
20. Saad, *Social History of Timbuktu,* 110.
21. Schmitz, *Florilège.*
22. Al-Naqar, *Pilgrimage Tradition.*
23. John Ralph Willis, "The Torodbe Clerisy: A Social View," *Journal of African History* 19, no. 2: 195–212; Hiskett, *Development of Islam,* 52.
24. Scholars diverge on when he lived. One authority on the Jakhanke, Yale professor Lamin Sanneh, argued that he lived in the thirteenth century (Sanneh, *Jakhanke Muslim Clerics*). Another authority, Ivor Wilks, believed that he lived in the fifteenth century: Ivor Wilks, "The Juula and the Expansion of Islam into the Forest," in Levtzion and Pouwels, eds., *History of Islam in Africa,* 93–115, 96–98. In support of his claim, Wilks shows that Suwari taught the Qur'anic exegesis coauthored by 'Abd al-Rahman al-Suyuti, which was completed in the late fifteenth century.
25. Wilks, "The Juula," 98.
26. Ibid.
27. Hiskett, *Development of Islam,* 170.
28. Robinson, "Revolutions in the Western Sudan," in Levtzion and Pouwels, eds., *History of Islam in Africa* (Athens, OH: Ohio University Press, 2000), 131–152, 133.
29. Hiskett, *Development of Islam,* 140.
30. Boubacar Barry, *Senegambia and the Atlantic Slave Trade* (Cambridge: Cambridge University Press, 1998); *idem,* "La Guerre des marabouts dans la région du Fleuve Sénégal de 1673 à 1677," *BIFAN* sér B XXXIII, no. 3 (1971): 565–589.
31. Hiskett, *Development of Islam,* 20.
32. Ibid., 27.

33. El-Bara, *Al-Majmu'a al-kubra*, 1, 74.

34. Hiskett, *Development of Islam*, 7.

35. El-Bara, *Al-Majmu'a al-kubra*, 1, 83.

36. Ibid., 1, 83–84.

37. Known as the *Al-Burda* (The Mantle, in Arabic), the full title of this panegyric of the Prophet is *al-kawakib al-duriyya fi madh khayr al-bariyya* (The Shining Planets, or the Eulogy to the Best of All Creatures), and it was composed by Sharaf al-din al-Busiri al-Sanhaji (1226–1294). For a French translation, see Sharafu-d-Din al-Busiri, *Al-Burda (le manteau). Poème consacré au Prophète de l'islam*, trans. Hamza Boubakeur (Montreuil: Imprimerie TIPE, 1980).

38. Hunwick, "Towards a History of the Islamic Intellectual Tradition," 7.

39. For a synthesis of the Wangara presence in its historical and geographical breadth in Africa, see Andreas W. Massing, "The Wangara. An Old Soninke Diaspora in West Africa," *Cahiers d'études africaines* 158 (2000): 281–308; Philip Curtin, "The Lure of the Bambuk Gold," *Journal of African History* 14, no. 4 (1973): 623–631; F. Fuglestad, "A Reconsideration of Hausa History before the Jihad," *Journal of African History* 19 (1978): 319–339; Dierk Lange, "From Mande to Songhay: Towards a Political and Ethnic History of Medieval Gao," *Journal of African History* 35 (1994): 275–301; Paul E. Lovejoy, "The Role of the Wangara in the Economic Transformation of the Central Sudan in the 15th and 16th Centuries," *Journal of African History* 19 (1978): 173–193; Paul Lovejoy, *Ecology and Ethnography of Muslim Trade in Muslim West Africa* (Trenton, NJ: Africa World Press, 2005); S. K. McIntosh, "A Reconsideration of Wangara/Palolus the Island of Gold," *Journal of African History* 22, no. 2 (1981): 145–158; Ivor Wilks, "A Medieval Trade-Route from the Niger to the Gulf of Guinea," *Journal of African History* 3, no. 2 (1962): 337–340; Ivor Wilks, "Wangara, Akan and Portuguese in the 15th and 16th Centuries," *Journal of African History* 23 (1982): 333–349, 463–472; Julius O. Adekunle, "Borgu and Economic Transformation 1700–1900: The Wangara Factor," *African Economic History* 22 (1994): 1–18; O Akinwumi and A. Y. Rayi, "The Wangara Factor in the History of Nigerian Islam: An Example of Kano and Borgu," *Islamic Studies* (Islamabad) 29, no. 4 (1990): 375–385; Musa Baba Idris, "The Role of the Wangara in the Formation of the Trading Diaspora in Borgu," International Conference on Manding Studies, London (1972); Robin Law, "'Central and Eastern Wangara': An Indigenous West African Perception of the Political and Economic Geography of the Slave Coast as Recorded by Joseph Dupuis in Kumasi, 1820," *History in Africa* 22 (1995): 281–305; Nehemia Levtzion, "The Wangara in Hausaland," International Conference on Manding Studies (London: 1972); Paul E. Lovejoy, "Notes on the Asl al-Wangariyin," *Kano Studies* 1, no. 3 (1978): 46–52; Scarsbrick and P. J. Carter, "An Expedition to Wangara," *Ghana Notes and Queries* 1 (1961): 4–5; Heinz Soelken, "Wangara: Afrikanistische Betrachtungen zur alten Geographie des Sudan," *Frankfurter Geographische Hefte* 37 (1961): 201–225; Ivor Wilks, "Consul Dupuis and Wangara: A Window on Islam in Early 19th Century Asante," *Sudanic Africa* (1995): 55–72.

40. John Hunwick, "Leo Africanus Description of the Middle Niger," in Hunwick, *Timbuktu and the Songhay Empire.*
41. McIntosh, "A Reconsideration of Wangara/Palolus the Island of Gold," 158.
42. Vincent Monteil, "Al-Bakrî (Cordoue 1068). Routier de l'Afrique blanche et noire du Nord-Ouest (Kitâb al-Masâlik wa-l-Mamâlik)," *Bulletin de l'IFAN* Série B XXX, no. 1 (1968): 39–116, 59.
43. See "Leo Africanus Description of the Middle Niger, Hausaland and Borno" in Hunwick, *Timbuktu and the Songhay Empire*, 272–291, 288.
44. "Al-Idrisi," in Levtzion and Hopkins, *Corpus*, 107–108.
45. "Ibn Battuta," in Levtzion and Hopkins, *Corpus*, 279–304, 287.
46. Massing, "Wangara. An Old Soninke Diaspora," 18.
47. For a detailed study of the Jakhanke in Senegambia, see Sanneh, *Jakhanke Muslim Clerics;* Abdoul Kader Taslimanka Sylla, *Bani Israël du Sénégal ou Ahl Diakha peuple de diaspora* (Paris: Publibook, 2012).
48. It was published as Muhammad A. al-Hajj, "A Seventeenth-Century Chronicle on the Origins and Missionary Activities of the Wangarawa," *Kano Studies* 1, no. 4 (1968): 7–17.
49. H. R. Palmer, "Kano Chronicle," 70.
50. Al-hajj, "A Seventeenth-Century Chronicle," 8.
51. See Chapter 4, "Curriculum and Knowledge Transmission," for a further discussion of these texts.
52. Sanneh, *Jakhanke Muslim Clerics*, 7–8.
53. Al-Hajj, "A Seventeenth-Century Chronicle," 8.
54. Ibid.
55. Massing, "Wangara: An Old Soninke Diaspora," 30.
56. Sanneh, *Jakhanke Muslim Clerics*, 16.
57. Hiskett, *Development of Islam in West Africa*, 6.
58. Hunwick, "Toward a History of the Islamic Intellectual Tradition," 12.
59. For a discussion of these specializations and their various explanations, see Louis Brenner, *Controlling Knowledge: Religion, Power and Schooling in a West African Muslim Society* (London: Hurst, 2000), 24.
60. Dedoud Ould Abdallah, "Dawr al-Shanaqita fi nashr al-thaqafa al-'arabiyya al-islamiyya bi-Gharb Ifriqiyya hatta nihayat al-qarn al-thamina 'ashar li 'l-milad" (Contribution of Shanaqita to the Spread of Arab-Islamic Culture until the End of the Eighteenth Century), *Annales de la Fac. des Lettres et des Sciences Humaines de l'Univ. de Nouakchott* (1989): 13–33.
61. 'Abd al-'Aziz 'Abdallah Batran, "A Contribution to the Biography of Shaikh Muhammad Ibn 'Abd al-Karim Ibn Muhammad ('Umar-A'mar) al-Maghili al-Tilimsani," *Journal of Africa History* XIV, no. 3 (1973): 381–394, 394.
62. Ibid, 391.
63. See 'Abd al-Karim al-Maghili, "'Taj al-Din fi ma yajib 'ala al-muluk' or 'The Crown of Religion: Concerning the Obligations of Princes,'" in Hassan I.

Gwarzo, Kamal I. Bedri, and Priscilla Starratt, eds., *Kano Studies* (new series) 1, no. 2 (1974–1977): 15–28.

64. For a French version, see El-Haji Ravane Mbaye (translation and annotation), "Un aperçu de l'islam songhay ou Réponses d'Al-Maghili aux questions posées par Askia el-Hadji Muhammad, empereur de Gao," *Bulletin de l'IFAN* Série B XXXIV, no. 2 (1972): 237–267; for an English version, see John Hunwick, ed. (with an introduction and commentary), *Shari'a in Songhay. The Replies of Al-Maghili to the Questions of Askia al-Hajj Muhammad* (Oxford: Oxford University Press, 1985).

65. E. Ann McDougall, "The Economies of Islam in the Southern Sahara: The Rise of the Kunta Clans," in Levtzion and Fisher, *Rural and Urban Islam in West Africa*, 39–54, argues that their economic and religious influence was "unmatched among Southern Sahara zawaya," 39.

66. Abdel Wedoud Ould Cheikh, "A Man of Letters in Timbuktu: al-Shaykh Sidi Mukhtar al-Kunti," in Jeppie and Diagne, *Meanings of Timbuktu*, 231–247; Yahya Ould el Bara, "The Life of Shaykh Sidi al-Mukhtar al-Kunti," in Jeppie and Diagne, *Meanings of Timbuktu*, 193–211; Aziz Batran, *The Qadiriyya Brotherhood in West Africa and the Western Sahara: The Life and Times of Shaykh al-Mukhtar al-Kunti (1729–1881)* (Rabat: Institut des Etudes Africaines, 2001).

67. Hiskett, *Development of Islam*, 49.

68. E. Ann McDougall, "Economies of Islam," 39; Ould el-Barra, *Life of Sidi Mukhtar al-Kunti*, 198.

69. For a biography and exhaustive compilation of several generations of Kunta Scholars, see John Hunwick, "The Saharan Fringes of Mali: 1 The Kunta," in Hunwick, *Arabic Literature of Africa. Vol. 4, The Writings of Western Sudanic Africa*, 67–148; Ross, "Historical Geography," 26; Mohammed Ibrahim El-Kettani, "Les manuscripts de l'Occident africain dans les bibliothèques du Maroc," in Attilio Gaudio, ed., *Les Bibliothèques du desert* (Paris: L'harmattan, 2002); Abdallah wuld Mawlud wuld Daddah, "Shaykh Sidi Muhammad wuld al-Mukhtar al-Kunti: Contribution à l'histoire politique et religieuse de Bilad al-Shinqit et des régions voisines, notamment d'après les sources arabes inédites," PhD diss., Université de Paris IV, Sorbonne, 1977.

70. Winifred Marie Johnson, "The Tijaniyya Sufi Order amongst the Idaw 'Ali of Western Sahara," accessed December 2012, http://i-epistemology.net/history/369-the-tijaniyya-sufi-brotherhood-amongst-the-idaw-ali-of-the-western-sahara.html.

71. See Brenner, "Muslim Divination and the Study of Religion in Africa," in John Pemberton, ed., *Insight and Artistry in African Divination* (Washington and London: Smithsonian Institution Press, 2000), 45–59.

72. Hunwick, "Towards a History of the Islamic Intellectual Tradition," 14.

73. Robin Horton, "Stateless Societies in the History of West Africa," in J. F. Ade Ajayi and Michael Crowder, *History of West Africa*, Vol. 1 (London: Longman, 1985), 87–128, 13.

74. On the pre-colonial curriculum of the Fulbe, see Hiskett, "Material Related to the State of Learning," and A. D. Bivar and Mervyn Hiskett, "The Arabic Literature of Nigeria to 1804: A Provisional Account," *Bulletin of the School of Oriental and African Studies* (1962): 104–114; al-Hadi Mabruk al-Dali, *Qaba'il al-Fullan. Dirasa watha'iqiyya* (Tripoli: al-Sharika al-'amma li al-waraq wa al-tiba'a, 2002–2003).

75. R. M. Dilley, *Islamic and Caste Knowledge Practices among Haal Pulaar'en in Senegal: Between Mosque and Termite Mound* (Edinburgh: Edinburgh University Press, 2004), 95.

76. For a comprehensive list of their works, see chapters 2, 3, and 4 of John Hunwick, *Arabic Literature of Africa*, Vol. II, *The Writings of Central Sudanic Africa*: "The Fodiawa (1) Shaykh 'Uthman b. Muhammad Fudiye," 52–85; "The Fodiawa (2) 'Abd Allah b. Muhammad Fudiye," 86–113; "The Fodiawa (3) Muhammad Bello," 114–149. For a more detailed analysis of the styles, themes, and contents provided in chapter 5 of Ali Abu Bakr, see *Al-thaqafa al-'arabiyya fi Nigeria,* "al-intaj al-adabi fi al-qarn al-tasi' 'ashar" (The Intellectual Production of the Nineteenth Century), 246–322.

77. Jean Boyd and Murray Last, "The Role of Women as 'Agents Religieux' in Sokoto," *Canadian Journal of African Studies* 19, no. 2 (1985): 283–300, 286.

78. Boyd and Mack, *Collected works of Nana Asma'u;* Jean Boyd and Beverly Mack, *One Woman's Jihad: Nana Asma'u, Scholar and Scribe* (Bloomington: Indiana University Press, 2000); J. Boyd, *The Caliph's Sister, Nana Asma'u, 1793–1865: Teacher, Poet & Islamic Leader* (Bloomington: Indiana University Press, 2000).

79. John Hunwick, "The Arabic Literature of Africa Project," in Jeppie and Diagne, *Meanings of Timbuktu,* 306.

80. M. A. Al-Hajj, "The Writings of Shehu Uthman Dan Fodio: A Plea for Dating and Chronology," *Kano Studies* 1, no. 2 (1974–1977): 5–14, 9.

81. Last, "Book in the Sokoto Caliphate," 141; Boyd and Last, "Role of Women as 'Agents Religieux,'" 290.

82. Beverly Mack, "Muslim Women Scholars in the Nineteenth and Twentieth Centuries: Morocco to Nigeria," in Jeppie and Diagne, eds., *Meanings of Timbuktu,* 165–179, 167; Balaraba B. M. Sule and Priscilla Starratt, "Islamic Leadership Positions for Women," in C. Coles and B. Mack, eds., *Hausa Women in the Twentieth Century* (Madison: University of Wisconsin Press, 1991).

83. Beverly Mack, "Muslim Women Scholars," in Jeppie and Diagne, *Meanings of Timbuktu,* 178, n. 22.

84. Barry, *Senegambia and the Atlantic Slave Trade,* 95–102.

85. David Robinson, *Chiefs and Clerics. Abdul Bokar Kan and Futa Toro, 1853–1891* (Oxford: Clarendon Press, 1975); Barry, *Senegambia and the Atlantic Slave Trade,* 102–106.

86. Bintou Sanankoua, *Un empire peul du XIX e siècle: La Diina du Macina* (Paris: Karthala, 1990).

87. See David Robinson, *The Holy War of Umar Tal: The Western Sudan in the*

Mid-Nineteenth Century (Oxford: Clarendon Press, 1985). In addition to the excellent study of Robinson, two other biographies that better reflect the Tall family's perspective on Umar Tall are provided by his great granddaughter and his great grandson. The first in the French language is Madina Ly Tall, *Un Islam militant en Afrique de l'ouest au XIXe siècle: la Tijaniyya de Saiku Umar Futiyu contre les pourvoirs traditionnels et la puissance coloniale* (Paris: L'Harmattan, 1991), and the second, monumental one of more than a thousand pages in Arabic is Muhammad al-Muntaqa Ahmad Tall, *Al-Jawahir wa al-durar fi Sirat al-Shaykh Al-Hajj Umar Tall* (Beirut: Dar al-Buraq, 2005).

88. Titled *Rimah Hizb al-Rahim 'ala Nuhur Hizb al-Rajim* (The Spear of the Merciful against the Throat of the Reviled), this text has still not been translated into a European language. For an analysis of the text, see John Hunwick, "An Introduction to the Tijani Path: Being an Annotated Translation of the Chapter Headings of the Kitab al-Rimah of Al-Hajj 'Umar Tall," *Islam et Societies au Sud du Sahara* 6 (1992): 17–32.

89. Hill, "Divine Knowledge"; Eric Ross, "Marabout Republics Then and Now: Configuring Muslim Towns in Senegal," *Islam et Sociétés au Sud du Sahara* 16 (2002): 35–65.

90. Ka, *Ecole de Pir-Saniokhor.*

91. Cheikh Gueye, *Touba: La capital des Mourides* (Paris: Karthala, 2002).

92. Much of our discussion is focused on West Africa. For a discussion of the formation of Shurafa communities in East Africa, see Abdul Hamid M. el-Zein, *The Sacred Meadows: A Structural Analysis of Religious Symbolism in an East African Town* (Evanston, IL: Northwestern University Press, 1974).

93. David Robinson, *Muslim Societies in African History* (Cambridge: Cambridge University Press, 2004), 52–53.

4. Curriculum and Knowledge Transmission

1. See Shaykh Hadi Niasse, "Celebration of the birthday of the Prophet Muhammad," a lecture delivered in New York in 2002, and translated from Wolof by the author. A narrative with some similarity by Shaykh Ibrahim Niasse is reported in John Paden, *Religion and Political Culture in Kano* (Berkeley: University of California Press, 1973), 134–135.

2. Sean O'Fahey, *Enigmatic Saint: Ahmad Ibn Idris and the Idrisi Tradition* (Evanston, IL: Northwestern University Press, 1990), 175.

3. See Zachary Wright, *On The Path of the Prophet. Shaykh Ahmad Tijani and the Tariqa Muhammadiyya* (Atlanta: The African American Islamic Institute, 2005, 128–133.

4. For an elaborate discussion of Muhammadan reality and its centrality in Tijaniyya Sufism, see Ogunnaike, "Sufism and Ifa," chapter 3.

5. See Bruce Hall and Charles Stewart, "The Historic 'Core Curriculum' and the Book Market in Islamic West Africa," in Krätli and Lydon, eds., *Trans-Saharan*

Book Trade, 109–174. Others who offer a good overview of circulating texts in specific regions of the Sahel include Dedoud Ould Abdallah, *Dawr al-Shanaqita,* 29, which covers Saharan scholarship; Ka, *Ecole de Pir Saniokhor,* which covers Senegambian Islamic scholarship; Hunwick, *Timbuktu and the Songhay Empire,* which deals with Islamic scholarship in the Middle Niger; and, finally, Hiskett, "Material Relating to the State of Learning," and Bivar and Hiskett, "The Arabic Literature of Nigeria to 1804," which cover Islamic scholarship in the central Sudan.

6. http://www.islamweb.net/emainpage/index.php?page=showfatwa&Option =FatwaId&Id=91087

7. Denny, *Encyclopaedia of Islam II.*

8. Ibid.

9. Cheikh Hamidou Kane, *Ambiguous Adventure* (London: Heinemann, 1972), 1.

10. Hall and Stewart , "Historic 'Core Curriculum,'" 118.

11. See A. Rippin, "Tafsir," *Encyclopaedia of Islam II.*

12. Levtzion, "Islam in the Bilad al-Sudan to 1800," 70.

13. See Hunwick, *Timbuktu and the Songhay Empire,* 51, 59.

14. John Hunwick, "Note on a Late Fifteenth-Century Document concerning al-Takrur," in C. Allen and R. W. Johnson, *African Perspectives: Papers in the History, Politics and Economics of Africa presented to Thomas Hodgkin* (Cambridge: Cambridge University Press, 1970), 29–30; Levtzion, *Islam in the Bilad al-Sudan to 1800,* 73.

15. Ibrahim Niasse, *Removal of Confusion,* 10, n. 16.

16. See Ousmane Kane, *Handlist of Manuscripts in the Libraries of Shaykh Serigne Mor Mbaye Cissé, al-Hajj Malick Sy & Shaykh Ibraahim Niasse* (London: Al-Furqan, 1997).

17. See Shaykh Ibrahim Niasse, *Fi Riyad al-Tafsir li l-Quran al-karim,* six volumes, compiled by Muhammad b. 'Abdallah (Lemden, Mauritania: Muhammad b. Shayh 'Abdallah Publishers, 2010).

18. See Niasse Ibrahim, *Translation and Interpretation of the Holy Quran in Wolof 1950–1960* (New York: Sall Family Publishers, 1998).

19. Ibrahim Niasse, *Jawahir al-Rasa'il,* Being a Collection of Letters Written by the Author, part II (Borno: Abul Fath 'Ali al-Yarawi Publisher, n.d.), 59.

20. Joseph Hill, "Divine Knowledge," 2; Michael Lambek and Andrew Strathern, "Body and Mind in Mind. Body and Mind in Body. Some Anthropological Interventions in a Long Conversation," in *Bodies and Persons. Comparative Perspectives from Africa and Melanesia* (Cambridge: Cambridge University Press, 1998); Michael Lambek, "Certain Knowledge Contestable Authority: Power and Practice on the Islamic Periphery," *American Ethnologist* 17 (1990): 23–40.

21. Andrea Brigaglia, "Learning, Gnosis and Exegesis: Public Tafsir and Sufi Revival in the City of Kano (Northern Nigeria)," *Die Welt Des Islams* 49, no. 2 (2009): 334–366.

22. This paragraph draws from Wael Hallaq, *Introduction to Islamic Law,* 7–11.

23. Hall and Stewart, "Historic 'Core Curriculum,'" 29–30.

24. Vincent Cornell, *Realm of the Saint: Power and Authority in Moroccan Sufism* (Austin: University of Texas Press, 1998), xxiv.

25. Lansine Kaba, *The Wahhabiyya: Islamic Reform and Politics in French West Africa* (Evanston IL: Northwestern University Press, 1971); Ousmane Kane, *Muslim Modernity in Postcolonial Northern Nigeria: A Study of the Society for the Removal of Innovation and Reinstatement of Tradition* (Leiden: Brill, 2003); Roman Loimeier, *Islamic Reform and Political Change in Northern Nigeria* (Evanston, IL: Northwestern University Press), 1997.

26. See John Hunwick, *Timbuktu and the Songhay Empire,* 65–67, or Mukhtar b. Yahya al-Wangari, "Shaykh Baghayogho al-Wangari and the Wangari Library in Timbuktu," in Jeppie and Diagne, *Meanings of Timbuktu,* 281–82.

27. Hall and Stewart, "Historic 'Core Curriculum,'" 132.

28. Ibid., 133. The first local commentary on the Mukhtasar was composed by Mahmud B. 'Umar Aqit (1463–1548), who popularized it while teaching in Timbuktu. Stefan Reichmuth, "Islamic Education in Sub-Saharan Africa," in Levtzion and Pouwels, eds., *History of Islam,* 427.

29. See 'Uthman b. Fudi, *Bayan wujub al-hijra,* 48.

30. See Chapter 5 for a discussion of fatwas on slavery.

31. John Hunwick, *Shari'a in Songhay. The Replies of Al-Maghili to the Questions of Askia al-Hajj Muhammad* (Oxford: Oxford University Press, 1985); El Hadj Ravane Mbaye, "Un aperçu de l'islam Songhay ou Réponses d'Al-Maghili aux questions posées par Askia el-Hadji Muhammad, empereur de Gao," *Bulletin de l'IFAN,* série B, XXXIV, no. 2, 1972, 237–67.

32. For an elaborate discussion of the paradigm shifts in the understanding of knowledge in medieval Islamic history, see Franz Rosenthal, *Knowledge Triumphant: The Concept of Knowledge in Medieval Islam* (Leiden and Boston: Brill, 1970).

33. J. Robson, "Hadith," *Encyclopaedia of Islam II.*

34. Ibid.

35. This is found in many West African collections. I also found copies of this poem in all Senegalese collections that I catalogued. See Kane, *Handlists of Islamic Manuscripts.*

36. See Sharafu-d-Din, al-Busiri, *Al-Burda.*

37. Muhammad b. Suleyman al-Jazuli, *Dala'il al-khayrat wa shawariq al-anwar fi dhikr al-salat 'ala al-nabi al-mukhtar,* translated as *Guide to Goodness* by Andrey Hassan Rosowsky (Chicago: Great Books of the Islamic World, 2006).

38. See Ousmane Kane and John Hunwick, "Senegambia III: Writers of the Murid Tariqa," in Hunwick, *Arabic Literature of Africa,* Vol. IV, 396–452; Dumont, *La Pensée religieuse d'Ahmadou Bamba.*

39. See Ousmane Kane, *The Homeland Is the Arena: Religion, Transnationalism, and the Integration of Senegalese Immigrants in America* (New York: Oxford University Press, 2011), chapter 5.

40. Loimeier, *Islamic Reform;* Kane, *Muslim Modernity;* Kaba, *Wahhabiyya.*
41. W. Raven, "Sira," *Encyclopeadia of Islam II* on whom this paragraph relies.
42. Ibid.
43. Ibid.
44. Malik, Al-Muwatta, "hadith 1614," accessed December 26, 2012, http://www
    .dailyhadithonline.com/2011/02/01/the-prophet-was-sent-to-perfect-good
    -character/.
45. See Wilks, "Transmission of Learning," 168.
46. Literally, "nothing happened to me."
47. Niasse, Celebration of the birthday of the Prophet Muhammad." Our transla-
    tion from the Wolof language.
48. See Hunwick, *Timbuktu and the Songhay Empire,* 65–67, or Mukhtar b. Yahya
    al-Wangari, "Shaykh Baghayogho al-Wangari and the Wangari Library in Tim-
    buktu," in Jeppie and Diagne, *Meanings of Timbuktu,* 281–282.
49. Khassim Diakhaté, "Al-Sanusi, un Africain ash'arite au 15ème siècle," *Ethio-
    piques,* 66–67, 2001, 69–84. Louis Brenner, *Réflexion sur le savoir islamique en Af-
    rique noire* (Bordeaux: Centre d'étude d'Afrique noire, 1985), chapter 3, "Ensei-
    gnement théologique en fulfulde."
50. Brenner, *Réflexion,* 57.
51. Muhammad al-Wali b. Abdallah al-Fulani, *Al-manhaj al-farid fi ma'rifat 'ilm
    al-tawhid,* in Arabic Literature of Africa, Vol. IV, 267; Brenner, *Réflexion,* 57.
52. Brenner, *Réflexion,* 62.
53. Hall and Stewart , "Historic 'Core Curriculum,'" 140. The same argument was
    made earlier by Michel Chodkiewicz, a leading expert on Ibn 'Arabi. See
    M. Chodkiewicz, "The Diffusion of Ibn 'Arabi's doctrine," *Journal of the Muhyid-
    din Ibn 'Arabi Society* IX (1991): 36–57.
54. Bernd Radtke, "Studies on the Sources of the *Kitab Rimah Hizb al-Rahim* of
    'Umar Tall," *Sudanic Africa* 6: 73–113, has compiled all citations. He is the main
    source of information for this paragraph.
55. Radtke, "Studies on the Sources of the *Kitab Rimah.*"
56. See Said Bousbina, "Les mérites de la Tijaniyya d'après "Rimah" d'Al-Hajj
    'Umar," *Islam et sociétés au Sud du Sahara* 3 (1989): 253–260.
57. *Geschichte der Arabischen Litteratur,* II, 335, S, II, 464.
58. *Geschichte der Arabischen Litteratur,* S, II, 876.
59. *Geschichte der Arabischen Litteratur,* II, 462, S II, 704.
60. For more on Zarruq, see Ali Fahmi Kashim, *Zarruq, The Sufi: A Guide in the Way
    and a Ladder to the Truth, A Biographical and Critical Study of a Mystic from North
    Africa* (London: Outline Series, 1976); Scott Kugle, *Rebel between Spirit and
    Law: Ahmad Zarruq: Sainthood and Authority in Islam* (Bloomington: Indiana
    University Press, 2006).
61. Hall and Stewart , "Historic 'Core Curriculum,'" 123.
62. Ibid., 121.

63. Last, "Book in the Sokoto Caliphate," 143.

64. See "Al-Bakri," in Levtzion and Hopkins, *Corpus,* 82.

65. Ousmane Kane, "Reconciling Islam and Non Islamic Beliefs: Reflection on a Talismanic Textile of the Art Institute of the Chicago," *Islam et Sociétés au Sud du Sahara* 2: 137–161.

66. Levtzion, "Islam in the Bilad al-Sudan," 69.

67. See Chapter 5.

68. Aziz Batran, *Tobacco Smoking under Islamic Law: Controversy over Its Introduction* (Beltsville, MD: Amana Publications, 2003).

69. Al-Naqar, *Pilgrimage Tradition.*

70. Chanfi Ahmed, *West African 'ulamā' and Salafism in Mecca and Medina* (Leiden and Boston: E. J. Brill, 2015), back cover.

5. Shaping an Islamic Space of Meaning: The Discursive Tradition

1. Talal Asad, "The Idea of Anthropology of Islam," *Qui Parle?* 17, no. 2 (Spring 2009), 24.

2. John Hunwick, "The Arabic Literature of Africa Project," in Jeppie and Diagne, *Meanings of Timbuktu,* 303–310, 314.

3. Muhsin J. Al-Musawi, *The Medieval Islamic Republic of Letters. Arabic Knowledge Construction* (Notre Dame, IN: University of Notre Dame Press, 2015), 92. I thank Professor Mamadou Diouf for drawing my attention to this work.

4. See, for example, Abdullahi Mahadi, "The State and the Economy."

5. Hamidu Bobboye, "Ajami Literature and the Study of the Sokoto Caliphate," in Jeppie and Diagne, eds., *Meanings of Timbuktu,* 123–133, 129.

6. This is a classical definition of politics. See Harold Lasswell, *Politics: Who Gets What, When and How?* (New York: Meridian Books, 1958).

7. John Fage, "Slavery and the Slave Trade in the Context of West African History," *Journal of African History* X, no. 3 (1969): 393–404.

8. Academic coverage of the subject includes that by Allan Fisher and Humphrey Fisher, *Slavery and Muslim Society in Africa: The Institution in Saharan and Sudanic Africa, and the Trans-Saharan Trade* (London: Hurst, 1970); John Ralph Willis, ed., *Slaves and Slavery in Muslim Africa* (London, England; Totowa, NJ: F. Cass, 1985); James L. A. Webb, *Desert Frontier: Ecological and Economic Change along the Western Sahel, 1600–1850* (Madison: University of Wisconsin Press, 1995); Hall, *History of Race in Muslim Africa.*

9. Bruce Hall, "Enslaved Paths of Circulation in the Sahara and Sahel. Commercial Networks and Slave Agency between Ghadames (Lybia) and Timbuktu (Mali) in the 19th Century," in Chouki el Hamel and Paul Lovejoy eds., *Confluence of Cultures,* (Princeton: Marcus Wiener, forthcoming). I thank Bruce Hall for granting permission to cite this piece.

10. John Hunwick and Fatima Harrak (annotated and translated by), *Mi'raj al-Su'ud:*

Ahmad Baba's Replies on Slavery (Rabat: Institute of African Studies, 2000). The book is referred to henceforth as Ahmad Baba, *Ladder of Ascent.* It was composed in 1615 in Timbuktu. See Cleaveland, Ahmed Baba al-Timbukti, 42.

11. M. A. Cherbonneau, "Essai sur la littérature arabe au Soudan d'après le Tekmilet ed-Dibaje d'Ahmed Baba le Tombouctien, *Annales de la Société archéologique de Constantine* ii (1854–1855): 1–42.

12. On Ahmad Baba, see Cleaveland, "Ahmad Baba and His Islamic Critique of Slavery in the Maghreb"; Hunwick, *Arabic Literature of Africa,* IV: 17–31; Brockelmann, Gesc*hichte der Arabischen Litteratur* II: 618; Supplementbänden II: 715–716; Mahmoud A. Zouber, *Ahmad Baba (1556–1627). Sa vie et son œuvre* (Paris: Maisonneuve et Larose, 1977); John Hunwick, "Ahmad Baba and the Moroccan Invasion of the Sudan (1591)," *Journal of the Historical Society of Nigeria* 2, no. 1 (1962): 311–328; John Hunwick, "A New Source for the Study of Ahmad Baba al-Timbukti (1556–1627)," *Bulletin of the School of Oriental and African Studies* 27 (1964): 568–593; Mohamed Zaouit, "Mi'raj as-su'ud et les Ajwiba: Deux consultations juridiques d'Ahmad Baba de Tombouctou relatives à l'esclavage des noirs au Bilad al-Sudan au XVIème et début du XVIIème siècle: édition critique et analyse historique," PhD diss. in history, University of Paris 1, 1997; ISESCO, *Ahmad Baba al-Timbukti: Buhuth al-nadwa allati 'aqadatha ISESCO bi-munasabat murur arba'a qurun wa nisf 'ala wiladatihi,* Proceedings of a symposium organized by ISESCO four centuries and a half after the birth of Ahmad Baba (Marrakesh: ISESCO, 1993).

13. There is no consensus on his place of birth. Paul Farias states that Arawan, 250 kilometers north of Timbuktu, is his place of birth, and Tim Cleaveland claims that he was born in Timbuktu. See Cleaveland, Ahmed Baba al-Timbukti, 45.

14. Paulo F. de Moraes Farias, "Ahmad Baba."

15. Levtzion, "Islam in the Bilad al-Sudan," 74.

16. Hunwick and Boyle, *Hidden Treasures of Timbuktu,* 134.

17. See Hunwick, *Timbuktu and the Songhay Empire,* chapter 23, titled "Pasha Mahmud's Campaigns: Arrest of Timbuktu Scholars," 218–236.

18. Paulo F. de Moraes Farias "Ahmad Baba."

19. Ibid.; Hunwick and Boyle, *Hidden Treasures of Timbuktu,* 133.

20. Titled *Nayl al-Ibtihaj fi Tatriz al-Dibaj,* it was written as a supplement to *Al-Dibaj al-Mudhahhab fi ma'rifat a'yan 'ulama al-madhhab* by Ibrahim b. Ali b. Farhun. See Hunwick, *Arabic Literature of Africa,* Vol. IV, 23.

21. See, for example, a treatise by a leading exponent of the Maliki jurisprudence: Khalil b Ishaq al-Jundi, *Al-Mukhtasar,* Paris, 1318/1900, translated by G.-H. Bousquet as *Abrégé de la loi musulmane selon le rite de l'imam Malek* (Alger, 1956), 209.

22. Ahmad Baba, *Ladder of Ascent,* 14.

23. Ibid., 23.

24. Ibid.

25. Ibid., 24.

26. Hunwick and Harrak in Ahmad Baba, *Ladder of Ascent*, 13, n. 11.

27. Al-Jirari's questions in Hunwick and Harrak, 17.

28. Abdel Wedoud Ould Cheikh, "Islam et esclavage en Mauritanie," unpublished paper, 13. I am grateful to the author for supplying me a copy of this paper.

29. Ahmad Baba, *Ladder of Ascent*, 27–29.

30. Ibid., 16–17.

31. Ibid., 30–31.

32. Ibid., (n. 86 by Hunwick and Harrak, 46).

33. Ibid., 41–43.

34. Ibid., 43–48.

35. David Robinson, "Umar Tall" in John Esposito ed. *The Oxford Encyclopedia of the Modern Islamic World*, (New York: Oxford University Press, 2001), vol. 4, 265-266, 266.

36. Ousmane Kane, "Islamism. What Is New, What Is Not? Lessons from West Africa," *African Journal of International Affairs* 11, no. 2: 157–187.

37. Hiskett, *Sword of Truth*, 133.

38. Muhammad al-Hajj, "The Writings of Shehu Usman Dan Fodio." This paragraph relies on al-Hajj. Ahmad Kani suggested a slightly different periodization: a pre-jihad period (1774–1804), a jihad period (1804–1810), and a post-jihad period (1810 to the death of the shaykh in 1817). Ahmed Kani, "Some Reflections on the Writings of Shaykh 'Uthman b. Fudi," *Kano Studies* (new series) 2, no. 1 (1980): 1–9.

39. Last, *Sokoto Caliphate*, 6.

40. Ibid., 8.

41. Ibid., 9.

42. Shehu Uthman Dan Fuduye, *The Revival of the Sunna and the Destruction of Innovation*, translation and introduction by Alfa Umar Muhammad Sharif bin Farid (Sennar, Sudan: Sankore, 1998).

43. In the appendix of the English translation, Sharif mentions forty-three different sources. See Fudiye, *Revival of the Sunna*, 266–267. Ahmad Kani mentions sixty-five sources. (Kani, "Some Reflections," 4). This divergence may be due to slight differences in the surviving copies of the work.

44. Last, *Sokoto Caliphate*, 12.

45. 'Uthman Dan Fodio, *Bayan Wujub al-hijra*, 176–177. Along the same lines *as Revival of Sunna and Destruction of Innovation*, Dan Fodio draws from fifty-five different works of forty-five authors.

46. See Hiskett, "Kitab al-Farq."

47. Hiskettt, "Kitab al-Farq," 567–569.

48. For an overview of the Sokoto Borno conflict debate, see Louis Brenner, "The Jihad Debate between Sokoto and Borno, Historical Analysis of Islamic Political Discourse in Nigeria," in J. F. Ade Ajayi and J. D. Y. Peel, eds., *People and Empires in African History* (London: Longmans, 1992), 21–43. For a Borno perspective on the war, see Muhammad al-Kanami, "The Case against the Jihad

1813," in Collins, ed., *Documents from the African Past*. For a Sokoto perspective, see Muhammad Bello Infaq al-Maysur, in Arnett, *The Rise of the Sokoto Fulani*.

49. See Bintou Sanankoua, *La Diina. Un empire peul du XIX e siècle*.

50. The Arabic title is *Sayf al-Haqq al-mu'tamad fi bayan ma waqa'a baynahu wa bayn Ahmad b. Ahmad*. Several authors have commented on and translated the text partially or fully. For a full translation and commentary, see Sidi Mohamed Mahibou and Jean-Louis Triaud, *Voilà ce qui est arrivé. Bayan Ma waqa'a d'al-Hagg 'Umar al-Futi. Plaidoyer pour une guerre sainte en Afrique de l'Ouest*. See also Muhammad al-Muntaqa Ahmad Tall, *Al-Jawahir wa al-durar*, 735.

51. See Mahibou and Triaud, 127–130, in which Umar elaborates the five types of *muwalat*, invokes several sources in Maliki jurisprudence, and in particular cites Al-Maghili and Abdullah Dan Fodio to make his point.

52. Umar Tall, *Sayf al-Haqq* in *Mahibou and Triaud, Voilà ce qui est arrivé*, 138.

53. For a study of how the *sarauta* system was restored in post-jihad Kano, see Abdullahi Mahadi, "The State and the Economy."

54. For a complete list of his works, see John Hunwick, *Arabic Literature of Africa: The Writings of Central Sudanic Africa*, Vol. 2 (Leiden: Brill, 1995), 86–113; Sidi Mohamed Mahibou, *Abdullahi Dan Fodio*; Zahradeen, "Abdullahi b. Fodio"; Abdullahi, *On the Search for a Viable Political Culture*.

55. *Diya -Hukkam fi-ma lahum wa 'alayhim min ahkam, Diya al-Sultan wa ghayrihi min al-ahkam, Diya al-Siyasa wa fatawi wa nawazil.*

56. Mahibou, *Abdullahi Dan Fodio*, 56–57.

57. Ibid., 63–64.

58. As noted by Ahmad Kani, these issues are extensively discussed by 'Abd al-Qadir b. Mustafa in his *Masa'il al-khilaf* (Controversial Issues), completed in 1864. See Ahmad Kani, *Intellectual Origin of Sokoto Jihad*, 96–98, on which I rely in this paragraph.

59. Hunwick, *Timbuktu and the Songhay Empire*, chapters VI, IX, X, and XI.

60. Hamel, *La vie intellectuelle islamique dans le Sahel ouest-africain*.

61. Al-Shinqiti, *Al-Wasit*.

62. See, for example, Djibril Tamsir Niane, "Mythes, légendes et sources orales dans l'oeuvre de Mahmoud Kati" *Recherches Africaines* (études guinéenes) nouvelle série; 1, 1964, 36–42. Sekene Mody Cissokho, "L'intelligentsia de Tombouctou aux XVe et XVIe siècles," *Bulletin de l'IFAN* 4 (1969); idem, *Tombouctou et l'Empire Songhay*, (Dakar and Abidjan: Nouvelles Editions Africaines, 1975); Paulo F. de Moraes Farias, "Intellectual Innovation and Reinvention of the Sahel: The Seventeenth-Century Timbuktu Chronicles," in Jeppie and Diagne, eds., *Meanings of Timbuktu*, 95–108.

63. Moraes Farias, "Intellectual Innovation," 95–97.

64. Hamel, *Vie intellectuelle islamique*, 38–39.

65. Ibid.

66. See Hamel, *Vie intellectuelle islamique*, 79–81, on which this paragraph relies.

67. Al-Shinqiti, *Al-Wasit*.

68. Asad "Idea of Anthropology of Islam," 20.

6. Islamic Education and the Colonial Encounter

1. Cheikh Tidiane Gaye, "Takwin al-'atilin" (training the [future] jobless), cited in Hunwick, *Arabic Literature of Africa*, Vol. 4, 386.

2. In regard to French West Africa, this process was analyzed in a major conference convened in 1994, the proceedings of which were published as David Robinson and Jean-Louis Triaud, eds., *Le temps des marabouts: Itinéraires et stratégies islamiques en Afrique occidentale française v. 1880–1960* (Paris: Karthala, 1997). Another major work of accommodation in Senegambia is David Robinson's *Paths of Accommodation: Muslim Societies and French Colonial Authorities in Senegal and Mauritania 1880–1920* (Athens, OH: Ohio University Press, 2000).

3. In Mauritania, French colonial rule found support among Sufi leaders including Sidiya Baba (d. 1927). See Alan Verskin, *Oppressed in the Land? Fatwas of Muslims Living under Muslim Rule from the Middle Ages to the Present* (Princeton: Markus Wiener, 2013), 104–111. Shaykh Sa'ad Buh, who discouraged his brother, Mal 'Aynayn, from opposing the French, is another supporter of French rule. See Dedoud Ould Abdallah, "Guerre Sainte ou sédition blamable," in Robinson and Triaud, *Temps des Marabouts*. Many prominent Sufi leaders of Senegambia endorsed French colonial rule. See Robinson, *Paths of Accommodation*.

4. Mamdani, *Citizen and Subject: Contemporary Africa and the Legacy of Late Colonialism* (Princeton: Princeton University Press, 1996), chapter 1.

5. Mamdani, *Citizen and Subject*, 73.

6. Ibid.

7. Ibid.

8. Ibid.

9. One such movement is the Sanusiyya, a Saharan Sufi organization founded by Muhammad b. 'Ali al-Sanusi (1789–1857), with ramifications in Chad and Niger. At the beginning of the twentieth century, the Sanusiyya confronted the French, the British, and the Italians militarily as the latter were vying for colonial occupation of Africa. See Jean-Louis Triaud, "Sanusiyya" *Encyclopaedia of Islam II*, or the most comprehensive study of this movement by the same author: *La Légende Noire de la Sanusiyya: Une confrérie musulmane saharienne sous le regard français 1840–1930* (Paris: Editions de la Maison des Sciences de L'Homme, 1995).

10. Several Mahdist movements have been suppressed during and after colonial rule. See, for example, Asma'u G. Saeed, "The British Policy towards the Mahdiyya in Northern Nigeria: The Study of Arrest, Detention and Deportation of Sa'id B. Hayat 1923–1959," *Kano Studies* (new series) 2, no. 3 (1982): 95–119; Alhaji Hamidu Alkali, "The Mahdi of Toranke," *Kano Studies* 1, no. 4 (1968): 92–95; Hamidou Dialla, "Mousa Aminou, le Mahdi de Ouani," in Robinson and Triaud, eds., *Le Temps des marabouts*, 373-393.

11. Ironically, the most loyal such Muslim figure, Seydou Nourou Tall, a descendant Umar Tall, was appointed by the French as caliph general of West Africa. See Sylvianne Garcia, "Al-Hajj Seydou Nourou Tall, 'grand marabout' tijani: L'histoire d'une carrière (v. 1880–1980)," in Triaud and Robinson, eds., *Le temps des marabouts.*

12. Catherine Boone, *The Political Topography of African States* (Cambridge: Cambridge University Press, 2003); Mamdani, *Citizen and Subject.*

13. http://fbcusl.8k.com/history.htm

14. Reinhard Wittman, "Was There a Reading Revolution at the End of the 18th Century?" in Guglielmo Cavallo and Roger Chartier, eds., *A History of Reading in the West* (Amherst and Boston: University of Massachusetts Press, 2003).

15. Guglielmo Cavallo and Roger Chartier, "Introduction" in Cavallo and Chartier, eds., *A History of Reading in the West*, 1–36, 24–25.

16. Ibid.

17. Cavallo and Chartier, "Introduction," 25.

18. Despite the presence of substantial native black Arabic-speaking communities in French-speaking countries, for example, Arabic is taught in public school as a foreign language.

19. Thanks to Ebrima Sall and Ayodeji Ogunnaike for alerting me to the fact that this existed not just in Francophone but also in Anglophone countries.

20. Ngugi Wa Thiong'o, *Decolonizing the Mind. The Politics of Language in African Literature* (London, Nairobi, Portsmouth: James Currey, Heinemann Kenya, Heinemann New Hampshire, 1986) 11.

21. Kane, *Ambiguous Adventure.*

22. Mamadou Dia, *Essais sur l'islam: Socio-anthropologie de l'islam* (Dakar, Abidjan, Lomé: Les Nouvelles Editions Africaines, 1980); *idem, Islam: Sociétés africaines et culture industrielle* (Dakar, Abidjan: Les Nouvelles Editions Africaines, 1975); *idem, Islam et civilisations négro-africaines* (Dakar, Abidjan, Lomé: Les Nouvelles Editions Africaines, 1979).

23. Mudimbe, *Invention of Africa, X.*

24. Brenner, *Controlling Knowledge,* 40. Brenner's work is the most authoritative survey of the modernization of Islamic education in twentieth-century West Africa, and its epistemological implications are discussed in greater detail in the epilogue.

25. Brenner, *Controlling Knowledge,* 42.

26. Ibid., 40.

27. Ibid., 44.

28. Governor Closel, cited in Brenner, *Controlling Knowledge,* 41–42.

29. Brenner, *Controlling Knowledge,* 50.

30. Ibid.

31. J. F. Ade Ajayi, *Christian Missions in Nigeria, 1841–1891: The Making of an Educated Elite* (London: Longmans, 1965); Michael Crowder, *The Story of Nigeria* (London and Boston: Faber and Faber, 1962), 118–119.

32. Kane, *Muslim Modernity*, 63–64.
33. On the role of Al-Azhar in training African students, see A. Chanfi Ahmed, "Islamic Mission in Sub-Saharan Africa. The Perspectives of Some Ulama Associated with the Al-Azhar University (1960–1970)," *Die Welt des Islams* 41, no. 3 (2001): 348–378.
34. Mark T. Berger, "After the Third World? History, Destiny and the Fate of the Third World," *Third World Quarterly* 25, no. 1 (2004): 9–39.
35. Zeghal, *Gardiens de l'islam*, 29.
36. The information on reform in this paragraph comes from Ahmed, "Islamic Mission," 352.
37. See Shawqi Ataillah, *Al-Azhar wa dawruhu al-siyasi wa l-hadari fi Ifriqiyya* (Cairo: Al-Hay'a al-misriyya lil –kitab, 1988), 34–35, quoted by Ahmed, 352, n. 8.
38. Mamadou Youri Sall, *Al-Azhar d'Egypte, l'autre institution d'enseignement des Sénégalais: Indicateurs statistisques, contributions explicatives et bases de données*, 22. The Arabic version published in the same volume is titled *Al-Azhar al-Sharif. Al-Mu'assassat al-ta'limiyya al-ukhra li ahl al-Sinighal. Mu'ashshirat ihsa'iyya wa maqalat tafsiriyya ma'a qa'idat al-bayanat* (Cairo: Dar al-Ittihad li al-tiba'a wa al-nashr wa al-tawzi', 2009), 22. *Note:* All references here are to the French version.
39. Roman Loimeier, "Cheikh Touré: Du réformisme à l'islamisme, un musulman sénégalais dans le siècle," *Islam et sociétés au sud du Sahara* 8 (1994): 55–66, 57.
40. Hanspeter Mattes, "La da'wa libyenne entre le coran et le livre vert," in René Otayek, ed., *Le radicalisme islamique au sud du Sahara. Da'wa, arabisation et critique de l'Occident* (Paris: Karthala, 1993), 37–73, 50.
41. Mattes, "La da'wa libyenne," 42–43.
42. Jalal Bahri, "Le lycée de Rekada: Une filière de formation pour les arabisants d'Afrique noire en Tunisie," in Otayek, ed., *Le radicalisme islamique au sud du Sahara*, 76.
43. Bahri, "Le lycée de Rekada," 90.
44. Nicole Grandin Blanc, "Al-markaz al-islami al-ifriqi bi 'l-Khartoum: La République du Soudan et la propagation de l'islam en Afrique noire (1977–1991)," in Otayek, ed., *Le radicalisme islamique au sud du Sahara*, 98–99.
45. Grandin Blanc, "Al-markaz al-islami al-ifriqi," 107.
46. Ibid., 113.
47. Ibid., 99.
48. http://www.iua.edu.sd/english/
49. Al-Naqar, *Pilgrimage Tradition*.
50. Fouad Al Farsy, *Modernity and Tradition: The Sa'udi Equation* (London and New York: Kegan Paul International, 1990), 295.
51. Suleiman Nyang, "Saudi Arabian Foreign Policy toward Africa," *Horn of Africa* 5, no. 2 (1982): 3–17, 13.
52. Ibid.
53. Bahri, "Le lycée de Rekada," 89.

7. Modern Islamic Institutions of Higher Learning

1. Baffa Aliyu Umar, "Research Methods and Areas in the Islamization of knowledge Undertaking," in Bashir Shehu Galadanci, *Islamization of Knowledge: A Research Guide* (Kano: International Institute of Islamic Thought Nigeria Office, 2000), 52-69.

2. For a discussion of such reforms, see Bernard Lewis, *The Emergence of Modern Turkey* (New York: Oxford University Press, 1961); Niyazi Berkes, *The Development of Secularism in Turkey* (Montreal: McGill University Press, 1964).

3. For a discussion of these reforms, see Zeghal, *Gardiens de l'Islam*, 90–126; J. Jomier "Al-Azhar," *Encylopaedia of Islam II.*

4. Some prominent scholars include the French Vincent Monteil at the Université de Dakar, the Briton John Hunwick at the University of Ibadan, Mervyn Hiskett at Abdullahi Bayero College. As we have seen in Chapter 1, these scholars and their African students spearheaded the study of the Islamic intellectual tradition in sub-Saharan Africa in the post-colonial period, producing critical editions and translations of major works and important historical sources for the study of West African history.

5. Aliyu Umar Baffa, "Issues in Islamization of knowledge Research," in Bashir Shehu Galadanci, *Islamization of Knowledge: A Research Guide* (Kano: The International Institute of Islamic Thought Nigeria Office, 2000), 37-51, 38.

6. Ibid.

7. Mumtaz Ahmad, "Islamic Fundamentalism in South Asia: The Jamaat-i-Islami and the Tablighi Jamaat," in Martin Marty and R. Scott Appelby, *Fundamentalism Observed* (Chicago: University of Chicago Press, 1991), 457-530.

8. Ahmad, "Islamic Fundamentalism in South Asia."

9. For an initial statement of the project, see, for example, International Institute of Islamic Thought, *Islamization of Knowledge. General Principles and Work Plan* (Herndon VA: IIIT, 1989). For an updated discussion on the progress of the project, see Rafiu Ibrahim Adebayo, *Islamization of Knowledge: Global Developments, Individual Efforts and Institutional Contributions* (Kaduna: Islamic Heritage Foundation, 2008).

10. Taha Jaber Al-Alwani, *Apostasy in Islam: A Historical and Scriptural Analysis* (Malta: Gutenberg Press for IIIT, 2011), ix.

11. Michael Lofchie, "The New Political Economy of Africa," in David Apter and Carl Rosberg, eds., *Political Development and the New Realism in Sub-Saharan Africa* (Charlottesville: University Press of Virginia, 1994), 145–183; Robert Bates, *Markets and States in Tropical Africa: The Political Basis of Agricultural Policies* (Berkeley: University of California Press, 2005); World Bank, *Accelerated Development in Sub-Saharan Africa: An Agenda for Action* (Washington, DC: World Bank, 1981).

12. See Rafiu Ibrahim Adebayo, "The Islamic Universities," in Julius Okojie, Is-Haq Oloyede, and Pai Obanya, eds., *50 Years of University Education in Nigeria:*

Evolution, Achievements and Future Directions (Ilorin: Ilorin University and National Universities Commission, 2010).

13. Al-Amana al-'Amma li-Munazzamat al-Mu'tamar al-Islami, Al-Dalil al-i'lami li al-Jami'a (Mecca: Matba'at al-Safa, 1988).

14. Interview with Aboubacar Touré, secretary general of the Université islamique de Say, Niamey, November 2010.

15. http://www.iuiu.ac.ug/home/

16. Interview with the staff of the university in Mbale, Uganda, in April 2011.

17. For the impact of Sufism in Lamu, see also el-Zein, *Sacred Meadows*; Ulrike Freitag, "Hadramaut: A Religious Centre for the Indian Ocean in the Late 19th and Early 20th Century," *Studia Africana* (1999): 165–183; Anne K. Bang, *Sufis and Scholars of the Sea: Family Networks in East Africa, 1860–1925* (London and New York: Routledge Curzon, 2003).

18. Ahmed bin Sumeit Khitamy, "The Role of the Riyadah Mosque College in enhancing the Islamic Identity in Kenya," Mohammed Bakari and Saad S. Yahya, eds., *Islam in Kenya: Proceedings of the National Seminar on Contemporary Islam in Kenya* (Nairobi: Mewa Publications, 1995), 269–277; Abdulaziz A. Ahmed, "The Impact of Hadrami Scholarship on Kenyan Islam," in Bakari and Yahya, eds., *Islam in Kenya*, 158–167; Salih Muhammad Ali Badawi, *Al-Riyad bayna Madihi wa Hadirihi* (Zanzibar: Al-Kayria Press, 1989).

19. Interview with Salih Muhammad Ali Badawi, Lamu, 2009.

20. Interview with the dean of the faculty of Islamic studies, Nairobi, 2011.

21. Interview with Ahmad Ndack Lo, Pire, December 2010.

22. Ahmad Ndack Lo, ibid.

23. Mohamed Dahiru Sulaiman, "Shiaism and the Islamic Movement in Nigeria 1979–1991," *Islam et sociétés au sud du Sahara* 7 (1993): 5–16, 8.

24. See Mara Leichman, *Shi'i Cosmopolitanisms in Africa: Lebanese Migration and Religious Conversion in Senegal* (Bloomington: Indiana University Press, 2015), *idem* "Shi'a Lebanese Migrants and Senegalese Converts in Dakar," in Sabrina Mervin, ed., *The Shi'a Worlds and Iran* (London: Saqi Books, 2010), 215–251; *idem*, "Revolution, Modernity and (Trans)National Shi'i Islam: Rethinking Religious Conversion in Senegal," *Journal of Religion in Africa* 39, no. 3 (2009): 319–351.

25. Interview with Shaykh Jawad, principal of Madrasat al-Rasul al-Akram, Niamey, November 2010.

26. It was established by the Nasrul-Lahi-L-Fatih Society of Nigeria (NASFAT) in Oshogbo, Nigeria. Created just about a decade ago, in Yorubaland, the Nasrul-Lahi-L-Fatih movement has become one the most powerful Islamic societies in Nigeria, apparently copying the methods of Pentecostals in organizing meetings, holding retreats, building schools, and trying to promote education.

27. Interview with the librarian, Fountain University, Oshogbo, Nigeria, February 2011.

28. Interview with Rafiu Ibrahim Adebayo, Fountain University, Oshogbo, Nigeria, February 2011.

29. Interview with Dr. Mubarak S. Lubaga, lecturer at the Department of Arabic Studies, Mbale, Uganda, March 2011.

30. Interview with the dean of the College of Islamic Studies, Thika, Kenya, April 2011.

31. Interview with Seydou Aboubacar Touré, Niamey, July 2007 and November 2010.

32. Guide de la Fédération des universités du monde islamique, Maroc, ISESCO, 2004.

33. Interview with Abdul Karim Toffar, academic dean, International Peace Varsity of South Africa, Cape Town, July 2011.

34. Interview with Abdul Qadir Badawi, dean of the College of Islamic Studies, Lamu, Nairobi, Kenya, March 2011.

8. Islam in the Post-colonial Public Sphere

1. Aliyu Dawuda, "The Falsity of Nigeria's Secular Claims," Kano, Muslim Corpers Lecture Series, 1989. I am grateful to Aliyu Dawuda for supplying me with a copy of the text of the lecture.

2. See the editorial of the rector of the university, published in the first issue of the journal: Abdul 'Ali al-Wadghiri, "Kalimat al-'Adad," *Annals of the Université islamique de Say* 1 (1995): 3–5, 2.

3. Jean-Louis Triaud, "Présentation," *Islam et sociétés au sud du Sahara* 1 (1987): 7–9.

4. Abdal-Baqi Hamd Bello, "Ma Huwa al-Zanji" (What Is a Negro?), *Al-Ittihad* (March 1, 2007): 22–24.

5. Mouhamed Diouf, "Al-'alam al-thalith," *Sawt al-Rabita* (1992): 11–16, 14–15 (my translation).

6. See, for example, the section "Explaining Global Patterns of Inequality," in John Dickenson, *Geography of the Third World* (London and New York: Routledge, 1996), 3–30.

7. Diouf, "Al-'Alam al-thalith," 16 (my translation).

8. Dorothea E. Schultz, *Muslims and New Media in West Africa: Pathways to God* (Bloomington: Indiana University Press, 2012), 98–135; Hamadou Adama, "Islamic Associations in Cameroon: Between the Umma and the State," in Benjamin Soares and René Otayek, eds., *Islam and Muslim Politics in Africa* (New York: Palgrave Macmillan, 2007), 227–241; Benjamin Soares, "Islam in Mali in the Neoliberal Era," in Soares and Otayek, eds., *Islam and Muslim Politics,* 211–226.

9. Dale Eickelman, "The Religious Public Sphere in Early Muslim Societies," in Mirian Hoexter, Shmuel N. Eisensenstadt, and Nehemia Levtzion, eds., *The Public Sphere in Muslim Societies* (Albany: State University of New York University Press, 2002), 1–8, 2.

10. Mark Bray, *Universal Primary Education in Nigeria* (London: Routledge and Kegan Paul, 1981), 1.

11. Ruth Marshall, *Political Spiritualities: The Pentecostal Revolution in Nigeria* (London and Chicago: University of Chicago Press, 2009), 11; Mathews Ojo, "The Contextual Significance of the Charismatic Movements in Independent Nigeria," *Africa* 58, no. 2 (1988); *idem*, "The Growth of Campus Christianity and Charismatic Movements in Western Nigerian," PhD diss., SOAS, University of London, 1987.

12. Toyin Falola, *Violence in Nigeria: The Crisis of Religious Politics and Secular Ideologies* (Rochester, NY: University of Rochester Press, 1998); Jibrin Ibrahim, "Religion and Political Turbulence in Nigeria," *Journal of Modern African Studies* 29 (1991), 115–136; *idem*, "The Politics of Religion in Nigeria: The Parameters of the 1987 Crisis in Kaduna State," *Review of African Political Economy* (1989): 65–82.

13. Kane, *Muslim Modernity;* Loiemeir, *Islamic Reform and Political Change.*

14. Kane, *Muslim Modernity.*

15. Peter Cole, "Borderline Chaos? Stabilizing Libya's Periphery," in Frederic Wehrey and Anouar Boukhars, eds., *Perilous Desert: Insecurity in the Sahara* (Washington, DC: Carnegie Endowment for Peace, 2013), 54.

16. For an informed analysis of the resurgence of the veil in the Middle East and among Muslim women in the West, see Leila Ahmed, *A Quiet Revolution: The Veil's Resurgence from the Middle East to America* (New Haven and London: Yale University Press, 2011), 148. For a discussion of the veil in Senegal, see Erin Auges, "Religion, Religiousness, and Narrative: Decoding Women's Practice in Senegalese Islamic Reform," *Journal for the Scientific Study of Religion* 51, no. 3 (2012): 429–441.

17. Adama, "Islamic Associations in Cameroon," 227.

18. O'Fahey, "Arabic Literature in the Eastern Half of Africa," 334.

19. Moustapha Barry, *Histoire des medias au Sénégal: De la colonisation à nos jours* (Paris: L'Harmattan, 2013).

20. For a history of the group, see the autobiography of the founder, Sidi Lamine Niasse: *Un arabisant entre presse et pouvoir* (Dakar: Edition Groupe Walfadjri, 2003), foreword by Amadou Makhtar Mbow.

21. Fabienne Samson, *Les marabouts de l'islam politique: Le Dahiratoul Moustachidina Wal Moustarchidati. Un mouvement néo-confrérique sénégalais* (Paris: Karthala, 2005).

22. Fiona McLaughlin, "Islam and Popular Music in Senegal: The Emergence of a New Tradition," *Africa* 67: 560–581.

23. Mauritania did not allow the formation of a political party based on religion. See Zekeria Ould Ahmed Salem, "Islam in Mauritania between Political Expansion and Globalization: Elites, Institutions, Knowledge, and Network," in Soares and Otayek, eds., *Islam and Muslim Politics in Africa,* 27–46, 27; *idem*, *Prêcher dans le désert: Islam politique et changement social en Mauritanie* (Paris: Karthala, 2013), 53; *Constant Hamès,* "Le role de l'islam dans la république mauritanienne," *Politique africaine* 55 (1994): 54.

24. Amsatou Sow Sidibe, *Le pluralisme juridique en Afrique: L'exemple du droit successoral sénégalais* (Paris: Librairie générale de droit et de jurisprudence, 1991).

25. John Esposito, *Islam: The Straight Path* (New York: Oxford University Press, 1991).

26. Sulaiman, "Shiaism and the Islamic Movement in Nigeria."

27. Ahmad, "Islamic Fundamentalism in South Asia."

28. See Ayatollah Khomeini, "Islamic Government," in Roxanne L. Euben and Muhamad Qasin Zaman, eds., *Princeton Readings in Islamist Thought: Texts and Contexts from al-Banna to Bin Laden* (Princeton and Oxford: Princeton University Press, 2009), 166.

29. Sayyid Qutb, "Signposts along the Road," in Euben and Zaman, eds., *Princeton Readings in Islamist Thought*, 138.

30. Sayyid Abu 'l-A'la Maududi, "The Islamic Law," in Euben and Zaman, eds., *Princeton Readings in Islamist Thought*, 92.

31. Qutb, "Signposts along the Road,"138.

32. Rosenthal, *Knowledge Triumphant.*

33. John Paden, *Faith and Politics in Nigeria: Nigeria as a Pivotal State in the Muslim World* (Washington, DC: United States Institute Of Peace Press, 2000).

34. Dawuda, Falsity of Nigeria's Secular Claims.

35. Ould Ahmed Salem, *Prêcher dans le désert*, 52.

9. Arabophones Triumphant: Timbuktu under Islamic Rule

1. William Miles, "West Africa Transformed: The New Mosque-State Relationship," in Miles, ed., *Political Islam in West Africa* (Boulder, CO: Lynne Rienner, 2007), 183.

2. Matthew Hassan Kukah, "An Assessment of the Intellectual Response of the Nigerian Ulama to the Shari'a Debate since Independence," *Islam et Sociétés au Sud du Sahara* 7 (1993): 35–55; Paul Lubeck, "Nigeria. Mapping a Shari'a Restorationist Movement," in Robert Hefner, *Shari'a Politics. Islamic Law and Society in the Modern World* (Bloomington and Indianapolis: Indiana University Press, 2011), 244–279.

3. Ousmane Kane, "Political Islam in Nigeria," in Michael Broening and Holger Weiss, eds., *Politischer Islam in Westafrika: Eine Bestandsaufnahme* (Berlin: Lit Verlag und Friedrich Ebert Stiftung): 153–178, 170; Kukah, "An Assessment," 49.

4. William Miles, "West Africa Transformed"183–184.

5. See Ousmane Kane, "Moderate Revivalists: Islamist Inroads in Sub-Saharan Africa," *Harvard International Review* vol. 29 , no. 2, 2007, 64-68.

6. Pew Forum on Religion and Public Life, "Tolerance and Tension: Islam and Christianity in Sub-Saharan Africa," accessed July 16, 2013, http://www.pewforum.org/2010/04/15/executive-summary-islam-and-christianity-in-sub-saharan-africa/.

7. Pew Forum on Religion and Public Life, "Tolerance and Tension, ii.

8. Ibid.

9. Ibid.

10. Ibid., 11.

11. The questions were asked to Muslims in eastern Africa (Djibouti, Tanzania, Uganda, Ethiopia, Kenya), West Africa (Mali, Senegal, Ghana, Nigeria, Liberia, Guinea Bissau), southern Africa (Botswana, Mozambique, Zambia, South Africa, Botswana), and Central Africa (Rwanda, Cameroon, DRC).

12. Mahmood Mamdani, *Good Muslim, Bad Muslim: America, the Cold War, and the Roots of Terror* (New York: Pantheon Books, 2004.)

13. Gunnar J. Weimann, *Islamic Criminal Law in Northern Nigeria. Politics, Religion, Judicial Practice* (Amsterdam: University of Amsterdam Press, 2010), 26–29.

14. http://www.nigeria-law.org/ConstitutionOfTheFederalRepublicOfNigeria.htm

15. Human Rights Watch, *"Political Shari'a?": Human Rights and Islamic Law in Northern Nigeria,* September 21, 2004, http://www.refworld.org/docid/415c02ae4.html, 97. Accessed July 18, 2013.

16. Sanusi Lamido Sanusi, "Class, Gender and a Political Economy of "Sharia" 1 in www.nigerdeltacongress.com Accessed August 2007.

17. Sanusi, "Class, Gender," 3.

18. Ibid., 5.

19. Hawa Ibrahim, *Practicing Shariah Law: Seven Strategies for achieving Justice in Shariah Courts* (Chicago: American Bar Association, 2012), 44.

20. Human Rights Watch, "Political Shari'a," 5.

21. Paul Newman, "The Etymology of Hausa Boko," at http://lah.soas.ac.uk/projects/megachad/publications/Newman-2013-Etymology-of-Hausa-boko.pdf.

22. Abdalla Uba Adamu, "Muslim Religious Extremism, Radicalization and Militancy in Northern Nigeria" unpublished paper, National Institute for Policy and Strategic Studies, Kuru, Plateau State Nigeria, 2012, 31.

23. The most recent work on Boko Haram is Mike Smith, *Boko Haram. Inside Nigeria's Unholy War* (London: I B Tauris, 2015). Another recent collective volume of eleven contributors explore the social base, ideology, relations with the state and other Muslims, changing tactics, and modes of financing of Boko Haram. See Marc-Antoine Perouse de Montclos, ed., *Boko Haram: Islamism, Politics, Security and the State in Nigeria* (Leiden: African Studies Center, 2014). Other works on Boko Haram include Abdalla Uba Adamu, "Muslim Religious Extremism, Radicalization and Militancy in Northern Nigeria," P. Ostien, "A Survey of the Muslims of Nigeria's North-Central Geo-Political Zone," Oxford: Nigeria Research Network, Working Paper, n° 1, 2011; Adam Higazi and Florence Brisset-Foucault, "Les origines et la Transformation de l'insurrection Boko Haram au Nord du Nigéria," *Politique africaine,* 130: 2013, 137–164; Anonymous, "The Popular Discourses of Salafi Radicalism and Salafi Counter-Radicalism in Nigeria: A Case Study of Boko Haram," *Journal of Religion in Africa,* 42, 2012, 118–44; Adesoji Abimbola, "Between Maitatsine and Boko Haram: Islamic Fundamentalism and the Response of the Nigerian State," *Africa Today* 57, no. 4 (2011): 98-119; *idem,* "The Boko Haram Uprising and Islamic Revivalism in

Nigeria," *Africa Spectrum,* 45, 2, 2010, 95–108; Roman Loimeier, "The Development of a Militant Religious Movement in Nigeria," *Africa Spectrum,* 2, 3, 2012, 137–155; Andrea Brigaglia, "Ja'far Mahmoud Adam, Mohammed Yusuf and Al-Muntada Islamic Trust: Reflections on the Genesis of the Boko Haram Phenomenon in Nigeria," *Annual Review of Islam in Africa,* 11, 2012, 35–44.

24. Anonymous, "The Popular Discourses."

25. Higazi and Brisset-Foucault, "Les origines et la Transformation de l'insurrection Boko Haram au Nord du Nigéria."

26. Ibid.; Brigaglia, "Ja'far Mahmoud Adam," 38; Anonymous, "Popular Discourses of Salafi Radicalism."

27. Brigaglia, "Ja'far Mahmoud Adam," 38.

28. See Qur'an 2–256: "There is no compulsion in religion: true guidance has become distinct from error, so whoever rejects (taghut) false gods and believes in God has grasped the firmest hand-hold, one that will never break. God is all hearing, all knowing."

29. Hijazi and Brisquet, "Les origines et la Transformation de l'insurrection Boko Haram."

30. Anonymous, "Popular Discourses," on which this paragraph relies.

31. Ibid.

32. Hijazi and Brisquet, "Les origines et la Transformation de l'insurrection Boko Haram"; Brigaglia, "Ja'far Mahmoud Adam," 37.

33. For a biography of Surur, see Stephane Lacroix, "Muhammad Surur Zayn al-'Abidin" in Roel Meijer, ed., *Global Salafism: Islam's New Religious Movement* (New York: Columbia University Press, 2009), 435–436.

34. Brigaglia, "Ja'far Mahmoud Adam," 40.

35. For a biography of Malam Ja'far, see Kane, *Muslim Modernity,* and Andrea Brigaglia, "Ja'far Mahmoud Adam."

36. http://www.aljazeera.com/news/africa/2010/02/201029811494949112.html. Accessed August 2013.

37. For a detailed account of this and other attacks, including death toll, see Freedom Onuoha, "Boko Haram and the Evolving Salafi Jihadist Threat in Nigeria," in Perouse de Montclos, ed., *Boko Haram,* 174.

38. Abdul Kareem Ogori, "Return of the Boko Haram," *The Politico,* January 1 2011, http://the-politico.com/cover/return-of-the-boko-haram/5. Accessed August 19, 2013.

39. See presidential address by President Goodluck Jonathan on the declaration of a state of emergency in Borno, Yobe, and Adamawa States, http://saharareporters.com. Accessed August 2013.

40. http://www.channelstv.com/home/2013/08/19/boko-haram-leader-shekau-may-have-died-of-gunshot-wounds-jtf/. Accessed August 19, 2013.

41. See Hunwick and Boyle, *Hidden Treasures.*

42. Ibid.

43. Pierre Boiley, "AQMI et le terrorisme islamiste au Sahel. Isolement ou Enracin-

ement," in Odile Goerg and Anna Pondopoulo, eds., *Islam et Sociétés en Afrique sub-saharienne à l'épreuve de l'histoire: Un parcours en compagnie de Jean-Louis Triaud* (Paris: Karthala, 2012), 379–389.

44. Jean-Louis Triaud, "Sanusiyya," *Encyclopaedia of Islam II*, or the comprehensive study of this movement by the same author: *La Légende Noire de la Sanusiyya*.

45. See D. B. Devon, "The Crisis in Mali. A Historical Perspective on the Tuareg People" on which the discussion in this paragraph on Tuareg rebellion is based. http://www.globalresearch.ca/the-crisis-in-mali-a-historical-perspective-on-the -tuareg-people/5321407. Accessed August 17, 2013.

46. Anouar Bohkhars, "*The Paranoid Neighbour,*" in Frederic Wehrey and Anouar Boukhars, eds., *Perilous Desert: Insecurity in the Sahara* (Washington DC: Carnegie Endowment for Peace, 2013), 91.

47. Wolfram Lacher, "Organized Crime and Conflict in the Sahel-Sahara Region" in Wehrey and Boukhars, *Perilous Desert*, 61–85.

48. Gilles Kepel, *Jihad: The Trail of Political Islam* (New York: I. B. Tauris Publishers, 2002), chapter 11.

49. See Luis Martinez, *The Algerian Civil War 1990–1998* (London: Hurst & Company, 2000).

50. An abundant literature is emerging on jihadis in northern Mali and their international ramifications. See Samuel Laurent, *Sahelistan: De la Libye au Mali. Au cœur du nouveau jihad* (Paris: Seuil, 2013); Michel Galy, ed., *La Guerre au Mali: Comprendre la Crise au Sahel et au Sahara. Enjeux et Zones d'Ombre* (Paris: La Découverte, 2013); Isabelle Lasserre and Thierry Oberlé, *Notre Guerre Secrète au Mali* (Paris: Fayard, 2013); Atmane Tazaghart, *AQMI: Enquête sur les héritiers de Ben Laden au Maghreb et en Europe* (Paris: Jean Picollec, 2011); Jeremy Keenan, *The Dark Sahara. America's War on Terror in Africa* (New York: Pluto Press, 2009); Weherey and Anouar, *Perilous Desert;* International Crisis Group, "Mali, Security, Dialogue and Meaningful Reform," *Africa Report* 201, accessed April 11, 2013, http://www.crisisgroup.org/en/regions/africa/west-africa/mali/201-mali -security-dialogue-and-meaningful-reform.aspx; CERI, ed., *Le Sahel dans la Crise malienne* (Paris: CERI), accessed July 2013, http://www.sciencespo.fr/ceri /fr/content/dossiersduceri/le-sahel-dans-la-crise-malienne.

51. For a complete biography of Mokhtar Belmokhtar, see Lemine Ould M. Salem, *Le Ben Laden du Sahara. Sur les traces du jihadiste Mokhtar Belmokhtar* (Paris: Editions de la Martinière, 2014).

52. Boukhars, "Paranoid Neighbour," 94.

53. Serge Daniel, *AQMI Al-Qaida au Maghreb Islamique: L'industrie de l'enlèvement* (Paris: Fayard, 2012).

54. Boukhars, "Paranoid Neighbour," 94.

55. http://www.jeuneafrique.com/Articles/Dossier/JA2698p024–033.xml7/mali -mauritanie-terrorisme-attentatmali-hamada-ould-mohamed-kheirou-le -cerveau-du-mujao.html. Accessed August 18, 2013.

56. Moussa Kaka, http://www.rfi.fr/emission/20131108–1-syndrome-stress-post -traumatique. Accessed November 8, 2013.

57. Daniel, *AQMI.*

58. Lasserre and Oberlé, *Notre Guerre Secrète au Mali.*

59. Boukhars, "Paranoid Neighbour," 92.

60. Ibid.

61. Interview of Abdoulaye Cissé, curator of Ahmad Baba Institute by RFI journalist Christine Muratet, March 12, 2013.

62. For an Arabic version and English translation of parts of the document, see http://hosted.ap.org/specials/interactives/_international/_pdfs/al-qaida-manifesto.pdf. Accessed August 18, 2013.

63. Ibid.

64. Ould Ahmed Salem, "Islam in Mauritania between Political Expansion and Globalization," 29.

Epilogue

1. Cheikh-skiredj.com, accessed August 2014.

2. Dore Gold, *Hatred's Kingdom: How Saudi Arabia Supports the New Global Terrorism* (Washington, DC: Regnery Publishing, 2003).

3. Niang, "Le Transnational pour argument," 315.

4. See Abdullai Iddrisu, *Contesting Islam in Africa: Homegrown Wahhabism and Muslim Identity in Northern Ghana, 1920–2012* (Durham, NC: Carolina Academic Press, 2013).

5. David Owusu-Ansah, *Islamic Talismanic Tradition in Nineteenth-Century Asante* (Lewiston, NY: Edwin Mellen Press, 1991); *idem*, "Prayer, Amulets, and Healing," in Levtzion and Pouwels, *History of Islam in Africa,* 477–488.

6. Shaykh Niasse was approached to mediate political conflicts in Nigeria during his lifetime. After his death, Madina Kaolack has attracted those who sought political mediation. President Obasanjo of Nigeria visited Kaolack in 2012 to seek mediation for the resolution of the Boko Haram crisis. Members of Madina Kaolack elites have also been received by former president Goodluck Jonathan for the same reasons.

7. Eleanor Abdella Dumato, *Getting God's Ear: Women, Islam and Healing in the Gulf and Saudi Arabia* (New York: Columbia University Press, 2000); Madawi al-Rashid, *A Most Masculine State: Gender, Politics and Religion in Saudi Arabia* (Cambridge: Cambridge University Press, 2013), 46.

8. Kepel, *Jihad: The Trail of Political Islam.*

9. See Malcom H. Kerr, *The Arab Cold War 1958–1964: A Study of Ideology in Politics* (London: Oxford University Press, 1965), 21–22; James Piscatori, "Ideological Politics in Saudi Arabia," in J. Piscatori, ed., *Islam in the Political Process* (Cambridge: Cambridge University Press, 1983), 59; Edward E. Curtis "Islamism and Its African American Muslim Critics. Black Muslims in the Era of the Arab

Cold War," in Manning Marable and Hishaam Aidi, *Black Routes to Islam* (New York: Palgrave Macmillan, 2009), 48–68, 51–52.

10. Brenner, *Controlling Knowledge*, 7.

11. Ibid., 8.

12. Ibid., 307.

13. Schoeler, *The Oral and the Written in Early Islam* (London ; New York : Routledge, 2006.), 45; Robinson, *Islamic Historiography*, 145.

14. See Henrietta L. Moore and Todd Sanders, eds., *Magical Interpretations, Material Realities: Modernity, Witchcraft, and the Occult in Postcolonial Africa* (New York, Routledge, 2011).

15. Oludamini Ogunnaike, "Sufism and Ifa: Ways of Knowing in Two West African Traditions," PhD diss. in African studies, Harvard University, August 2015, 348.

16. Ibid., 351.

17. Kane, *The Homeland Is the Arena*, chapter 3.

18. Mazrui, *The Africans.*

19. See, for example, the findings of a CODESRIA working group on endogenous knowledge in Paulin J Hountondji, ed., *Endogenous Knowledge: Research Trails* (Dakar: Codesria, 1997).

20. Abdou Moumouni, *L'éducation en Afrique* (Paris: François Maspéro, 1964)

21. UNESCO and International Social Sciences Council, *Knowledge Divides*, World Social Sciences Report, http://unesdoc.unesco.org/images/0018/001883/188333e.pdf.

Glossary

'Abd al-Karim Al-Maghili An influential fifteenth century Algerian scholar who argued for jihad against unbelievers, is credited with introducing the Qadiriyya brotherhood into the Bilad al-Sudan, and advised the rulers of Kano and Songhay.

'Abdallah b. Yasin Reformist who led the initial Almoravid movement, credited with the establishment of the Maliki *madhhab* that replaced earlier Kharijite influences in the Bilad al-Sudan. (d. 1055 CE)

Abdullahi Dan Fodio Brother of Uthman Dan Fodio and ruler of the western half of the Sokoto Caliphate. He also wrote many works on politics, Sufism, tafsir, and poetry. (c. 1766–1828 CE)

Abu 'l A'la Maududi Pakistani Islamist scholar who argued strongly against secularization and for the Islamization of the state. (1903–1979 CE)

Ahmadu Bamba Mbacké Shaykh and founder of the Muridiyya Sufi brotherhood and its holy city, Touba in Senegal. He was also a prolific writer of both poetry and scholarly works. (1853–1927 CE)

Ahmadu Bello Prominent Nigerian politician and first premier of the Northern Nigerian region. Ahmadu Bello University in Zaria, Nigeria is named in his honor. (1910–1966 CE)

Ahmadu Lobbo Leader of the jihad that created the Masina State who received a flag for his jihad from Uthman Dan Fodio. He was also a student of Sidi Mukhtar al-Kunti. (c. 1776–1845 CE)

Ahmad Baba One of the most famous West African scholars whose advice and opinions were sought by scholars and rulers throughout West and Northern Africa. He was exiled from his home in Timbuktu in 1591 when the Sultan of Morocco toppled the Songhay Empire, but he was allowed to return in 1608. (1556–1627 CE)

Ajami African languages written in Arabic script. A tradition that became widely practiced after the establishment of Islam and contains a great deal of knowledge that is as yet unmined by Europhone intellectuals. [Arabic]

Almoravid Medieval state that stretched from Andalusian Spain in the north to present-day Mauritania in the south. Founded by 'Abdallah b. Yasin, its name is derived from the Arabic word "ribat" meaning "fortress." (1040–1147 CE)

Ansar Dine A rebel Tuareg group from Northern Mali that emerged in 2011 and sought to create an Islamic state in its part of the country. It attracted former soldiers of deposed Colonel Khaddafi in Libya and deserters from the Malian army.

'Aqida Theology. [Arabic]

AQIM Al-Qaida in the Islamic Maghreb. Based in northern Mali and southern Algeria, its members played a large role in the revolt against the Malian government in 2011 and the destruction of manuscripts and shrines in important locations like Timbuktu before they were driven out.

Arabophone A member of the intellectual tradition carried out in the Arabic language. To be contrasted with "Europhone" although the two are not mutually exclusive.

Arma Soldiers that invaded and defeated the Songhay Empire in 1591. They established a brief Moroccan vassal state, and the events of this episode are recorded in al-Sa'di's *Tarikh al-Sudan*.

Al-Azhar One of the greatest institutions of higher learning in the Islamic world. Founded in 972 CE and located in Cairo, Egpyt, it has attracted students and scholars from all over the Islamic world including the Bilad al-Sudan practically since its inception.

Al-Bakri A famous Andalusian geographer who wrote one of the earliest sources on West Africa called *Kitab al-Masalik wa al-Mamalik* "Book of Routes and Realms" that contains information on the Almoravid Empire, the Empire of Ghana, and important trans-Saharan trade routes. (1014–1094 CE)

Batin Inner, hidden, or esoteric dimension of a text or other aspects of Islam. [Arabic]

Bilad al-Sudan Arabic for "Land of the Blacks" and used to refer to Sub-Saharan Africa.

Boko Haram A radical jihadi group in northeastern Nigeria founded in 2003 that does not recognize the legitimacy of the secular Nigerian state. The name in Hausa means "deceitful knowledge is sinful."

Borno Currently the name for a state in northeastern Nigeria, but was an important part of the Kanem-Borno Empire which was one of the first West African states to embrace Islam.

Al-Burtuli Mauritanian scholar and author of the biographical dictionary *Fath al-Shukur* (1727/28–1805 CE)

Caillié, René French explorer who was one of the first Europeans to visit Timbuktu and left a written account of his experience there in the early nineteenth century. (1799–1838 CE)

CEDRAB *Centre de documentation et de recherches Ahmad Baba* created in 1973 in Mali and based in Timbuktu. It has been renamed Institut des Hautes Études et de Recherches Islamiques Ahmad Baba.

Ceerno A master, teacher, or guide especially in a religious context. [Pulaar]

Cheikha Marieme Ibrahim Niasse A prominent Senegalese religious and educational figure. Over the past six decades, thousands of students from West Africa, Europe and the US attended and graduated from schools she has founded and run. She is also the daughter of Shaykh Ibrahim Niasse and the mother of the author.

Da'wah "Call" or propagation of Islam. [Arabic]

Dhikr "Remembrance" or the ritual recitation of Divine names and frequently the first part of the *shahadah*: *la ilaha illa Allah*, "There is no God but God." [Arabic]

Du'a Prayer of supplication which is separate from the mandatory five daily prayers or *salat*. [Arabic]

Europhone A term developed by Kwame Anthony Appiah to refer to a member of the intellectual tradition carried out in European languages. To be contrasted with "Arabophone" although the two are not mutually exclusive.

Fadima bint Uthman Dan Fodio One of the well educated and intellectually accomplished daughters of Uthman Dan Fodio.

Al-Falah A Senegalese Sunni reformist movement that has been very active in proselytizing and larger social strategies such as promoting the wearing of headscarves, using modern multimedia to broadcast its message, and promoting access to modern education.

Fatwa (s)/Fatawa (p) Legal cases, opinions, or rulings. [Arabic]

Fayda Outpouring or deluge referring to what is commonly called "the divine flood" predicted by Ahmad al-Tijani and actualized by Shaykh Ibrahim Niasse which greatly enhanced spiritual enlightenment and membership in the Tijaniyya Sufi brotherhood. [Arabic]

Fiqh Islamic jurisprudence. [Arabic]

Fourah Bay College Founded in 1827 CE in Freetown, Sierra Leone, it is the first western-style university founded in West Africa.

Fulani Ethnic group stretching across the Sahel that has produced a large number of prominent Muslim scholars since the sixteenth century CE. Other names for this group include Peul and Fulbe, but this name is usually used to refer to those in Northern Nigeria.

Fulbe Ethnic group stretching across the Sahel that has produced a large number of prominent Muslim scholars since the twelfth century CE. Other names for this group include Peul and Fulani.

Al-Furqan Foundation A charitable foundation established by the 1990s by Sheikh Ahmad Zaki Yamani for the purpose of preserving the Islamic written heritage.

Futa Jallon A region straddling present-day Senegal, Mali, and Guinea where a theocratic state was established by the Fulbe in about 1727 CE.

Futa Toro A region around the Senegal River basin where a different theocratic state was established by Fulbe scholars in the 1770s.

Gao A city in present-day Mali that was previously an important hub of trans-Saharan trade dating back to the ninth century CE. It also became part of the Mali empire and served as the capital of the Songhay Empire until its collapse after the Arma invasion in 1591.

Ghana A fabled West African Empire that covered parts of present-day Mali and Mauritania that derived much of its power from the lucrative gold and salt trade around and in the Sahara. Not to be confused with the contemporary state of Ghana which is located in a different part of West Africa. (c. 350–1236 CE)

GIA *Groupe Islamique Armé,* initially the military arm of the Algerian *Front Islamique du Salut*. Became unpopular when its members launched a campaign of terror targeting indiscriminately the military, journalists, and intellectuals.

GSPC *Groupe Salafi pour la Prédication et le Jihad,* the movement that later became Al-Qaida in the Islamic Maghreb (AQIM). Its origins lie in the suppressed Islamist movement that was driven from Algeria into Northern Mali where it supported rebel Tuareg groups such as Ansar Dine and MNLA.

Habsatu bint Uthman Dan Fodio One of the well educated and intellectually accomplished daughters of Uthman Dan Fodio.

Hadith Sayings of the Prophet Muhammad or accounts and traditions about his life whose study forms one of the most important bases for Islamic science and law.

Hafiz (m)/Hafiza (f) A person who has memorized the Qur'an. The term literally means "guardian" in English. [Arabic]

Al-Hajj Salim Suwari A Jakhanke scholar who developed a theology for the peaceful existence of Muslims under a non-Muslim government called the Suwarian Tradition. This tradition had an important impact on Muslim societies for centuries in West Africa. He argued against military jihad and proselytizing as contrary to God's will and was most likely active between the thirteenth and fifteenth centuries.

Haqiqa A truth or fact, especially divine reality. [Arabic]

Hausa A very large ethnic group found across many contemporary West and Central African countries such as Nigeria, Cameroon, Niger, and Chad. The Sokoto Caliphate established by Uthman Dan Fodio was centered in Hausaland in present-day Northern Nigeria.

Hifz Memorization of the Qur'an and a central aspect of Islamic education. [Arabic]

Hijra Flight or emigration usually referring to the Prophet Muhammad's flight from Mecca to Medina, or later migrations by other Muslims based on the original *hijra*. It is also used as the starting point for dating in the Islamic calendar, corresponding to 622 CE. [Arabic]

Ibadis A part of a larger group called the *Kharijites* who withdrew support from 'Ali when he agreed to arbitration to settle a succession dispute. Many of them moved to Algeria and their form of Islam was the first to reach West Africa as they dominated Saharan trade at the time.

Ibn Battuta The famous Moroccan traveler who visited numerous places in the world, including the ancient Mali Empire in 1353 CE, and wrote about his travels and experiences in his book called *al-Rihla* or "The Journey." (1304–1369 CE)

Ibn Hawqal Arab geographer who wrote the first comprehensive account of the Saharan trade routes in his work *Surat al-Ard* "Picture of the World." (c. 988 CE)

Ibrahim Niasse One of the most prominent and influential Sufi shaykhs in modern times, his Qur'anic commentaries and other works are widely studied in West Africa and beyond. Through establishing a new and faster method for disciples to attain *ma'rifa*, he transformed his branch of the Tijaniyya brotherhood into one of the largest Sufi organizations in the world with millions of adherents both in Africa and abroad. He founded the city of Madina Kaolack in Senegal and is the grandfather of the author. (1900–1975 CE)

Al-Idrisi A twelfth century Andalusian geographer who is famous for his *Tabula Rogeriana* in Latin or *Book of Roger* in English which he composed in 1154 CE for Norman king Roger II of Sicily. One of the most impressive early maps and geographical descriptions, it includes descriptions of Saharan trade routes taken from al-Bakri's *Book of Routes and Realms.*

IFAN Originally titled *Institut français d'Afrique Noire*, which has been since renamed *Institut Fondamental d'Afrique Noire* or "Fundamental Institute of Black Africa." It is affiliated with the Université Cheikh Anta Diop of Dakar and has done a great deal of work collecting and cataloguing Arabic and Ajami manuscripts from the Bilad al-Sudan in addition to other projects.

Ijaza A license or certificate that allows a person to teach a text, transmit knowledge, or instruct others in certain ritual practices. [Arabic]

Ijtihad Independent juridical reasoning or the process of deriving legal rulings and opinions from the Qur'an and the Sunna. [Arabic]

'Ilm al-Hadith The science of *hadith* or traditional accounts of the life and sayings of the Prophet Muhammad. [Arabic]

IRSH *Institut de Recherche en Sciences Humaines*, a Nigerien institute that houses a large repository of Arabic and Ajami documents due in large part to the efforts of former president of the National Assembly Boubou Hama.

Islamic University in Uganda Established in 1988 after the recommendation of the Organization of Islamic Cooperation in 1974 to serve the Anglophone students of East Africa as a complement to the Francophone Université islamique de Say in Niger.

Islamiyya School A hybrid primary or secondary school that blends modern academic training and disciplines with traditional Islamic education and often includes language instruction in European languages and Arabic.

Jakhanke Also called the *Wangara*, they are one of the first clerical groups in West Africa that spread Islam in the region. Involved in trade, subsistence agriculture, and clericalism, they spread and assimilated into many of the major societies and groups of West Africa, bringing the practice of Islam with them.

Jalal al-Din al-Suyuti One of the most widely known and respected scholars in West Africa for teaching many scholars who came to learn from him in Cairo and his consultation with Timbuktu scholars on issues such as permissible association with non-Muslims and the use of amulets. He is also one of the authors of the widely studied *Tafsir al-Jalalayn*. (1445–1505 CE)

Jamaatou Ibadourahmane A Senegalese Sunni reformist movement that has been very active in proselytizing and larger social strategies such as promoting the wearing of headscarves, using modern multimedia to broadcast its message, and promoting access to modern education.

Jingerer Ber Mosque Built in 1327 CE and commissioned by the famously wealthy Malian king Mansa Musa, it is one of the large mosque colleges in Timbuktu that was a center of Islamic learning in the medieval period.

Kanem-Borno A medieval Empire in what is called the Central Bilad al-Sudan and was comprised of territory in present-day Nigeria, Niger, Chad, and Libya. Most likely originating in the seventh century CE, its Sayfawa dynasty embraced Islam in the eleventh century, and the empire lasted until the mid-nineteenth century.

Kano The most populous city in Northern Nigeria, and historically a very important town in Saharan trade and Islamic scholarship. The *Kano Chronicle* contains a great deal of information about the spread of Islam into this city, in Hausaland and northern Nigeria in general.

Khalifa A successor who inherits spiritual and sometimes political authority from the founder of a Sufi order but also from the Prophet Muhammad himself (sometimes called "caliph" in English). [Arabic]

Khalwa Ritual seclusion aimed to prepare a devotee for spiritual enlightenment. [Arabic]

Kharijites A sectarian group that withdrew support from the Caliph 'Ali when he accepted arbitration in a succession dispute. They can be found in present-day Oman and Algeria, and the *Ibadis* are a smaller sub-set of this group.

Khidma "Service" usually for a community or a spiritual master. [Arabic]

Kunta A clan of Islamic scholars from the larger Zawaya group and one of the most influential clerical group in the Bilad al-Sudan in the eighteenth and nineteenth centuries. Various factions of the Kunta tribe spread all over West and North Africa were united by Sidi Mukhtar al Kunti, and many of them are still very influential in important areas such as the Senegambia.

Leo Africanus A famous fifteenth century Andalusian diplomat and author originally named Hassan ibn Muhammad al-Wazzan al-Fasi who wrote the book *Descrittione dell'Africa* and enjoyed the patronage of the de Medici family, making his name and his work widely recognized in Europe. His book includes a description of his travels to Timbuktu and the Bilad al-Sudan.

Madh Devotional poetry usually about the Prophet Muhammad. [Arabic]

Madhhab (s)/Madhahib (p) A school of Islamic jurisprudence or *fiqh*. There are four recognized Sunni madhahib (Maliki, Hanafi, Hanbali, and Shafi'i), two Shi'I madhahib (Ja'fari and Zaidi), as well as the Ibadi and Zahiri madhahib. [Arabic]

Madina Kaolack The city founded by Shaykh Ibrahim Niasse in Senegal and the religious center of the Ibrahimiyya branch of the Tijaniyya brotherhood.

Madrasa (s)/Madaris (pl) Literally a "school" which could refer to lower level educational institutions or even to higher level colleges such as Qayrawan in Tunisia. [Arabic]

Mahmud Ka'ti Was believed to be the author of seventeenth century chronicle *Tarikh al-Fattash* that documents the history of the Songhay Empire.

Majlis (s)/Majalis (p) Literally a place for sitting, it is a gathering for a specific purpose such as saying the rites for a Sufi brotherhood or holding instructional sessions or lectures in an educational setting. [Arabic]

Malam A master, teacher, or guide especially in a religious context. [Hausa]

Maliki School of Law One of the four recognized Sunni *madhahib*, and the dominant school of law in the Bilad al-Sudan after the *Almoravids* instituted it in place of the previous *Ibadi* ideology.

Mansa Musa The legendarily wealthy king of the Mali Empire who went on hajj in 1324 CE with an enormous entourage and brought back books and scholars, which greatly strengthened the Islamic intellectual tradition in Mali and the region in general. (1280–1337 CE)

Ma'rifa Gnosis or mystical knowledge of God. [Arabic]

Maryam bint Uthman Dan Fodio One of the well educated and intellectually accomplished daughters of Uthman Dan Fodio.

Masina (Islamic state of) The state that Umar Tall attacked in the nineteenth century on account of it not adhering properly to Islamic principles in his opinion. It also is referred to as the Caliphate of Hamdullahi or the Diina.

Médersa French hybrid schools established in Mali and in Mauritania that combine Islamic and modern forms of education along the lines of Islamiyya schools.

MNLA *Movement National de Liberation de l'Azawad* another rebel Tuareg movement that emerged in Mali in 2011 and was lead by Iyad Ag Ghali.

Mori A master, teacher, or guide especially in a religious context. [Manding]

Mufti Islamic jurisconsult. [Arabic]

Muhammadan Reality *Al-Haqiqa al-Muhammadiyya* in Arabic and an important concept in Sufism, particularly the Akbarian tradition of Ibn Arabi. It refers to the nature and existence of the Prophet Muhammad before the creation of any other being through which all things were brought into being.

MUJAO *Mouvement pour l'Unicité et le Jihad en Afrique de l'Ouest*, a splinter group that split from AQIM on the grounds that black Africans were not given any major positions in AQIM and did not receive a fair share of its booty.

Al-Mukhtar al-Kunti al-Kabir The most prominent and famous member of the Kunta lineage, credited with uniting the clan and revitalizing the Maliki tradition and the Qadiriyya Sufi brotherhood in West Africa. (1729–1811 CE)

Al-Mukhtasar A leading treatise on Maliki jurisprudence written by Khalil Ibn Ishaq al-Jundi.

Muqaddam A deputy or intermediary authority figure who is authorized to initiate others into the secrets and practices of a Sufi Brotherhood. [Arabic]

Murid A spiritual disciple, particularly in a Sufi brotherhood or a member of the *Muridiyya*, the Sufi brotherhood founded by Shaykh Ahmadu Bamba. [Arabic]

Musa Kamara One of the most prominent Senegalese Arabophone who authored various texts in Arabic and Pulaar on such different fields as history, geography, the hydrology of the Senegal River from Guinea to Saint Louis, literature, sociology, anthropology, jurisprudence, traditional medicine, and Sufism. His most famous work is entitled *Zuhur al-basatin fi tarikh al-sawadin* (Flowers from the Gardens in the

History of the Black People) and constitutes a major source of information on economic and social life in the valley of the Senegal River. (1864–1945 CE)

Nahw Grammar. [Arabic]

Nana Asma'u Daughter of Shaykh Uthman Dan Fodio and a prolific author on various topics in various languages including Arabic, Hausa, and Fulfulde. She played an active role in continuing and strengthening the tradition of women's religious education and leadership in Fulani society and led the group of educated women called Yan Taru. Her poems are still widely studied and memorized in the area today. (1793–1864 CE)

Qadi A judge who interprets and implements Islamic law. [Arabic]

Qadiriyya The earliest and one of the most prominent Sufi brotherhoods found in West and North Africa founded by Shaykh Abd al-Qadir Jilani in Baghdad. Prominent members of this brotherhood are 'Abd al-Karim al-Maghili, Sidi Mukhtar al-Kunti, and Uthman Dan Fodio.

Qawa'id Legal maxims. [Arabic]

Qayrawan An ancient city in modern-day Tunisia and the name of the oldest college in the world, founded in 859 CE. The scholars responsible for establishing the Maliki *madhhab* studied here.

Risala An important treatise on Maliki *fiqh* written by Ibn Abi Zaid al-Qayrawani and studied all over the Bilad al-Sudan.

Riwaq (s)/Arwiqa (pl) Hostels at important mosques and institutions of higher learning. One was established at al-Azhar in Cairo for students coming from the central Bilad al-Sudan dating as far back as 1258. [Arabic]

Safiya bint Uthman Dan Fodio One of the well educated and intellectually accomplished daughters of Uthman Dan Fodio.

Salafi A person who follows the ideology of Salafism. [Arabic]

Salafism A conservative reform movement in Islam which emphasizes imitation of the Prophet Muhammad and his earliest followers the *Salaf*. It is often divided into three categories or factions: quietists who are uninterested in modern politics, activists who are intensely concerned with politics, and a smaller group of jihadists.

Sanad Support or the chain of transmitters of *ijaza* who initiate others into a Sufi order and its practices. [Arabic]

Sanhaja A sub-group within the Berber ethnicity who converted to Islam relatively early through contact with Ibadi traders, but were converted to the Maliki *madhhab* by Abdallah ibn Yasin and formed the Almoravid Empire.

Sankoré Mosque An important Islamic institution of higher learning in Timbuktu founded in the fourteenth century that is used as the paradigm for knowledge production and transmission in this book. At its height it was one of the most prominent intellectual centers in the entire Muslim world.

Sayyid Qutb An Egyptian Islamist scholar who argued against secularism and for the Islamization of the state. (1906–1966 CE)

Serin A master, teacher, or guide especially in a religious context. [Wolof]

Shari'a Islamic law derived from the Qur'an and Sunna. [Arabic]

Sharif A descendant of the Prophet Muhammad who is often afforded a great deal of respect as a result. [Arabic]

Shaykh (m)/Shaykha (f) A spiritual master or guide, specifically in the context of Sufism.

Shinqit An important intellectual and commercial hub found in present-day central Mauritania.

Shirk Association of Allah's power and nature with something else. Sometimes also used to refer to polytheism or idolatry. [Arabic]

Sidi Yahya al-Tadallisi Also refered to as Sidi Yahya al-Andalusi. He was the first imam and lead scholar at the Sidi Yahya Mosque in Timbuktu and is still considered by many to be a saint.

Sidi Yahya Mosque One of the large college mosques completed in Timbuktu in 1440 CE and named after the celebrated Sidi Yahya al-Tadallisi.

Silsila A chain of initiation or transmission. [Arabic]

Sira Biography of the Prophet Muhammad [Arabic]

SOAS School of Oriental and African Studies at the University of London. One of the leading institutions for the study of Africa and the Middle East.

Sokoto A major city in Northwestern Nigeria that was the capital of the Sokoto Caliphate established by Uthman Dan Fodio and still an important religious center today.

Songhay The last of the prominent medieval West African Empires. Ruled first by the Sonni dynasty from the capital Gao, it was later replaced by the Askya dynasty until the Moroccan invasion in 1591 CE effectively ended the empire. Much of what we know about this empire is taken from the two Timbuktu chronicles *Tarikh al-Sudan* and *Tarikh al-Fattash*.

Soninke An ethnic group that founded and led the Empire of Ghana. They later scattered all over the Bilad al-Sudan.

Sonni Ali Ber First King of the Songhay Empire in the later fifteenth century. Under his rule Songhay eclipsed the previous Mali Empire and captured the important cities of Timbuktu and Jenne.

Sudani Adjective referring to the land of the black people or to black people themselves. Not to be confused with present-day Sudan, whose name also comes from the Arabic word for "black." [Arabic]

Sufism A term referring to the esoteric, mystical, and inner aspects of Islam. Organized into various brotherhoods or *tariqas*, Sufi Islam became the normative form of Islam in the Bilad al-Sudan and is still of paramount importance in the region. Prominent brotherhoods include the Qadiriyya, the Tijaniyya, and the Muridiyya.

Sunna The transmitted sayings, actions, teachings, and lived examples from the life of the Prophet Muhammad and his companions that form an important basis for Islamic law and practice. [Arabic]

Tafsir Qur'ānic exegesis or commentary. [Arabic]

Tafsir al-Jalalayn Literally "The Exegesis of the Two Jalals," it is a widely known and studied commentary on the Qur'an written by Jalal al-Din al-Suyuti and Jalal al-Din al-Mahalli.

Tajwid Established methods of reciting and pronouncing the Qur'an. [Arabic]

Takfir Declaring self-identified Muslims as unbelievers. [Arabic]

Takrur One of the first Islamized medieval West African states. It controlled a number of important trade routes, and because of its high profile in Egypt and the Hijaz, West African Muslims were often referred to as people of Takrur or *Takruri*.

Tarbiyya spiritual training towards an ultimate goal of direct knowledge of and union with God. [Arabic]

Tarikh al-Fattash A seventeenth century West African chronicle attributed for a long time to Mahmud Ka'ti that documents the history of the Songhay Empire.

Tarikh al-Sudan The other seventeenth century chronicle documenting the Songhay Empire, which was written by 'Abd al-Rahman al-Sa'di.

Tariqa A path or way, usually used to refer to a Sufi brotherhood. [Arabic]

Tasawwuf Islamic mysticism. [Arabic]

Tawhid Term referring to the "oneness" of God that is a fundamental aspect of Islamic philosophy and Theology. [Arabic]

Tijaniyya The most popular Sufi brotherhood in West Africa founded by Shaykh Ahmad al-Tijani after he received the authority to do so from the Prophet Muhammad in a vision.

Timbuktu One of the most fabled intellectual and commercial centers in West Africa. It is home to many important scholars such as Ahmad Baba and Sidi Mukhtar al-Kunti and celebrated institutions such as the Sankoré Mosque, Sidi Yahya Mosque, and the Jingerer Ber Mosque.

Tuareg A traditionally pastoralist and nomadic subgroup within the larger Berber ethnicity that was heavily involved in Saharan trade.

Umar Tall One of the most prominent scholars and warriors of the nineteenth century in the western Sudan who led a jihad against the non-Muslim Bambara states and the Islamic state of Masina after learning a great deal from his connections with Uthman Dan Fodio's lineage in Sokoto. (1797–1864 CE)

Université islamique de Say Located in Say, Niger and inaugurated in 1987 after the recommendation of the Organization of Islamic Cooperation in 1974 to serve the Francophone students of West Africa as a complement to the Anglophone Islamic University in Uganda.

Usul Religious principles. [Arabic]

Uthman Dan Fodio A towering Fulani scholar and reformist who established the Sokoto Caliphate in Northern Nigeria at the beginning of the nineteenth century after leading a successful jihad against the Hausa rulers in the area. He established the model for the later jihads of the nineteenth century, was a prolific writer of theological treatises and poetry, and helped to establish the Qadiriyya brotherhood in Northern Nigeria. (1754–1817 CE)

Wahhabi A person who follows the ideology of Wahhabism. [Arabic]

Wahhabism An ideology based on the writings of the eighteenth century scholar Muhammad bin Abd al-Wahhab that claims to purify Islam from any influences not found in the life of the Prophet Muhammad or the Qur'an. It is the official state ideology in Saudi Arabia and has gained adherents in West Africa and influenced movements such as the Yan Izala in Nigeria.

Wali (s)/Awliya' (p) A saint or friend of God. [Arabic]

Wangara Also called the *Jakhanke* in Senegambia, they are one of the first clerical groups in West Africa that helped to spread Islam in the region. Involved in trade, subsistence agriculture, and clericalism, they spread and assimilated into many of the major societies and groups of West Africa, bringing the practice of Islam with them.

Walata An important intellectual and commercial town in present-day southeastern Mauritania.

Walaya Friendship with or closeness to God, sainthood. [Arabic]

Wird (s)/Awrad (p) Litany or daily ritual supererogatory prayers. [Arabic]

Wolof An ethnic group in Senegambia and also the language spoken by this group. They are most involved in the teaching and spreading of Islam in the area, often through collaboration with extant political powers, and many commentaries on the Qur'an, poems, and other Ajami documents are written in this language.

Wuld version of "son" derived from *walad*; a common part of male names. [Hassani-yya Arabic]

Yan Izala Officially called the Society for the Removal of Innovation and Reinstatement of Tradition, a reformist movement established in Northern Nigeria in 1978 by the former students of Shaykh Abubakar Gumi. The argued against the practice of Sufism, sought to reform many social practices that did not have strictly Islamic origins, and emphasized access to education for both men and women. [Hausa]

Yan Taru An educational and religious group of women led by Nana Asma'u in Northern Nigeria. It is still active in Northern Nigeria. The name means "Those who have come together." [Hausa]

Zahir The apparent, manifest, or outward, "exoteric" dimension of a text or other aspects of Islam. [Arabic]

Zawaya One of the most important ethnic groups in the history of Islam in West Africa. They specialized in the production, reproduction, and dissemination of Islamic knowledge and were also largely responsible for the introduction and establishment of Sufism in the western Bilad al-Sudan. They trace their ancestry to the Arab Banu Hilal and Banu Sulaym tribes and the Almoravids. Prominent Zawaya families are the Kunta and the Idaw 'Ali.

Zawiya A corner or a Sufi lodge or meeting place. [Arabic]

Ziyara A pilgrimage or trip to a sacred site. [Arabic]

Acknowledgments

Harvard University Press Executive Editor Sharmila Sen commissioned this book in 2009. I am extremely grateful to her and her colleagues for guidance and support during the many years of its preparation.

The roots of this book go much deeper, to my undergraduate training in Middle Eastern Studies at the Institut National des Langues et Civilisations Orientales and my graduate training in Middle Eastern Studies and Political Science at the Institut d'Etudes Politiques de Paris, both in France. That I have written down the intellectual history of Islam in West Africa was in part thanks to my interaction with, and learning from, some leading Africanists over the past twenty years. The intellectual debt I owe them will be obvious to the reader of the book. To those mentors, notably Habibu Sani Babura, Boubacar Barry, Louis Brenner, Christian Coulon, Mamadou Diouf, John Hunwick, Jibrin Ibrahim, Lansine Kaba, Murray Last, Mahmood Mamdani, René Otayek, Abdel Wedoud Ould Shaykh, John Paden, David Robinson, Jean Schmitz, Charles Stewart, and Jean-Louis Triaud, I offer my heartfelt thanks.

In Senegal, the Council for the Development of Social Science Research in Africa (CODESRIA) expressed an interest in this project and commissioned a concept paper published in French in 2003 as "Intellectuels non Europhones," subsequently translated into English by Victoria Bawtree, and into Spanish and Arabic. Sections of "Intellectuels non Europhones" are included in Chapters 1, 3, and 6 of this book with CODESRIA's permission.

Several friends, colleagues, and some of my students read drafts of the manuscript and offered useful comments. My thanks to Boubacar Barry, Louis Brenner, Marianne Czisnik, Mamadou Diouf, Murray Last, Ayodeji Ogunnaike, Oludamini Ogunnaike, Ebrima Sall, Farah al-Sharif, and Matthew Steele. Likewise, two Harvard University Press reviewers provided helpful suggestions to improve the book. One of those reviewers is Chouki El Hamel, with whom I have maintained a long intellectual friendship, and whose suggestions helped me outline the argument of the book in the introduction. I benefitted very much from conversations with Leila Ahmed, Emmanuel Akyeampong, Joe Caruso, Bachir Diagne, Najam Haidar, Fatima Harrak, Brian Larkin, Roman Loimeier, Greg Mann, Brinkley Messick, Tim Mitchell, Ahmed Boukar Niang,

Sidina Ali Niasse, Jacob Olupona, Ruediger Seeseman, Rudolph Ware, and Zachary Wright. Ulrike Guthrie, Ayodeji Ogunnaike, Darlene Slagle, and David Owen offered critical editorial assistance.

As well as being the fruit of my academic studies, this book is even more fundamentally an intellectual history of Islam in Africa as I have lived it. I am grateful to my mother, Cheikha Marieme Ibrahim Niasse; my late father, Al-Hajj Oumar Kane; and my extended family for nurturing me in this tradition and encouraging me to learn and interact with the world beyond it. Without their support, I would not have been able to narrate this story.

I received two major grants to support my research on Islamic Education in West Africa from the United States Institute of Peace and the Gerda Henkel Stiftung, which I gratefully acknowledge.

My former and current employers Columbia University (2002–2012) and Harvard University (2012–) granted research leaves, which enabled me to devote my time to reflecting and writing. I thank my family for tolerating my long absences and moments of isolation during the preparation of this book.

A section of *Kitab al-Farq* by Uthman Dan Fodio, translated into English by Mervyn Hiskett, is reprinted with the permission of Cambridge University Press. Sections of the translation of Ahmad Baba's *Mi'raj al-Su'ud* by John Hunwick and Fatima Harrak are quoted with the permission of the Institut d'Etudes Africaines, Université Mohammed V Rabat Morocco.

Index